MILITARY BIBLIOGRAPHY OF THE CIVIL WAR

VOLUME III

Military Bibliography of the Civil War

Volume I

Originally published as: Regimental Publications and Personal Narratives of the Civil War: Northern States

In 7 parts:

1. Illinois
2. New York
3. New England States
4. New Jersey and Pennsylvania
5. Indiana and Ohio
6. Iowa, Kansas, Michigan, Minnesota, and Wisconsin
7. Index of Names

Volume II

Regimental Publications and Personal Narratives: Southern, Border, and Western States and Territories; Federal Troops

Union and Confederate Biographies

Volume III

General References

Armed Forces

Campaigns and Battles

Military Bibliography of the Civil War

Compiled by C. E. DORNBUSCH

Volume Three

General References; Armed Forces; and Campaigns and Battles

New York

The New York Public Library

Astor, Lenox and Tilden Foundations

1 9 7 2

THIS VOLUME HAS BEEN PUBLISHED WITH HELP
FROM THE EMILY ELLSWORTH FORD SKEEL FUND

*   *   *

Library of Congress Catalog Card Number: 72–137700
International Standard Book Number: 0–87104–117–0

Table of Contents

General References

Armed Forces

Campaigns and Battles

Table of Contents ix

Preface

MOST OF THE work of compiling the *Military Bibliography of the Civil War* was accomplished while the compiler was a member of the staff of The New York Public Library, from which he retired in 1963. Volume I, originally entitled *Regimental Publications and Personal Narratives of the Civil War: Northern States*, was published in seven parts in 1961 and 1962, and reprinted in 1971 in one clothbound volume, under the title *Military Bibliography of the Civil War*, Volume I; in 1967 Volume II of the *Bibliography* was published, encompassing Regimental Publications and Personal Narratives: Southern, Border, and Western States and Territories; Federal Troops; and Union and Confederate Biographies (see the contents list, p ii). Many revisions and additions have accumulated for these first volumes since their original publication, and it is hoped that the supplementary material for Volumes I and II will find publication within the next few years.

Compilation of Volume III was completed for the most part in 1962. Some additions and revisions have been made during the intervening years, but the indexing of periodicals effectively terminated in 1961. This volume is divided into three major parts: General References, Armed Forces, and Campaigns and Battles. The entries of the first part are arranged by subject (in alphabetical order), such as General Histories, Prisons and Prisoners of War, and Veterans and Their Organizations. The second part of the volume has three subdivisions: General References (for which the entries are arranged alphabetically by subject, such as Artillery, Medical Services, and Rosters), and Confederate Army and Union Army (under units within the respective army). The subdivisions of the third part of the volume, Campaigns and Battles, are General References, Official Reporting of Military Operations, Listing of Battles, Joint Congressional Committee on the Conduct of the War, Official Records of the War of the Rebellion, and Individual Battles Listed by State. For the final subdivision, battles are listed chronologically within each state; states are listed in a geographical arrangement which takes into account the order of campaigns and the most important battles. The authors of entries in this subdivision are civilians or staff officers. The user of this part of the *Bibliography* who is seeking additional narratives of enlisted men, line officers, or other participants, may, by determining the regiment(s) taking part in the engagement in question, find further materials in Volumes I and II of the *Bibliography*.

Location symbols used to record the holdings of libraries are those of the National Union Catalog. Since the main portion of the work on Volume III was done at the Henry E. Huntington Library in San Marino, California, and at other libraries visited, the location symbols for the holdings of The New York Public Library (NN) were sometimes omitted when the works were available elsewhere.

The compiler wishes to thank the Huntington Library for financial assistance which enabled him to spend three months at that institution. Production costs of this publication have been financed by The New York Public Library's Emily E. F. Skeel Fund, which has also supported the project since its inception in 1959. As was noted above, the publication of a supplementary volume is being planned. For inclusion there, as well as for his own interest in the subject, the compiler would be glad to receive additions, corrections, and other correspondence in connection with the *Bibliography*: his address is Strong Road, Cornwallville, New York 12418.

Abbreviations

LHQ	Louisiana historical quarterly (Louisiana historical society)
LWL	Land we love, Charlotte, N. C.
MA	Military affairs (American military institute)
MC&H	Military collector & historian, Washington
MHM	Maryland historical magazine (Maryland historical society)
MHR	Missouri historical review (State historical society of Missouri)
MHSMP	Military Historical Society of Massachusetts. Papers
MOLLUS	Military order of the loyal legion of the United States. [The personal narrative series published by the individual Commanderies are indicated by the state abbreviations following *MOLLUS*]
MVHR	Mississippi Valley historical review (Mississippi Valley historical association)
NCHR	North Carolina historical review (North Carolina. Historical commission)
Nicholson Catalogue	Nicholson, John Page. Catalogue of library of Brevet Lieutenant-Colonel John Page Nicholson relating to the War of the rebellion, Philadelphia, 1914 (Title 12, Volume III)
NMHR	New Mexico historical review (Historical society of New Mexico)
OLOD	Our living and our dead [issued with different subtitles] (Southern historical society)
PMHS	Publications, Mississippi historical society [entitled *Collections* after 1st year of publication]
PMHSM	Papers of the Military historical society of Massachusetts
PNRISSHS	Personal narratives, Rhode Island soldiers and sailors historical society
RKHS	Register, Kentucky state historical society
Sabin	Sabin, Joseph. Bibliotheca americana, New York, 1868–1936
SB	Southern bivouac; a monthly literary and historical magazine
SCHM	South Carolina historical magazine (South Carolina historical society)

SCQ	Historical society of southern California. Quarterly
Shetler	Shetler, Charles. West Virginia Civil war literature, Morgantown, 1963 (Title 1499A, Volume II)
SHM	Southern Historical Monthly
SHSP	Southern historical society. Papers
SHST	Southern historical society. Transactions
SM	Southern magazine, Baltimore (Southern historical society)
SWHQ	Southwestern historical quarterly (Texas state historical association)
THM	Tennessee historical magazine (Tennessee historical society)
THQ	Tennessee historical quarterly (Tennessee historical society; Tennessee. Historical Commission)
TMH	Texas military history (National guard association of Texas)
US	United service, Philadelphia
VMHB	Virginia magazine of history and biography (Virginia historical society)
Wright	Wright, Marcus Joseph. Tennessee in the war, 1861–1865, New York [1908] (Title 960, Volume II)
WTHSP	West Tennessee historical society. Papers
WVH	West Virginia history; a quarterly magazine (West Virginia. Dept of archives and history)

Errata

Title 735: for *VMBH* read *VMHB*

Title 2001: for *USCAJ* read *JUSCA*

General References

General References

BIBLIOGRAPHY

Abbot, George Maurice
Contributions toward a bibliography of the Civil war in the United States. I. Regimental histories. By Geo. Maurice Abbot. Philadelphia, 1886. v, 6–34 p. 24cm.　　NN　**1**
"150 copies reprinted from January Bulletin of the Library company of Philadelphia."

Bartlett, John Russell, 1805–1886.
The literature of the rebellion. A catalogue of the books and pamphlets relating to the Civil war in the United States, and on subjects growing out of that event, together with works on American slavery, and essays from reviews and magazines on the same subjects. Compiled by James Russell Bartlett. Boston, Draper and Halliday, 1866. iv, [5]–477 p. 29½cm.
　　NN　**2**
"250 copies printed in royal octavo; 60 copies [the edition described] in quarto."

Boston. Public Library.
A list of regimental histories and official records of the individual states in the Civil war in this library. *Monthly bulletin* s 2 IX (1904) 289–314.　　**3**

Cox, Jacob Dolson, 1828–1900, editor.
Bibliography of the Civil war period. *In The literature of American history*, edited by J. N. Larned, 1902, 213–60.　　**4**

Eldridge, James William, 1841–1900.
Catalogue of books, pamphlets, etc., formed by James W. Eldridge relating to the Civil war. . . . Offered for sale by William H. Murray. . . . Roslindale [1910] 2 v. (106, 38 p.) 23cm.　　CSmH NN　**5**
I locates William H. Murray at Hartford.

Freeman, Douglas Southall, 1886–1953.
The South to posterity, an introduction to the writing of Confederate history, by Douglas Southall Freeman. New York, Charles Scribner's Sons, 1939. xii, (1), 235 p. 21cm.
　　NN　**6**

Grimes, Maxyne Madden and Patti Carr Black
Confederate imprints and Civil war newspapers on file in the Mississippi Department of archives and history. *JMH* XXIII (1961) 231–54.　　**7**

Hodgkins, William Henry, 1840–1905.
. . . Catalogue . . . of the extensive private library of the late Major Wm. H. Hodgkins of Somerville, Mass., comprising large collections of books and pamphlets relating to the Civil war, slavery and Confederate states. . . . Boston, 1906–07. 2 v. 24cm.　　CSmH NN　**8**

Auction sale at C. F. Libbie & co.
[I] April 16–18, 1906; II April 10–11, 1907.

Houston Civil War Round Table.
Houston Civil war round table, 1954–1967, compiled by Cooper K. Ragan. History, programs and members. Houston, Lone Star press, 1967. 23 p. 20cm.　　**8A**

Kelly, James
A list of pamphlets, sermons, and addresses on the Civil war in the United States, from 1861 to 1866. *In his* The American catalogue of books, 1866, 241–82.　　**9**

Lambert, William Harrison, 1842–1912.
Library of the late Major William H. Lambert of Philadelphia. Part III, Civil war. To be sold March 9 and 10, 1914 . . . at the Anderson galleries, Metropolitan art association. New York, 1914. 126, (1) p. front. (port.). 23cm.
　　NN　**10**

Mebane, John, 1909–
Books relating to the Civil war, a priced check list, including regimental histories, Lincolniana, and Confederate imprints. Compiled by John Mebane. New York, Thomas Yoseloff [c1963] 144 p. 26cm.　　NN　**11**

Nicholson, John Page, 1842–1922.
Catalogue of library of Brevet Lieutenant-Colonel John Page Nicholson relating to the War of the rebellion, 1861–1866. Philadelphia [John T. Palmer co.] 1914. 1022 p. front. (illus.). 24½cm.　　CSmH NN　**12**
"300 copies privately printed."
The collection was acquired by the Henry E. Huntington library and art gallery — see *Pennsylvania magazine of history and biography* LI (1927) 331.

United States. War Department. Library.
. . . Bibliography of State participation in the Civil war, 1861–1866. War department library subject catalogue no. 6. Third edition. Washington, Govt. print. office, 1913. 1140 p. 23cm.　　CSmH NN　**13**
At head of title: War department: Office of the Chief of staff. War college division, General staff, no. 19.

—— —— Charlottesville, Allen pub. co., 1961. 1140 p. 23cm.　　**14**
A photographic reprinting.

COLLECTED BIOGRAPHY

Generals of Iowa Civil war regiments, by Richard Hellie. *Annals of Iowa*. s 3 XXXVI (1962/63) 498–99.　　**15**
Alphabetical list giving birth and death years, where death occurred, year of coming to Iowa, and profession.

Collected Biography, continued

Memoirs of the War of '61. Colonel Charles
Russell Lowell, friends and cousins. Boston,
Press of Geo. H. Ellis co., 1920. xvi, 66 p.
plates (ports.). 20½cm.   **15A**
"Foreword" signed: Elizabeth C. Putnam.

The war and its heroes. Richmond, Ayres &
Wade, 1864. 88 p. ports. 23½cm.
                CSmH DLC NcD Vi   **16**
On cover: First series.
Plates are paged.
Crandall 2609.

Armstrong, Zella
The last of the Confederate Generals.
Munsey's magazine XXXI (1904) 387–93. ports.
                                            17

Bradford, Gamaliel, 1863–1932.
Union portraits, by Gamaliel Bradford. Bos-
ton, Houghton Mifflin co. [1916] xvi, 350 p.
front. (port.). 19cm.   GEU   **18**
Includes McClellan, Hooker, Meade, Thomas, and
Sherman.

Bramhall, Frank J
The military souvenir, a portrait gallery of
our military and naval heroes, by Frank J.
Bramhall . . . New York, J. C. Buttre, 1863.
plates (ports.). 30½cm.   GEU NN   **19**
Engraved title page adds: v. 1.

[Brockett, Linus Pierpont] 1820–1893.
Our great Captains, Grant, Sherman,
Thomas, Sheridan, and Farragut. . . . New
York, Charles B. Richardson, 1865. 251 p.
plates (ports.). 19cm.   CSmH   **20**

——— ——— New York, Charles B. Richardson,
1865. 292 p. maps, plates (ports.). 19cm.
                                CSmH   **20A**
The "Contents" page references are those of the
251 page edition, though the biographies have been
expanded.
The author's name appears on the title page.

Cuyler, Telamon Smith
A roster of the surviving general officers of
the Confederate states army, 1861–1865, by
Telamon Smith Cuyler. Privately printed.
Mamaroneck, N. Y., 1905. 5 folios. 28cm.
                                CSmH   **21**
"The impression is limited to fifty copies."
"Of the Beverwyck quartos this is the first."

Dickinson, Sally Bruce
Confederate leaders [by] Sally Bruce Dickinson. Staunton, Printed by McClure co.
[c1937] 198 p. front. (port.). 23½cm.
                                  NcD   **22**

Dudley, Dean, 1823–1906.
Officers of our Union army and navy, their
lives, their portraits. vol. I. Boston, L. Prang
& co., c1862. viii, [9]–148 p. plates (ports.).
13½cm.   CSmH DLC   **23**

"Preface" signed: Dean Dudley, Boston, 24 Feb.,
1862.
No further volumes published.

Eliot, Ellsworth, 1864–
West Point in the Confederacy, by Ellsworth Eliot, Jr. New York, G. A. Baker & co.,
1941. xxxii, 491 p. 22cm.   NN   **24**

Hamersly, L. R. & co., Philadelphia.
Officers of the army and navy (regular and
volunteer) who served in the Civil war. Philadelphia, L. R. Hamersly & co., 1894. 177 p.
ports. 32cm.   CSmH   **25**
Portraits printed on rectos. There is no text.

Harwell, Thomas Fletcher, 1866–1947.
Eighty years under the Stars and bars, including biographical sketches of "100 Confederate soldiers I have known." Information concerning the organization of the United Confederate veterans. Organization and history of
Camp Ben McCulloch, United Confederate
veterans, near Driftwood, Hays county, Texas.
By Thomas Fletcher Harwell. [Kyle, Texas,
c1947] 108 p. illus., ports. 22½cm.
     Cover illustrated in color.   NcD   **26**
     Copyright by W. Turner Harwell.

Hastings, Hugh, 1856–1917.
About Generals, a paper read before the
Albany institute, Albany, N. Y., January 18,
1898, by Hugh Hastings, State historian of
New York. Albany, James B. Lyon, printer,
1898. 30 p. 23cm.   CSmH   **27**

Hill, Frederick Trevor, 1866–1930.
. . . On the trail of Grant and Lee, a narrative history of the boyhood and manhood of
two great Americans, based upon their own
writings, official records, and other authorita-
tive information, by Frederick Trevor Hill.
Illustrations in color by Arthur E. Becher. New
York, D. Appleton and co., 1911. xiv, 305 p.
facsims., plans, col. plates (illus.). 22cm.
                           CSmH DLC   **28**
At head of title: National holiday series. . . .

Johnson, Sidney Smith, 1840–
Texans who wore the Gray, by Sid S. John-
son, Capt. 3rd Texas cavalry . . . volume one.
[Tyler, 1907] 407 p. ports. 21½cm. NN   **29**

Larke, Julian K
Strong's pictorial and biographical record of
the great rebellion, containing sketches of departed heroes, prominent personages of the
past, facts, incidents and stories connected
with that important epoch of the history of
America. Compiled and edited by Julian K.
Larke. New York, T. W. Strong [1866?] 288 p.
ports. 34cm.   CSmH DLC   **30**
Text in three columns and within ruled double
border.

Macartney, Clarence Edward Noble, 1879–
Grant and his Generals, by Clarence Edward Macartney. New York, McBride co. [c1953] xiv, 352 p. plates (ports.). 21cm.
DLC NcD **31**
"Western [Eastern] theatre of conflict . . . ," maps on endpaper.

Marsh, Margaret Mitchell, 1900–1949.
Georgia Generals for Stone mountain memorial, by Peggy Mitchell. *Atlanta historical bulletin* no 34 (May 1950) 67–99. **32**
Reprinted from the *Atlanta journal Sunday magazine*, November 29 – December 13, 1925.
Generals John B. Gordon, Pierce M. Butler, Thomas R. R. Cobb, Henry Benning, and Ambrose R. Wright.

Mickle, William English, 1846–
Well known Confederate veterans and their war records. New Orleans, Wm. E. Mickle, 1907. 74, xxxix p. ports. 29½cm.
DLC GEU LNHT MoHi **33**
On cover: Vol. I.
"Alphabetical roster of soldiers, C.S.A.," with military biography, xxxix p.
Portraits of veterans with their military biographies, 74 p.

Military Order of the Loyal Legion of the United States. Illinois Commandery.
Memorials of deceased companions of the Commandery of the State of Illinois, Military order of the loyal legion of the United States. Chicago, 1901–23. 3 v. ports. 23½cm.
DLC NHi NN **34**
I From May 8, 1879, when the Commandery was instituted, to July 1, 1901.
II From July 1, 1901, to December 31, 1911.
III From January 1, 1912, to December 31, 1922.

Moore, Frank, 1828–1904.
Heroes and martyrs, notable men of the time. Biographical sketches of the military and naval heroes, statesmen and orators, distinguished in the American crisis of 1861–62. Edited by Frank Moore. New York, G. P. Putnam [c1861] iv, [3]–253 p. plates (ports.). 27½cm. CSmH DLC **35**
On p. 253: End of vol. I.
"First published in 20 parts; no more issued," *Sabin.*

Morrow, John P
Confederate Generals from Arkansas. *ArHQ* xxi (1962) 231–46. plate (4 ports.). **36**

Piatt, Donn, 1819–1891.
Memories of the men who saved the Union, by Donn Piatt. New York, Belford, Clarke & co., 1887. xxvi, [27]–302 p. plates (illus., ports.). 19½cm. CSmH DLC **37**
Partial contents: Major-General George H. Thomas, 172–279; McClellan's own story, 280–95.

—— —— [Second edition] New York, Belford, Clarke & co., 1887. xxvi, (16), [27]–302 p. plates (illus., ports.). 19½cm.
CSmH DLC **38**

"Preface to second edition," dated May 27, 1887, (16) p.

Pollard, Edward Alfred, 1828–1872.
Lee and his Lieutenants, comprising the early life, public services, and campaigns of General Robert E. Lee and his companions in arms, with a record of their campaigns and heroic deeds . . . by Edward A. Pollard. New York, E. B. Treat & co., 1867. vi, (1), [9]–851 p. plates (1 illus., ports.). 24cm.
CSmH DLC **39**

Powell, William Henry, 1838–1901.
Officers of the army and navy (regular) who served in the Civil war. Edited by Major William H. Powell and Medical-Director Edward Shippen. Philadelphia, L. R. Hamersley & co., 1892. 487 p. ports. 30½cm.
CSmH DLC **40**
Text printed in double columns.

—— Officers of the army and navy (volunteers) who served in the Civil war. Edited by Lieutenant-Colonel William H. Powell. Philadelphia, L. R. Hamersly & co., 1893. 419 p. ports. 31½cm. **41**

—— Powell's record of living officers of the United States army, by William H. Powell. Philadelphia, L. R. Hamersly & co., 1890. 689 p. 23½cm. CSmH **42**

Shea, John Dawson Gilmary, 1824–1892.
The American nation illustrated in the lives of her fallen brave and living heroes, by John Gilmary Shea. With fine portraits on steel. New York, Thomas Farrell & Son, 1862. 165, 463 p. plates (ports.). 27cm. CSmH **43**
P. 1–224 (of the 463-page section) are a reprinting of the author's The fallen brave, 1861.
"Directions to the binder" would indicate publication in parts.

—— The fallen brave: a biographical memorial of the American officers who have given their lives for the preservation of the Union. Edited by John Gilmary Shea. With eight portraits on steel by J. A. O'Neill. New York, Charles B. Richardson & co., 1861. 224 p. plates (ports.). 28cm. CSmH **44**
Added engraved title page.
Biographical sketches are signed by their authors.

Sherrill, Samuel Wells, 1869–
Heroes in Gray, by Samuel W. Sherrill. Nashville, Claude J. Bell [c1909] 170 p. 19½cm. CSmH DLC NcD TxU **45**

Snow, William Parker, 1817–1895.
Southern Generals, who they are, and what they have done. New York, Charles B. Richardson, 1865. 473 p. plates (ports.). 23cm.
Published anonymously. DLC **46**

—— Southern Generals, their lives and campaigns, by William Parker Snow. New York,

Collected Biography, continued

Charles B. Richardson, 1866. 500 p. plates
(ports.). 24cm.   CSmH DLC   **47**
The plates of the 1865 edition have been used with
the addition of some material.

—— Lee and his Generals, by Capt. Wm. P.
Snow. New York, Richardson & co., 1867.
500 p. plates (ports.). 23cm.
CSmH DLC   **48**

Steiner, Paul E
Physician-Generals in the Civil war, a study
in nineteenth mid-century American medicine,
by Paul E. Steiner. Springfield, Ill., Charles C.
Thomas [1966] xv, 194 p. ports. 24cm.
NN   **49**

Stratton, Robert Burcher, 1835–1924?
A father's talks with his children about three
great characters, by a Confederate soldier.
Lynchburg, J. P. Bell co., printers, 1892. 36 p.
23½cm.   NcD   **50**
"Preface" signed: R. B. Stratton.
Lee, Jackson and Stuart.

Strong, Henry
U. S. Grant and Robert E. Lee, a comparison by a Northern soldier. *SB* n s ii (1886/87)
279–83.   **51**

Townsend, Thomas Seaman, 1829–1908.
Specimen pages of Our heroes, dead and
living, a memorial record of all officers and
men in the military and naval service, whose
names have received honorable mention in
official reports, newspaper correspondence,
obituary notices, and otherwise. Compiled by
Thomas S. Townsend. Vol. i, April 13, 1861 –
April 13, 1863, containing 5000 names. New
York, Charles D. Richardson, 1866. 15, (1) p.
24cm.   CSmH   **52**
"Never published, the specimen pages contain a
large amount of information," *Nicholson Catalogue.*

Victor, Orville James, 1827–1910.
Men of the time, being biographies of Gen-
erals Halleck, Pope, Siegel, Corcoran, Prentiss,
Kearney, Hatch, Augur. New York, Beadle and
co. [c1862] 100 p. front. (port.), ports. 16cm.
CSmH DLC   **53**
Introduction signed: O. J. V.

—— —— Butler, Banks, Burnside, Baler,
Stevens, Wilcox, Weber. New York, Beadle
and co. [c1862] 100 p. front. (port.), ports.
16cm.   CSmH DLC   **54**
Plates are paged.

—— —— Hooker, Rosecrans, Grant, Mc-
Clernand, Mitchell. New York, Beadle and co.
[c1863] 99 p. front. (port.), ports. 16cm.
Plates are paged.   CSmH DLC   **55**

Walker, Charles D
Memorial Virginia military institute. Biographical sketches of the graduates and élèves

of the Virginia military institute who fell dur-
ing the War between the States, by Charles
D. Walker. Philadelphia, J. B. Lippincott &
co., 1875. 585 p. 23cm.   CSmH DLC   **56**
"Errata" slip inserted.
Index identifies authors of biographies.

Ward, William H
Records of members of the Grand army of
the Republic, with a complete account of the
twentieth national encampment, being a care-
ful compilation of biographical sketches. . . .
A history of the growth, usefulness, and important events of the Grand army of the Republic,
from its origin to the present time. Edited by
William H. Ward. San Francisco, H. S. Crocker
& co., 1886. 624 p. front. (port.). 26cm.
DLC NcD   **57**
An additional page in NcD's copy announces the
publication of a second volume in 1887.

Warner, Ezra Joseph, 1910–
General in Blue, lives of the Union com-
manders, by Ezra J. Warner. [Baton Rouge]
Louisiana State University press [1964] xxix,
(1), 679, (1) p. ports. 25cm.   NN   **58**
Title on two leaves.
"Bibliography," 673–[80]
Text in double columns.

—— Generals in Gray, the lives of the Con-
federate commanders, by Ezra J. Warner.
[Baton Rouge] Louisiana State University
press [1959] xxvii, 420 p. ports. 25cm.
Title on two leaves.   NN   **59**
"Bibliography," 401–20.
Text in double columns.

Yeary, Mamie
Reminiscences of the boys in Gray, 1861–
1865, compiled by Miss Mamie Yeary. Dallas,
Published for the author by Smith & Lamar
[1912] 904 p. plates (illus., 1 col.; ports.).
25½cm.   NHi   **60**

CANALS

Sanderlin, Walter Stanley, 1920–
The vicissitudes of the Chesapeake and
Ohio canal during the Civil war. *JSH* xi (1945)
51–67.   **61**

CEMETERIES

Confederate soldiers, sailors and civilians who
died as prisoners of war at Camp Douglas, Chicago, Ill., 1862–1865. Kalamazoo, Edgar Gray
publications [1968] [107] p. front. (2 illus.).
28cm.   **61A**

Kentucky Confederates buried at Camp Douglas, Illinois. *RKHS* xlvi (1949) 404–09.   **62**

Foote, Frank H
. . . A roster of departed comrades, buried
in the several cemeteries of Port Gibson, Clai-

borne county, State of Mississippi, from April, 1861, to date, May 1, 1917, and command in which they served. [n. p., 1917] 12 p. 15½cm.

MsHa 63

"Closing of the ranks" signed: Frank H. Foote.

Garnett, Alexander Yelverton Peyton, 1820–1888.
Burial ceremonies of Confederate dead. Oration by A. Y. P. Garnett. Ode by Rt. Rev. Wm. Pinkney. December 11, 1874. Washington, D.C. S. & R. O. Polkinhorn, printers, 1875. 16 p. 23cm.   CSmH NcD TxU   64

The reinterment of soldiers killed in Early's raid of 1864.

Hollywood Memorial Association, Richmond, Va.
Register of the Confederate dead, interred in Hollywood cemetery, Richmond, Va. Richmond, Gary, Clemmitt & Jones, printers, 1869. 116, (1) p. front. (fold. plan), illus. on t. p. 24½cm.   CSmH   65

"Explanatory," (1) p.

Ladies' Memorial Association, Charleston, S. C.
Confederate Memorial day at Charleston, S. C. Re-interment of the Carolina dead from Gettysburg. Address of Rev. Dr. Girardeau, odes, &c. Charleston, William G. Mazyck, printer, 1871. 36 p. 22½cm.

CSmH NN   66

"List of South Carolinians who fell at Gettysburg whose remains have been removed to Magnolia cemetery," 32–36.

Osborne, John Ball, 1868–
The story of Arlington, a history and description of the estate and National cemetery, containing a complete list of officers interred there, with biographical sketches of heroes of the Civil and Spanish wars, and notable memorial addresses and poems, by John Ball Osborne. . . . Washington, D.C. [Press of John F. Sheiry] 1899. 106, (1) p. plates (illus., plan, port.). 23cm.   CSmH DLC   67

"Errata," (1) p.

Titus, William A
A Wisconsin burial place of Confederate prisoners of war. *Wisconsin magazine of history* xxxvi (1953) 192–4. 1 illus., 1 port.   68

Underwood, John C
Report of proceedings incidental to the erection and dedication of the Confederate monument, reception and entertainment of renowned Southern Generals and other distinguished personages, at Chicago, Illinois . . . by Jn. C. Underwood. Souvenir edition. Chicago, Wm. Johnston print. co., 1896. x, (2) 285 p. front. (illus.), facsims., illus., ports. 27½cm.

NN   69

Dedication of the Confederate monument in Oakwoods cemetery, Chicago, under the auspices of the ex-Confederate association of Chicago, Camp no 8 United Confederate veterans.
"The autographic edition is limited to three hundred copies."

United Confederate Veterans, Charles Broadway Rouss Camp no 1191, Washington, D.C.
Report on the re-burial of the Confederate dead in Arlington cemetery and attention called to the care required for the graves of Confederate soldiers who died in Federal prisons and military hospitals now buried in Northern states. . . . Washington, D.C., Judd & Detweiler, printers, 1901. 47 p. fold. plan. 23½cm.   DLC   70

United Confederate Veterans. Division of the Northwest.
Appeal for pecuniary aid to care for and monument the remains of the Confederate dead buried on Johnson's island and at Columbus, Ohio. Cincinnati, Cohen & co., printers, 1892. 71, (1) p. fold. table. 18cm. TxU   71

List arranged by state and regiment.

United Confederate Veterans, Illinois.
Register of Confederate soldiers who died in Camp Douglas, 1862–65, and lie buried in Oakwoods cemetery, Chicago, Ills. Cincinnati, Cohen & co., 1892. 58 p. 18cm.   TxU   72

On cover: Appeal for monumental aid and roster of Confederate dead buried in Oakwoods cemetery, Chicago, Ills.
List arranged by state and regiment.

United Daughters of the Confederacy. Fitzhugh Lee Chapter, no 279.
Confederate dead buried in Mt. Olivet cemetery, Frederick, Maryland . . . compiled by Fitzhugh Lee Chapter, no 279, United Daughters of Confederacy. [n. p., 190–] [8] p. 18½cm.   73

Title from cover.

United States. Quartermaster General.
Statement of the disposition of some of the bodies of deceased Union soldiers and prisoners of war whose remains have been removed to National cemeteries in the Southern and Western states. Washington, Govt. print. office. 1868–69. 4 v. 22cm.   NHi   74

Published as General orders: I, 1868, no 8; II, 1868, no 21; III, 1868, no 33; IV, 1869, no 12.

United States Christian Commission.
Record of the Federal dead buried from Libby, Belle Isle, Danville & Camp Lawton prisons, and at City Point, and in the field before Petersburg and Richmond. Published by the U. S. Christian commission, from reports of its agents. Philadelphia, Jas. B. Rodgers, printer, 1865. 168 p. 22½cm.   NHi   75

CENTENNIAL OBSERVANCE

Ambrose, Stephen E   1936–
The Civil war round tables. *Wisconsin magazine of history* XLII (1958/59) 257–62.   **76**

Angle, Paul McClelland, 1900–
Tragic years, the Civil war and its commemoration. *South Atlantic quarterly* LX (1961) 375–89.   **77**

Franklin, John Hope, 1915–
The Civil war and the Negro-American. *Journal of negro history* XLVII (1962) 77–107.   **78**

Hesseltine, William Best, 1902–
The Civil war industry. *Michigan history* XLII (1958) 421–34.   **79**

CHRONOLOGY

Chronology of the great rebellion, and war map, showing the localities of all the battle fields, Cincinnati, Chas. Tuttle [1863?] 72 p. fold. map. 13cm.   CSmH   **80**
Title and imprint from cover.
P. 62–72 are printed in smaller type.

The chronology of the rebellion, a complete history of the war, showing the progress and decline of the most terrible rebellion the world has ever known. Boston, G. W. Tomlinson [c1865] 16 p. 13½cm.   CSmH DLC   **81**

Soldiers' and citizens' album of military and civil record, including a chronological and statistical history of the Civil war. Chicago, Grand Army pub. co., 1891. 372 p. plates (illus., ports.). 26½cm.   CSmH   **82**
Text in double columns.
P. 161–334 are ruled forms for personal military and civil record, personal biography, roster of company, etc.
Copyright by H. O. Brown.

[Bridgeman, Raymond Landon] 1848–1925.
Calendar of the Civil war including every military and naval engagement (except the smallest skirmishes), the secession conventions, Presidential nominations, calls for troops, peace negotiations, important army movements, and other events of interest. Boston, Press of Rockwell and Churchill, 1890. 24 p. 23½cm.   TxU   **83**

Carey, James P
Carey's record of the great rebellion, a carefully compiled chronological history of the war, from the dawn of the rebellion to the dawn of peace, by James P. Carey. New York, Dick & Fitzgerald [c1865] 16 p. 23½cm.
Text in double columns.   CSmH   **84**

Clarke, H   C
Diary of the War for separation, being a daily chronicle of the leading events and his-

tory of the present revolution, from the inauguration of Abraham Lincoln, to the battle of Shiloh, containing full and minute statements of all the battles, skirmishes and engagements, lists of killed and wounded, number of forces engaged, etc. Also, notes of the war, with biographical sketches of the Confederate Generals, remarkable events, etc. Edited by H. C. Clarke. Vicksburg, Clarke's Southern pub. house, 1862. 56 p. 22½cm.
                   CSmH NcU   **85**
On cover: The first year of the War for separation. Events are reported through April 13, 1862.
Crandall 2619.

—— Diary of the War for separation, a daily chronicle of the principal events of the history of the present revolution, to which is added notes and descriptions of all the great battles, including Walker's narrative of the battle of Shiloh. By H. C. Clarke, Vicksburg, Miss. [Augusta, Press of Chronicle and Sentinel, 1862] 191 p. 21½cm.
      CSmH DLC GEU NcD   **86**
"Narrative of the battle of Shiloh, by Alexander Walker of the New Orleans Delta," 114–47.
A reprinting and continuation of the preceding title.
Events are reported through November 1862.
Crandall 2618.

Fisher, Richard Swainson
A chronological history of the Civil war in America . . . by Richard Swainson Fisher. . . . New York, Johnson and Ward, 1863. iv, [5]–160 p. 2 fold. and 8 double maps. 22cm.
       CSmH DLC TxU   **87**
Text in double ruled border.

Hitchcock, Benjamin W
Hitchcock's chronological record of the American Civil war, giving every event in the order of its occurrence, from November 8th, 1860, to June 3d, 1865. Also, a complete list of the vessels captured by the Confederate navy. New York, Benjamin W. Hitchcock, 1868. 106, 561–[65] p. front. (port.). 22½cm.
Text in double columns.   NN CSmH   **88**
"List of Federal vessels captured by the Confederate navy," p. 561–[65], reprinted from the *Commercial and financial chronicle*.
Illus. on p. [1, 3, 4] of cover; map on p. [2] of cover.

Knight, Edward H
The Union war chart. New York, Lorenzo Dow, c1866. col. illus. broadside, 76½cm x 104cm. in boards 15 x 10cm.   CSmH   **89**
Col. illus. of Corps badges in margins.
Cover title: The Union war chart and statistics of the War for the Union.
Copyright by Edward H. Knight.

Niven, Alexander C
Civil war day-by-day, a chronology of the principal events of the war's first year. Compiled by Alexander C. Niven. Edited by Arthur

W. Monks. Cambridge, Mass., Berkshire pub. co. [c1961] 64 p. illus., ports. 20½cm.
Cover illustrated in color. TxU **90**

Scott, Allen M
Chronicles of the great rebellion, by Rev. Allen M. Scott. Fifth edition. Cincinnati, C. F. Vent & co., 1864. 344 p. 19½cm.
NcD **91**
Concludes with the capture of Vicksburg.
Written in scriptural language.
CSmH has reprintings, 22nd edition, 1864, and 26th edition, 1868; TxU has 13th edition, 1864.

United Daughters of the Confederacy. St. Louis Chapter 624.
Dixie dates. St. Louis [c1912] [60] p. col. front. (illus.). 22½. CSmH **92**
Title from cover.
"Erratum" slip included.

United States. Adjutant General's Office.
List of events of which reports are on file in the Adjutant-General's office, 1860–1865. [Washington, 1883] 93 p. 21½cm.
Errata slips inserted. CSmH **93**

United States. Pensions Bureau.
. . . Service in and close of War of rebellion, Act 27, 1890. [Washington, 1895] 8 p. 23cm.
CSmH **94**
Caption title. At head of title: No. 215. Department of the interior, Washington, D.C., April 5, 1895.
Establishes terminal dates for enlistments as service in the Civil war.

United States. War Records Office.
Memorandum of events from January 1, 1863, to May 26, 1865. [Washington, War Records office, 1883] 109 p. 23cm.
CSmH **95**

[Westcott, Thompson] 1820–1888.
Chronicles of the great rebellion against the United States of America, being a concise record and digest of the events connected with the struggle, civil, political, military and naval, with the dates, victories, losses and results, embracing the period between April 23, 1860, and October 31, 1865. Philadelphia, A. Winch [c1867] 136, (4) p. 24cm. CSmH **96**
Text in double columns.
"Names of Governors of States and Territories 1861–'65," (4) p.

COMPENDIUMS

The Union army, a history of military affairs in the loyal states, 1861–65. Records of the regiments in the Union army. Cyclopedia of battles. Memoirs of commanders and soldiers. . . . Madison, Federal pub. co., 1908. 8 v. plates (ports.). 24cm. DLC NN **97**
Contents: i–iv Military affairs and regimental histories.

v–vi Cyclopedia of battles.
vii The navy.
viii Biographical.

Boatner, Mark Mayo, 1921–
The Civil war dictionary, by Mark Mayo Boatner III. Maps and diagrams by Major Allan C. Northrup and Lowell I. Miller. New York, David McKay co. [c1959] xvi, 974 p. maps. 22cm. NN **98**
Two theater maps with calendars of campaigns, end papers.

Campbell, Robert Allen
The rebellion register, a history of the principal persons and places, important dates, documents and statistics, military and political, connected with the Civil war in America. To which is added a citizen's manual, containing national documents, proclamations, and statistics, political platforms, Grant's report, parliamentary rules, &c., alphabetically arranged. Compiled from official and other authentic sources, by Robert A. Campbell. Kalamazoo, R. A. Campbell, 1866. 378, (1) p. 19½cm. CSmH **99**
"Index," (1) p.

—— —— Indianapolis, A. D. Streight, 1867. 378, (1) p. 19½cm. NHi **100**

Carnahan, J Worth
History of the easel-shaped monument and a key to the principals and objects of the Grand army of the Republic and its co-workers . . . Chicago, Dux pub. co. [1893] vi, 424 p. front. (illus.), illus., plate (9 ports.). 22½cm.
DLC NN **101**
"Author's preface" signed: J. W. Carnahan.
Partial contents: List of Union army regiments, 92–9; List of battles and engagements, 101–94; Roster of the posts of the Grand army of the Republic, 213–409; Naval engagements, 195–212.

—— Manual of the Civil war and key to the Grand army of the Republic and kindred societies, by J. Worth Carnahan. Revised edition. Chicago, Easel Monument Association, 1897. 255 p. illus., ports. 22½cm. DLC **102**
Includes Corps engagements, lists of battles and campaigns, and ruled pages for an individual record.

—— Military record with historic reference. [Washington, D.C., Army and Navy Historical Association, 1899?] 255 p. facsims., illus., ports. 22cm. CSmH **103**
Title from cover.
P. 231–47 are ruled blank pages for "reminiscences." Pockets on covers for individual records and portraits.
A re-issue, the title page omitted and some changes of text at the end of the author's Manual of the Civil war, Chicago, 1897.

Dyer, Frederick Henry, 1849–1917.
A compendium of the War of the rebellion, compiled and arranged from official records of

Compendiums, continued

the Federal and Confederate armies, reports of the Adjutant generals of the several states, the army registers and other reliable documents and sources, by Frederick H. Dyer. Including in three departments the matter as here outlined. Organization of the several military divisions, Departments, Armies, Army Corps, Divisions, Brigades and other important commands of the United States army formed during the War of the rebellion, 1861–1865, showing the troops assigned to each and the various commanders of each formation to its discontinuance. A complete record of the battles, engagements, combats, actions, skirmishes and important operations, tabulated by States and showing the Union troops engaged in each event. A concise history of each and every regiment, battery, battalion and other organizations mustered by the several States for service in the Union army during the period referred to. Des Moines, Dyer pub. co., 1908. 1796 p. 30½cm.   DLC NN   **104**

"The following errors have been discovered since publication, February 15, 1909, to date, May 1, 1910," leaf laid in NN's copy.

—— —— With a new introduction by Bell Irvin Wiley. New York, Thomas Yoseloff [1959] 3 v. (1796 p.) illus., maps, ports. 28cm.   NN   **105**

A photographic reprinting with the addition of illustrative material.

La Bree, Benjamin, 1847?–1935.

The Confederate soldier in the Civil war, 1861–1865, prefaced by an eulogy by Major-General Fitzhugh Lee. A complete history of the foundation and formation of the Confederacy and the secession of the Southern states and prominent parts taken by Hon. Jefferson Davis and others. Campaigns, battles, sieges, charges, skirmishes, by General Robert E. Lee . . . [57 names] and others. The Confederate states navy . . . by Admiral Franklin Buchanan . . . [12 names]. Edited by Ben La Bree. Louisville, Courier-journal print. co., 1895. 480 p. col. front. (illus.), facsims., illus., maps, ports. 32cm.   DLC NHi   **106**

"Flags of the Confederate states of America," four col. illus.
Text in triple columns.
DLC has an 1897 reprinting.

—— The Confederate soldier in the Civil war. The campaigns, battles, sieges, charges and skirmishes described by . . . [15 names] and other military leaders. The foundation and formation of the Confederacy, described by Jefferson Davis, Alexander H. Stephens, Judah P. Benjamin and others. The Confederate navy, described by Franklin Buchanan, Raphael Semmes and other naval leaders. Eulogy

by Fitzhugh Lee. Edited by Ben La Bree. Preface by John S. Blay. Paterson, N. J., Pageant Books [1959] 480 p. facsims., illus., maps, ports. 41½cm.   NN   **107**

"Flags of the Confederate states of America," 4 col. illus. [5]

Lord, Francis Alfred, 1911–

Civil war collector's encyclopedia, arms, uniforms, and equipment of the Union and Confederacy, by Francis A. Lord. Harrisburg, Stackpole co. [c1963] 360 p. illus. 29cm.   NN   **108**

Alphabetical arrangement of entries with cross references.
Col. illus, end paper.

Manson, George J

A diary of the Grand army of the Republic and hand-book of military information . . . by George J. Manson. New York, Fowler & Wells co. [c1894] 122 p. 16cm.   CSmH   **109**

"Chronological history of the Civil war," 41–73.

Pakula, Marvin H

Centennial album of the Civil war, by Marvin H. Pakula, in collaboration with William J. Ryan and David K. Rothstein. New York, Thomas Yoseloff [c1960] 299 p. 20 col. plates (illus.), ports. 36½cm.   NN   **110**

Except for those of Lincoln and Davis, the "Command roster," the portraits are on rectos with descriptive text on facing versos.

Wood, Robert C

Confederate hand-book, a compilation of important data and other interesting and valuable matter relating to the War between the States, 1861–65. . . . [New Orleans, L. Graham & Son, c1900] 126, (1), xix p. 1 illus., 2 col. plates (illus.), port. on t. p. 23cm.   CSmH TxU   **111**

"Introduction" signed: Robt. C. Wood.
"Table of contents," (1) p.
Advertising matter, xix p.
"Errata" slip inserted.

Conscientious Objectors

Cartland, Fernando Gale

Southern heroes; or, the Friends in war time, by Fernando G. Cartland. With an introduction by Benjamin F. Trueblood. . . . Third edition. Poughkeepsie, Fernando G. Cartland, 1897. xxviii, 480 p. plates (illus., ports.). 21cm.   CSmH TxU   **112**

Foster, Ethan

The conscript Quakers, being a narrative of the distress and relief of four young men from the draft for the war in 1863. Cambridge, Printed at the Riverside press, 1883. 29 p. 16cm.   CSmH DLC NB   **113**

—— —— Second edition. Cambridge, Printed at the University press, 1855, 42 p. 21cm.   CSmH   **114**

DEFENSE OF THE SOUTHERN CAUSE

Cave, Robert Catlett
The men in Gray, by Robert Catlett Cave. . . . Nashville, Confederate Veteran, 1911. 143 p. front. (port.), 2 plates (illus., 1 col.). 19½cm.
CSmH **115**

Christian, George Llewellyn, 1841–1924.
The Confederate cause and its defenders, an address delivered before the Grand camp of Confederate veterans of Virginia at the annual meeting held at Culpepper C. H., October 4, 1898, by George L. Christian. . . . Richmond, Wm. Ellis Jones, printer, 1898. 27 p. 23½cm.
CSmH **116**

Cussons, John, 1838–1912.
A glance at current history, by John Cussons. Glen Allen, Va., Cussons, May & co., 1899. 172 p. front. (port.). 18cm.
CSmH DLC **117**
"A glance at current history," 11–71, also published separately, 1900, "United States history as the Yankees makes and takes it."

——— United States "history" as the Yankees makes and takes it, by a Confederate soldier. Glen Allen, Va., Cussons, May & co., 1900. 99 p. 17½cm.
WvU **118**
At head of title: Third edition. . . .

Harrison, W   H
Capt. W. H. Harrison shows that Cooper's history does not do the South justice. [Atlanta, 1898] 5 p. 23cm.
CSmH NN **119**
"I was appointed to prepare and submit a written criticism of the school history recently written by Professors Cooper, Estill and Lemon, of Texas, and published by Ginn & co., of Boston, Mass."
Title from cover.

Meriwether, Elizabeth (Avery), 1824–
Facts and falsehoods concerning the war on the South, 1861–1865, by George Edmonds [pseud.]. Memphis, For sale by A. R. Taylor & co. [c1904] vii, (1), 271 p. 22cm.
CSmH DLC NbU GEU TxU **120**

Reed, John Calvin, 1836–1910.
The brothers' war, by John C. Reed of Georgia. Boston, Little, Brown, and co., 1906. xviii, 456 p. 21cm.
CSmH DLC **121**

Rutherford, Mildred Lewis, 1852–1928.
Truths of history, presented by Mildred Lewis Rutherford. A fair, unbiased, impartial, unprejudiced and conscientious study of history. Object: to secure a peaceful settlement of the many perplexing questions now causing contention between the North and the South. Athens [1920?] 114 p. 23½cm.
DLC MB **122**
Contents: The Constitution of the United States (1787) was a compact between sovereign states and

not perpetual nor national; Secession was not rebellion; The North was responsible for the War between the States; The War between the States was not fought to hold the slaves; The slaves were not illtreated in the South and the North was largely responsible for their presence in the South. . . .

Smith, John Julius Pringle
The War between the States, its causes and consequences as now described by Northern expositors. Also, a refutation of calumnies from the same quarter, and a vindication, sustained by documentary evidence, of the South and Southern character, against the slanders upon them . . . by J. Pringle Smith. Charleston, J. D. Parry, printer, 1880. 68 p. 23cm.
CSmH **123**

Sweeney, Talbot
A vindication from a Northern standpoint of Gen. Robt. E. Lee and his fellow officers who left the United States army and navy in 1861, from the Northern charge of treason and perjury, by Talbot Sweeney. Richmond, J. L. Hill print. co., 1890. 48 p. 22cm.
CSmH **124**

ENTERTAINMENT OF THE SOLDIER

Hutchinson, John Wallace, 1821–1908.
The book of brothers (second series), being a history of the adventures of John W. Hutchinson and his family in the camps of the Army of the Potomac. Boston, S. Chism, Franklin print. house, 1864. 24 p. port. on cover. 18cm.
CSmH **125**

Lovett, Robert W   1913–
The soldiers' free library. CWH VIII (1962) 54–63. **126**

Philadelphia.
First annual report of the soldiers' reading room. Re-opened October 13th, 1863. Location: 20th street, between Market & Chesnut streets. Philadelphia, Eckel, printer, 1863. 21 p. 18cm.
CSmH DLC **127**

Quenzel, Carrol Hunter, 1906–
Books for the boys in Blue. *Journal of the Illinois State historical society* XLIV (1951) 218–30. **128**

ETHNIC GROUPS
GENERAL

Lonn, Ella, 1879–1962.
Foreigners in the Confederacy [by] Ella Lonn. Chapel Hill, University of North Carolina press, 1940. xi, 566 p. plates (ports.). 24cm.
NbU **129**
"Confederate military companies composed for foreign born," 92–131; A list of foreign companies by States, 496–502.

CZECH

Cermak, Josef
Dějiny občanske války s připojením zkušeností českych vojínů sestavil Josef Čermak. Chicago, Tiskem a nákladem Augusta Geringera, 1889. 414, (6) p. illus., ports., plates (illus., maps). 26cm.   CSmH DLC   *130*
"Obsah," (6) p.

GERMAN

Kaufmann, Wilhelm
Die Deutschen im Amerikanischen Bürgerkrieg (Sezessionkrieg, 1861–1865), von Wilhelm Kaufmann. Munich, Druck und Verlag von R. Oldenbourg, 1911. xii, 588 p. maps. 22½cm.   NN   *131*
Partial contents: Biographischer Teil, Deutsche Unionsoffiziere, 443–566; Deutsche Konföderierte, 566–75.

Rosengarten, Joseph George, 1835–1921.
The German soldier in the wars of the United States, an address read before the Pioneer-Verein . . . by J. G. Rosengarten. . . . Philadelphia, J. B. Lippincott co., 1886. 49 p. 23cm.   CSmH DLC   *132*
"Reprinted from the United service magazine," July and August, 1885.

—— The German soldier in the wars of the United States, by J. B. Rosengarten. Philadelphia, J. B. Lippincott co., 1886. 175 p. 18½cm.
                                     CSmH DLC   *133*
Includes a list of Civil war officers who were of German extraction.

—— —— Second edition, revised and enlarged. Philadelphia, J. B. Lippincott co., 1890. 298 p. 18½cm.   CSmH DLC   *134*

HUNGARIAN

Pivany, Eugene
Hungarians in the Civil war, by Eugene Pivany. Illustrated by John Kemeny. . . . Cleveland, 1913. 61 p. illus., ports. 19cm.
                                     CSmH NN   *135*
"Reprinted from 'Dongo,' tenth anniversary number."

Vasvary, Edmund
Lincoln's Hungarian heroes, the participation of Hungarians in the Civil war, 1861–1865, by Edmund Vasvary. Washington, Hungarian Reformed Federation of America, 1939. 171 p. facsim., illus., ports. 27½cm.
Includes roster.   WHi   *136*
Hungarian text, [103]–71.

IRISH

The Irish volunteers memorial meeting and Military hall festival, October – November

1877. Charleston, News and Courier presses, 1878. 35, (4) p. 21½cm.   NHi ScU   *137*
Contents of (4) p.: Roll of the Irish volunteers that volunteered . . . September 16th, 1860; Roll of the Irish volunteers, Company "K," First regiment of South Carolina; Roll of Irish volunteers mustered into Confederate service, as Company "C," Charleston battalion; To the Irish volunteers, by James Power. Text in double columns.

Garland, John Lewis
Irish soldiers of the American Confederacy. *Irish sword* I (Dublin, 1949/53) 174–80. *138*

Kilpatrick, Hugh Judson, 1836–1881.
The Irish soldier in the War of the rebellion [delivered in Boston theatre, 1874]. [Deckertown, N. J., Independent print, 1880] 11 p. port. on cover.   CSmH   *139*
Title from cover.

O'Connell, J   C
The Irish in the Revolution and the Civil war. Revised and enlarged embracing the Spanish-American and Philippine wars and every walk of life. By Dr. J. C. O'Connell. Washington, D.C., Trades Unionist press [c1903] 116 p. 19½cm. CSmH DLC   *140*

JEWISH

Katz, Irving Isaac, 1907–
The Jewish soldier from Michigan in the Civil war [by] Irving I. Katz. Detroit, Wayne State University press, 1962. x, 62 p, illus., ports. 21cm.   Vi   *141*
"Michigan regimental records" with list of Jewish soldiers, 16–31. "Biographical sketches," 32–41.

Korn, Bertram Wallace, 1918–
American Jewry and the Civil war, by Bertram Wallace Korn. With an introduction by Allan Nevins. Philadelphia, Jewish pub. society, 1951. xii, 331 p. facsims., plates (ports.). 24cm.   DLC Vi   *142*

Meyer, Isadore Solomon, 1903–
The American Jew in the Civil war. Catalog of the exhibit of the Civil war centennial Jewish historical commission. Edited by Isadore S. Meyer. New York, American Jewish Historical Society, 1962. 162 p. facsims., plates (illus., facsims., ports.). 24cm.   NN   *143*
"The text of this volume is a reprint of the Publication of the American Jewish historical society, volume L, number 4 (pages 257–424)."

Wolf, Simon, 1836–1923.
The American Jew as patriot, soldier and citizen, by Simon Wolf. Edited by Louis Edward Levy. Philadelphia, Levytype co., 1895. xiii, (2), 576 p. front. (illus.), plate (illus.). 22½cm.   CSmH DLC Vi   *144*
"Errata," [xv]

Partial contents: Jewish staff officers in the Union army, 114–15: List of Jewish soldiers in the Union and Confederate armies during the Civil war, classified according to States and alphabetically arranged, 117–409; Soldiers of the Civil war, unclassified as to commands, 410–22; Addenda to lists of soldiers, 423. Contributed articles are signed.

FLAGS

[Eight color plates illustrating 48 Union and Confederate regimental Flags] "The list of battle flags with descriptions and explanations," 15–65. *In* My story of the war, by Mary A. Livermore, 1890.   NN   *145*

Armstrong, William Jackson, 1841–
The captured battle flags. *Magazine of American history* xviii (1887) 252–5.   *146*
In the possession of the War department.

Bennett, O   W
Battle flags captured and re-captured during the late Civil war in the United States, and now in the custody of the War department at Washington, D.C., giving name and organization to which they belonged at time of capture, and where known, name and rank of the soldier capturing the same, as well as the command to which he was attached, and the time and place of capture. Compiled from official records. Philadelphia, O. W. Bennett, c1890. 31 p. 18½cm.   CSmH DLC   *147*

Chestney, M   Jemison
The service of the Confederate flags, by M. Jemison Chestney. [Macon, c1926] [14] p. illus. 23cm.   NcD   *148*
Title from cover.

Conrad, Mary Lynn
Confederate banners, by Mary Lynn Conrad. Harrisonburg, Va., [1907] 20 p. cover illus. in color. 18cm.   CSmH   *149*

Coulter, Ellis Merton, 1890–
The flags of the Confederacy. *GHQ* xxxvii (1937) 188–89. col. plate (illus.).   *150*

Hill, Maynard
Return of the Confederate flags. *Michigan history magazine* xxvi (1942) 5–23. illus. *151*

Iowa. Battle Flag Committee
"Battle flag day," August 10, 1894. Ceremonials attending the transfer of the battle flags of Iowa regiments from the Arsenal to the Capitol. [Des Moines, F. R. Conaway, State printer, 1896] 85 p. illus. 22cm. NN *152*

New York State. Military Statistics Bureau.
History of flags now in charge of the Bureau. *In its* Fifth annual report, 1868, 169–265.
          NN   *153*

United Confederate Veterans.
The flags of the Confederate states of America, by authority of the United Confederate veterans. Baltimore, A. Hoen & co. [c1907] [6] p. col. plate (illus.). 23½cm. NcD   *154*
Title and imprint from cover.

United States. Quartermaster Department.
Flags of the Army of the United States carried during the War of the rebellion, 1861–1865, to designate the headquarters of the different armies, army corps, divisions and brigades. Compiled under direction of the Quartermaster general U. S. army. Philadelphia, Burke & McFetridge, Lith., 1887. vol. of 85 col. plates (illus.). 36cm.   NN   *155*

United States. War Department. Ordnance Museum.
Catalogue of Rebel flags captured by Union troops, since April 9, 1861, deposited in the Ordnance museum, War department. [Washington, n. d.] 31 p. 23cm. CSmH NN   *156*
Entries close with no 540, Rebel battle-flag brought from Richmond by Master Tad Lincoln.

Ware, Charles E
The flags of the Confederate armies returned to the men who bore them by the United States government. [St. Louis, Designed, engraved and printed by Buxton & Skinner] 1905. [56] p. col. illus. 25½cm.
          CSmH DLC   *157*
Copyright by Charles E. Ware.
"Souvenir presented to the Confederate veterans at their reunion, at Louisville, Ky., June 14th, 1905, with the compliments of the Passenger department, 'Cotton belt route.'"

West Virginia. Archives and History Department.
The battle flags, banners and guidons of West Virginia, as they are and what is known of them forty-one years after the close of the Civil war. *In its* Biennial report, 1904/06, 61–79.   NN   *158*

——— ——— [Supplementary] *In its* Biennial report, 1906/08, 67–8.   NN   *159*

Williams, Rebecca Yancey
Inauguration of a display of returned battle flags of the Confederacy [Battle Abbey]. *VMHB* lv (1955) 282–5.   *160*

Wisconsin State Historical Society.
I. Confederate battle flags in the Museum of the Wisconsin historical society. II. Photographs of Confederate officers and monuments in the Library of the Society. Madison, 1906. [11] p. plates (illus.). 23cm.   NcD   *161*

FLIGHT OF JEFFERSON DAVIS

Ashmore, Otis, 1853–
The story of the Confederate treasure. *GHQ*
II (1918) 119–38.   *162*

Barbee, David Rankin, 1874–1958.
The capture of Jefferson Davis. [1947] 36,
(1) p. 2 plates (illus.). 23cm.   DLC   *163*
"Reprinted from Tyler's quarterly historical and
genealogical magazine July, 1947."
Title from cover.

Davis, Jefferson, 1808–1889.
A letter by . . . relating to events preceding his capture. *GHQ* XXXI (1947) 30–3. *164*

Davis, Nora Marshall
Jefferson Davis's route from Richmond, Virginia, to Irwinville, Georgia, April 2 – May 10,
1865. *Proceedings of the South Carolina historical association* (1941) 11–20.   *165*

Dimick, Howard T
The capture of Jefferson Davis. *JMH* IX
(1947) 238–54.   *166*

—— The mythical Confederate "treasure."
JMH XI (1949) 243–9.   *167*

Hanna, Alfred Jackson, 1893–
Flight into oblivion, by A. J. Hanna. [Rich-
mond] Johnson pub. co. [c1938] xiii, 306 p.
illus., maps, ports. 21½cm.   NN   *168*

Reagan, John Henniger, 1818–1905.
Flight and capture of Jefferson Davis. *AW*
147–59.   *169*

Tilghman, Tench Francis,   –1867.
The Confederate baggage and treasure train
ends its flight in Florida, a diary of . . . by
A. J. Hanna. *FHQ* XVII (1938/39) 159–80.
map.   *170*

Wilson, James Harrison, 1837–1925.
How Jefferson Davis was overtaken. *AW*
554–89.   *171*

GENERAL HISTORIES

The comprehensive history of the great Civil
war, from Bull run to Appomattox, containing
correct accounts of the leading statesmen and
Generals, both in the Union and Confederate
councils and battle fields. Together with full
and vivid accounts of all the important sieges,
battles, and naval engagements. New York,
World Manufacturing co., c1885. 552 p. front.
(illus.). 19½cm.   LNHT   *172*

Lloyd's battle history of the great rebellion,
complete from the capture of Fort Sumter,
April 14, 1861, to the capture of Jefferson

Davis, May 10, 1865, embracing General
Howard's tribute to the volunteer. . . . New
York, H. H. Lloyd, 1865. 566 p. plates (illus.;
maps, partly fold.; ports.). 23½cm.
Text within ornamental border.   GEU   *173*
Portraits are accompanied by biographical sketches.

Abbott, John Stevens Cabot, 1805–1877.
Geschichte des Bürgerkrieges in Amerika.
Eine vollständige und unparteiische Beschrei-
bung des Ursprungs und Fortgangs der Rebellion, der verschiedenen Kämpfe zu Wasser
and zu Land, der Heldenthaten von Heeren
wie von einzelnen und von ergreifenden Vor-
fällen auf dem Schlachtfelde, im Lager, Hospital und Schiffe. Von John S. C. Abbott.
Ueberetzt [sic] von Julius Würburger und
Georg Dietz. Illustrirt mit Karten, Abrissen
und zahlreichen Stahlstichen und Portraits
ausgezeichneter Männer nach Original-Zeich-
nungen von Darley und andern vozüglichen
Künstlern. Springfield, Verlag von Gurdon
Bill, 1863–66. 2 v. maps and plans, plates
(illus., ports.). 25cm.   IaHi   *174*

—— The history of the Civil war in America,
comprising a full and impartial account of the
origin and progress of the rebellion, of the
various naval and military engagements, of the
heroic deeds performed by armies and individuals, and of touching scenes in the field, the
camp, the hospital, and the cabin, by John S.
C. Abbott. Illustrated . . . from original de-
signs by Darley and other eminent artists. . . .
Springfield, Gurdon Bill, 1863–66. 2 v. maps
and plans, plates (illus., ports.). 25½cm.
                             CSmH DLC IsHi   *175*

Barber, John Warner, 1798–1885.
The loyal West in the times of the rebellion;
also, before and since, being an encyclopedia
and panorama of the Western states, Pacific
states and territories of the Union . . . by John
W. Barber and Henry Howe. Cincinnati, F. A.
Howe, 1865. 764 p. illus., plates (illus., ports.).
23cm.   CSmH DLS   *176*

Barnes, Eric Wollencott
The War between the States, by Eric
Wollencott Barnes. Illustrated by W. N. Wilson. New York, Whittlesey House [1959] 143,
(1) p. illus., 2 maps. 25½cm.   PGC   *177*

Catton, Bruce, 1899–
The centennial history of the Civil war . . .
[by] Bruce Catton. E. B. Long, Director of
research. Garden City, Doubleday & co., 1961–
65. 3 v. plates (2 charts, maps). 24½cm.
                                           NN   *178*
Contents: 1. The coming fury, 1961; 2. Terrible
swift sword, 1963; 3. Never call retreat, 1965. Maps
on end papers.

Childs, Emery E
A history of the Civil war in the United States, 1861–1865. New York [M. H. Green, printer] 1885. 52 p. 15cm.   CSmH   **179**
Copyright by Emery E. Childs.

Coulter, Ellis Merton, 1890–
The Confederate States of America, by E. Merton Coulter. [Baton Rouge] Louisiana State University press, 1950. x, (4), 644 p. plates (illus., double map). 24cm. (A history of the South, vol. VII).   **180**

Crafts, William Augustus, 1819–1906.
The Southern rebellion, being a history of the United States, from the commencement of President Buchanan's administration through the War for the suppression of the rebellion. Containing a record of political events, military movements, campaigns, expeditions, battles, skirmishes, etc. Prepared from official documents and other authentic sources. By W. A. Crafts. Boston, Samuel Walker & co., 1866–67. 2 v. plates (maps, 1 double; ports.). 30cm.   CSmH   **181**
Text in double columns.
Chapters are continuously numbered.

Davis, Jefferson, 1808–1889.
The rise and fall of the Confederate government, by Jefferson Davis. London, Longmans, Green and co., 1881. 2 v. maps, plates (fold. maps, ports.). 25cm.   CSmH   **182**

—— —— Richmond, Garrett and Massie [1938] 2 v. fronts. (ports.), 1 illus., maps, ports. 23½cm.   TxU   **183**
"United daughters of the Confederacy memorial edition."

—— —— New York, Thomas Yoseloff [c1958] 2 v. plates (maps, ports.). 23½cm.
            TxU   **184**
A photographic reproduction of the 1881 edition.
Additional material, "Foreword by Bell I. Wiley."

Derry, Joseph Tyrone, 1841–1926.
Story of the Confederate states; or, history of the War for Southern independence. Embracing a brief but comprehensive sketch of the early settlement of the country, trouble with the Indians, the French revolutionary and Mexican wars, and a full complete and graphic account of the great four years' war between the North and the South, its causes, effects, etc. By Joseph T. Derry, with an introduction by Gen. Clement A. Evans. . . . Richmond, B. F. Johnson pub. co., 1895. xvi, 19–448 p. illus., maps, ports. 24cm.   MsHa   **185**

Dowdey, Clifford, 1904–
The land they fought for, the story of the South as the Confederacy, 1832–1865, by Clifford Dowdey. Garden City, Doubleday & co., 1955. viii, 438 p. 24cm.   CSmH   **186**

"Mainstream of America series, edited by Lewis Gannett."
Map on end paper.

Draper, John William, 1811–1882.
History of the American Civil war, by John William Draper. New York, Harper & Brothers, 1867–70. 3 v. maps and plans. 25cm.
Contents: CSmH   DLC   **187**
I The causes of the war, and the events preparatory to it, up to the close of President Buchanan's administration.
II From the inauguration of President Lincoln to the Proclamation of emancipation of the slaves.
III To the end of the war.

Duyckinck, Evert Augustus, 1816–1878.
National history of the War for the Union, civil, military and naval, founded on official and other authentic documents, by Evert A. Duyckinck. Illustrated . . . by Alonzo Chappel and Thomas Nast. New York, Johnson, Fry and co. [186–] 3 v. plates (illus., ports.). 28½cm.   CSmH   **188**
Added engraved title pages: History of the War for the Union. Copyright dates are 1861, 1862 and 1868.
Appeared in parts with title: History of the War for the Union, by E. A. Duyckinck. Illustrated by Alonzo Chappel.
Text in double columns and within border lines.

—— National Geschichte des Krieges für die Union, politisch und militärisch, nach offiziellen und andern authentischen Dokumenten beschrieben, von Evert A. Duyckinck. Deutsch bearbeitet von Friedrich Kapp. Mit seinen Stahltischen von See- und Landschlachten und Porträts berühunter Generale und Seeheldon nach Originalgemälden von Alonzo Chappel und Thomas Nast. New York, Johnson, Fry & co. [186–] 2 v. plates (illus., ports.). 28cm.   NN   **189**
Added engraved title page: History of the War for the Union, civil, military & naval, by E. A. Duyckinck. Illustrated by Alonzo Chappel.
Text in double columns and within border lines.
Originally issued in parts with cover title: Geschichte des Krieges. . . .

Eaton, Clement, 1898–
A history of the Southern Confederacy [by] Clement Eaton. New York, Macmillan co., 1954. ix, (2), 351 p. 21½cm.   NN   **190**

Eggleston, George Cary, 1839–1911.
The history of the Confederate war, its causes and its conduct, a narrative and critical history, by George Cary Eggleston. New York, Sturgis & Walton, 1910. 2 v. 21½cm
            CSmH   DLC   **191**

Ferree, Peter V   1822–1868.
The heroes of the War for the Union and their achievements: a complete history of the great rebellion, consisting of biographical sketches of officers and statesmen, pictures of great battles . . . by Rev. P. V. Ferree. First

General Histories, continued

series. Cincinnati, R. W. Carroll & co., 1864.
viii, [11]–512 p. front. (port.). 18cm.
                        CSmH MoHi   **192**
"Preface" dated: Somerset, Perry co., Ohio, June 6,
1864.

Formby, John
    The American Civil war, a concise history
of its causes, progress, and results, by John
Formby. New York, Charles Scribner's Sons,
1910. xvii, 520 p. 22½cm.
    "Errata" slip inserted.   CSmH DLC   **193**
    Maps in separate volume.

Frost, Jennett Blakeslee
    The rebellion in the United States; or, the
war of 1861, being a complete history of its
rise and progress . . . by Mrs. J. Blakeslee
Frost. Boston, Degen, Estes and Priest [c1862]
xiv, 11–388 p. plates (illus., ports.). 23½cm.
    Text within double ruled border. CSmH   **194**

Garrett, William Robertson, 1839–1904.
    . . . The Civil war from a Southern stand-
point, by the late William Robertson Garrett
and Robert Ambrose Halley. Printed and published for subscribers only. Philadelphia,
George Barrie & Sons [c1905] xxv, 547 p.
plates (facsims.; illus.; maps, 1 double; ports.).
21½cm.   CSmH DLC   **195**
    At head of title: The history of North America,
volume fourteen.

Greeley, Horace, 1811–1872.
    The American conflict, a history of the great
rebellion in the United States of America,
1860–'64, intended to exhibit especially its
moral and political phases, with the drift and
progress of American opinion respecting
human slavery, from 1776 to the close of the
War for the Union, by Horace Greeley. Hartford, O. D. Case & co., 1864–66. 2 v. maps and
plans, plates (illus., ports.). 24½cm.
                                CSmH   **196**
    Text in double columns and within ruled border.

—— The American conflict, a history by
Horace Greeley. . . . Washington, National
Tribune, 1899. 2 v. maps and plans, plates
(illus., ports.). 26cm.   CSmH   **197**
    Text in double columns.
    A reprinting.

Hanson, Harry, 1884–
    The Civil war, by Harry Hanson. New York,
Duell, Sloan and Pierce [c1962] 672 p. maps.
21½cm.   NN   **198**

Headley, Joel Tyler, 1813–1897.
    The great rebellion, a history of the Civil
war in the United States, by J. T. Headley.
Hartford, Hurlbut, Williams & co., 1865–66.
2 v. plates (illus., ports.). 23cm. DLC   **199**

Added engraved title page in I.
"Sold by subscription only."

Hedrick, Mary A
    . . . Incidents of the Civil war during the
four years of its progress, by Mary A. Hedrick. Lowell, Vox Populi press: S. W. Huse &
co., 1888. 179 p. front. (illus.), plates (illus.).
30½cm.   CSmH DLC TxU   **200**

    The plates are "Fac-similes of envelopes used dur-
ing the rebellion." "As they were taken at random
from the papers of the day, I can give no credit to
any paper or to any writer unless the name or initials
were attached."

Henry, Robert Selph, 1889–
    The story of the Confederacy, by Robert
Selph Henry. Indianapolis, Bobbs-Merrill co.
[c1931] 514 p. maps, plates (illus., ports.).
24cm.   CSmH   **201**
    Map on end paper.
    "A synoptic table of events of the War between the
States," 472–93.

Herbert, George B
    . . . A history of the Civil war in America,
by Captain George B. Herbert. A sketch of
the Grand army of the Republic. Also, a collection of anecdotes of the rebellion. [New
York, W. S. Trigg, 1889] xx, [21]–352 p. illus.,
ports. 18cm.   CSmH   **202**
    "Leisure hour library, no. 265."
    At head of title: The mammouth encyclopedia, vol-
ume III, containing.
    A cheap reprinting of his: The popular history of
the War in America, 1884, through p. 413.

—— The popular history of the Civil war in
America (1861–1865), a complete narrative
of events, military, naval, political and Congressional . . . by Capt. George B. Herbert.
New York, F. M. Lupton, 1884. xx, [21]–
415 p. illus., ports. 17½cm.
                        CSmH DLC   **203**

—— —— New York, F. M. Lupton, 1885.
xx, [21]–552 p. illus., ports. 18½cm.
                                MoU   **204**
    "The Grand army of the Republic," 414–44;
"Anecdotes of the rebellion," 445–552.

Howe, Henry, 1816–1893.
    The times of the rebellion in the West, a
collection of miscellanies, showing the part
taken in the war by each Western state, notices
of eminent officers, descriptions of prominent
battles, conspiracies in the West to aid the rebellion, incidents of guerrilla and border warfare, individual adventures, anecdotes illustrating the heroism of Western soldiers, etc., by
Henry Howe. Cincinnati, Howe's Subscription
Book concern, 1867. 252 p. col. front. (illus.),
illus. 22cm.   CSmH NHi   **205**

Humphrey, Willis C
    The great contest, a history of military and
naval operations during the Civil war in the

United States of America, 1861–1865, by Willis C. Humphrey. . . . Detroit, C. H. Smith & co., 1886. 691 p. front. (port.). 24cm.
CSmH DLC TxU **206**
"It will be sold only by subscription," from prospectus in CSmH's copy.
Officers of the United States army, 1860, and Civil war Major and Brigadier Generals volunteers, 633–71. List of battles by States, 672–91.

Johnson, Edwin Rossiter, 1840–1931.
A short history of the War of secession, 1861–1865, by Rossiter Johnson. Boston, Ticknor and co., 1888. xiv, 552 p. maps and plans. 23½cm. CSmH GEU **207**

—— The story of a great conflict, a history of the War of secession, 1861–1865, by Rossiter Johnson. Special contributions by Gen. O. O. Howard [and] Gen. John B. Gordon. New York, Bryan, Taylor & co., 1894. xvi, 604 p. maps and plans, plates (illus., ports.). 23cm.
CSmH DLC GEU **208**
"Second edition." A reprinting of his: A short history of the War of secession, 1888, with additional text.
"Important history suggested by a picture of Sherman and his Generals, by General O. O. Howard," 535–57.
"Last days of the Confederacy, by Gen. John B. Gordon," 558–65.

Jordan, Thomas, 1819–1895.
Beginnings of the Civil war in America. *Magazine of American history* xiv (1885) 25–40, 113–37, 269–87. facsims., illus., plans, ports. **209**

Kennedy, John
A history of the Civil war in the United States, from its commencement in 1861, to January, 1862. To be continued to the termination of the war. By John Kennedy. Philadelphia, Kennedy & Greely [c1861] 308 p. plates (illus., ports.). 21cm.
CSmH DLC GEU **210**

Kettell, Thomas Prentice
History of the great rebellion, from its commencement to its close . . . by Thomas P. Kettell . . . Furnished to subscribers only. Worcester, L. Stebbins, 1862–63. 2 v. (806 p.). maps, plates (illus., ports.). 22cm.
i "Two vols.;" ii "Three vols." TxU **211**
Text within border lines.
P. 797 is followed by p. 806.

—— —— Hartford, L. Stebbins, 1865. 778 p. maps, plates (illus., ports.). 22cm.
CSmH **212**

—— —— Hartford, L. Stebbins, 1866. 778, (4) p. maps, plates (illus., ports.). 22cm.
CSmH **213**
"Military terms," (4) p.

Lee, Guy Carlton, 1862–1936.
The true history of the Civil war, by Guy Carleton Lee. Philadelphia, J. B. Lippincott co., 1903. 421 p. plates (facsims., maps, ports.). 20½cm. CSmH GEU NbU **214**

Liddell, John R
Liddell's record of the Civil war. *SB* n s i (1885/86) 411–20, 529–35. port. **215**

Lossing, Benson John, 1813–1891.
A history of the Civil war, 1861–65, and the causes that led up to the great conflict, by Benson J. Lossing. And a chronological summary and record of every engagement between the troops of the Union and of the Confederacy and showing the total losses and casualties together with maps of localities. Compiled from the official records of the War department. Illustrated with fac-simile photographic reproductions of the official war photographs taken at the time by Mathew B. Brady. . . . New York, War Memorial Association [c1912] 512 p. illus., maps, ports., col. plates (illus.). 30½cm. CSmH DLC **216**
First copyright, 1895.
"Issued in sixteen sections."

—— Pictorial history of the Civil war in the United States of America, by Benson J. Lossing. Illustrated by many hundred engravings on wood, by Lossing and Barritt, from sketches by the authors and others. Philadelphia, George W. Childs (ii-iii, Hartford, T. Belknap), 1866–68. 3 v. fronts. (ports.), facsims., illus., maps and plans, ports. 25cm. CSmH DLC **217**

—— Pictorial field book of the Civil war in America, by Benson J. Lossing. Illustrated by many hundred engravings on wood, by Lossing and Barritt, from sketches by the authors and others. New York, T. Belknap & co., 1868. 3 v. fronts. (ports.), facsims., illus., maps and plans, ports. 24½cm. CSmH **218**
A reprinting of the Pictorial history.

—— —— New Haven, Geo S. Lester, 1877–78. 3 v. fronts. (ports.), facsims., illus., maps and plans, ports. 25½cm. TxU **219**
iii published in 1877 with title, Pictorial history of the Civil war . . . , and statement, "Three volumes in one."
"Preface" dated, September, 1873; the copyright date, 1866.

Luecke, Martin
Der Bürgerkrieg der Vereinigten Staaten, 1861–'65, nach den neuesten offiziellen Quellen bearbeitet, von Martin Lücke. St. Louis, Druck und Verlag von Louis Lange, 1892. vii, (1), 414 p. illus., maps, ports., double plates (illus.), plates (ports.). 22cm.
NN TxU **220**
"Vorwort" signed: Dr. H. Dumling, Redakture der Abendschule.
CSmH and DLC have "Dritte Auflage," a reprinting.

General Histories, continued

Macartney, Clarence Edward Noble, 1879–
Highways and byways of the Civil war, by
Clarence Edward Macartney. . . . Philadelphia,
Dorrance and co. [c1926] 274 p. plates (illus.,
ports.). 21½cm.   Vi   *221*

——— ——— Pittsburgh, Gibson press, 1938.
xiii, 304 p. plates (maps). 21cm. DLC   *222*
"Second edition."
"Western [Eastern] theatre of conflict . . . ," maps
on end papers.

Mathews, Alfred
Chronological history of the War of the rebellion founded on the "Official records of the
Union and Confederate armies," and approved
historical authorities, with biographical notes,
by Alfred Mathews. Supplemented by battlefield maps from government sources, showing
the positions of troops in all important engagements. Also, by numerous illustrations of decisive battles, portraits of army and corps commanders, etc. Philadelphia, L. H. Everts & co.
[n. d.] 68 p. maps, plates (illus., ports.).
35½cm.   CSmH   *223*
A prospectus for a work that was not published.

Moore, James
A complete history of the great rebellion;
or, the Civil war in the United States, 1861–
1865, comprising a full and impartial account
. . . biographical sketches of the principal
actors in the great drama, by Dr. James Moore.
With an introduction by Dr. Shelton Mackenzie. Philadelphia, Quaker City pub. house,
1875. 552 p. plates (illus., ports.). 21cm.
Biographical sketches, 508–52. CSmH   *224*

Nevins, Allan, 1890–
The War for the Union . . . by Allan Nevins.
New York, Charles Scribner's Sons [c1959–60]
2 v. maps and plans, plates (illus., ports.).
24cm.   NN   *225*
Contents: I The improvised war, 1861–62; II War
becomes revolution.

Newman, Ralph Geoffrey, 1911–
The Civil war digest . . . by Ralph Newman
and E. B. Long. Introduction by Allan Nevins.
Maps by Barbara Long. New York, Grosset &
Dunlap [c1956, 1960] xiii, (1), 274 p. facsims.,
illus., maps and plans, ports. 21cm. NN   *226*
Text in double columns.
Plates are paged.
"New and enlarged edition of The Civil war: the
picture chronicle."

Paris, John
The soldier's history of the war, containing
a narrative of events, campaigns and battles.
. . . *OLOD* I (1874/75) 289–303, 401–18,
529–45; II (1875) 1–18, 131–52, 259–79, 389–
406; III (1875) 1–20, 147–61, 291–311, 435–
48, 577–92; IV (1876) 3–18.   *227*

Chapters I-XI.
"To be continued."
Author was Chaplain of the 54th North Carolina.

Paris, Louis Philippe Albert d'Orleans, comte
de, 1838–1894.
Histoire de la guerre civile en Amérique,
par le Comte de Paris. Paris, Calmann Lévy
Frères, 1874–90. 7 v. 23½cm.
                      CSmH DLC TxU   *228*
I-IV were published by Michael Lévy Frères.
Publication dates: I 1874; II 1874; III 1875; IV
1875; V 1883; VI 1883; VII 1890.

——— ——— Cartes et planches. Paris, Michael
Lévy Frères, 1974–83 6 parts in 3. 45½cm.
                      CSmH DLC   *229*

——— History of the Civil war in America, by
the Comte de Paris. . . . Philadelphia, Porter
& Coates (I-II Jos. H. Coates & co.) 1876–[88]
4 v. front. IV (port.), fold. maps. 24½cm.
                                 CSmH   *230*
Title of I-II continues: Translated with the approval
of the author, by Louis F. Tasistro. Edited by Henry
Coppee.
"Editor's note" III-IV signed: J. P. Nicholson.
III 1883; IV 1888.

——— ——— Translated with the approval of the
author, by Louis F. Tasistro. Edited by Henry
Coppee. New edition revised by Bvt. Lieut.
Colonel John P. Nicholson. Philadelphia, John
C. Winston co., 1907. 2 v. fold. maps. 23cm.
A reprinting of volumes I-II.   CSmH   *231*

Paxson, Frederic Logan, 1877–
The Civil war, by Frederic L. Paxson. New
York, Henry Holt and co. [c1911] x, 11–256 p.
4 maps. 17cm.   CSmH DLC   *232*
Half title: Home university library of modern
knowledge, no. 25.

Pollard, Edward Alfred, 1831–1872.
La cause perdue, histoire de la guerre des
Confederes d'apres des rapports officiels et des
documents authentiques, par Edward A. Pollard. Traduction française de Jules Noblom.
Edition illustrée et augmentée de notes et de
renseignements complimentaires concernant La
Louisiane. New Orleans, La Renaissance Loui-
sianaise, 1867. 420, (3) p. plates (3 maps,
ports., mounted port.). 30½cm. LNHT   *233*
Text in double columns.
"Table des matieres," "Pagination des gravures,
cartes et plans," (3) p.
"La cause perdue," mounted port. of the Confederacy leaders against a camp background.

——— The first year of the war, by Edward A.
Pollard. . . . Richmond, West & Johnston,
1862. viii, [17]–374 p. 23cm.
Crandall 2643.   DLC GEU   *234*

——— ——— Corrected and improved edition.
Richmond, West & Johnston, 1862. xvi. [17]–
406 p. 22½cm.   CSmH DLC   *235*
Crandall 2645.

—— —— Corrected and improved [second] edition. Richmond, West & Johnston, 1862. 389 p. plates (map, port.). 23½cm.
   Crandall 2644.   DLC   **236**

—— —— Third edition. Richmond, West & Johnston, 1863. viii, [17]–406 p. 23cm.
   Crandall 2646.   MBAt NcU   **237**

—— Life of Jefferson Davis, with a secret history of the Southern confederacy, gathered "behind the scenes in Richmond." Containing curious and extraordinary information on the principal Southern characters in the late war, in connection with President Davis, and in relation to the various intrigues of his administration. By Edward A. Pollard. . . . Philadelphia, National pub. co., [c1869] viii, 536 p. front. (port.). 22½cm.   CSmH DLC   **238**

—— The lost cause, a new Southern history of the war of the Confederates, comprising a full and authentic account of the rise and progress of the late Southern Confederacy. The campaigns, battles, incidents, and adventures of the most gigantic struggle of the world's history. Drawn from official sources, and approved by the most distinguished Confederate leaders. By Edward A. Pollard. Sold only by subscription. New York, E. B. Treat & co., 1866. xxx, (1), [33]–752, p. plates (ports.). 24cm.   CSmH   **239**

—— The second year of the war, by Edward A. Pollard. . . . Richmond, West & Johnston, 1863. x, [xvii]–326 p. 22½cm. CSmH   **240**
   Crandall 2650.

—— Southern history of the war. The first year of the war. Reprinted from the Richmond corrected edition. New York, Charles B. Richardson, 1863. 389 p. plates (fold. map, ports.). 23cm.   CSmH   **241**

—— Southern history of the war. The second year of the war, by Edward A. Pollard. New York, Charles B. Richardson, 1864. iv, [5]–10, [17]–386 p. plates (fold. map, ports.). 23cm.   CSmH   **242**

—— Southern history of the war. The Third year of the war, by Edward A. Pollard. New York, Charles B. Richardson, 1865. 391 p. plates (ports.). 23cm.   CSmH   **243**
  "Appendix. Jail journal of the author in Fort Warren, etc.," 323–86.

—— Southern history of the war. The last year of the war, by Edward A. Pollard. New York, Charles B. Richardson, 1866. 363 p. plates (ports.). 23cm.   CSmH   **244**

—— Southern history of the war . . . by Edward A. Pollard. New York, Jack Brussel, the Blue & the Gray press [1960] 4 v. 17cm.
  Photographic reprinting.   NN   **245**

Contents: ɪ The first year of the war. ɪɪ The second year of the war. ɪɪɪ The third year of the war. ɪv The last year of the war.

Robertson, James Irvin, 1930–
The Civil war, by James I. Robertson, Jr. Washington, U. S. Civil War Centennial Commission, 1963. 63, (1) p. illus., double map, ports. 23cm.   NN   **246**

Roland, Charles P   1918–
The Confederacy, by Charles P. Roland. . . . [Chicago] University of Chicago press [c1960] xiii, 218 p. 4 maps, plates (illus., ports.). 21cm.   NN   **247**
  Title on two leaves. "The Chicago history of American civilization. Daniel J. Boorstin, editor."

Schmucker, Samuel Mosheim, 1823–1863.
The history of the Civil war in the United States, its cause, origin, progress and conclusion, containing full, impartial and graphic descriptions of the various military and naval engagements . . . and biographical sketches of its heroes. By Samuel M. Schmucker. Revised and completed by Dr. L. P. Brockett. Philadelphia, Jones Brothers & co. [c1865] 1021 p. plates (illus., maps, ports.). 24½cm.
         CSmH DLC GEU   **248**
  Text within ruled border.

Schouler, James, 1839–1920.
History of the United States of America, under the Constitution, by James Schouler, vol. vɪ, 1861–1865. New York, Dodd, Mead & co. [c1899] xxii, 647, (1) p. front. (double map). 21cm.   CSmH DLC   **249**
  "Author's final notes, 1916," (1) p.

Snyder, Ann E
The Civil war from a Southern standpoint, by Mrs. Ann E. Snyder. . . . Printed for the author. Nashville, Pub. House of the M. E. Church, South, 1890. 308 p. plates (illus.). 19cm.   DLC NcD   **250**

—— —— Revised and arranged for use in schools and colleges. Printed for the author. Nashville, Pub. House of the M. E. Church, South, 1893. 356 p. plates (illus., maps and plans). 19cm.   CSmH DLC   **251**
  "Flag presentations," 303–16.

Stephens, Ann Sophia (Winterbotham), 1813–1886.
Pictorial history of the War for the Union, a complete and reliable history of the war, from its commencement to its close, giving a graphic picture of its encounters, thrilling incidents, frightful scenes, hairbreadth escapes . . . by Mrs. Ann S. Stephens. New York, Benjamin W. Hitchcock, 1866–67. 2 v. front. ɪ (group ports.), illus., map, ports. 23cm.
         CSmH DLC   **252**

General Histories, continued

Added illus. title page I.
Plates are paged.

Storke, Elliot G   1811–1879?
. . . A complete history of the great American rebellion, embracing its causes, events and consequences. With biographical sketches and portraits of its principal actors, and scenes and incidents of the war . . . By Elliot G. Storke and L. P. Brockett. Auburn, Auburn pub. co. [c1865] 2 v. (1612 p.). fronts. (illus., port.), illus., maps and plans, ports., plates (illus.). 23½cm.   CSmH   253
At head of title: Published only for subscribers.
TxU has I c1863, with Storke's name alone on the title page.

Tenney, William Jewett, 1814–1883.
The military and naval history of the rebellion in the United States, with biographical sketches of deceased officers, by W. J. Tenney. New York, D. Appleton & co., 1865. x, 843 p. illus., maps and plans, plates (col. illus., ports.). 25½cm.   CSmH   254
Text in double columns.
"Biographical sketches," arranged chronologically by date of death, 719–805.
CSmH has an 1866 reprinting; TxU an 1867.

Tomes, Robert, 1817–1882.
Der Krieg mit dem Süden, unfassende Schilderung des Ursprungs und Verlaufs der Rebellion, nebst biographischen Skizzen der hervorragendsten Staatsmänner u.s.w. Nach dem Englischen des Robert Tomes. Fortgeführt von Anfang des Jahres 1864 bis zum Schluss des Krieges, von Benjamin G. Smith. . . . New York, Virtue und Yorston [c1863] 2 v. (1361 p.). plates (illus., maps, ports.). 27cm.   TxU   255
The added engraved title pages of the English edition have been used as well as its plates without translation.
Text in double columns and within ruled border.

—— The war with the South, a history of the great American rebellion, with biographical sketches of the leading statesmen and distinguished naval and military commanders, etc. By Robert Tomes, continued from the beginning of the year 1864, to the end of the war, by Benjamin G. Smith. London, New York, Virtue & Yorston [1862–66] 3 v. plates (illus., maps, ports.). 29cm.   NN   256
Added engraved title pages.
Text in double columns and within ruled border.

—— The great Civil war, a history of the late rebellion with biographical sketches of leading statesmen and distinguished naval and military commanders, etc., by Robert Tomes and Benjamin G. Smith. New York, R. Worthington [n. d.] 3 v. plates (illus., 2 maps, ports.). 27cm.   CSmH   257

A reprinting. The "Preface" has been rewritten.
Text in double columns.

Victor, Orville James, 1827–1910.
The history, civil, political and military, of the Southern rebellion, from its incipient stages to its close. Comprehending, also, all important state papers, ordinances of secession, proclamations, proceedings of Congress, official reports of commanders, etc. By Orville J. Victor. New York, James D. Torrey [1861–66] 4 v. maps and plans, plates (illus., fold. maps, ports.). 26cm.   CSmH   258
Added engraved title pages.
Text in double columns and within ruled border.

Washington Star, Washington, D.C.
Mirror of the war, the Washington star reports the Civil war. Compiled and edited by John W. Stepp and I. William Hill. Englewood Cliffs, N. J., Prentice-Hall [c1961] vi, 378 p. illus., ports. 28cm.   NN   259
Title on two leaves.
Text in double columns.

Werner, Edgar Albert
Historical sketch of the War of the rebellion from 1861 to 1865. Movements of the Federal and Confederate armies; chronological list of engagements, reconstruction proceedings, proclamations, statistical tables, etc. Compiled and edited by Edgar A. Werner. Albany, Weed, Parsons and co., 1890. viii, 270 p. front. (illus.). 20½cm.   CSmH DLC OMC TxU   260

Whitney, Lorenzo Harper, 1834–1912.
The history of the war for the preservation of the Federal Union. . . . Also, the military and naval engagements between the Union and Confederate armies and navies, interwoven with which are sketches of the lives and characters of prominent leaders on both sides. . . . By Lorenzo H. Whitney. . . . In two vols., vol. I. Philadelphia, Printed for the author, by Lippincott & co., 1863. xiii, 25–516 p. plates (illus., ports.). 23cm.   CSmH NcD   261
Only Vol. I published.
I closes with action at Big Bethel, June 10, 1861.

Williams, George Forrester, 1837–1920.
The memorial war book as drawn from historical records and personal narratives of the men who served in the great struggle, by Major George F. Williams. Illustrated by two thousand magnificent engravings, reproduced largely from photographs taken by the U. S. government photographers, M. B. Brady and Alexander Gardner. . . . New York, Lovell Brothers co., c1894. 610, (3) p. facsims., illus., ports. 31cm.   CSmH DLC   262
"Index," (3) p.

Wilson, John Laird, 1832–1896.
The pictorial history of the great Civil war, its causes, origin, conduct and results, embrac-

ing full and authentic accounts of its battles by land and sea, with graphic descriptions of heroic deeds achieved by armies and individuals, narratives of personal adventures . . . containing carefully prepared biographies of the leading Generals and naval commanders of both the North and South. By John Laird Wilson, special correspondent of the New York Herald. Philadelphia, Staley & Hawes [c1881] iv, 5–976 p. plates (illus., maps and plans). 26cm. CSmH TxU **263**
Text in double columns.

GUERRILLAS

Quantrel, the guerrilla chieftain from his own diary. [n. p., 189–?] 59 p. 19½cm.
A fictitious narrative. CSmH MoHi **264**

Appler, Augustus C 1828–1917.
The guerrillas of the West; or, the life, character and daring exploits of the Younger brothers, with a sketch of the life of Henry W. Younger, father of the Younger brothers, who was assassinated and robbed by a band of Jayhawkers. Also, the war record of Quantrell during the three years that Cole and James Younger were with him. Also, a sketch of the life of the James boys. . . . By Augustus C. Appler. St. Louis, Eureka pub. co., 1876. iv, 5–208 p. plates (illus.). 21½cm.
On cover: Younger bros. MoHi **265**

—— The life, character and daring exploits of the Younger brothers, with a sketch of the life of Henry W. Younger. . . . By Augustus C. Appler. Chicago, Belford, Clarke & co. [c1875] viii, [9]–287 p. illus. 19½cm. NN **266**
Published with Train and bank robbers of the West, a romantic but faithful story of bloodshed and plunder perpetuated by Missouri's daring outlaws. . . . Chicago, Belford, Clarke & co., 1883.

—— The Younger brothers, their life and character, by A. C. Appler. With a foreword by Burton Rascoe. New York, Frederick Fell [1955] 245 p. illus., ports. 21cm. MoHi **267**

Breihan, Carl W 1915–
Quantrill and his Civil war guerrillas, by Carl W. Breihan. Denver [Alan Swallow, 1959] 174 p. facsim., plates (illus., ports.). 23½cm.
"Sage books." DLC MoHi TxU **268**
"Roster of guerrillas . . . a verified and complete list of the names of the men who, at one time or another, rode with Quantrill," 166–74.

—— Younger Brothers, by Carl W. Breihan. San Antonio, Naylor co. [c1961] xiii, 260 p. illus., plates (illus., ports.). 21½cm.
Title on two leaves. TxU **269**
Civil war, 1–57.

Brownlee, Richard S 1918–
Gray ghosts of the Confederacy, guerrilla warfare in the West, 1861–1865 [by] Richard S. Brownlee. Baton Rouge, Louisiana State University press [c1958] xi, 274 p. maps, plates (1 illus., ports.). 22cm. TxU **270**
Title on two leaves.
"Known members of Quantrill's, Andersons's and Todd's guerrillas," 253–61.
"The Union military districts in Missouri, 1861–1865," map end paper.

Burch, John P
Charles W. Quantrell, a true history of his guerrilla warfare on the Missouri and Kansas border during the Civil war of 1861 to 1865, by John P. Burch, as told by Captain Harrison Trow, one who followed Quantrell through his whole course. [Vega, Texas, c1923] 266 p. illus., ports. 20½cm. GEU NHi **271**

Castel, Albert E 1928–
William Clarke Quantrill, his life and times, by Albert Castel. New York, Frederick Fell [c1962] 250 p. plates (maps, ports.). 21cm.
Title on two leaves. TxU **272**

Connelley, William Elsey, 1855–1920.
Quantrill and the Border wars, by William Elsey Connelley. Cedar Rapids, Torch press, 1910. 542 p. front. (port.), illus., plans, fold. map and plan. 24½cm. CSmH DLC **273**

Dalton, Kit, 1843–
Under the black flag, by Captain Kit Dalton, a Confederate soldier, a guerrilla Captain under the fearless leader Quantrell. . . . [Memphis] Lockard pub. co. [1914] 252 p. ports., plate (illus.). 19cm. TxU **274**
Cover illus. in color.

Edwards, John Newman, 1839–1889.
Noted guerrillas; or, the warfare of the border, being a history of the lives and adventures of Quantrell, Bill Anderson, George Todd, Dave Poole, Fletcher Taylor, Peyton Long, Oll Shepherd, Arch Clements, John Maupin, Tuck and Woot Hill, Wm. Gregg, Thomas Maupin, the James Brothers, the Younger Brothers, Arthur McCoy. And numerous other well known guerrillas of the West. By John N. Edwards. St. Louis, Bryan, Brand & co., 1877. xi, [13]–488 p. plates (1 illus., ports.). 22cm. CSmH DLC **275**
TxU and NN have an 1879 reprinting.

—— —— St. Louis, J. W. Marsh, 1880. 302 p. plates (1 illus., ports.). 19cm. TxU **276**
A reprinting through the first two lines of p. 302 of the 1877 edition. Two paragraphs have been added closing the text.

Lieber, Francis, 1800–1872.
Guerrilla parties considered with reference to the laws and usages of war. Written at the request of Major-General Henry W. Halleck . . . by Francis Lieber, in the month of August, 1862. New York, D. Van Nostrand, 1862. 22 p. 18cm. CSmH DLC **277**
"Errata" slip inserted.

Guerrillas, continued

McCorkle, John, 1838–
Three years with Quantrell, a true story, told by his scout, John McCorkle. Written by O. S. Barton. Armstrong, Mo., Armstrong Herald print [c1914] 157 p. plates (ports.). 24cm.   MoHi TxU   **278**

Sawyer, William E
Martin Hart, Civil war guerrilla. *TMH* III (1963) 146–53.   **279**

Sensing, Thurman, 1900–
Champ Ferguson, Confederate guerrilla, by Thurman Sensing. Nashville, Vanderbilt University press, 1942. xi, 256 p. front. (port.). plate (map). 23½cm.   TxU   **280**

Watts, Hamp B
The babe of the Company, an unfolded leaf from the forest of never-to-be-forgotten years, by Hamp B. Watts. Fayette, Mo., Printed by the Democrat-Leader press, 1913. 32, (1) p. illus., ports. 23½cm.   MoHi   **281**
Officers of the Richmond Greys chapter no. 148, United daughters of the Confederacy, (1) p.

Williams, Robert H   1831–
With the Border ruffians, memories of the Far West, 1852–1868, by R. H. Williams, sometime Lieutenant in the Kansas rangers and afterwards Captain in the Texan rangers. Edited by E. W. Williams. London, John Murray, 1907. xviii, 478 p. plates (illus., ports.). 22cm.   GEU   **282**
Partial contents: Texas, 1860–62, 145–226; In the Confederate service, 227–392.

HISTORIOGRAPHY

Boynton, Henry Van Ness, 1835–1905.
Criticisms on the histories now in use in the public schools of the District of Columbia, by Gen. Henry V. Boynton, President of the Board of education. [Washington, D.C., 1901] 10 p. 23½cm.   CSmH   **283**
Caption title.

—— Errors in school histories, compared with the official record, by General H. V. Boynton. The Civil war period. Washington, D.C., Speech pub. co., 1903. 17 p. 23cm.
                                       CSmH NN   **284**
Title and imprint from cover.

INDIANS

Abel, Annie Heloise, 1873–1962.
The American Indian as participant in the Civil war, by Annie Heloise Abel. Cleveland, Arthur H. Clark co., 1919. 403 p. plates

(facsims., double map, port.). 24½cm.
                                              MoU   **285**
II of the author's The slaveholding Indians.

—— The Indians in the Civil war. *Magazine of history* XII (1910) 9–26.   **286**

Buchanan, Elliott M
The part Indians played in the Confederacy. *AHQ* v (1943) 59–65.   **287**

Cunningham, Frank, 1911–
General Stand Watie's Confederate Indians, by Frank Cunningham. San Antonio, Naylor co. [1959] xiv, 242 p. illus., plates (ports.). 22½cm.   NN   **288**

MEDALS

Belden, Bauman Lowe, 1862–1931.
American insignia. *Proceedings of the American numismatic and archaeological society* 1894/96 87–97; 1900/01 41–61; 1901/02 46–65.   **289**
Title of sections varies: 1st, The insignia of the patriotic hereditary societies of the United States; 2nd, Insignia of American military societies since the War of 1812.

—— Department badges of the Grand army of the Republic. *Proceedings of the American numismatic and archaeological society* 1901/02 42–7. plates (illus.).   **290**

Grand Army of the Republic. Department of West Virginia.
Medal list, a list of medals unclaimed, and in the hands of George B. Crawford, Ass't Adjutant General, Department of West Virginia, G.A.R. Wellsburg [1891] 22 folios. 28½ × 14cm.   NN (E)   **291**
List arranged by regiments and companies.
"Notes" signed by I. H. Duval, Dep't commander, Aug. 1st, 1891, p. 4 of cover.
Title from cover.

Stafford, Frederick H
. . . Medals of honor awarded for distinguished service during the War of the rebellion. Compiled under the direction of Brigadier General Richard C. Drum, Adjutant general U. S. army, by Frederick H. Stafford. Washington, 1886. 32 p. 22½cm. NN   **292**
At head of title: Adjutant general's department.
An alphabetical list with rank, organization, date of issue, action and date when the medal was won and the citation.

United States.
Report of a Board of officers appointed by Special orders, No. 131, June 4, 1902, Headquarters of the army, Adjutant general's office, of which Major General S. B. M. Young was President, to examine and report upon applications and recommendations for medals of

honor and certificates of merit. Washington, Govt. print. office, 1904. 82 p. 19½cm.   **293**

United States. War Department.
. . . Medals of honor issued by the War department, up to and including September 1, 1904. Published by direction of the Secretary of war. Washington, Govt. print. office, 1904. 153 p. 28cm.   **294**
At head of title: <Circular>.
An alphabetical list with date of issue, place and date of action and citation.

MISCELLANEOUS

Barr, Thomas Francis, 1837–1916.
Costs and compensations of the war, a paper read before the Illinois commandery of the Military order of the loyal legion of the United States, December 13th, 1888, by Lieut. Col. Thomas F. Barr. 10 p. 21cm.   CSmH   **295**
Also published *MOLLUS-Ill* I 519–28.

Bivins, Viola (Cobb)
Echoes of the Confederacy, by Viola Cobb Bivins. Longview, Texas, Mrs. J. K. Burns [Dallas, Manufactured by Banks, Upshaw and co., c1950] 197 p. front. (illus.). 23cm.
     DLC   **296**

Catton, Bruce, 1899–
. . . America goes to war. Middletown, Wesleyan University press [c1958] 126 p. illus., port. 21cm.   NN   **297**
At head of title: Bruce Catton.
Contents: The first modern war; The citizen soldier; Making hard war; The era of suspicion; The General as President; The heritage of victory.

Cockrell, Monroe Fulkerson, 1884–
Notes and articles by Monroe F. Cockrell for his maps of the War between the States. [Evanston, Ill.] c1950. 1 v. printed on rectos. front. (port.), plates (illus., ports.), fold. maps in pocket. 29cm. mimeographed. GEU   **298**
"Twenty-two copies privately printed," ms. note signed in GEU's copy.

Columbia University. Library
The Townsend library of national, State, and Civil war records at Columbia University, New York city. [New York, Press of Styles & Cash, 1897] 15 p. front. (port.). 21½cm.
     NcD   **299**
"A history of the Library, by J. Henry Hager," 12–15.

Davis, Burke
Our incredible Civil war, by Burke Davis. Drawings by Raymond Houlihan. New York, Holt, Rinehart and Winston [c1960] 249 p. illus., ports. 23½cm.   NN   **300**
"Book is a sampler of some of my favorite tales, facts, coincidences, and oddities of the strange, romantic, brutal conflict."

Donald, David Herbert, 1920–
Why the North won the Civil war. Essays by . . . [5 names]. Edited by David Donald. [Baton Rouge] Louisiana State University press [c1960] xv, 128, (1) p. 22cm.
     Title on two leaves.   CSmH DLC   **301**
Contents: God and the strongest battalions, by Richard N. Current; The military leadership of North and South, by T. Harry Williams; Northern diplomacy and European neutrality, by Norman A. Graebner; Died of democracy, by David Donald; Jefferson Davis and political factors in Confederate defeat, by David M. Potter.

Halsey, Ashley
Who fired the first shot? And other untold stories of the Civil war, by Ashley Halsey, Jr. New York, Hawthorn Books [1963] 223 p. illus., ports. 21cm.   NN   **302**

Johnson, Edwin Rossiter, 1840–1931.
Turning points in the Civil war. *Annual report of the American historical association* 1894, 39–53.   **303**

Stewart, Lucy Shelton, 1875–
The reward of patriotism, a refutation of the present-day defamations of the defenders and preservers of the Union in the Civil war and an exposition of the cause which they overcame, by Lucy Shelton Stewart. New York, Walter Neale, 1930. 484 p. plates (2 maps, ports.). 24cm.   DLC NcD   **304**

Wellman, Manly Wade
They took their stand, the founders of the Confederacy [by] Manly Wade Wellman. New York, G. P. Putnam's Sons [1959] 258 p. 22cm.   NN   **305**

Wilson, Edmund, 1895–
Patriotic gore, studies in the literature of the American Civil war, by Edmund Wilson. New York, Oxford University press, 1962. xxxii, 816 p. 19½cm.   NN   **306**

MONUMENTS

The South's battle abbey. [Atlanta, Respess co., 1896?] 32 p. cover illus. in color. 18cm.
     Title from cover.   LNHT NcD   **307**
Text in double columns.
"Introduction" signed: J. R. McIntosh, Chairman; J. A. Chaleron, W. R. Garrett — Committee.

Emerson, Bettie Alder (Calhoun), 1840–
Historic Southern monuments, representative memorials of the heroic dead of the Southern confederacy, compiled by Mrs. B. A. C. Emerson. New York, Neale pub. co., 1911. 466 p. illus., port. 22½cm. DLC NcD   **308**

Roe, Alfred Seelye, 1844–1917.
Monuments, tablets and other memorials erected in Massachusetts to commemorate the

Monuments, continued

services of her sons in the War of the rebellion, 1861–1865 . . . collected and arranged by Alfred S. Roe. Boston, Wright & Potter print. co., 1910. 132 p. plates (illus.). 23½cm.

NN   *309*

NAME OF THE WAR

Coulter, Ellis Merton, 1890–
A name for the American war of 1861–1865. *GHQ* XXXVI (1952) 109–31.   *310*

Meany, Edward Stephen, 1862–1935.
Name of the American war of 1861–1865. [Seattle, 1910] [18] p. 22½cm.
Caption title.   CSmH DLC   *311*
Republishes the debate in the United States Senate, January 11, 1907.

NEGROES

Free military school for applicants for commands of colored troops, no. 1210 Chestnut street, Philadelphia. Established by the Supervisory committee for recruiting colored regiments. John A. Taggert, 12th regiment Pennsylvania reserves, preceptor. Philadelphia, King & Baird, printers, 1863. 12 p. 23cm.
Issued December 28, 1863.   NB   *312*

—— Second edition. Philadelphia, King & Baird, printers, 1864. 43 p. 22cm. NB   *313*
"Roll of students . . . March 31st, 1864," 33–43. Taggart in title as "chief preceptor."

Notes on colored troops and military colonies on Southern soil, by an officer of the 9th army corps. New York, 1863. 16 p. 22½cm.
Copyright by S. B. Brague.   TxU   *314*

Adams, Julius Walker,   –1865.
Letter to the Secretary of war, on the examination of field officers for colored troops. Second edition enclosed in a letter to the officers of the Army of the Potomac, by Julius W. Adams. . . . Printed but not published. New York, John F. Trow, printer, 1863. 24 p. 22½cm.   CSmH   *315*
Title from cover, p. [1]

Aptheker, Herbert, 1915–
Negro casualties in the Civil war, by Herbert Aptheker. Washington, D.C., Association for the Study of Negro Life and History [n. d.] 73 p. 25cm.   NbU   *316*

—— The negro in the Civil war [by] Herbert Aptheker. New York, International publishers [c1938] 48 p. 20cm.   NcD   *317*
WyU has "second printing," 1940.

Blassingame, John W
The recruitment of negro troops in Maryland. *MHM* LVIII (1963) 20–29.   *318*

Brown, William Wells, 1816?–1884.
The negro in the American rebellion, his heroism and his fidelity, by William Wells Brown. Boston, Lee & Sheppard, 1867. xvi, 380 p. 20cm.   CSmH   *319*
Partial contents: Fifty-fourth Massachusetts regiment; Battle of Port Hudson; Assault on Fort Wagner; Sixth regiment United-States volunteers.

—— —— New edition. Boston, A. G. Brown & co., 1880. xvi, 380 p. front. (port.). 19½cm.
NNC RPB   *319A*

Clark, Peter H
The Black brigade of Cincinnati, being a report of its labors and a muster-roll of its members, together with various orders, speeches, etc. relating to it, by Peter H. Clark. Cincinnati, Printed by Joseph B. Boyd, 1864. 30 p. 22½cm.   CSmH NN   *320*
Muster-roll of the Black brigade, [22]–30.

Colyer, Vincent, 1825–1888.
Report of the services rendered by the freed people to the United States army, in North Carolina in the Spring of 1862, after the battle of Newbern, by Vincent Colyer, Superintendent of the poor under General Burnside. . . . New York, Vincent Colyer, 1864. 63, (1) p. front. (illus.), illus. 22cm.   NN   *321*

Cornish, Dudley Taylor, 1915–
The sable arm, negro troops in the Union army, 1861–1865, by Dudley Taylor Cornish. New York Longmans, Green and co., 1956. xiii, (1), 337 p. 22cm.   GEU   *322*

Furness, William Eliot
The negro as a soldier, read November 12, 1891. *MOLLUS-Ill* II 456–87.   *323*

Hay, Thomas Robson
The South and the arming of the slaves. *MVHR* VI (1919) 34–73.   *324*

O'Reilly, Henry, 1806–1886.
First organization of colored troops in the State of New York to aid in suppressing the slaveholders' rebellion . . . collated for the "New York association for colored volunteers," by Henry O'Reilly, Secretary. New York, Baker & Goodwin, printers, 1864. 24 p. 23cm.
CSmH NNC   *325*
Title and imprint from cover.

Quarles, Benjamin, 1904–
The negro in the Civil war, by Benjamin Quarles. Boston, Little Brown and co. [c1953] xvi, (1), 379 p. 21cm.   TxU   *326*

Reid, William G
Confederate opponents of arming the slaves, 1861–1865. *JMH* xxii (1960) 249–70.   **327**

Rollin, Frank A
Life and public services of Martin R. Delany, Sub-assistant commissioner Bureau relief of refugees, freedmen, and of abandoned lands, and late Major 104th U. S. colored troops. By Frank A. Rollin. Boston, Lee and Shepard, 1868. 367 p. 19½cm.   CSmH DLC   **328**

Spender, Edward, 1834–1883.
Confederate negro enlistments. AW 536–53.   **329**

United States. Adjutant General's Office.
Correspondence, etc. relating to muster and pay of officers of colored troops. Washington, Govt. print. office, 1880. 20 p. 23cm.
DNW NN(M)   **330**

Williams, George Washington, 1849–1891.
A history of the negro troops in the War of the rebellion, 1861–1865. Preceeded by a review of the military services of negroes in ancient and modern times. By George W. Williams. New York, Harper & Brothers, 1888. xvi, 353 p. front. (port.), plates (illus.). 21cm.
CSmH DLC   **331**

Wilson, Joseph Thomas, 1836–1891.
The black phalanx, a history of the negro soldiers of the United States in the wars of 1775–1812, 1861–'65, by Joseph T. Wilson, late of the 2nd reg't La. native guard, 54th Mass. vols. Hartford, American pub. co., 1888. 528 p. front. (port.), plates (illus.). 23cm.
CSmH NN   **332**

PENSIONS

Association of the Maryland Line.
Memorial of the Association of the "Maryland line" to the Legislature of the State of Maryland, Baltimore, February 8th, 1888. 15 p. 21½cm.   CSmH   **333**
Title from cover.
State and not Federal pensions for Confederate soldiers.

United States. Record and Pension Office.
Memorandum relative to the probable number and ages of the army and navy survivors of the War of the rebellion. [Washington, 1890] 10 p. 20cm.   CSmH   **334**
Title from cover.

———— ———— and the possible number of beneficiaries under and possible cost of certain proposed pension laws . . . April 14, 1896. [Washington, Govt. print. office, 1896] 15 p. 23cm.
CSmH   **335**

PERIODICALS

The acme haversack of patriotism and song. Syracuse, 1887–96. 36 nos. 17cm.   **336**
Collation: vol. 1–10, no 1 (whole no 1–36); July 1887 – March 1896. Only fragmentary files are held by any collections.
Title varies slightly.

The annals of the Army of Tennessee and early Western history, including a chronological summary of battles and engagements in the Western armies of the Confederacy. Edited by Dr. Edwin L. Drake, Lieutenant-Colonel C.S.A. Volume 1, April – December, 1878. Nashville, Printed by A. D. Haynes, 1878. vi, 432, 97 (1) p. fold. map. 20½cm.
"Errata," (1) p.   CSmH DLC NN   **337**
"Chronological summary of battles . . . by Edwin L. Drake," 97, (1) p. was also published separately.

The army and navy official gazette, containing reports of battles, also important orders of the War department, record of courts-martial, etc. Published by order of the War department. Washington, D.C., Printed at the office of F. & J. Rives, 1864–65. 2 v. 30½cm.
CSmH   **338**
Weekly, July 7, 1863, to June 20, 1865.
Annual indexes.
1 Printed at the office of John C. Rives.

Confederate annals, a semi-monthly magazine, reciting facts and incidents of the war in the South. Issued from the rooms of the Southern historical and benevolent association. St. Louis, J. W. Cunningham, editor and publisher, 1883. 84 p. 23cm. vol. 1, no. 1–2; June – August, 1883.   CSmH   **339**

The Confederate knapsack, published monthly by A. Meynier, Jr., Private Co. "C," 8th La. vols. New Orleans, 1883–84. 2 nos. illus. 32cm.   CSmH   **340**
Collation: v 1, no 1–2; December 1883 – January 1864.

The Confederate veteran, published monthly in the interest of Confederate veterans and kindred topics. . . . Nashville, 1893–1932. illus., maps, ports. 27cm. IHi [1–2]–40.   **341**
Collation: v 1–40; January 1893 — December 1932.
Officially represents United Confederate veterans, United daughters of the Confederacy, Sons of veterans, Confederated southern memorial association, and other organizations.

The land we love. Charlotte, N. C., 1866–69. 6 v. occasional fronts. (1 illus., ports.). 21cm.   **342**
Collation: v 1–6, no 5; May 1866 – March 1869. Monthly.

The lost cause, a Confederate war record. Louisville, 1898–1904. 10 v. illus., ports. 30cm.
NN   **343**

Periodicals, continued

June 1898 – April 1904. Benjamin La Bree, editor, I-II; Mrs. General Basil Duke, editor, III-X 1; Florence Barlow, associate editor, III-X 1, editor, X 2–10.
"Owned, controlled and edited by women, Daughters of the Confederacy."

The Maine bugle, campaign 1 [–5] January, 1894 [–October 1898]. . . . Rockland [1894–98] 5 v. 24½cm.   NHi   *344*

Quarterly. "Organ of the men of Maine who served in the War of the rebellion. . . . Also the organ of the Cavalry society of the armies of the United States . . . Editors, committees from Maine regiments."
Preceded by 1st Maine cavalry record of proceedings at the 1st [–11th] annual re-union held Sept. 26, 1872 [–1882] and First Maine bugle, campaign 2–3, July 1890 – October 1893.

The National tribune library. Washington, D.C., 1895–97. 21 nos. illus., music, plates (ports.). 23cm.   CSmH NB   *345*

"Weekly." Collation: v 1, no 1–22; October 26, 1895 – September 18, 1897.
Each issue a monograph, those with Civil war interest:
1 Statistics of the war.
2 Words of Lincoln.
3 Miscellaneous memoranda: events which began the war; events which ended the war; personal characteristics of the Union volunteer; General officers killed.
4 Pension statistics; history of slavery in the U. S., by John McElroy.
7/8 Commanders of the United States army, by John McElroy.
10 Life of Maj.-Gen. George H. Thomas, by John McElroy.
12 Gen. Philip Henry Sheridan, by John McElroy.
13 Chronological list of battles, etc., during the War of the rebellion, compiled by H. E. Weaver.
14 Life of Admiral Farragut, by John McElroy.
15 Fun of the war.
18 Some poetry of the war.
19 Life of Gen. U. S. Grant, by John McElroy.
20 Memorial day poetry and oratory, compiled by H. E. Weaver.

The National tribune repository, good stories of experience and adventure. Washington, D.C., 1907–08. 3 nos. 22½cm.   WHi   *346*

Collation: v 1, no 1–3; November 1907 – January 1908.

The Northern monthly, a magazine of original literature and military affairs. Edward P. Weston, editor and proprietor. Volume I, 1864. Portland, Bailey & Noyes, 1864. iv, 730 p. 23½cm.   NN   *347*

Monthly. Each issue includes Military appointments [Maine] and Position of Maine troops. Publishes numerous brief references to Maine units and unsigned articles on the Civil war.

Atchison, Ray M
The land we love: a Southern post-bellum magazine of agriculture, literature, and military history. *NCHR* XXXVII (1960) 506–15.

See Title 342.   *348*

Cresap, Bernarr, 1919–
The Confederate veteran. *AR* XII (1959) 243–57.   *349*

See Title 341.

Society for Civil War Information.
Bulletin. Evanston, 1935–41. 69 nos. 28cm. mimeographed.   NN   *350*

Indexes: 1–12, 13–24, 25–36, 37–48, 49–60, 61–72. Issued by Miss Lucy S. Stewart, Secretary. October 1935 – December 1941. Monthly. For article on the periodical, see *CWH* IX (1963) 430–2.

Southern Historical Society.
Southern historical papers. Richmond, 1876–1959. 52 v. 24cm.   NN   *351*

Annual and irregular: 1876–1877, two volumes a year. 1914–1959 also numbered, n s nos 1–14.
L-LII published by the Virginia historical society. XLIV-LII are Proceedings of . . . Confederate Congress.

CAMP NEWSPAPERS

Lutz, Earle, 1890–
The Stars and stripes of Illinois boys in Blue. *Journal of the Illinois state historical society* XLVI (1953) 132–41.   *352*

Price, Beulah M   D'Olive
The Corinth war eagle. *JMH* XX (1958) 244–50.   *353*

Wiley, Bell Irvin, 1906–
Camp newspapers of the Confederacy. *NCHR* XX (1943) 327–35.   *354*

PERSONAL NARRATIVES
(ANONYMOUS AND UNIDENTIFIED)

Bob's letter, Cowan, Tenn., Aug. 23d, 1862, 10 p. m. [n. p., 186–?] 6 p. 23cm.
Caption title.   CSmH   *357*
The writer was from Philadelphia.

Civil war notes of a French volunteer. *Wisconsin magazine of history* XLV (1962) 239–45. illus.   *358*

Originally published in 1864 in La vie parisienne, by an unidentified author who seems to have been in personal association with both Generals Fremont and Hooker.

The lady Lieutenant. A wonderful, startling and thrilling narrative of the adventures of Miss Madeline Moore, who, in order to be near her lover, joined the army, was elected Lieutenant and fought in Western Virginia under the renowned General McClellan; and afterwards at the great battle of Bull run. Her own and her lover's perilous adventures and hair-breadth escapes are herein graphically delineated. The reader may rely upon this narrative as being strictly authentic. Philadelphia, Barclay & co., 1862. 40 p. front. and 2 plates (illus.). 23½cm.

Wright 1499.   CtY DLC MWA NN   **359**

Opium eating, an autobiographical sketch, by an habituate. Philadelphia, Claxton, Remsen & Heffelfinger, 1876. xii, 13–150 p. 19cm.

DLC NN PP   **360**

Enlisted as a drummer, 1861; captured September 19, 1863; released February 1865.
Civil war, 13–49.

Von Achten der Letzte, Amerikanische Kriegsbilder aus der Südarmee des Generals Robert E. Lee, von einem ehemaligen königl. preuss. Einjährig-Freiwilligen. Wiesbaden, Julius Riedner, 1871. vii, 276 p. 18cm.

ICI IU PU   **361**

"Druckfehler," unpaged leaf following viii.

Barber, Joseph
War letters of a disbanded volunteer, embracing his experiences as Honest old Abe's bosom friend and unofficial advisor. . . . New York, Frederic A. Brady, 1864. 312 p. front. (illus.). 18½cm.   CSmH NhHi   **362**

Bixby, O   H
Incidents in Dixie, being ten month's experiences of a Union soldier in the military prisons of Richmond, N. Orleans and Salisbury. Published for the benefit of Maryland state fair for the Christian and Sanitary commissions. Baltimore, Printed by James Young, 1864. 89 p. 14½cm.   CSmH DLC   **363**

Cunnington, W   H
Generals fight and fraternize. *B&G* I (1893) 383–5.   **364**

De Witt, James M
Reminiscences of army life. *Public spirit* I 6 (Troy, Sept. 1867) 45–59.   **365**

Franke, Fred E
Aus einem verfehlten Leben, Skizzen von F. E. F. Hermann, Mo., Graf print. co. [190–] [52] folios. 29cm.   CSmH(M)   **366**

Collation from positive photostat in MoHi made from copy in possession of Mrs. Clarence Hasse of Hermann.
A translation by William Wilke was published in the *Washington citizen*, February 18 – September 22, 1955.
Text in triple columns.

Hogan, Benedict, 1841?–
Ben Hogan's wild career in both armies. Bounty jumping, blockade running and spying. His battles in the ring and gambling career. [Chicago, Radcliffe & Manny, printers, 1887] 46 p. port. p. [3] of cover. 17cm.

Caption title.   DLC   **367**

"A startling life!," Bradford, Pa. *Evening star,* p. [1–2] of cover. "A peculiar sermon. Ben Hogan's first attempt to preach on the prodigal son, to miners, in Montana," p. [3–4] of cover.

Murray, George W
A history of George W. Murray, and his long confinement at Andersonville, Ga. Also, the starvation and death of his three brothers at the same place, by himself. Sold for the benefit of the author. Springfield [Northampton, Trumbull & Gere, printers, n. d.] 30 p. 18½cm.   NN   **368**

—— —— Springfield [Samuel Bowles and co., printers, n. d.] 30 p. 18cm.

CtHT-W   NjJ   **369**

—— —— Sold by himself for the benefit of himself and family. [Hartford, Press of Case, Lockwood and co., n. d.] 30 p. 19cm.

OMC   **370**

—— —— Written by himself. Sold by himself alone, for the benefit of the author and family. Cincinnati, Printed for the author by the Elm Street print. co. [n. d.] 23 p. 20½cm.

IHi   **371**

—— Incidents in the life of George W. Murray, during four years of service in the War for the Union, and his long confinement and sufferings in Libby prison. . . . Cleveland, Printed by Fairbanks, Benedict & co., 1865. 28 p. 14½cm.   WHi   **372**

—— The life and adventures of Sergt. G. W. Murray, a soldier in the Army of the Potomac, and his long confinement at Andersonville prison, Georgia. Also, the starvation and death of his three brothers. Minneapolis, Herald pub. house, 1872. 45, (1) p. 21½cm. MnHi   **373**

"Errata," (1) p. "Minneapolis, Published by Manley & Dada, 1872," preliminary leaf.

Yvan [pseud.]
From Vicksburg to New Orleans, through the enemy's country. *B&G* II (1894) 159–61.

374

—— Daring exploit at Donaldsville. *B&G* III (1894) 281–2.   **375**

PERSONAL NARRATIVES
(COLLECTIONS)

Anecdotes of the rebellion, a collection of humorous, pathetic and thrilling narratives of actual experiences during the war. . . . New York, F. M. Lupton, 1886. 16 p. 29cm.

CSmH   **376**

At head of title: The leisure hour library, new series, vol. 1, no. 113.
Publisher's advertisement of the series, 16.

Personal Narratives (Collections), continued

The annals of the war, written by leading participants, North and South, originally published in the Philadelphia weekly times. Philadelphia, Times pub. co., 1879. iv, ii, 17–800 p. 22½cm.   CSmH NN   **377**

> Articles are signed.
> CSmH has mounted clippings of the original newspaper publication, March 3, 1877, to February 21, 1878, which include minor articles omitted from the published volume.

A bundle of war letters. *University of North Carolina magazine* xLvii (1916/17) 205–11, 265–70, 316–20.   **378**

Civil war stories retold from St. Nicholas. New York, Century co., 1905. 201 p. illus., ports. 19½cm.   CSmH   **379**

> Contributions are signed.
> Plates are paged.

Famous adventures and prison escapes of the Civil war. New York, Century co., 1893. x, 338 p. illus., ports. 20½cm.   DLC   **380**

—— Edited by G. W. Cable and others. London, T. Fisher Unwin, 1894. x, 338 p. illus., ports. 20½cm.   NN   **381**

The grayjackets and how they lived, fought and died, for Dixie. With incidents & sketches of life in the Confederacy. Comprising narratives of personal adventure, army life, naval adventure, home life, partisan daring, life in the camp, field and hospital. Together with the songs, ballads, anecdotes and humorous incidents of the war for Southern independence . . . By a Confederate. Richmond, Jones Brothers & co. [c1867] 574 p. plates (maps and ports., partly fold.). 21cm. CSmH NN   **382**

> Contents: i Narratives of personal daring and adventure; ii The grayjackets in camp, field and hospital; iii Partisan life and adventure; iv The grayjackets on the high seas; v Home life in Dixie.

The haversack.   **383**

> A collection of soldiers' stories published in *The land we love* i-vi (1866–69). For the page references, see the Index of each volume. In iii the entry for Haversack appears in the "S" alphabet. v is without an Index; the running title must be used to locate the Haversack articles.
> See Title 342.

Hero tales of the American soldier and sailor, as told by the heroes themselves and their comrades. The unwritten history of American chivalry. [n.p.] Hero pub. co. [c1899] x, 33–503 p. col. double front. (illus.), plates (illus.). 25cm.   CSmH   **384**

> Civil war, 355–453.
> Copyright by A. Hollaway.
> Preface with caption "Glory crowns the brave" signed: W. Buel.

Incidents of American camp life, being events which have actually transpired during the present rebellion. New York, T. R. Dawley [1862] vi, 7–72 p. front. (illus.). 17cm.
CSmH   **385**

—— Second edition. New York, Hurst & co., c1866. vi, 7–104 p. front. (illus.). 17cm.
CSmH TxU   **386**

> A reprinting with the addition of new text, 73–104.
> At head of cover title: Popular series of fiction, fancy and fact, number 1.
> Copyright by T. R. Dawley.

Incidents of the Civil war in America. New York, Frank Leslie, 1862. 100 p. front. (illus.), illus. 21cm.   CSmH CtHt-W NcD   **387**

> Cover title: Heroic incidents of the Civil war in America.
> Cover illustrated in color.

The National tribune scrap book number . . . , stories of the camp, march, battle, hospital and prison told by comrades. Washington, D.C. National Tribune [190–] 3 v. 22cm.
CSmH   **388**

The picket line and camp fire stories, a collection of war anecdotes, both grave and gay, illustrative of the trials and triumphs of soldier life, with a thousand-and-one humorous stories, told of and by Abraham Lincoln, together with a full collection of Northern and Southern war songs, by a member of G.A.R. New York, Hurst & co. [188–] 1 v. 19cm.   DLC   **389**

> Contents: [Soldiers' stories] 104 p.; Old Abe's jokes p. [21]–135; Ballads of the North p. [13]–72; Ballads of the South p. [17]–72.
> Contents of the first section pages, [v]-vi. The third and fourth sections are followed by an unpaged "Contents" leaf.
> On cover: Arlington edition.

The soldiers' and sailors' half dime magazine. New York, Soldiers' and Sailors' pub. co., 1868. 326 p. 19½cm.   CSmH   **390**

> "v. ii."
> i published as The soldiers' and sailors' half-dime tales of the late rebellion.

The soldiers' and sailors' half-dime tales of the late rebellion. New York, Soldiers' and Sailors' pub. co., 1868. 120, 360 p. illus., ports. 19½cm.
CSmH DLC   **391**

> The second pagination, Caption title: Soldiers' and sailors' tales of the rebellion; running title: Tales of the rebellion; text in double columns.
> Includes "Contents vol. I."
> Continued as The soldiers' and sailors' half dime magazine.

The story of American heroism, thrilling narratives of personal adventures during the great Civil war, as told by the medal winners and roll of honor men. Among the contributors are . . . [16 names] [Akron, Werner co., c1896] xxvi, [21]–798 p. illus., ports. 25cm.
NN   **392**

Distributors of this volume appear on the title pages as publishers.
CSmH has a reprinting, Philadelphia, B. T. Calvert co., 1897.

Strange stories of the Civil war, by Robert Shackleton, John Habberton, William J. Henderson, L. E. Chittenden, Capt. Howard Patterson, Gen. G. A. Forsyth and others. New York, Harper & Brothers, 1907. x, 218, (1) p. plates (illus.). 17½cm.　　　NN　　393

Tales of the Civil war pictured by pen and pencil, by celebrities of both sides, the men and women who created the greatest epoch of our Nation's history . . . Boston, Perry Mason & co., c1896. 592 p. illus., maps, ports. 29½cm.
　　　　　　　　　　　　　　　NcD　394
Running title: Tales of the Civil war as told by veterans.
Text is identical with Under both flags, a panorama of the great Civil war. (See entry for Vickers, George Morley.)
Text in double columns.
Copyright by C. R. Graham.

Two great raids. Col Grierson's successful swoop through Mississippi. Morgan's disastrous raid through Indiana and Ohio. Vivid narratives of both these great operations, with extracts from official records. John Morgan's escape, last raid, and death. Washington, D.C., National Tribune, 1897. 320 p. front. (port.), illus., maps, port. 21½cm. DLC MsHa　395
Excerpted from the accounts by Surby, Kautz and others.
"Old glory library, no. 8."

Under both flags, a panorama of the great Civil war . . .
See Vickers, George Morley (Title 520).

. . . The volunteers' roll of honor, a collection of the noble and praiseworthy deeds performed in the cause of the Union by the heroes of the Army and Navy of the United States. Edited by D. Brainerd Williamson . . . to be published in monthly numbers . . . Philadelphia, Barclay & co., 1864–66. 3 v. plates (illus.). 23½cm.　　　CSmH　396
Covers illustrated in color.
First issue is not numbered; at head of title: Second [-third] number.
Editor's name does not appear in the first issue.
Collation: [1] p. 21–30, 39–52, 61–74, 85–100; 2, p. 21–30, 39–52, 61–74, 83–100; 3, p. 21–30, 39–52, 61–74, 83–112. The text is continuous though there are breaks in the pagination. A plate at each break in the pagination may have significance.
See also Title 396A.

[Alexander, Charles Wesley, 1837–1927]
The volunteers' roll of honor, a collection of the noble and praiseworthy deeds performed in the cause of the Union by the heroes of the Army and Navy of the United States, by Wesley Bradshaw [pseud.] . . . To be published in monthly numbers. . . . Philadelphia, Bar-

clay and co. [1863] p. 21–30, 39–52, 63–74, 85–100. plates (illus.). 23½cm.
See also Title 396.　　DLC NN　　396A

Bankston, Marie Louise Benton
Camp-fire stories of the Mississippi valley campaign, by Marie Louise Benton Bankston . . . Louisiana series. New Orleans, L. Graham co., 1914. 171 p. illus., plates (illus., port.). 18½cm.　　　　　　　LNHT　397

Barstow, Charles Lester, 1867–
Century readings in United States history. The Civil war. Edited by Charles L. Barstow. New York, Century co., 1912. 224 p. front. (port.), facsims., illus., maps, ports. 19½cm.
Contributions are signed.　　CSmH　398

Bernard, George Smith, 1837–1912.
War talks of Confederate veterans, compiled and edited by Geo. S. Bernard, Petersburg, Va. Addresses delivered before A. P. Hill camp of Confederate veterans of Petersburg, Va., with addenda giving statements of participants, eye-witnesses and others, in respect to campaigns, battles, prison life and other war experiences. Petersburg, Fenn & Owen, 1892. xiii, 335, (2) p. plates (2 fold. maps, plan, ports.). 23½cm.　　　　CSmH MoU　399
Includes "Biographical sketches" of authors.
CSmH has "(Advance sheets)" of p. 1–76 and p. 149–230, two pamphlets.
"Errata," "Supplement to errata," (2) p.

Beyer, Walter Frederick, 1871–
Deeds of valor. How America's heroes won the Medal of honor. Personal reminiscences and records of officers and enlisted men who were awarded the Congressional Medal of honor for most conspicuous acts of bravery in battle, combined with an abridged history of our country's wars. Compilers, Walter F. Beyer and Oscar F. Keydel. Introduction by Brig.-Gen'l H. M. Duffield. Detroit, Perrien-Keydel co., 1901. 2 v. illus., ports., col. plates (illus.). 29½cm.　　　　　NN I　400
DLC has i as issued in 16 numbered parts.

—— —— Detroit, Perrien-Keydel co., 1902. 2 v. illus., ports., col. plates (illus.). 29cm.
　　　　　　　　　　　　　DLC　401

—— Deeds of valor. How America's heroes won the Medal of honor. A history of our country's recent wars in personal reminiscences and records of officers and enlisted men who were rewarded by Congress for most conspicuous acts of bravery on the battle-field, on the high seas and in Arctic explorations . . . Edited by W. F. Beyer and O. F. Keydel. Introduction by Brig. Gen'l H. M. Duffield. Detroit, Perrien-Keydel co., 1903. 2 v. illus., ports., col. plates (illus.). 28cm.　　　　　DLC　402

Personal Narratives (*Collections*), *continued*

—— Deeds of valor from records in the archives of the United States government. How American heroes won the Medal of honor. History of our recent wars and explorations, from personal reminiscences and records of officers and enlisted men who were rewarded by Congress for most conspicuous acts of bravery on the battle-field, on the high seas and arctic explorations . . . Edited by W. F. Beyer and O. F. Keydel. Introduction by Brig.-Gen'l H. M. Duffield. Detroit, Perrien Keydel co., 1906. 2 v. illus., ports., col. plates (illus.). 28½cm.   CSmH   **403**
Copyright 1901, 1906.

—— —— Detroit, Perrien Keydel co., 1907. 2 v. illus., ports., col. plates (illus.). 28½cm.
CSmH   **404**

Bill, Ledyard, 1836–1907.
Pen pictures of the war. Lyrics, incidents, and sketches of the rebellion, comprising a choice selection of pieces by our best poets, also, current and well authenticated anecdotes and incidents of the war. Together with a full account of many of the great battles. Also, a complete historical record of all events, both civil and military, from the commencement of the rebellion. Compiled by Ledyard Bill. Second edition. Sold only by subscription. New York [Printed by C. A. Alvord] 1864. x, [11]–344 p. front. (illus.). 21½cm.
CSmH TxU   **405**
Contents: Lyrics of the war, 11–100; Anecdotes, incidents and pictures of the war, 101–200; The great battles and record of events, 201–344.

—— —— Sixth edition. Sold only by subscription. New York, 1866. x, [11]–368 p. front. (illus.). 22½cm.   CSmH   **406**
A reprinting with the addition of p. 345–68, completing the Record of battles and events.

Blaisdell, Albert Franklin, 1847–1927.
Stories of the Civil war, by Albert F. Blaisdell. Boston, Lee and Shepard, 1890. 245 p. ports., plates (illus.). 18cm.   CSmH   **407**

Brockett, Linus Pierpont, 1820–1893.
The camp, the battle field and the hospital; or, lights and shadows of the great rebellion, including adventures of spies and scouts, thrilling incidents . . . by Dr. L. P. Brockett. Philadelphia, National pub. co. [1866] 512 p. plates (illus., ports.). 23cm.   CSmH TxU   **408**

—— Battle-fields and hospitals; or, lights and shadows of the great rebellion, including thrilling adventures, daring deeds, heroic exploits, and wonderful escapes of spies and scouts . . . by Dr. L. P. Brockett. Philadelphia, Hubbard Brothers, 1888. 512 p. plates (illus.). 23cm.   NHi   **409**

A reprinting of his The camp, the battle field and the hospital, 1866.

—— Scouts, spies, and heroes of the great Civil war, including thrilling adventures, daring deeds, heroic exploits . . . by Captain Joseph Powers Hazelton [pseud.] Jersey City, Star pub. co., [c1892] 512 p. plates (illus., ports.). 23cm.   CSmH   **410**
A reprinting of his The camp, the battle field and the hospital, 1866. TxU has another reprinting, Providence, W. W. Thompson & co., 1893, copyright by J. Frank Beale, Jr.

—— Scouts, spies and detectives of the great Civil war, including thrilling adventures, daring deeds, heroic exploits, and wonderful escapes, by Captain Joseph Powers Hazelton [pseud.] Washington, D.C., National Tribune, 1899. 248 p. plates (illus.). 20½cm.   **411**
Here the plates of Brockett's 1866 publication became two books. The second title follows.

—— Daring enterprises of officers and men, by Captain [Hazelton, pseud.] Washington, National Tribune, 1899. 256, (1) p. illus. 20½cm.   CSmH   **412**
With altered paging, a reprinting of p. 267–503 of Brockett's 1866 work.

Brooks, Ulysses Robert, 1846–1917.
Stories of the Confederacy, edited by U. R. Brooks. Columbia, S. C., State co., 1912. 410 p. plates (illus., ports.). 23½cm.
CSmH DLC NN   **413**

Bruce, Philip Alexander, 1856–1933.
Brave deeds of Confederate soldiers, by Philip Alexander Bruce. Philadelphia, George W. Jacobs & co. [1916] 351 p. plates (illus.). 21½cm.   IHi TxU   **414**

Burnett, Alfred, 1823?–
Incidents of the war, humorous, pathetic, and descriptive, by Alf Burnett. Cincinnati, Rickey & Carroll, 1863. xi, 13–310 p. front. (port.), plates (illus.). 19cm. CSmH   **415**
"Sketch of the author, by Enos B. Reed," iii–vi.

—— Humorous, pathetic, and descriptive incidents of the war, by Alf Burnett. Cincinnati, R. W. Caroll & co., 1864. x, 13–310 p. front. (port.), plates (illus.). 19cm.   NcD   **416**
A reprinting.

Calvert, Bruce T   1866–1940.
. . . Our country's defenders, thrilling stories of desperate battles, heroic deeds, brave personal encounters, reckless daring, bold achievements, terrible suffering, wondrous fortitude and lofty patriotism of the men who fought for the Union with individual records of the rank and file . . . Edited by Bruce T. Calvert. Volume I. Philadelphia, Keystone pub. co., 1894. 478 p. illus., maps, ports., col. plates illus.). 24cm.   DLC   **417**

At head of title: Soldier's memorial edition.
Printed from the plates of Sparks from the camp-fire; or, tales of the old veterans, edited by Joseph W. Morton, 1893, duplicating pages 15–478.

Chattahooche Valley Historical Society.
War was the place, a centennial collection of Confederate soldier letters . . . [Alexander City, Ala.] 1961. *In its* Bulletin no 5, 1–123.
TxU   **418**

Coffin, Charles Carleton, 1823–1896.
Stories of our soldiers. War reminiscences, by "Carleton" and by soldiers of New England. Collected from the series written especially for the Boston journal. Illustrated by J. S. Barrows. Boston, Journal Newspaper co., 1893. 2 v. fronts. (facsims.), illus., ports. 21cm.   CSmH TxU   **419**
On spine: Boston journal war tales.
Plates are paged.
Text in double columns.

Confederate Veterans Association of Savannah, Ga.
Addresses delivered before the Confederate veterans association of Savannah, Ga., to which is appended the President's annual report. . . . Savannah, Braid & Hutton, printers, 1893–1902. 5 vols. 25cm.
DLC 1893–1898. GU-De   **419A**
Comprises separate volumes for the years 1893, 1895, 1896, and 1898, and a combined issue for 1898 to 1902.

Davis, Washington
Camp-fire chats of the Civil war, being the incident, adventure and wayside exploit of the bivouac and battle field, as related by members of the Grand army of the Republic . . . by Washington Davis. Containing an authentic history of the G.A.R. and other valuable information. Chicago, A. B. Gehman & co., 1886. xii, 15–346, (1) p. illus. 18½cm. IaHi   **420**
"Picture of Andersonville, (page 107)," (1) p., explanatory text.
Copyright 1884, 1886.

——— ——— as related by veteran soldiers themselves. Embracing the tragedy, romance, comedy, humor and pathos in the varied experiences of army life, by Washington Davis. Also, a history of the Grand army of the Republic, from its beginning to the present date, including the 20th national encampment at San Francisco, Cal., August, 1886, and other valuable information by a comrade. Chicago, Sidney C. Miller & co., 1887. xiv, 15–404 p. illus. 20cm.   CSmH NN TxU   **421**

Camp-fire chats of the Civil war, being the incident, adventure and wayside exploit of the bivouac and battle field, as related by veteran soldiers themselves . . . by Washington Davis. Also a history of the Grand army of the Repub-

lic, from its beginning to the present date, and other valuable information, by a comrade. Chicago, Sidney C. Miller co., 1888. xiv, 15–420 p. illus. 21cm.   IHi   **421A**
Copyright 1886 by A. B. Gehman & co.
Printed imprint of A. B. Gehman & co. covered by paster with the Sidney C. Miller co. imprint.

——— ——— Chicago, A. B. Gehman & co., 1889. xiv, 15–420 p. illus. 21cm.   IHi   **422**

Devens, Richard Miller
The pictorial book of anecdotes and incidents of the War of the rebellion, civil, military, naval and domestic, embracing the most brilliant and remarkable anecdotical events of the great conflict in the United States . . . by Frazar Kirkland [pseud.] Published by subscription only. Hartford, Hartford pub. co., 1866. 705 p. illus., ports., plates (illus.). 24cm.   CSmH DLC OMC IHi   **423**
Text in double columns.
Added col. illus. title page.

——— ——— Des Moines, W. E. Bliss & co., 1884. 705 p. illus., ports., plates (illus.). 25cm.
A reprinting.   IaHi   **424**

——— ——— Hillsdale, Mich., Hall & Ellis pub. co., 1887. 705 p. illus., ports, plates (illus.). 25cm.   TxU   **425**
A reprinting of the 1866 volume.
Copyright by W. E. Allen.

——— The pictorial book of anecdotes of the rebellion; or, the funny and pathetic side of the war . . . by Frazer Kirkland [pseud.] With an introduction by . . . Benson J. Lossing. St. Louis, J. H. Mason [c1889] 705 p. illus., ports, plates (illus.). 25½cm.
DLC MoHi NcD   **426**
A reprinting of the 1866 volume.

——— Reminiscences of the Blue and Gray, '61–'65, embracing the most brilliant and thrilling short stories of the Civil war . . . By Frazar Kirkland [pseud.]. . . . Chicago, Preston pub. co. [1895] 705 p. illus., ports., plates (illus.). 28cm.   IHi   **427**
A reprinting of the 1866 volume.

Dupre, Louis J
Fagots from the camp fire, by "the newspaper man." Washington, D.C., Emily Thornton Charles & co., 1881. 199 p. front. (port.). 22cm.   CSmH DLC NB   **428**
Copyright by L. J. Dupre.

Eggleston, George Cary, 1839–1911.
Southern soldier stories, by George Cary Eggleston. With illustrations by R. F. Zogbaum. New York, Macmillan co., 1898. xi, 251 p. front. (port.), plates (illus.). 19½cm.   CSmH NHi   **429**

Personal Narratives (Collections), continued

Eisenschiml, Otto, 1880–
The American Iliad, the epic story of the Civil war as narrated by eyewitnesses and contemporaries, by Otto Eisenschiml and Ralph Newman. Indianapolis, Bobbs-Merrill co. [c1947] 720 p. maps and plans, plates (facsims., illus., ports.). 22cm.   NN   *430*

Elliott, M   A
The garden of memory, stories of the Civil war as told by veterans and daughters of the Confederacy. Compiled by Mrs. M. A. Elliott, historian, H. L. G. Grinstead chapter U.D.C., Camden, Arkansas . . . Camden, Brown print. co. [1911] 96, (2) p. illus., ports. 25½cm.
CSmH DLC TxU   *431*
"History of the Appeal battery, by C. C. Scott," 56–60. Roster of Hugh McCollum camp, 1911, 94–6. Cover title adds: 1861–'65. "They bore the flag of a Nation's trust."

Goodhue, Benjamin W
Incidents of the Civil war, by Benjamin W. Goodhue. Chicago, J. D. Tallmadge, 1890. 158 p. front. (port.), ports. 19½cm.
Contributions are not signed.   TxU   *432*

Greene, Charles Shiel, 1829–1903.
Thrilling stories of the great rebellion, comprising heroic adventures and hair-breadth escapes of soldiers, scouts, spies, and refugees . . . by a disabled officer. Philadelphia, John E. Potter, 1865. 384 p. col. plates (illus.). 18cm.   CSmH OMC   *433*

—— —— by Lieutenant-Colonel Charles S. Greene. Philadelphia, John E. Potter & co., 1866. 494 p. 4 plates (3 col. illus., port.). 22cm.   CSmH DLC   *434*
A reprinting with additional text, 384–494.
Text in ruled border.
Author served in the 61st Penn infantry.

—— "A photograph of our old life," sparks from the camp fire, thrilling stories of heroism, adventure, daring and suffering, re-told by the boys who were there . . . Illustrated by . . . Mr. F. L. Fithian. Compiled by Lieut.-Col. Charles S. Greene. New York, Houghton, 1889. 528 p. plates (fold. facsim., illus., plan). 20½cm.   CSmH NN   *435*
A reprinting with additional text, 484–528.
See Title 489.

Hale, Edward Everett, 1822–1900.
Stories of war, told by soldiers, collected and edited by Edward E. Hale. Boston, Roberts Brothers, 1879. 264 p. 17½cm.   NN   *436*

—— —— Boston, Little, Brown, and co., 1907. 264 p. 17½cm.   DLC   *437*
A reprinting.

Hallum, John, 1833–
Reminiscences of the Civil war, by John Hallum. . . . Little Rock, Tunnah & Pittard, printers, 1903. 400 p. 20cm.
NN NcD TxU   *438*
"Volume I." "This volume will be followed at an early date by a volume entitled "Three years in the secret service of General Forrest" and then by another volume of "Reminiscences of the Civil war.""

—— Speciman advance sheets of Reminiscences of the Civil war, by John Hallum . . . volume I. Little Rock, Tunnah & Pittard, printers, 1903. 34 p. 19½cm.   LNHT   *439*
Subscription forms are included.

Hanaford, Phoebe Ann (Coffin), 1819–1921.
Field, gunboat, hospital, and prison; or, thrilling records of the heroism, endurance, and patriotism displayed in the Union army and navy during the great rebellion, by Mrs. P. A. Hanaford. . . . Boston, C. M. Dinsmoor and co., 1866. 379 p. front. (port.). 19½cm.
CSmH   *440*

Hart, Albert Bushnell, 1854–1943, editor.
. . . The romance of the Civil war, selected and annotated by Albert Bushnell Hart, with the collaboration of Elizabeth Stevens. New York, Macmillan co., 1903. xiv, 418 p. front. (illus.), illus. 18½cm.   NN   *441*
At head of title: Source-readers in American history, no. 4.
Authors of the selections are identified but not the works from which they are taken.

Harwell, Richard Barksdale,   editor.
The Confederate reader, edited by Richard B. Harwell. New York, Longmans, Green and co., 1957. xxvi, 389 p. facsim., illus., front. (port.), plate (2 illus.). 23½cm. NN   *442*

—— The Union reader, edited by Richard B. Harwell. New York, Longmans, Green and co., 1958. xxii, 362 p. plates (facsims., illus.). 23½cm.   NN   *443*

—— The war they fought, edited by Richard B. Harwell. New York, Longmans, Green & co., 1960. xviii, 389, x, 362 p.   NN   *444*
A reprinting of The Confederate reader, 1957, and The Union reader, 1958.

Herbert, George B
Anecdotes of the rebellion, compiled and arranged by George B. Herbert. Springfield, Ohio, Mast, Crowell & Kirkpatrick, c1894. 110 p. 19cm.   CSmH   *445*
"Farm and fireside library, October, 1894, no. 116."

Hood, B   H
Records and reminiscences of Confederate soldiers in Terrell county, compiled by Mrs. B. H. Hood and Mrs. W. S. Dozier. Edited by

Mrs. James M. Griggs, Historian Mary Brantley chapter, U.D.C. Dawson, Ga., News print. co. [1914?] 152, (9) p. 23½cm. GEU **446**

"Records of Confederate soldiers taken from tax receiver's books and pension lists in Ordinary's office, Dawson, Terrell County, Ga.," (9) p.
"Roll of the Dawson volunteers Co. E, 5th Georgia regiment," 4–7.

Hull, Susan Rebecca (Thompson), 1833–
Boy soldiers of the Confederacy, collated by Susan R. Hull. New York, Neale pub. co., 1905. 256 p. plates (ports.). 21½cm.
CSmH GEU NHi **447**

Hutchins, Edward Ridgeway
The war of the 'sixties, compiled by E. R. Hutchins. New York, Neale pub. co., 1912. 490 p. 22½cm. CSmH NHi **448**

Illinois Central Magazine.
The story of the Illinois central lines during the Civil conflict, 1861–5. 1913–6. **449**

Series commenced with an article, The part played by the Illinois central and its employees in the Civil war, in the February 1913 issue, which also contained the first of a five part article on Abraham Lincoln. The series continued until September 1916 publishing biographies and personal narratives of Union and Confederate soldiers.

Jackson, Edgar, editor.
Three Rebels write home, including the letters of Edgar Allan Jackson (September 7, 1860 – April, 1863), James Fenton Bryant (June 20, 1861 – December 30, 1866) [and] Irvin Cross Wills (April 9, 1862 – July 29, 1863) and miscellaneous items. [Franklin, Va., News pub. co.] 1955. 103, (2) p. 23cm.
NN ViHi **450**
"(This edition limited to 150 copies)."
Foreword signed: Edgar Jackson.

Joel, Joseph A
Rifle shots and bugle notes; or, the national military album of sketches of the principal battles, marches, picket duty, camp fires, love adventures, and poems connected with the late war, by Joseph A. Joel, and Lewis R. Stegman. Illustrations by Darley, Leslie, and other well known artists. New York, Grand army pub. co., 1884. x, [11]–564 p. plates (illus., ports.). 27½cm.
CSmH NN NcD TxU **451**

Jones, Buehring H 1823–1872.
The sunny land; or, prison prose and poetry, containing the productions of the ablest writers in the South, and prison lays of distinguished Confederate officers, by Col. Buehring H. Jones, 60th Virginia infantry. Edited with Preface, biographies, sketches, and stories, by J. A. Houston. . . . Baltimore [Innes & co., printers] 1868. viii, 540 p. 20cm.
CSmH DLC Vi **452**

"Errata," inserted leaf.
"The sunny land, a story of the cruel war," 1–246, fiction.

Kelsey, D M
Deeds of daring by both Blue and Gray, thrilling narratives of personal adventure . . . during the great Civil war, by D. M. Kelsey. . . . Philadelphia, Scammel & co., 1883. xxi, (1), 23–608 p. front. (illus.), illus., ports. 23½cm. CSmH DLC **453**

—— —— Boston, D. L. Guernsey, 1884. xxi, 23–608 p. illus., ports. 22cm.
NHi NcD TxU **454**

—— —— New revised, enlarged and illustrated edition. Philadelphia, Scammel & co., 1890. xxi, 23–672 p. front. (col. illus.), illus., ports. 22cm. MoHi **455**
With the chapters re-arranged and seven new ones added.

—— Deeds of daring by the American soldier, North and South, thrilling narratives of personal adventure, exploits of scouts and spies . . . by D. M. Kelsey. Revised edition. Chicago, Werner co., 1898. xxi, 23–672 p. front. (illus.), illus., ports. 23½cm.
CSmH GEU **456**
OMC has an 1899 reprinting.

—— The Blue and the Gray. The American soldier, North and South, thrilling narratives of personal adventure . . . during the Civil war, by D. M. Kelsey. Revised edition. New York, etc., Saalfield pub. co., 1907. xi, 23–672 p. illus., ports. 23½cm. IaHi **457**
A reprinting of his Deeds of daring, 1898. Plates are paged.

Kilmer, George Langdon
Daring deeds of daring men, a collection of graphic accounts of deeds of individual heroism, hairbreadth escapes, acts of bravery, strategic movements, and other exciting adventures of the great war of modern times, by Capt. Geo. L. Kilmer. . . . New York, W. D. Rowland [1891] 172 p. illus., plans. 19½cm.
CSmH DLC **458**
"Leisure-time series, no. 2, Feb. 1891."
Text in double columns.

King, William C 1853–
Camp-fire sketches and battle-field echoes of 61–5, compiled by W. C. King and W. P. Derby of 27th Mass. regt. Springfield, Mass., W. C. King & co., 1887. 624 p. front. (illus.), illus. 24cm. DLC NB **459**

—— —— [another printing] Springfield, King, Richardson & co., 1888. 624 p. illus., plates (illus., ports.). 24cm. CSmH **460**
NN has an 1889 reprinting.

Personal Narratives (Collections), continued

LaBree, Benjamin, 1847?–1935.
Camp fire of the Confederacy, a volume of humorous anecdotes, reminiscences, deeds of heroism, thrilling narratives, campaigns . . . Confederate poems and selected songs . . . Edited by Ben LaBree. Louisville, Courier-Journal print. co., 1899. 560 p. illus., ports. 25cm.   CSmH NN   **461**
"The Battle abbey or memorial edition."

Lawson, Albert
War anecdotes and incidents of army life, reminiscences from both sides of the conflict between North and South. Cincinnati, Albert Lawson, 1888. 152, (2) p. 22½cm.
"Contents," (2) p.   CSmH TxU   **462**

Leland, Charles Godfrey, 1824–1903.
Ana of the war. *United States service magazine* III–v (1865–66).   **463**
For location of the eight articles, see the indexes.

[Lester, Charles Edwards] 1815–1890.
The light and dark of the rebellion. . . . Philadelphia, George W. Childs, 1863. 303 p. 18½cm.   DLC NcD   **464**

Lewis, Charles Bertrand, 1842–1914.
Field, fort and fleet, being a series of the most brilliant and authentic sketches of the most notable battles of the late Civil war, including many incidents and circumstances never before published in any form, by M. Quad [pseud.] . . . 1861–63. Detroit, Free Press pub. co., 1885. vii, 520 p. illus., plates (illus., ports.). 26½cm.   CSmH NN   **465**
"Sold by subscription only."

——— Field, fort and fleet . . . by M. Quad, to which is appended an outline history of the Grand army of the Republic, together with a history of the George Washington post no. 103, G.A.R., including biographical sketches of members, by Henry Whittemore. Detroit, Free Press pub. co., 1885. vii, 520, 87 p. illus., plates (illus., ports.). 26½cm.
                                    NN   **466**

McLeod, Martha Norris
Brother warriors, the reminiscences of Union and Confederate veterans. Edited with an introduction, notes and maps, by Martha Norris McLeod. Washington, D.C., Darling print. co., 1940. p. E-P, 358 p. plates (4 maps, ports.). 23cm.   IHi   **467**

Military Order of the Loyal Legion of the United States. California Commandery.
War paper no . . . Commandery of the State of California, Military order of the loyal legion of the United States. [San Francisco, 1888–1913] 24 nos. 22½cm.   CSmH   **468**

Title from cover.
The series title and numbering of the papers is the only text on the cover. In checking files and references, variations were noted in the numbering of the papers which may be explained by shuffling of the covers.

——— District of Columbia Commandery.
. . . War paper. [Washington, 1887–1916] 98 nos. 23½cm.   CSmH   **469**
At head of title, the name of the organization.
Nos 1–95 have title: War papers.

——— Illinois commandery.
Military essays and recollections, papers read before the Commandery of the State of Illinois, Military order of the loyal legion of the United States. [Chicago, 1891–1907] 4 v. 23½cm.   CSmH   **470**
Each volume is indexed.
Publisher's binding.

——— Indiana Commandery.
War papers read before the Indiana commandery, Military order of the loyal legion of the United States. Indianapolis [Press of Levey Bro's & co.] 1898. viii, 521 p. 3 plates (fold. map, 2 ports.). 25cm.   NHi   **471**
"Membership," 476–521.
Publisher's binding.

——— Iowa Commandery.
War sketches and incidents as related by companions of the Iowa commandery, Military order of the loyal legion of the United States. Des Moines, Kenyon press, 1893–98. 2 v. 23½cm.   NHi   **472**
Publisher's binding.

——— Kansas Commandery.
War paper. . . . [Kansas City, Kan., 1891–1903] 24 nos. 23½cm.   **473**
Title from cover.
Nos. 1–16 are not numbered.

——— ——— War talks in Kansas, a series of papers read before the Kansas commandery of the Military order of the loyal legion of the United States. Kansas City, Mo., Press of the Franklin Hudson pub. co., 1906. 391, (1) p. 22½cm.   CSmH   **474**
"Toasts gathered here and there from the reports of our banquets," 361–91.

——— Maine Commandery.
War papers read before the Commandery of the State of Maine, Military order of the loyal legion of the United States. Portland, 1898–1915. 4 v. 24½cm.   NHi   **475**
Each volume is indexed.
Publisher's binding.

——— Massachusetts Commandery.
Civil war papers read before the Commandery of the State of Massachusetts, Military order of the loyal legion of the United States.

Boston, Printed for the Commandery [F. H. Gilson co.] 1900. 2 v. (569, 62 p.). 24½cm.

CSmH   *476*

Officers since its organization and list of members, 62 p.
Publisher's binding.

—— Michigan Commandery.

War papers read before the Commandery of the State of Michigan, Military order of the loyal legion of the United States. Detroit, 1893–98. 2 v. 23½cm.   NHi   *477*

Contents:
ɪ From October 6, 1886, to April 6, 1893.
ɪɪ From December 7, 1893, to May 5, 1898.
Separately published, the papers of ɪ were collected and bound with a title page and table of contents.

—— Minnesota Commandery.

Glimpses of the nation's struggle [first-sixth series] papers read before the Minnesota commandery of the Military order of the loyal legion of the United States. St. Paul, Minneapolis, 1887–1909. 6 v. 23cm. CSmH   *478*

ɪ is not numbered nor its contents dated on the title page.
ɪɪ 1887–1889.
ɪɪɪ 1889–1902.
ɪᴠ 1892–1897.
ᴠ 1897–1902; includes Register . . . July 1, 1903.
ᴠɪ 1903–1908.
Publisher's binding.

—— Missouri.

War papers and personal reminiscences, 1861–1865, read before the Commandery of the State of Missouri, Military order of the loyal legion. St. Louis, Becktold & co., 1892. vi, 451 p. 24cm.   NHi   *479*

Volume is indexed.
Publisher's binding.

—— Nebraska Commandery.

Civil war sketches and incidents, papers read by companions of the Commandery of the State of Nebraska, Military order of the loyal legion of the United States. vol ɪ. Omaha [Burkley ptg. co.] 1902. 277 p. 24½cm.

NHi   *480*

—— New York Commandery.

Personal recollections of the War of the rebellion. Addresses delivered before the Commandery of the State of New York, Military order of the loyal legion of the United States [first-fourth series]. . . . New York, G. P. Putnam's Sons, 1891–1912. 4 v. 23cm.

The first series is not numbered.   NN   *481*
Editors: ɪ James G. Wilson and Titus M. Coan; ɪɪ-ɪᴠ A. Noel Blakeman.
Each volume is indexed.
Publisher's binding.

—— Ohio Commandery.

Papers and personal reminiscences read before the Ohio commandery of the Military order of the loyal legion of the United States,

by members of the Commandery. Cincinnati, Henry C. Sherrick, 1885–87. 2 v. 22½cm.

NHi   *482*

Separately published, the papers were collected and bound with a title page.
Publisher's binding.

—— —— Sketches of war history, 1861–1865, papers prepared for the Commandery of the State of Ohio, Military order of the loyal legion of the United States. Cincinnati, Robert Clarke co., 1888–1908. 6 v. 24½cm.

ɪ-ɪɪ "Papers read before."   CSmH   *483*
ɪ-ᴠ are indexed.
Later sketches were separately published.
Publisher's binding.

—— Oregon Commandery.

War paper no . . . Oregon commandery M.O.L.L.U.S. Portland, 1890–96. 4 nos. 23cm.

Title from cover.   DLC   *484*

—— Vermont Commandery.

War paper no. 1 [–5] Vermont commandery of the Loyal legion. Burlington, 1892–95. 5 nos. 23½cm.   NHi   *485*

Title from cover.

—— Wisconsin Commandery.

War papers read before the Commandery of the State of Wisconsin, Military order of the loyal legion of the United States. Milwaukee, 1891–1914. 4 v. 23cm.   CSmH   *486*

Each volume is indexed.
Publisher's binding.

Mitchell, Joseph Brady, 1915–

The badge of gallantry, recollections of Civil war Congressional medal of honor winners, letters from the Charles Kohen collection [by] Lt. Col. Joseph B. Mitchell. New York, Macmillan co. [1968] xvii, 194 p. illus., ports. 24½cm.

IHi NcD   *486A*

"The theatre of war; or, the stage as set for the opening scenes of 1861," map originally published in 1893, endpaper.

Moore, Frank, 1828–1904.

Anecdotes, poetry and incidents of the war, North and South, 1860–1865. Collected and arranged by Frank Moore, Printed for the subscribers. New York, 1866. 560 p. plates (ports.). 25cm.   CSmH DLC   *487*

Text in double columns.

—— —— [New York] P. F. Collier, 1889. 560 p. plates (illus.). 26½cm.   DLC   *488*

Morton, Joseph W

A photograph of our old life. Sparks from the camp fire; or, tales of the old veterans. Thrilling stories of heroic deeds, brave encounters, desperate battles . . . New and revised edition with contributions from one hundred and fifty comrades. Edited by Joseph W. Mor-

Personal Narratives (Collections), continued

ton. Philadelphia, Keystone pub. co., 1890.
580 p. fold. facsim., illus., maps and plans,
ports., col. plates (illus.). 24½cm.
                            CSmH   **489**
Black and white plates are paged.
"History of the Grand army of the Republic,"
479–580.
The editor's note, "this new and enlarged edition
of Sparks from the camp fire," refers to the same
title, compiled by Charles S. Greene and issued by
the same publisher in 1889. See Title 435.

—— —— Philadelphia, Keystone pub. co.,
1892. 629 p. illus., maps, ports, plates (fold.
facsim., col. illus.). 24½cm.   OMC   **490**
"History of the Grand army of the Republic;
Chronology of the order; Feminine allies of the
G.A.R.; Woman's relief corps and its officers; Chronology by Departments; Sketch of the Sons of veterans, U.S.A.; 479–620.

—— —— Philadelphia, Keystone pub. co.,
1893. 648 p., illus., maps, ports., plates (fold.
facsim., col. illus.). 24½cm.   CSmH   **491**

—— —— Philadelphia, Keystone pub. co.,
1895. 688 p. illus., maps, ports., plates (fold.
facsim., col. illus.). 24½cm.
                        CSmH NcD   **492**

—— —— as retold today around the modern
camp fire. New and revised edition with contributions from one hundred and fifty comrades. Edited by Joseph W. Morton, Jr. Washington, D.C. National Tribune, 1899. 469 p.
illus. 25½cm.   NeHi   **493**
A reprinting omitting History of the Grand army
of the Republic.

Mulholland, St. Clair Augustine, 1839–1910.
   Military order Congress Medal of honor
legion of the United States [by] Brevet Major-
General St. Clair A. Mulholland. Philadelphia
[Town print. co.] 1905. 694 p. plates (4 col.
illus., ports.). 29½cm.   CSmH NN   **494**

New York Tribune.
   . . . The story of our mess and other stories
of the war, told by soldiers and sailors. Re-
printed from the New York weekly tribune.
New York, John W. Lovell co. [c1887] 164 p.
18cm.   CSmH   **495**
Contributions are signed.
At head of title: The Tribune prize war stories.
"Lovell's library, vol. 20, no. 966, May 7, 1887."

—— . . . The three bummers and other
stories of the war told by soldiers and sailors.
Reprinted from the New York Weekly Tribune. New York, John W. Lovell co. [c1887]
171 p. 18cm.   CSmH   **496**
At head of title: The Tribune prize war stories.
"Lovell's library, no. 967."

Patrick, Robert W
   Knapsack and rifle; or, life in the grand
army, war as seen from the ranks. Pen pictures and sketches of camp, bivouac, marches,
battle-fields and battles, commanders, great
military movements, personal reminiscences
and narratives . . . By one of the boys. Copi-
ously and finely illustrated by E. B. Williams.
Philadelphia, Calypso pub. co., 1886. x, 11–
429 p. illus., ports., plates (illus., map, ports.).
23cm.   GEU   **497**
Dedication signed: by Robert W. Patrick.
NB has "Fifth edition," 1887, a reprinting.

—— —— Portland, Oregon, J. K. Gill & co.,
1889. x, 11–430 p. illus., ports., plates (illus.,
map, port.). 21cm.   NB NN   **498**
A reprinting with an additional page of text.

Poe, Clarence Hamilton, 1881–
   True tales of the South at war, how soldiers
fought and families lived, 1861–1865. Collected and edited by Clarence Poe. Betsy Sey-
mour, assistant editor. Chapel Hill, University
of North Carolina press [c1961] xiii, 208 p.
21cm.   DLC   **499**
Personal narratives of soldiers and civilians from
unpublished manuscripts.

Post, Lydia Minturn
   Soldier's letters from camp, battle-field and
prison . . . edited by Lydia Minturn Post. Published for the U.S. sanitary commission. New
York, Bunce & Huntington, 1865. 472 p.
19½cm.   CSmH NHi NN   **500**

Reed, Peter Fishe, 1819–1887.
   Incidents of the war; or, the romance and
realities of soldier life [by] P. Fishe Reid.
[Indianapolis] Asher & co., c1862. 96 p. 18cm.
                  CSmH DLC   **501**

—— —— by P. Fishe Reed. [Indianapolis]
Asher & co., c1862. 112 p. 18cm.
                  CtHT-W   **502**

Reunion Society of Vermont Officers.
   Proceedings of the . . . with addresses de-
livered at its meetings by . . . and a roster of
the Society. Burlington, 1885–1906. 2 v.
23½cm.   NN   **503**
Contents:
[I] 1864–1884.
II 1886–1905.

Rhode Island Soldiers and Sailors Historical
     Society.
   Personal narratives of events in the War of
the rebellion, being papers read before the
Rhode Island soldiers and sailors historical society. . . . Providence, Published by the Society,
1878–1915. 100 nos. plates (illus., ports.).
21cm.   NHi   **504**

Published in seven series of ten numbers each, with the exception of the 2nd, 3rd and 4th series which each had 20 numbers.

Printer varies: 1st series, Sidney S. Rider; 2nd series, nos 1–17, N. Bangs Williams & co.; 2nd series, nos 18–20, Sidney S. Rider, with 19–20 adding "Agt."

No 10 of the 7th series includes list of authors with their military record, list of Rhode Island soldiers awarded the Congressional Medal of honor, and a table of contents.

Rodenbough, Theophilus Francis, 1838–1912.
The bravest five hundred of '61, their noble deeds described by themselves, together with an account of some gallant exploits of our soldiers in Indian warfare. How the Medal of honor was won. Compiled by Theo F. Rodenbough. New York, G. W. Dillingham, 1891. xii, 496 p. facsims., illus., ports. 23cm.
CSmH NN   505

—— Sabre and bayonet, stories of heroism and military adventure, collected and edited by Theo F. Rodenbough. New York, G. W. Dillingham co., 1897. 361 p. facsims., illus., ports. 20½cm.   CSmH NN   506

—— Uncle Sam's Medal of honor, some of the noble deeds for which the Medal has been awarded, described by those who won it, 1861–1866, collected and edited by Theo. F. Rodenbough. New York, G. P. Putnam's Sons [1886] xiv, 424 p. facsims., illus., plan, ports. 21½cm.
CSmH NN   507

Rohrbacher, (Mrs.) L   E   C
Prose, poetry, and song of the Southern Confederacy, comprising the traditions, manners, and customs of the South. Biographical sketches of its statesmen, Generals, and authors. The battles of the Civil war, with its thrilling incidents, its daring adventures, and its romantic reminiscences. Its flag, its music, and its minstrelsy. Edited by Mrs. L. E. C. Rohrbacher. Galveston, M. Strickland & co. [1884] 192 p. plates (ports.). 33½cm.
TxU   508
Many of the contributions are signed.
Issued in 8 parts, hand numbered.
Plates have guard sheets.

Rouse, E   S   S
The bugle blast; or, spirit of the Conflict, comprising naval and military exploits, dashing raids, heroic deeds, thrilling incidents, sketches, anecdotes, etc. . . . by E. S. S. Rouse. Philadelphia, James Challen & Son, 1864. 336 p. 19cm.   CSmH NHi TxU   509

Scoville, Samuel, 1872–
Brave deeds of Union soldiers, by Samuel Scoville, Jr. Philadelphia, George W. Jacobs & co. [1915] 397 p. plates (illus.). 21½cm.
DLC NcD   510

Smith, Edward Parmalee, 1827–1876.
Incidents among shot and shell, the only authentic work extant giving the most tragic and touching incidents that came under the notice of the United States Christian commission during the long years of the Civil war, by Rev. Edward P. Smith, Field secretary of the Commission. [Philadelphia?] Edgewood pub. co. [c1868] 512 p. illus., plates (illus., ports.). 23cm.   CSmH GEU DLC   511

—— Incidents of the United States Christian commission, by Rev. Edward P. Smith. Philadelphia, J. B. Lippincott & co., 1869. 512 p. illus., plates (illus., ports.). 23cm.
A reprinting.   CSmH   512
Added engraved illus. leaf precedes title page.

Sons of Veterans. Michigan. Charles T. Foster Camp No. 4.
Old veterans' stories. *Michigan history magazine* ii (1918) 484–90; iii (1919) 220–30, 652–62; iv (1920) 781–98; v (1921) 452–60.
513

Straley, W
Soldiers and their deeds, compiled by W. Straley. Hico, Texas, Hico print. co., 1913. 24 p. plates (map; ports., 1 fold.). 22½cm.
NN   514
"Originally printed in the 'Old soldiers edition' of the Hico news-review."
Unit roster, company K, 8th Texas cavalry, 23–4.

Stratton, Robert Burcher, 1835–1924?
The heroes in Gray, by a Confederate soldier. . . . Lynchburg, Gregory Brothers, 1894. 140 p. 23½cm.   LNHT Vi   515
Inserted slip "Comrade" signed: R. B. Stratton.

Tramp, Tim [pseud.]
War life, illustrated by stories of the camp and field, compiled by Tim Tramp. New York, Callender, Perce & Welling, 1862. vi, [7]–144 p. col. illus. cover. 19cm.
CSmH DLC OMC   516
"Stories of the War for the Union," 7–84.

Truesdale, John
The Blue coats and how they lived, fought and died for the Union, with scenes and incidents in the great rebellion, comprising narratives of personal adventure, thrilling incidents, daring exploits, heroic deeds, wonderful escapes, life in the camp, field and hospital, adventures of spies and scouts, together with songs, ballads, anecdotes and humorous incidents of the war, by Captain John Truesdale. . . . Philadelphia, Jones Brothers & co. [1867] 510 p. 2 fronts. (ports.), fold. plates (illus., ports.). 22cm.   CSmH NN TxU   517
"Issued by subscription only."

Personal Narratives (Collections), continued

United Daughters of the Confederacy. North
Carolina Division. Pamlico Chapter,
Washington.
The Confederate reveille memorial edition.
Published by the Pamlico chapter of the
Daughters of the Confederacy, Washington,
N. C., May 10, 1898. Raleigh, Edwards &
Broughton, printers, 1898. 162 p. front. (port.).
23cm.   DLC NcD   *518*

Advertising matter, 151–62.

—— South Carolina Division. John K. McIver
Chapter.
Treasured reminiscences, collected by John
K. McIver chapter, U.D.C. Columbia, State
co., printers, 1911. 86 p. 23cm.   ScU   *519*

Title from cover.
"Editing committee: Lieut. W. E. James [and]
Sergt. C. D. Evans."

[Vickers, George Morley] 1841–
Under both flags, a panorama of the great
Civil war, as represented in story, anecdote,
adventure, and the romance of reality, written
by celebrities of both sides, the men and
women who created the greatest epoch of our
Nation's history . . . Indianapolis, Union pub.
co., c1896. 592 p. illus., plans, ports. 29½cm.

Contributions are signed.   CSmH DLC   *520*
Copyright by C. R. Graham.
Also: Philadelphia, World Bible House, c1896,
CSmH; Philadelphia, St. Louis, People's pub. co.,
c1896, DLC.

Victor, Orville James, 1827–1910.
Incidents and anecdotes of the war, with
narratives of great battles, great marches, great
events, and a record of heroic deeds and daring
personal achievements, which characterized
the great conflict for the Union. Edited by
Orville J. Victor. New York, James D. Torrey
[c1866] vi, [9]–495 p. plates (illus.). 23cm.

Added illus. title page.   CSmH   *521*

Watson, Annah Walker (Robinson), 1848–
On the field of honor, by Annah Robinson
Watson. . . . Detroit, Sprague pub. co. [1902]
226 p. plates (illus., ports.). 17cm.
                              DLC NB NN   *522*

Westcott, Mary W
Footfalls of loyalty, by Mary W. Westcott.
Swanton, Neb. Lincoln, Journal co., 1886. vi,
191 p. 18½cm.   NB NN   *523*

Collection of soldiers' letters.

Winchester-Frederick County Historical
Society.
Diaries, letters and recollections of the War
between the States. Printed by the Winchester-

Frederick county historical society. Editorial
committee . . . [4 names] [Staunton, McClure
co.] 1955. 133 p. 22½cm. (Its Papers III).
                                          VHi   *524*

PICTORIAL WORKS

The Civil war through the camera . . . The
new text history, by Henry W. Elson. . . . New
York, McKinlay, Stone & Mackenzie [c1912]
1 v. illus., ports., col. plates (illus.). 27cm.
                                          NN   *525*

Originally published in sixteen numbered parts by
the Patriot pub. co. of Springfield, Mass, who hold
the copyright for this work.

Frank Leslie's scenes and portraits of the Civil
war . . . by such well known artists as Becker,
Crane, Beard . . . and others. With an introduction by Joseph B. Carr, Major-General. New
York, Mrs. Frank Leslie [c1894] 1 v. illus.,
ports. 42cm.   CSmH   *526*

"This series . . . will consist of thirty parts, twenty-
six of which will be devoted to illustrations, and four
to reading matter."
The illustrations are not paged; the text, [417]–80.
No more published vols?
The illustrations are reprinted from Frank Leslie's
pictorial history of the Civil war, edited by E. G.
Squier, 1861–62.

Frank Leslie's illustrated famous leaders and
battle scenes of the Civil war . . . by such well-
known artists as Becker, Crane, Beard, Schell
. . . Edited by Louis Shepheard Moat. With an
introduction by Joseph B. Carr, Major-General.
New York, Mrs. Frank Leslie [c1896] 544 p.
illus., ports. 42cm.   CSmH   *527*

Text, 449–543, in three columns and captioned:
A concise history of the Civil war.

Pictorial envelopes of the Civil war. *Bulletin
Missouri historical society* v (1948/49) 306–
10. plates (illus.)   *528*

Based on the collection assembled and mounted
in a scrapbook by Lieutenant Nathan Appleton of the
5th Mass. battery.

Pictorial war record. Battles of the late Civil
war . . . First series. v. 1–2; v. 3, no. 1–19;
whole number 1–23. [New York, Stearns & co.,
1881–84] illus., maps, ports. 42cm.

Caption title.   CSmH DLC   *529*
No more published.

American Heritage
The American heritage picture history of the
Civil war, by the editors of American heritage.
Editor in charge, Richard M. Ketchum. Narra-
tive by Bruce Catton. New York, American
Heritage pub. co. [c1960] 629 p. partly col.
facsims., illus., ports. (partly double). 28½cm.

Title on two leaves.   TxU   *530*

Blay, John S
The Civil war, a pictorial profile [by] John S. Blay. New York, Thomas Y. Crowell co. [1958] 342 p. illus., maps, ports. 28½cm.
NN   531

Brady, Matthew, 1823–1896.
Brady's national photographic collection of war views, and portraits of representative men. . . . New York, Raymond & Caulon, printers [1866] 103 p. 19cm.   CSmH   532

—— —— New York, C. A. Alvord, printer, 1870. 139, (1) p. 18½cm.   CSmH   533

Donald, David Herbert, 1920–
Divided we fought, a pictorial history of the war, 1861–1865. Picture editors, Hirst D. Milhollen, Milton Kaplan and Hulen Stuart; author of the text and general editor, David Donald. New York, Macmillan co., 1953. x, (1), 452 p. illus., ports. 29cm. DLC   534
Title on two leaves.

Forbes, Edwin, 1839–1895.
A Civil war artist at the front, Edwin Forbes' life studies of the great army. Edited by William Forrest Dawson. New York, Oxford University press, 1957. front. (illus.), 40 numbered illus. on rectos with text on facing versos. 20½ x 26½cm.   NcD   535
Front. is a "sketch for plate 26."

—— Life studies of the great army, by Edwin Forbes. . . . A historical work of art, in copperplate etching, containing forty plates, illustrating the life of the Union armies during the years 1862–'3–'4–'5. New York, E. Forbes [c1876] cover title, 40 plates. 61cm.
Proofs on tinted plate paper.   CSmH   536

—— Thirty years after, an artist's story of the great war, told and illustrated with nearly 300 relief etchings after sketches in the field, and 20 half-tone equestrian portraits from original oil paintings, by Edwin Forbes. New York, Fords, Howard & Hulbert [c1890] 319 p. illus., ports., plates (illus., ports.). 35cm.
CSmH NcD   537
Re-issued April 5 – August 16, 1894 in 20 numbered weekly parts with cover title, The army sketch book, and with series title, Army life series.
The plates are paged except for the illus. and ports., which are reproduced by the photogravure process.

Gardner, Alexander, 1821–1882.
Gardner's photographic sketch book of the war. Washington, D.C., Philip & Solomons [1865–66] 2 v. 100 mounted photographs. 36 x 47cm.   PU   538
Engraved title pages.
Each plate accompanied by a leaf of descriptive letterpress.
Sabin 26635.

—— —— New York, Dover publications [c1959] 1 v. illus. 27½ x 22cm.   NN   539

Guernsey, Alfred Hudson, 1825–1902.
Harper's pictorial history of the great rebellion, by Alfred H. Guernsey and Henry M. Alden. New York, Harper & Bros. [1866–68] 2 v. (836 p.). facsim., illus., maps and plans, ports. 41½cm.   CSmH DLC   540
Contents:
i To the close of the Peninsula campaign of 1862.
ii [Closing with "Reconstruction, 1864–67"]
Text in double columns.

—— —— [Another printing] Chicago, McDonnell Bros. [1894–96] 2 v. (836 p). facsim., illus., maps and plans, ports. 41½cm.
CSmH   541
ii Star pub. co.
NcD has original parts of ii, 17 (April 16 – May 28, 1894).

Horan, James David, 1914–
Matthew Brady, historian with a camera, by James D. Horan. Picture collation by Gertrude Horan. New York, Crown pub. [c1955] xix, 244 p. facsims., illus., ports. 31cm.   542
"A picture album," [91–228].
Plates are paged.

Johnson, Edwin Rossiter, 1840–1931.
Campfire and battlefield, an illustrated history of the campaigns and conflicts of the great Civil war, by Rossiter Johnson . . . [6 names] Art editors, Frank Beard [and] George Spiel. New York, Bryan, Taylor & co., c1894. 551 p. front. (port.), illus., maps, ports. 34½cm.
Text in double columns.   DLC   543

Joinville, François Ferdinand Philippe Louis Marie d'Orleans, prince de, 1818–1900.
A Civil war album of paintings by Prince de Joinville. Preface by the Comte de Paris. Texts by André Maurois and General James M. Gavin. New York, Atheneum [Paris, Presses de I.P.E.] 1964. 33. (1) p. 20 col. plates (illus.). 25 x 33cm.   NN   544
Illus. on rectos, text on facing versos.

Kurz and Allison, engravers.
Battles of the Civil war, 1861–1865, a pictorial presentation. [Little Rock] Pioneer press, Civil War publications, [c1960] 36 col. plates (illus.). 47½ x 62½cm.   545
Plates accompanied by sheets of varying widths with descriptive text on rectos and versos.

Mottelay, Paul Fleury, 1841–
The soldier in our Civil war, a pictorial history of the conflict, 1861–1865, illustrating the valor of the soldier as displayed on the battlefield, from sketches drawn by Forbes, Waud, Taylor, Hall, Becker, Lovie, Schell, Crane and numerous other eye-witnesses to the strife. Edited by Paul F. Mottelay, assisted by the

Pictorial Works, continued

most notable Generals and commanders of both
sides. With an introduction by Robert B.
Beath. History of the Grand army of the Republic, by Paul Vandervoort. History of the
Sons of veterans, by A. P. Davis. New York,
J. H. Brown pub. co., 1884–85. 2 v. illus.,
maps and plans, ports. 42cm.   TxU   **546**
"Chronological list of events (1860–1865) and
miscellaneous statistics, compiled and arranged by
T. Campbell-Copeland," II 393–456, 465–73. The
second pagination is the Index of the Chronological
list. It is possible that the text of 457–64 is considered a part of the Chronological list.
"Engraving and composition at the establishment
of Mrs. Frank Leslie."
Text in triple columns.

—— —— Edited by Paul F. Mottelay and T.
Campbell-Copeland assisted by the most nota-
ble Generals and commanders of both sides.
With an introduction by Robert B. Beath. History of the Grand army of the Republic, by
Paul Vandervoort. History of the Sons of the
veterans, by A. P. Davis and Frank P. Merrill.
New York, G. W. Carleton & co., 1886. 2 v.
front. (ports.), illus., maps and plans, plates
(col. illus., port.). 43½cm.   CSmH   **547**
"Sold only by subscription."
"Chronological list of events (1860–1865) and
miscellaneous statistics, compiled and arranged by
T. Campbell-Copeland," 393–474, 483–8. The second
pagination is the Index of the Chronological list. It is
possible that the text of 475–82 is considered a part
of the Chronological list.
Text in triple columns.

—— —— New York, Stanley Bradley pub.
co., 1890. 2 v. fronts. (ports.), illus., maps and
plans, plates (col. illus., port.). 43½cm.
A reprinting on heavier paper.   CSmH   **548**
"The chronological list . . . ," I 423–74; II 393–
432.

—— Frank Leslie illustrations. The soldier in
our Civil war. Columbian memorial edition. A
pictorial history of the conflict, 1861–1865,
illustrating the valor of the soldier as displayed
on the battle field, from sketches drawn by
Forbes, Waud, Taylor, Hillen, Becker, Lovie,
Schell, Crane, Davis, and numerous other eye-
witnesses to the strife. Edited by Paul F.
Mottelay and T. Campbell-Copeland, assisted
by the most notable Generals and commanders
of both sides. With an introduction by Robert
B. Beath. History of the Grand army of the
Republic, by Paul Vandervoort. History of the
Confederate veterans' association, by Col. I.
W. Avery. History of the Sons of veterans, by
A. P. Davis and Frank P. Merrill. . . . New
York, Stanley Bradley pub. co., 1893. 2 v.
fronts. (ports.), illus., maps, ports. 43½cm.
"Sold only by subscription."   NcD   **549**
Half-title: Frank Leslie's the soldier in our Civil
war.
Text in triple columns.

Pratt, Fletcher
Civil war in pictures, by Fletcher Pratt. New
York, Henry Holt and co. [c1955] 256 p. illus.,
ports. 28½cm.   DLC   **550**
Title on two leaves.

Reed, C   W
Bits of camp life, by C. W. Reed and Louis
K. Harlow. Dedicated to the Grand army of
the Republic by the artists. Munich, Obpacher
Bros., c1888. [14] leaves. col. plates (illus.,
music). 17½ x 25cm.   CSmH DLC   **551**

Simpson, Harold Brown, 1917–
Matthew Brady, Civil war cameraman
(presentation given by Colonel Harold B.
Simpson before the Civil war round table of
Wiesbaden, Germany, on Monday evening,
November 18, 1957, at the Von Steuben
hotel). 13 folios. 27cm. mimeographed.   **552**

Squier, Ephraim George, 1821–1888.
Frank Leslie's pictorial history of the Ameri-
can Civil war, edited by the Hon. E. G. Squier.
New York, Frank Leslie [1861]–62. 2 v. illus.,
maps, ports. 58½cm.   CSmH   **553**
I complete with title page, indexes to literature and
engravings, xvi, 400 p.; II 88 p.
No more published.
Caption title: History of the war of 1861 [–2]
descriptive, statistical, and documentary.
Issued in 33 "semi-monthly parts."
Text in triple columns.

Thompson, William Fletcher
Illustrating the Civil war. *Wisconsin magazine of history* XLV (1961/62) 10–20.   **554**

Wright, Marcus Joseph, 1831–1922.
Official and illustrated war record, embracing nearly one thousand pictorial sketches by
the most distinguished American artists of battles by land and sea, camp and field scenes,
insignia of rank in the Civil war. Comprehensive and impartial histories of military and
naval operations, compiled from the official
data furnished by Union and Confederate departments, commands, corps, divisions and
brigades. Portraits and biographies of Northern and Southern leaders. Elaborate maps,
army and navy rosters, battle-lists and descriptions, alphabetically and chronologically
arranged. Numerous tabular statements of
cemeteries, prisoners, casualties, expenditures,
and martial matters not hitherto accessible.
Authentic articles by eminent officials on the
uses of a navy, closing days of conflict, origin
and meaning of corps badges, object and status
of the Grand army of the Republic and Confederate veterans' association. Carefully written and edited by: Gen. Marcus J. Wright,
Col. Benjamin La Bree [and] James P. Boyd.
Washington, 1898. 560 p. illus. (partly col.),
maps, ports., fold. plates (illus.). 45½cm.
                                    CSmH   **555**

POETRY AND SONG

Our war songs, North and South. Cleveland, S. Brainard's Sons, c1887. 638 p. plates (ports.), music. 36½cm.   CSmH   **556**
Title page illus. in color.

Allan, Francis D
Allan's Lone star ballads, a collection of Southern patriotic songs, made during Confederate times . . . Compiled and revised by Francis D. Allan. Galveston, J. D. Sawyer, 1874. iv, [5]–222, (2) p. 15cm. CSmH **557**
Advertising matter, [201] to end of volume.

Browne, Francis Fisher, 1843–1913.
Bugle-echoes, a collection of poems of the Civil war, Northern and Southern, edited by Francis F. Browne. New York, White, Stokes, & Allen, 1886. x, [13]–336 p. 20cm.
                                          CSmH   **558**

Brownell, Henry Howard, 1820–1872.
Gulf-weed third annual reunion of the Society of the army and navy of the Gulf, Newport, July 7th, 1871. By Henry Howard Brownell. Broadside, 35½ x 21½cm.
Poetry.   CSmH   **559**
Text in double columns.

—— Lyrics of a day; or, newspaper-poetry, by a volunteer in the U.S. service. Second edition. New York, Carleton, 1864. ix, [11]–192 p. 17½cm.   NN   **560**
"Votes and bayonets; or, lays of the Civil war," [11]–63.
The author served as a Navy Ensign through Farragut's special favor.
c1862 by Henry Howard Brownell.

Brownlee, James Henry, 1846–
Martial recitations, heroic, pathetic, and humorous for the veterans' camp-fire. Collected and arranged by James Henry Brownlee . . . Chicago, Werner co. [1896] 232 p. 19½cm.
                                          CSmH   **561**
"Vol. III, no. 1. The practical series. Issued quarterly."

Bruce, Wallace, 1844–1914.
The candle parade, by Wallace Bruce, read by the author at the eighteenth annual reunion of the Society of the Army of the Potomac, held at Saratoga Springs, N. Y., June 22, 1887. 16 folios. 15½cm.   CSmH   **562**
Title from cover.
"Just before the grand review in Washington, at the close of the war, a single company, each man carrying a lighted candle, started in procession through the camps of Alexandria. Regiments, battalions and brigades caught the infection, and fifty thousand candles . . ."
Poetry.

Childs, Bert B
Civil war musicians. *Annals of Iowa* s 3, xxv (1943) 122–8.   **563**

Davidson, Nora Fontaine M
Cullings from the Confederacy, a collection of Southern poems, original and others, popular during the War between the States, and incidents and facts worth recalling, 1862–1866, including the doggerel of the camp, as well as tender tribute to the dead . . . Compiled by Nora Fontaine M. Davidson. Washington, D.C., Rufus H. Darby print. co., 1903. 163 p. plates (illus., ports.). 23½cm.
                        CSmH DLC TxU   **564**

Didier, Eugene Lemoine, 1838–1913.
Some Southern war-songs and their authors. *B&G* II (1893) 464–8.   **565**

Duganne, Augustine Joseph Hickey, 1823–1884.
. . . Ballads of the war, by Augustine J. H. Duganne, splendidly and profusely illustrated by the best artists. New York, John Robins, c1862. p. [25]–36. illus. 25½cm. MB **566**
At head of title: Number 1. March to the Capitol.
"The march to the Capitol though the third of the series is published first, but is paged so as to bind up in chronological order as the third."
Title and imprint from cover.

—— —— Engraved by John Filmer. New York, John Robins, c1862. 12 p. front. (illus.), illus. 25½cm.   MB   **567**
At head of title: Number 2. Sumter.
Fourteen parts were advertised.

—— Manassas [poem] *Foederal American* LXVI (1865) 359–61.   **568**

[Dwyer, J   Henry]
Sheridan's battles in the Shenandoah, by Henry Horton [pseud.] Lynn, Mass., Press of Thos. P. Nichols, 1885. 16 p. 17cm.
Poetry.   CSmH DLC   **569**

Eggleston, George Cary, 1839–1911.
American war ballads and lyrics, a collection of the songs and ballads of the colonial wars, the Revolution, the War of 1812–15, the War with Mexico, and the Civil war. Edited by George Cary Eggleston. New York, G. P. Putnam's Sons [c1889] 2 v. fronts. (illus.). 14½cm.   CSmH   **570**
Civil war, I 165–226 and II.
"Knickerbocker nuggets."

Emurian, Ernest K
Stories of Civil war songs, by Ernest K. Emurian. Natick, Mass., W. A. Wilde co. [c1960] 96 p. 21cm.   TxU   **571**

Erdman, William Jacob, 1834–1903.
A cavalry raid, poem delivered before the alumni of Hamilton college, July 18, 1866, Rev. W. J. Erdman. Fayetteville, Printed by F. A. Darling, 1866. 14 p. 21½cm.
Running title: Alumni poem.   CSmH   **572**

Poetry and Song, continued

Fagan, William Long, 1838–
Southern war songs, camp-fire, patriotic and sentimental. Collected and arranged by W. L. Fagan. New York, M. T. Richardson & co., 1890. vi, 389 p. col. front. (illus.), illus., ports. 25½cm.   CSmH DLC   **573**

[Godfrey, John A   ]
Rhymed tactics, by "Gov. . . ." New York, D. Van Nostrand, 1862. 144 p. plates (ports.). 14½cm.   CSmH DLC   **574**
"The numbers placed in the margin correspond with the numbers of paragraphs in the last edition Regulation tactics."
The front. is a port. of Col. John A. Godfrey. Facing p. 15 is a port. of "Gov." With these statements the compiler registers his questioning of the ascription to Godfrey.

Gunn, Otis Berthoude, 1828–1901.
A tribute to the Union soldier, a poem, written by companion Major O. B. Gunn and recited by him before the Kansas commandery M.O.L.L.U.S. at Leavenworth, Kansas, February 7, 1894. 3 p. 21½cm.   CSmH   **575**
Caption title.

Hasson, Alexander Breckinridge,   –1877.
Contributions to the rhymes of the war, being a collection of pieces which were published from time to time in the papers of the day, by A. B. H., U.S.A. [Baltimore] J. D. Toy, print [1865] 25 p. 19½cm.
                                CSmH DLC   **576**
On cover: Baltimore, May, 1865.
Text in double ruled border.

Hayne, Paul Hamilton, 1830–1886.
Confederate war songs. *SB* n s i (1885/86) 35–43.   **577**

Hayward, John Henry
Poetical pen pictures of the war, selected from our Union poets, by J. Henry Hayward . . . Third edition. New York, Published by the Editor, 1864. 408 p. 19cm.
                                CSmH DLC   **578**
"Published for the purpose of founding a building fund for the 'Union home and school' established for the education and maintenance of our volunteers' children."

Heaps, Willard Allison, 1909–
The singing sixties, the spirit of Civil war days drawn from the music of the times, by Willard A. and Porter W. Heaps. Norman, University of Oklahoma press [c1960] xiv, 423 p. illus., music. 24½cm.   CSmH   **579**

Hubner, Charles William, 1835–1929.
War poets of the South and Confederate camp-fire songs . . . [n.p., 1896] viii, [17]–176 p. plate (illus.). 18½cm.
                                CSmH DLC   **580**

"Preface" signed: Charles W. Hubner, Atlanta, Ga.

James, Bushrod Washington, 1836–1903.
Echoes of battle, by Bushrod Washington James. Philadelphia, Henry T. Coates & co., 1895. 222 p. plates (illus.). 20½cm.
                                CSmH   **581**
"Poems [with] prose descriptive chapters."
Contents, Partial: Antietam — after the battle; Gettysburg — after the battle; Missing; March! March! march! march! 1861–1864.
The author was a volunteer surgeon with the Sanitary commission.

Jones, Walter Burgwyn, 1888–
War poems of the Southern Confederacy, address by Walter Burgwyn Jones, before the fifty-sixth annual reunion Confederate veterans . . . Edgewater park, Mississippi, October 7, 1946. 63 p. 4 illus., port. 22½cm.
                                MsHa MoU   **582**

Miles, Dudley
Poems of our Civil war. *Magazine of history* xxii (1916) 20–4.   **583**

Moore, Frank, 1882–1904.
Songs and ballads of the Southern people, 1861–1865. Collected and edited by Frank Moore. New York, D. Appleton and co., 1886. 324 p. 18cm.   CSmH DLC   **584**

Read, Thomas Buchanan, 1822–1872.
Sheridan's ride, by T. Buchanan Read. Privately printed. New York [Bradstreet press] 1867. 6 p. front. (port.). 32cm.
                                CSmH DLC   **585**
"Edition, 60 copies quarto."
Poetry.

Semmes, Raphael
Civil war song sheets, one of the collections of the Maryland historical society. *MHM* xxxviii (1943) 205–29. 2 facsims.   **586**

[Shepperson, William G   ]
War songs of the South. Edited by "Bohemian," correspondent Richmond dispatch . . . Richmond, West & Johnston, 1862. 216 p. 19cm.   CSmH DLC   **587**
Crandall 3154.

Silber, Irwin
Songs of the Civil war, compiled and edited by Irwin Silber. Piano and guitar arrangements by Jerry Silverman. New York, Columbia University press, 1960. 385 p. illus., music. 28½cm.
"References," p. 369–74.   DLC   **588**

Society of the Army of the Potomac.
Army of the Potomac. Seventeenth annual reunion, 1886. Veterans' hymn book, used at the banquet of the Society, at San Francisco, Cal., August 4th, 1886. Printed by courtesy of

the New York commandery of the Military order of loyal legion. [New York, Macgowan & Slipper, printers, 1886] 35 p. 17cm.
Title from cover.   CSmH   **589**
P. [1]–2 and 3 printed on cover.

Steinmetz, Lee, editor
The poetry of the American Civil war, edited by Lee Steinmetz. [Lansing] Michigan State University press [c1960] xii, 264 p. 23½cm.
NN   **590**

Townsend, Richard Walter, 1859–
The passing of the Confederate, by R. Walter Townsend. Suggested by the account given of the decrepit "appearance" of the Confederate veterans, during their march through the streets of Lumberton, N.C., at the unveiling of a monument to the memory of the Confederate dead from Robeson county, May 10, 1907. New York, Neale pub. co., 1911. 20 p. 18½cm.   CSmH DLC   **591**

Vickers, George Edward
Gettysburg, a poem, by George E. Vickers. [Philadelphia, 1890] [36] p. 24cm.
CSmH   **592**

—— Last charge at Gettysburg, by George Edward Vickers. Philadelphia, Herald co., 1899. 32 p. 21cm.   CSmH   **593**
Poetry with copious footnotes.

Wakeman, George
Our soldier's songs. *Public spirit* ii (1868) 533–8.   **594**

Walter, R   S
A ride for life at Gettysburg, by R. S. Walter. New York, A. T. De LaMare ptg. and pub. co., 1896. 101 p. 18½cm.   CSmH   **595**
c1896 by King, Schaarmann & co., Front Royal, Va.
Poetry.

Wharton, Henry Marvin, 1848–1928.
War songs and poems of the Southern Confederacy, 1861–1865. A collection of the most popular and impressive songs and poems of the war times, dear to every Southern heart. Collected and retold with personal reminiscences of the war, by H. M. Wharton. [Philadelphia, c1904] 412, (4) p. plates (illus., ports.). 24cm.   CSmH DLC   **596**
"Kind words of approval and endorsement," (4) p.

White, Richard Grant, 1821–1885.
Poetry, lyrical, narrative, and satirical of the Civil war, selected and edited by Richard Grant White. New York, American News co., 1866. xxii, 334 p. 19½cm.
DLC NcD   **597**

PRISONS AND PRISONERS OF WAR

General

Northern prison life. *LWL* ii (1866/67) 39–44, 102–07, 172–9.   **598**
Text signed: Sigma Chi, Fayetteville, N. C., May 8th, 1866.

Prisoners of war and military prisons, personal narratives of experience in the prisons at Richmond, Danville, Macon, Andersonville, Savannah, Millen, Charleston, and Columbia . . . by Asa B. Isham, Henry M. Davidson and Henry B. Furness. Cincinnati, Lyman & Cushing, 1890. xii, 571 p. illus., ports, plates (illus., fold. plan). 23cm.   CSmH NN   **599**
Contents:
Experience in Rebel prisons for United States officers at Richmond, Macon, Savannah, Charleston, and Columbia, by Asa B. Isham, 1–146.
Experience in Rebel prisons for United States soldiers at Richmond, Danville, Andersonville, Savannah, and Millen, by Henry M. Davidson, 147–398.
A general account of prison life and prisons in the South during the War of the rebellion, including statistical information relating to prisoners of war, by Henry B. Furness, 399–487.
Appendix. Military and naval officers in the United States service who were prisoners of war . . . from January 1, 1864, 489–554.
Coulter 142.

[Bartlett, John Russell] 1805–1886.
The barbarities of the Rebels, as shown in their cruelty to the Federal wounded and prisoners, in their outrages upon Union men, in the murder of negroes, and in their unmanly conduct throughout the rebellion, by Colonel Percy Howard [pseud.] late of the Royal horse guards. Providence, Printed for the author, 1863. 40 p. 23½cm.   CSmH IHi   **600**

Christian, George Llewellyn, 1841–1924.
Official report of the History committee of the Grand camp, C.V., Department of Virginia, by Hon. Geo. L. Christian, Chairman. Read at Wytheville, Va., October 23rd, 1902 . . . on the treatment and exchange of prisoners. . . . Pulaski, Press of B. D. Smith & Bros., [1902] 29 p. 23cm.   MsHA Vi   **601**
Title and imprint from cover.

Confederate Veteran, Nashville.
Names of six hundred Confederate officers who were subjected to severest prison fare and placed under fire of Confederate cannon in Charleston harbor. [Nashville, 189–?] [8] p. 28cm.   CSmH   **602**
Caption title.
Residence, regiment and place of capture is supplied.
Text in double columns.

Prisons & Prisoners of War, General, continued

Duckworth, William A
Escape of Iowa soldiers from Confederate prison. *Annals of Iowa* s 3, x (1910) 337–59. plates (ports.).   **603**

[Dunkle, John J   ]
Prison life during the rebellion, being a brief narrative of the miseries and sufferings of six hundred Confederate prisoners sent from Fort Delaware to Morris island to be punished. Written by Fritz Fuzzlebug [pseud.] one of their number. Published by the author. Singer's Glen, Va., Joseph Funk's Sons, printers, 1869. 48 p. 23cm.   CSmH DLC   **604**
Roster of prisoners includes rank, regiment and place of residence.

Early, Jubal Anderson, 1816–1894.
A letter from . . . Treatment of Federal prisoners in Confederate prisons. General John H. Winder. *SHM* I (1876) 173–83.   **605**

Green, Wharton Jackson, 1831–1910.
Prisoners of war and their treatment. *SHM* I (1876) 148–56.   **606**

Hemmerlein, Richard F
Prisons and prisoners of the Civil war, by Richard F. Hemmerlein. Boston, Christopher pub. house [c1934] 116 p. 21cm.
                          DLC NcD   **607**

Hesseltine, William Best, 1902–
Civil war prisons, a study in war psychology [by] William Best Hesseltine. Columbus, Ohio State University press, 1930. xi, 290 p. 23cm.
"Bibliography," 259–82.   DLC NN   **608**

—— The underground railroad from Confederate prisons to East Tennessee. *ETHSP* II (1930) 55–69.   **609**

Illinois State Association of Union Ex-Prisoners of War.
Ex-prisoners of war. Fourth annual re-union Illinois association, held at Decatur, Illinois, October 17 and 18, 1883. Decatur, Morning Herald print [1883] 103 p. 18cm.
                          CSmH   **610**
List of those in attendance with addresses, and place and date of imprisonment, 77–103.

Jeffrey, William Hartley, 1867–
Richmond prisons, 1861–1862, compiled from the original records kept by the Confederate government. Journals kept by Union prisoners of war. Together with the name, rank, company, regiment and State of the four thousand who were confined there, by William H. Jeffrey. St. Johnsbury, Vt., Republican press

[1893] 271 p. facsims., plates (illus., ports.). 20½cm.   NN   **611**

Lewis, Samuel Ebenezer, 1848–
. . . The treatment of prisoners-of-war, 1861–1865. Over 12 per cent Confederate soldiers died in Northern prisons. Less than 9 per cent Federal (Unionist) prisoners died in Southern prisons. The North held 220,000 Confederate soldiers as prisoners-of-war. The South held 270,000 Federal (Unionist) soldiers as prisoners-of-war. Prepared by Samuel E. Lewis, late Assistant surgeon, C.S. army. [Richmond, Wm. Ellis Jones, printer] 1910. 16 p. 23½cm
                          CU-SB GEU   **612**

Ohio Association of Union Ex-Prisoners of War.
Constitution and by-laws of the Ohio association of Union ex-prisoners of war, together with register of members and proceedings at the reunion, held at Cincinnati, Sept. 14, 15, 16, 1881 . . . Columbus, Ohio State Journal print. estab., 1882. 62 p. 23cm.   **613**
Rosters of members, 23–62, include regiment, date of capture, place and duration of imprisonment.

—— —— reunion held at Marietta, June 10 and 11, 1891 . . . Cincinnati, Thos. Mason, printer, 1892. 46, (1) p. 23cm. OMC   **614**
Notice of 1892 reunion, (1) p.

Ould, Robert, 1820–1882.
The exchange of prisoners. *AW* 32–59.   **615**

Tebault, Christopher Hamilton
Treatment of prisoners during the War between the States, 1861–1865, by C. H. Tebault . . . [1905] 15 p. 23½cm.   ViHi   **616**
Title from cover, p. [1]
"Reprint from the Southerner practitioner, June, 1905."
Read at the seventh annual meeting of the Association of medical officers of the army and navy of the Confederacy, June, 1904.

Wilson, Thomas L
Sufferings endured for a free government; or, a history of the cruelties and atrocities of the rebellion, by Thos. L. Wilson. Washington, D.C. Published by the author, 1864. x, 13–300 p. 19cm.   GEU   **617**
Contents:
I Treatment of prisoners of war by the Rebel government, 13–77.
II Persecution of Unionists in the revolted states . . . [79]–300.

—— —— Philadelphia, King & Baird, 1865. x, 13–372 p. front. (port.), plates (illus., ports.). 19cm.   OMC   **618**
Contents:
I Treatment of prisoners of war by the Rebel government, 13–77.
II Persecution of Unionists in the revolted states . . . [79]–372.

The South

(Individual Prisons)

ANDERSONVILLE

The demon of Andersonville; or, the trial of Wirz for the cruel treatment and brutal murder of helpless Union prisoners in his hands . . . Philadelphia, Barclay & co. [1865] 120 p. front. (plan), illus. 23cm.   DLC NB   **619**
Cover illus. in color with port.
Plates are paged.

[Asche, S   W   ]
The trial and death of Henry Wirz, with other matters pertaining thereto. Raleigh, E. M. Uzzell & co., printers, 1908. 62 p. 23cm.
CSmH MoU   **620**
"Introduction" signed: S. W. A.

Atwater, Dorence
A list of the Union soldiers buried at Andersonville, copied from the official record in the Surgeon's office at Andersonville . . . New York, Tribune Association, 1866. viii, 74 p. 25cm.   CSmH NjJ   **621**
Title from cover, p. [i]
Introductory remarks signed: Dorence Atwater.

——— ——— by Dorence Atwater. New York, Tribune Association, 1868. viii, 74 p. 25cm.
Title from cover, p. [i]   CSmH   **622**

——— ——— New York, Tribune Association, 1890. 72 p. 25½cm.   CSmH   **623**

Braun, Herman A
Andersonville, an object lesson on protection, a critical sketch, by Herman A. Braun. Milwaukee, C. D. Fahsel pub. co., 1892. xi, [13]–164, (2) p. 2 plates (plans). 16cm.
CSmH DLC NB NN(M)   **624**
"Index," (2) p.

Chipman, Norton Barker, 1836–1924.
The horrors of Andersonville Rebel prison. Trial of Henry Wirz, the Andersonville jailor. Jefferson Davis defense of Andersonville fully refuted. By General N. P. Chipman. San Francisco, Bancroft & co., 1891. 89 p. 17cm.
CSmH DLC NB   **625**

——— The tragedy of Andersonville, trial of Captain Henry Wirz, the prison keeper, by General N. P. Chipman . . . Second edition, revised and enlarged . . . [Sacramento, 1911] 532 p. front. (port.), illus., ports. 23½cm.
"Published by the author."   IHi   **626**

Chollett, Louise E
At Andersonville. *Atlantic monthly* xv (1865) 285–96.   **627**

Davis, Jefferson, 1809–1889.
Andersonville and other war prisons, by Jefferson Davis. New York, Belford co. [c1890] [27] p. 22cm.   CSmH   **628**
"From Belford's magazine."
Text dated: December 10, 1888.

Futch, Ovid
Prison life at Andersonville. *CWH* viii (1962) 121–35.   **629**

Gue, Benjamin F., 1828–1904.
The story of Andersonville. *Palimpsest* xlii (1961) 211–78. illus.   **630**
"Iowans buried at Andersonville," 246–78.
"Analysis of the roster," by William J. Petersen, 243–5.
"Taken verbatim from the Iowa State register of May 30, 1884."

Hamlin, Augustus Choate, 1829–1905.
Martyria; or, Andersonville prison, by Augustus C. Hamlin. Illustrated by the author. Boston, Lee and Shepard, 1866. 256 p. front. (illus.), illus., plates (plans, 1 fold.). 19½cm.
CSmH DLC IHi   **631**

Hanly, James Franklin, 1863–1920.
Andersonville, by J. Frank Hanly. Cincinnati, Jennings and Graham [c1912] 35 p. front. (illus.). 19cm.   CSmH   **632**
Address at the dedication of the Indiana monument.

Hesseltine, William Best, 1902–
Andersonville revisited, by William B. Hesseltine. [1956] 9 p. 25½cm.   NbHi   **633**
Title from cover.
"Reprinted from the Georgia review, volume x, number 1, Spring, 1956."

Jones, Joseph, 1833–1896.
Andersonville. The relations of the "Confederate government" to Federal prisoners. Letter of Prof. Joseph Jones of New Orleans to B. H. Hill. Letter of R. E. Lee on Federal and Confederate prisons. [New Orleans, 1876] broadside, 45 x 24cm.   CSmH LNHT   **634**
Text in four columns.

Jordan, Francis,   –1900.
Something about Andersonville. *US* vii (1882) 362–8.   **635**

King, Spencer Bidwell, 1904–
Yankee letters from Andersonville prison. Edited by Spencer B. King, Jr. *GHQ* xxxviii (1954) 394–8.   **636**

King, T   J
On the Andersonville circuit. *Century magazine* xli (1890) 100–65.   **637**

Park, Lemuel Madison
The "rebel prison pen" at Andersonville, Ga. *SM* xiv (1874) 528–37.   **638**

Prisons, The South, Andersonville, continued

Author was "stationed at Andersonville almost from the first establishment of the prison until the removal to Millen, Ga., or Camp Lawton," and a member of Co. G, 1st (Fannin's) Georgia infantry, Reserves.

Rutherford, Mildred Lewis
Facts and figures vs. myths and misrepresentations. Henry Wirz and the Andersonville prison [by] Mildred Lewis Rutherford. Athens [1921] 52, (3) p. 23cm.   IHi   *639*
Title from cover.
"Index," (3) p.

Spencer, Ambrose
A narrative of Andersonville, drawn from the evidence elicited on the trial of Henry Wirz, the jailer. With the argument of Col. N. P. Chipman, Judge advocate. By Ambrose Spencer. New York, Harper & Brothers, 1866. xiii, [15]–272 p. front. (illus.). 19½cm.
                                        CSmH DLC   *640*
Stevenson, Richard Randolph
The Southern side; or, Andersonville prison, compiled from official documents, by R. Randolph Stevenson . . . Together with an examination of the Wirz trial. A comparison of the mortality in Northern and Southern prisons. Remarks on the Exchange bureau, etc. An appendix, showing the number of prisoners that died at Andersonville, and the causes of death. Classified lists of all that died in stockade and hospital, etc. Baltimore, Turnbull Brothers, 1876. 488 p. front. (fold. plan), fold. facsim., plates (illus.). 23cm.
                                CSmH DLC TxU   *641*
List of Federal soldiers that died and were buried at Andersonville, arranged by State and alphabetically, 295–402.
List of officers imprisoned at Camp Asylum, Columbia, S. C., 405–38.

United States. Adjutant General.
. . . Trial of Henry Wirz. Letter from the Secretary of war ad interim in answer to a resolution of the House of April 16, 1866, transmitting a summary of the trial of Henry Wirz. [Washington, Govt. print. office, 1868] 850 p. 23cm.   MoHi   *642*
Caption title.
At head of title: 40th Congress, 2d session, House of representatives, Ex. doc., no. 23.
"Prepared in the office of the Adjutant general."

United States. Quartermaster General's
    Department.
. . . The martyrs who, for our country, gave up their lives in the prison pen in Andersonville, Ga. Washington, Govt. print. office, 1866. 225 p. 23cm.   CU-SB   *643*
Caption title: Report of the expedition to Andersonville, Ga., during the months of July and August, 1865.

The report is signed: James M. Moore, Captain and Assistant quartermaster, U. S. Army.
At head of title: Quartermaster general's office, General orders no. [corrected in ms. 69½]

Andersonville — State Monuments

Connecticut.
Dedication of the monument at Andersonville, Georgia, October 23, 1907, in memory of the men of Connecticut who suffered in Southern military prisons, 1861–1865. Published by the State. Hartford [Case, Lockwood & Brainard co.] 1908. 73 p. plan, plates (illus., ports.). 25½cm.   CSmH NN   *644*
"List of Connecticut soldiers buried in the Andersonville, Georgia, National cemetery, as per burial register, with a few notes and corrections," 47–58.

Indiana.
Report of the unveiling and dedication of Indiana monument at Andersonville, Georgia (National cemetery), Thursday, November 26, 1908. . . . Indianapolis, Wm. B. Burford, 1909. 128 p. front. (illus.), illus., ports. 25½cm.   NN   *645*
"List of Indiana soldiers . . . arranged regimentally," 73–102.

Maine.
Report of the Maine Andersonville monument commissioners. . . . Augusta, Kennebec Journal print, 1904. 31 p. 4 plates (illus.). 23½cm.   NN   *646*

Massachusetts.
Report of the Commission on Andersonville monument. [Boston, Wright & Potter print. co., 1902] front. (illus.). 23cm.   NcD   *647*
"A list of the Massachusetts soldiers known to be buried in the National cemetery, Andersonville, Ga.," 43–75.

Michigan.
Report of the Andersonville monument commission on erection of monument at Andersonville, Ga. Lansing, Robert Smith print. co., 1905. 57 p. plates (illus., plan, ports.). 23½cm.
                                        NHi   *648*
New Jersey.
Report of the Andersonville monument commission, 1899. Somerville, Unionist-Gazette Association, State printers, 1899. 18 p. 3 plates (illus.). 23cm.   CSmH   *649*
"List of New Jersey troops buried in Andersonville, Ga., National cemetery," 13–18.

New York.
A pilgrimage to the shrine of patriotism, being the report of the Commission to dedicate the monument erected by the State of New York, in Andersonville, Georgia, to commemorate the heroism, sacrifices and patriotism of

more than nine thousand of her sons who were confined in that prison . . . Albany, J. B. Lyon co., printer, 1916. 241 p. plates (illus., fold. plan, ports.). 27cm.   NN   *650*

"Veteran service record," forms, [14] p. at end.

Pennsylvania.

Pennsylvania at Andersonville, Georgia. Ceremonies at the dedication of the memorial erected by the Commonwealth of Pennsylvania in the National cemetery at Andersonville, Georgia . . . 1905. [Harrisburg, C. E. Aughinbaugh, printers to the State, 1909] 94 p. plates (illus., ports.). 22½cm.   NN   *651*

Copyright "by the editors and compiler, Col. James D. Walker."

Pennsylvania. Surgeon General's Office.

List of soldiers, (prisoners of war,) belonging to the Pennsylvania regiments, who died at the military prison at Andersonville, Georgia, from February 26, 1864, to March 24, 1865. [Harrisburg, Singerly & Myers, State printers, 1865] 24 p. 27cm. CSmH DLC NB   *652*

Rhode Island.

. . . Report of the Joint special committee on erection of monument at Andersonville, Ga. . . . Providence, E. L. Freeman & Sons, State printers, 1903. 60 p. plates (illus., fold. plan). 23½cm.   NN   *653*

At head of title: State of Rhode Island and Providence plantations.

Wisconsin.

Report of the Wisconsin monument commission appointed to erect a monument at Andersonville, Georgia, with other interesting matter pertaining to the prison. . . . Madison, Democrat print. co., 1911. vii, 296 p. illus., plan, ports. 23cm.   NN   *654*

"Personal reminiscences of prison life, by D. G. James, compiler of this book," 63–90.

CAHAWBA PRISON

Brannon, Peter Alexander, 1882–

The Cahawba military prison, 1863–1865. *AR* III (1950) 163–73. plan.   *655*

CAMP FORD

The old flag, first published by Union prisoners at Camp Ford, Tyler, Texas. [Bridgeport, c1864] 1 v. 29cm.   CSmH DLC   *656*

Title from cover.
Lithographed reproduction of the three numbers originally issued in manuscript.
"Preface," (1) p. signed: Wm. H. May [23rd Conn infantry]
I 1–3 (February 17 – March 13, 1864). Each issue, 4 p.
Includes "List of officers, prisoners of war at Camp Ford . . . giving rank, regiment, where and when captured," (3) p.

The Preface mentions a successor periodical, Ford city herald, which was not reproduced except for some advertisements and "A review of the market, July 14, 1864."

The old flag, 1864, fiftieth anniversary, 1914. First published by Union prisoners at Camp Ford, Tyler, Texas, 1864. Respectfully dedicated to "The old 72." Entered according to Act of Congress, in the year of 1864, by Wm. H. May . . . Reproduced by his comrades, Captain Alfred B. Beers, Major Thomas Boudren, Comrade Frank Miller, under the auspices of Elias Howe, jr. Post number three, Department of Connecticut, G.A.R., Decoration day, 1914. [Bridgeport, "The Old Flag" pub. co., 1914] [64] p. facsims., illus., ports. 32cm.   Ct   *657*

Lawrence, Francis Lee, 1926–

Camp Ford C.S.A., the story of Union prisoners in Texas, by F. Lee Lawrence and Robert W. Glover. Austin Texas Civil War Centennial Advisory Committee [c1964] 99 p. facsims., illus., ports. 24cm.   IHi   *658*

"Locations of known 'shebangs' and streets, Camp Ford, Texas, March, 1864," plan, end paper.
"550 copies of this book have been printed at El Paso, Texas, by Carl Hertzog."
A part of the illustrative material is in the text or paged.

Mitchell, Leon

Camp Ford, Confederate military prison. *SWHQ* LXVI (1962/63) 1–16.   *659*

CASTLE THUNDER

Confederate States of America. House of Representatives.

Evidence taken before the Committee of the House of Representatives, appointed to enquire into the treatment of prisoners at Castle Thunder. [Richmond, 1863] 58 p. 22½cm.

Caption title.   CSmH   *660*
Testimony taken April 11–13, 1863.
Crandall 592.

DANVILLE PRISON

Robertson, James Irvin, 1930–

House of horrors, Danville's Civil war prisons. *VMHB* LXIX (1961) 329–45. plate (3 illus.).   *661*

LIBBY PRISON

Walls that talk: a transcript of the names, initials and sentiments, written and graven on the walls, doors and windows of the Libby prison at Richmond, by the prisoners of 1861–65. . . . Richmond, Published by R. E. Lee Camp, no. 1, C. V., 1884. 19 p. 17cm. OMC   *662*

Prisons, The South, Libby Prison, continued

—— Richmond, R. E. Lee Camp, no. 1, C. V., 1884; republished by permission of . . . J. W. Randolph & English, 1889. 19 p. 18cm.
                      NjJ   **663**

Byrne, Frank L
   Libby prison: a study in emotion. *JSH* XXIV (1958) 430–44.   **664**

Kent, Will Parmiter
   The story of Libby prison, also some perils and sufferings of certain of its inmates. By Will Parmiter Kent. Compiled from personal narratives and various authentic sources. Second edition. Chicago, Libby Prison War Museum Association [1890] 60 p. illus., ports. 25cm.
   Cover illustrated in color. NbHi NN   **665**

Libby Prison War Museum Association.
   Libby prison war museum catalogue and program. Chicago, Foster Roe and Crone, printers, 1889. [32] p. facsim., music, port. 22½cm.   NN   **666**
   Title and imprint from cover.
   Color illus. on cover.

—— A trip through the Libby prison war museum, Chicago, with a brief synopsis of what you can see. [Chicago, 1893] 14, (1) p. 1 illus. 16 x 15½cm.   NN   **667**
   Title from cover.

Sclater, W   S
   A complete and authentic history of Libby prison, compiled by W. S. Sclater. Richmond, Southern Art Emporium, J. C. Weckert, printer, 1894. 28, (1) p.   NN(P)   **668**
   Sclater was the proprietor of the Southern art emporium which sold relics of the Civil war.
   Advertising matter, p. 28 and (1) p.

Waitt, Robert W
   Libby prison, Richmond, Virginia. [Richmond, Richmond Civil War Centennial Commission, 1961] [4] p. 2 illus. 23cm.   **669**
   Title and 2 illus. on cover.
   "Compiled by R. W. Waitt, jr."
   Inserted leaf: "Other Civil War prisons in Richmond," text recto; illus. verso.

SALISBURY PRISON

Maine.
   Report of the Maine commissioners on the monuments erected at Salisbury, N. C., 1908. . . . Waterville, Sentinel pub. co., 1908. 27, (5) p. 3 plates (illus.). 23½cm. NN   **670**
   "List of men buried at Salisbury, N. C.," (5) p.

Mangum, Adolphus Williamson, 1834–1890.
   History of the Salisbury, N. C., Confederate prison. *Publications of the Southern history association* III (1899) 307–36.   **671**

Pennsylvania.
   Pennsylvania at Salisbury, North Carolina. Ceremonies at the dedication of the memorial erected by the Commonwealth of Pennsylvania in the National cemetery at Salisbury, North Carolina, in memory of the soldiers of Pennsylvania who perished in the Confederate prison at Salisbury, North Carolina, 1864 and 1865. [Harrisburg, C. E. Aughinbaugh, printer] 1910. 70 p. plates (illus., plan, ports.). 22cm.
                        NN   **672**

The North
(*Individual Prisons*)
ALTON PRISON

Williamson, Hugh P
   Military prisons in the Civil war. *Bulletin Missouri historical society* XVI (1959/60) 329–32.   **673**

CAMP CHASE

Calhoun, Harrison M
   Memorial address delivered by H. M. Calhoun, of Franklin, W. Va., at Camp Chase, Ohio, on June 1, 1929. New Market, Va., Henkel press, 1929. 15, (2) p. front. (illus.). 21cm.   WvU   **674**
   "Appendix," (2) p.

Knauss, William H
   The story of Camp Chase, a history of the prison and its cemetery, together with other cemeteries where Confederate prisoners are buried, etc., by William H. Knauss. Nashville, Methodist Episcopal Church, South, 1906. xx, 407 p. facsims., illus., ports. 24cm.
        CSmH IHI TxU   **675**

—— The story of Camp Chase. *Ohio magazine* I (1906) 233–40. illus.   **676**

CAMP DOUGLAS

Bross, William, 1813–1890.
   Biographical sketch of the late B. J. Sweet. History of Camp Douglas, a paper read before the Chicago historical society, Tuesday evening, June 18th, 1873, by William Bross. Chicago, Jansen, McClurg & co., 1878. 28 p. 22½cm.   CSmH DLC NN OMC   **677**

Gilmore, James Roberts, 1822–1903.
   The Chicago conspiracy. *Atlantic monthly* XVI (1865) 108–20.   **678**

Tuttle, Edmund Bostwick, 1815–1881.
   The history of Camp Douglas, including official report of Gen. B. J. Sweet, with anecdotes of the Rebel prisoners, by Rev. E. B.

Tuttle, Post-Chaplain. Chicago, J. R. Walsh & co., 1865. 51 p. front. (illus.). 23cm.

IHi   *679*

CAMP MORTON

Carnahan, James Richard, 1840–1905.
Camp Morton, reply to Dr. John A. Wyeth, by R. Carnahan. Indiana commandery M.O. L.L.A., February 22, 1892. [Indianapolis] Baker-Randolph L. & E. co. [1892] 79 p. 22½cm.   CSmH NHi   *680*
"Concerning the charges published in the Century [XLI (1891) 844–52] by Dr. John A. Wyeth, concerning the treatment of Confederate prisoners at Camp Morton."
See Titles 682 and 683.

Holloway, W   R
A reply to "Cold cheer at Camp Morton." *Century magazine* XLII (1891) 757–70. illus., plan.   *681*
See Titles 682 and 683.

Wyeth, John Allen, 1845–1922.
Cold cheer at Camp Morton. *Century magazine* XLI (1891) 844–52. illus.   *682*

—— Rejoinder by Dr. Wyeth. *Century magazine* XLI (1891) 771–5.   *683*

ELMIRA PRISON CAMP

"A prisoner of war." *The XIX century* I/II (Charleston, 1869–70) 388–94.   *684*
"By 'High Private.'"

Holmes, Clayton Wood, 1848–
The Elmira prison camp, a history of the military prison at Elmira, N. Y., July 6, 1864, to July 10, 1865, by Clay W. Holmes. With an Appendix containing names of the Confederate prisoners buried in Woodlawn National cemetery. New York, G. P. Putnam's Sons, 1912. xvii, 467 p. plates (illus., ports.). 25cm.
CSmH DLC   *685*
Record of Confederate dead buried in Woodlawn cemetery, 377–461.

—— The Elmira prison camp. *MOLLUS-NY* IV 351–72.   *685A*

Robertson, James Irvin, 1930–
The scourge of Elmira. *CWH* VIII (1962) 184–201.   *686*

Taylor, Eva C
Holmes and his sources for "The Elmira prison camp." *Chemung historical journal* I (Elmira, 1955) 59–60.   *687*

FORT LAFAYETTE

"Fort-La-Fayette life," 1863–64, in extracts from the "Right flanker," a manuscript circu-lating among the Southern prisoners in Fort-La-Fayette, in 1863–64. . . . London, Simkin, Marshall & co., 1865. v, 102 p. double plate (facsim.). 17cm.   IHi NN NcD   *687A*
Reprinted extra no. 13 of the Magazine of history with notes and queries, 1911.

FORT WARREN

McLain, Minor H
The military prison at Fort Warren. *CWH* VIII (1962) 136–51.   *688*

JOHNSON'S ISLAND

An escape from Johnson's island. *SM* XI (1872) 535–44.   *689*

Burr, T   A
A romance of the great rebellion, a waif of history from the Philadelphia press. *Firelands pioneer* n s I (Norwalk, Ohio, 1882) 78–91.   *690*

Carpenter, Horace
Plain living at Johnson's island, described by a Confederate officer. *Century magazine* XLI (1891) 705–18.   *691*

—— "Poor Johnnies," plain living at Johnson's island, described by a Confederate officer. [n. p., 189–] [12] p. 21cm.   CSmH   *692*
Text signed: H. Carpenter.
Caption title.
Text in double columns.

Cook, S   N
Johnson's island in war days. *Ohio magazine* I (1906) 225–32. illus.   *693*

Downer, Edward T
Johnson's island. *CWH* VIII (1962) 202–17.   *694*

Frohman, Charles E.
Rebels on Lake Erie, by Charles E. Frohman. Columbus, Ohio Historical Society, 1965. v, 157 p. plates (facsims., illus., ports.). 26½cm.   NN   *694A*

Hicks, Irl
The prisoner's farewell to Johnson's island; or, valedictory address to the Young men's Christian association of Johnson's island, Ohio. A poem, by Irl Hicks. St. Louis, Southwestern book and pub. co., 1872. 29 p. 16cm.
CSmH   *695*

[Jones, Buehring H   ] 1823–1872.
Memorial of the Federal prison on Johnson's island, Lake Erie, Ohio, 1862–1864, contain-ing a list of prisoners of war, from the Confed-erate states army, and of the deaths among them. With "Prison lays," by distinguished

Prisons, The North, Johnson's Island, continued

officers. *Collections of the Virginia historical society,* n s VI (1887) 233–345. plates (illus.).
696

"Prisoners of war at Johnson's island, Lake Erie, Ohio, from November 22d, 1862, to September 5th, 1864," 239–325.

Shepard, Frederick J
The Johnson's island plot, an historical narrative of the conspiracy of the Confederates, in 1864, to capture the U. S. steamship Michigan on Lake Erie, and release the prisoners of war in Sandusky bay. *Publications of the Buffalo historical society* IX (1906) 1–51. 1 illus., plan. **697**

—— Burleigh and Johnson's island. *Magazine of history* I (1905) 306–15, 378–84. **698**

OLD CAPITOL PRISON

Colby, Newton T
The "Old Capitol prison." *AW* 501–12. **699**

POINT LOOKOUT

Manakee, Harold Randall, 1908–
Omenhausser's Confederate prisoners of war sketch. *MHM* LIII (1958) 177–9. **700**

ROCK ISLAND

Minnich, J   W
Inside of Rock island prison, from December, 1863, to June, 1865, by J. W. Minnich, Grand Island, La. Nashville, Publishing House of the M. E. Church, South, 1908. 59, (1) p. front. (port.), 1 illus., port. 18½cm.
CSmH DLC **701**
"History of Rock Island, Ill., 1863, paper read by Mrs. Kate E. Perry Mosher," [41]–59.

Tillinghast, Benjamin Franklin
Rock Island arsenal, in peace and in war . . . by B. F. Tillinghast. . . . Chicago, Henry O. Shepard co., printers, 1898. 112, lxxii p. illus., ports. 24cm.   CSmH DLC **702**
"The Island as a military prison," 31–5.

Walker, Theodore Roosevelt, 1903–
Rock Island prison barracks. *CWH* VIII (1962) 152–63. **703**

ST LOUIS

Hesseltine, William Best, 1902–
Military prisons of St. Louis, 1861–1865. *MHR* XXIII (1928/29) 380–99. **704**

RAILROADS
GENERAL

Abdill, George B
Civil war railroads, by Geo. B. Abdill. Seattle, Superior pub. co. [c1961] 192 p. illus. 22 x 27½cm.   NcD **705**

Ashcraft, Allan C   1928–
The Confederate "Inspector of railroads" for Texas. *TMH* III (1963) 33–5. **706**

Black, Robert Clifford, 1914–
The railroads of the Confederacy, by Robert C. Black III. Chapel Hill, University of North Carolina press [c1952] xiv, 360 p. facsims., plans, plates (illus., ports.). 24cm.
DLC NcD **707**
"The railroads of the Confederate states, as of June 1, 1861," fold. map at end.

—— Railroads in the Confederacy. *CWH* VII (1961) 231–8. **708**

—— The railroads of Georgia in the Confederate war effort. *JSH* XIII (1947) 511–34. **709**

Doster, James Fletcher, 1912–
Were the Southern railroads destroyed by the Civil war? *CWH* VII (1961) 310–20. **710**

Johnston, Angus James, 1916–
Virginia railroads in April 1861. *JSH* XXIII (1957) 307–30. **711**

—— Virginia railroads in the Civil war, by Angus Johnston, II. Chapel Hill, Published for the Virginia Historical Society by the University of North Carolina press, 1961. xiv, 336 p. maps, tables, plates (illus.). 24cm.
DLC NcD **712**

Murphey, Hermon King
The Northern railroads and the Civil war. *MVHR* V (1918) 324–38. **713**

Price, Charles L
North Carolina railroads during the Civil war. *CWH* VII (1961) 298–309. **714**

Riegel, Robert Edgar, 1897–
Federal operations of Southern railroads during the Civil war. *MVHR* IX (1922) 126–38. **715**

Turner, George Edgar
Victory rode the rails, the strategic place of the railroads in the Civil war, by George Edgar Turner. Maps by George Richard Turner. Indianapolis, Bobbs-Merrill co. [1953] xiv, 15–419 p. maps, plates (illus., ports.). 24cm.
NN **716**

Weber, Thomas, 1916–
The Northern railroads in the Civil war, 1861–1865, by Thomas Weber. New York, King's Crown press, 1952. xii, 316 p. 21cm.
DLC NcD   **717**

BALTIMORE AND OHIO

The Baltimore & Ohio railroad and the Civil war. *Book of the Royal blue* II 10 (July 1899) 1–7. illus.   **718**

Baltimore and Ohio Railroad.
Annual report of the President and directors to the stockholders. 35–39 (1860/61–1864/65).
NN   **719**
1860/61 was presented October 1, 1863; 1861/62 was presented October 1, 1864.

Porter, W   E
Keeping the Baltimore & Ohio in repair in war time was a task for Hercules. *Book of the Royal blue* x 9 (June 1907) 17–20.   **720**

Smith, William Prescott, 1822?–1872.
B & O in the Civil war, from the papers of Wm. Prescott Smith. Edited by William E. Bain. Denver, Sage Books [1966] 156 p. facsims., illus., map. 22½cm.   **720A**

Sumners, Festus Paul, 1895–
The Baltimore and Ohio in the Civil war, by Festus P. Sumners. New York, G. P. Putnam's Sons [c1939] xii, 15–304 p. facsims., maps, plates (illus.), front. (port.). 22½cm.
TxU   **721**
"The Baltimore and Ohio (1861)," "Battlefields on and near the Baltimore and Ohio" maps on end papers.

—— The Balitmore and Ohio, first in war. *CWH* VII (1961) 239–54.   **722**

FLORIDA RAILROAD COMPANY

Clarke, Robert L
The Florida railroad company in the Civil war. *JSH* XIX (1953) 180–92.   **723**

ILLINOIS CENTRAL

Sutton, Robert Mize, 1915–
The Illinois central, thoroughfare for freedom. *CWH* VII (1961) 273–87.   **724**

LOUISVILLE AND NASHVILLE

Tilford, John E
The delicate track, the L&N's role in the Civil war. *FCHQ* XXXVI (1962) 209–21.   **725**

NASHVILLE AND CHATTANOOGA

Burt, Jesse C
The Nashville and Chattanooga railroad, 1854–1872: the era of transition. *ETHSP* XXIII (1951) 58–76.   **726**

PHILADELPHIA, WILMINGTON, AND BALTIMORE

Philadelphia, Wilmington, and Baltimore Railroad.
Annual report of the President and directors to the stockholders. 24–28 (1860/61–1864/65).
NN   **727**

RICHMOND AND DANVILLE

Johnston, Angus James, 1916–
Lee's last lifeline, the Richmond and Danville. *CWH* VII (1961) 288–97.   **728**

RICHMOND, FREDERICKSBURG AND POTOMAC

Stuart, Meriwether, 1905–
Samuel Ruth and General R. E. Lee, disloyalty and the line of supply to Fredericksburg, 1862–1863. *VMHB* LXXI (1963) 35–109. plates (facsim., illus., map).   **729**

Turner, Charles Wilson, 1916–
The Richmond, Fredericksburg and Potomac, 1861–1865. *CWH* VII (1961) 255–63. **730**

VIRGINIA CENTRAL

Turner, Charles Wilson, 1916–
The Virginia central railroad at war, 1861–1865. *JSH* XII (1946) 510–33.   **731**

RELIGION

Bennett, William W
A narrative of the great revival which prevailed in the Southern armies during the late Civil war between the States of the Federal Union, by William W. Bennett. Philadelphia, Claxton, Remsen & Haffelfinger, 1877. vi, [7]–427 p. plates (illus., ports.). 19½cm.
CSmH DLC   **732**
Brown, William Young, 1827–1914.
The army chaplain: his office, duties, and responsibilities, and the means of aiding him, by Rev. W. Y. Brown, hospital chaplain. Philadelphia, William S. & Alfred Martien, 1863. 144 p. 15½cm.   CSmH DLC   **733**

Christian Association of the Stonewall Brigade.
Constitution, by-laws and catalogue of members of the Christian association of the

Religion, continued

Stonewall brigade, Johnson's division, Army of Northern Virginia. Organized May 19th, 1863. . . . Richmond, William H. Clemmitt, printer, 1864. 11, (1) p. 18½cm.
    Crandall 4956.   CSmH   **734**

Daniel, W   Harrison
    The Christian association, a religious society in the Army of Northern Virginia. *VMBH* LXIX (1961) 93–100.   **735**
    Includes list of members from the 2nd, 4th, 5th, 27th, and 33rd Virginia infantry regiments.

Hall, William Thomas, 1835–1911.
    Religion in the Army of the Tennessee. *LWL* IV (1867/68) 127–31.   **736**

Jones, John William, 1836–1909.
    Christ in the camp; or, religion in Lee's army, supplemented by a sketch of the work in the other Confederate armies [by] Rev. J. Wm. Jones. With an introduction by Rev. J. C. Granberry. Richmond, B. F. Johnson & co. [1887] 624 p. 2 col. fronts. (illus.). 22cm.
            DLC NN   **737**
    Roster of Chaplains, 529–34; the work of grace in other armies of the Confederacy, 535–624.

—— Christ in the camp; or, religion in Lee's army, by Rev. J. Wm. Jones. With an introduction by Rev. J. C. Granberry. Richmond, B. F. Johnson & co., 1887. 528 p. front. (port.), plates (illus.). 22cm.   NN   **738**
    A reprinting omitting p. 529–624.

—— —— Atlanta, Martin & Hoyt co. [c1904] 624 p. plates (illus., ports.). 22cm.
            DLC NN   **739**

Norton, Herman
    Rebel religion, the story of Confederate Chaplains, by Herman Norton. St. Louis, Bethany press [1961] 144 p. illus. 22½cm.
            PGC   **740**
    "A roster of Confederate Chaplains," 115–34, identifying their unit and denomination.

Pitts, Charles Frank
    Chaplains in Gray, the Confederate Chaplain's story. Nashville, Boardman press, c1957. xv, 166 p. 20½cm.   NN   **741**
    At head of title: Charles F. Pitts.
    Title on two leaves.

Quimby, Rollin W
    The Chaplain's predicament. *CWH* VIII (1962) 25–37.   **742**

Romero, Sydney James, 1917
    The Confederate Chaplain. *CWH* I (1955) 127–40.   **743**

Shepard, John
    Religion in the Army of Northern Virginia. *NCHR* xxv (1948) 341–76.   **744**

Silver, James W
    The Confederate preacher goes to war. *NCHR* XXXIII (1956) 499–509.   **745**

Swinton, William, 1833–1892.
    Notes on the religious sentiment in the Union / army and its influence on the war. *Hours at home* II (1865/66) 382–7.   **746**

Walker, Arthur L
    Three Alabama Baptist Chaplains. *Alabama review* xvi (1963) 174–84.   **747**

UNITED STATES MILITARY ACADEMY

Barnard, John Gross, 1815–1882.
    Letter to the editors of the National intelligencer, in answer to the charges against the United States military academy in the Report of the Secretary of war, of July, 1861, by Major J. G. Barnard. New York, D. Van Nostrand, 1862. 18 p. 22½cm.   CSmH   **748**
    "The defection of so many graduates of the Academy should suggest ungenerous and unjust charges."

Marshall, Edward Chauncey, 1824–1898.
    Are the West Point graduates loyal?, by Edward Chauncey Marshall. [New York, D. Van Nostrand, 1862] 8 p. 18½cm.
    Caption title.   CSmH NcU   **749**

Ness, George T
    Missouri at West Point, her graduates through the Civil war. *MHR* XXXVIII (1942/43) 162–9.   **750**

Williams, Thomas Harry, 1909–
    The attack upon West Point during the Civil war. *MVHR* xxv (1939) 491–504. **751**

VETERANS AND THEIR ORGANIZATIONS *

General

The army reunion: with reports of the meetings of the Societies of the Army of the Cumberland, the Army of the Tennessee, the Army of the Ohio, and the Army of Georgia. Chicago, December 15 and 16, 1868. . . . Chicago, S. C. Griggs and co., 1869. 330 p. plates (2 col. illus., ports.). 24cm.
         CSmH DLC NN   **752**
    Each Society's proceedings has its own title page.

---

* Associations of armies, corps, brigades, divisions, and regiments are entered with the unit.

Bericht über die 1. Zusammenkuft der in der Schweiz wohnenden Veteranen des amerikanischen Sezessions-Krieges (1861–1865), abgehalten in Luzern am 29. January 1899. 14 p. 22½cm. **753**

. . . Reunion of the Blue and Gray, Philadelphia brigade and Pickett's division, July 2, 3, 4, 1887, and September 15, 16, 17, 1906. John W. Frazier, Sergt. Co. C, 71st Penna. vol., Adjutant Philadelphia brigade association. Philadelphia, Ware Bros. co., 1906. 118 p. illus., ports. 23½cm.   CSmH MnHi **754**
At head of title: 1887 Gettysburg 1906.
Plates are paged.

Reunions of ex-soldiers of the North and South held at Luray, Virginia, July 21, 1881, and at Carlisle, Pennsylvania, September 28, 1881, with the addresses delivered on both occasions. Published under the auspices of Capt. Colwell post no. 201, Grand army of the Republic, of Carlisle, Pa. Carlisle, Herald and Mirror print [1881] 30 p. 22cm.
    CSmH **755**

Souvenir of the re-union of the Blue and Gray on the battlefield of Gettysburg, July 1, 2, 3, and 4, 1888. How to get there, and what is to be done during the year. New York, American Graphic co., 1888. 1 v. illus., fold. map, ports. 21½cm.   NB **756**
Advertising matter included.
Copyright by John Tregaskis of Tregaskis & co., publishers of the official program.

Gosson, Louis C
Post-bellum campaigns of the Blue and Gray, by Louis C. Gosson. Trenton, Naar, Day & Naar, printers, 1882. 192 p. front. (illus.). 19½cm.   OMC **757**

Noyes, Edward
The Civil war veteran and social affairs in Ohio. *Bulletin of the historical and philosophical society of Ohio* VIII (1950) 201–06.
    758

White, William W
The Confederate veteran, by William W. White. Tuscaloosa, Ala., 1962. 128 p. 21½cm. (Confederate centennial studies, no 22). **759**

INDIVIDUAL ORGANIZATIONS

Association of Veterans of Southwestern Iowa and Northwestern Missouri.
. . . A sketch of the ninth annual reunion, held at Creston, Iowa, August 17, 18, 19, '86, comprising a list of the registered members of the Association, with stenographic reports of speeches delivered in camp. . . . Creston, Gazette print, 1887. 33 p. port. 22cm.
    CSmH **760**
                *   *   *

Cavalry Society of the Armies of the United States.*
Constitution and record of proceedings of the meetings held in Providence, June 27, 1877, and Springfield, Mass., June 5, 1878. Providence, J. A. & R. A. Reid, printers, 1878. 12 p. 19cm.   CSmH **761**

———— ———— in Albany, June 18, 1879. New York, Livingston Middleditch, printers, 1880. 13 p. 19cm.   CSmH **762**

———— ———— in Burlington, Vt., June 16, 1880. New York, W. B. Dickie, printer, 1881. 13 p. 19cm.   CSmH **763**

———— ———— at Hartford, Conn., June 18th, 1881. New York, W. B. Dickie, printer, 1882. 13 p. 19cm.   CSmH **764**

———— ———— at Detroit, Mich., June 14th, 1882. New York, William S. Fowler, printer, 1883. 12 p. 19cm.   CSmH **765**

———— ———— at Washington, D.C., May 17th, '83. New York, Press of Wm. S. Fowler, 1883. 12 p. 18½cm.   CSmH **766**

———— ———— at New York and Brooklyn, June 10th and 11th, 1884. New York, Spectator co., printers, 1884. 25, (2) p. 23cm.
    CSmH **767**

———— ———— at Baltimore, Md., June 5, 1885. Elmira, Advertiser Assoc., pub. house, 1885. 15, (2) p. 23cm.   CSmH **768**

———— ———— at Mt. McGregor and Saratoga, N. Y., June 21st and 22nd, 1887. Elmira, J. S. Allen, print., 1887. 20 p. 23cm.
    CSmH **769**

———— ———— at Gettysburg, Pa., July 2 and 3, 1888. New York, Nicoll & Roy, printers, 1888. 18, (1) p. 23cm.   CSmH **770**
                *   *   *

Cincinnati Society of Ex-army & Navy officers.
Annual report of the Secretary, Treasurer and Executive committee. . . . October 7, 1881. Cincinnati, Robert Clarke & co., printers, 1881. 12 p. 21½cm.   CSmH **771**

———— ———— October 6, 1882. Cincinnati, Peter G. Thomson, printer, 1882. 23 p. 21½cm.
    CSmH **772**
On cover: Second annual report . . .

---

* Name of organization varies: 1877–1878 Society of the cavalry corps of the armies of the United States; 1879–1883 Society of the cavalry corps of the United States; 1884–1885 Society of the cavalry corps of the armies of the United States.

Individual Organizations, continued

—— Report of the proceedings and speeches of the seventh annual reunion and supper of the Cincinnati society of ex-army and navy officers, held at the Burnet house, January 12th, 1882. Cincinnati, Peter G. Thomson, printer, 1883. 49 p. 21½cm.   CSmH   **773**

—— Constitution and by-laws of the Cincinnati society of ex-army and navy officers. Cincinnati, 1878. 10 p. 13½cm.   CSmH   **774**
Includes list of members.

Mattox, Absalom Heiskell
A history of the Cincinnati society of ex-army and navy officers, with the name, army record, and rank of the members, alphabetically arranged. Written by A. H. Mattox. Cincinnati, Peter G. Thomson, 1880. 214 p. 25½cm.   CSmH DLC   **775**
P. 208–14 are blank for "Memoranda."

*   *   *

Confederate Survivors Association.
[Annual address of the President, Charles Colcock Jones, at the annual meeting, 1879–1892]
See Vol. II, Titles 2882–6.
In 1893 the custom of the presidential address was discontinued for an annual orator. Separate entries are given to the Annual address(es).

Owen, Edward
The Confederate veteran camp of New York. *National magazine* XVI (1892) 455–67.   **776**

Randolph, N   V
Address delivered by N. V. Randolph, before R. E. Lee camp, no. 1 C. V., December 3, 1886. . . . Richmond, Johns & co., printers, 1887. 15 p. 22½cm.   NHi   **777**
Dedication of a new hall, and the origin, growth, and present condition of the R. E. Lee camp.

*   *   *

Proceedings on the occasion of the reception and acceptance of the Stephenson Grand army memorial presented by the Grand army of the Republic, July 3, 1909. Washington, Govt. print. office, 1911. 48 p. plates (illus.). 27cm.   CSmH   **778**

Site of the organization of the Grand army of the Republic, Decatur, Ill., marked by the Department of Illinois woman's relief corps, April 6, 1915. *Journal of the Illinois state historical society* VIII (1915) 143–9. 3 plates (illus., 2 ports.).   **779**

Beath, Robert Burns, 1839–1914.
History of the Grand army of the Republic, by Robert B. Beath. With an introduction by General Lucius Fairchild. New York, Bryan, Taylor & co. [c1888] xv, 720 p. 3 col. plates (illus. of badges), ports. 25½cm.
                CSmH   **780**

Davies, Wallace E
The problem of race segregation in the Grand army of the Republic. *JSH* XIII (1947) 354–72.   **781**

Primm, James N
The G.A.R. in Missouri, 1866–70. *JSH* XX (1954) 356–75.   **782**

*   *   *

Hooker Association of Massachusetts.
Proceedings at the first annual meeting and dinner of. . . . American house, Boston, Tuesday, November thirteenth, nineteen hundred and six. 32 p. 18cm.   CSmH   **783**

*   *   *

Lee Monument Association.
Organization of the Lee monument association, and the Association of the Army of Northern Virginia, Richmond, Va., Nov. 3d and 4th, 1870. Richmond, J. W. Randolph & English, 1871. 52 p. front. (port.). 25cm.
                CSmH DLC   **784**

*   *   *

Medal of Honor Legion.
Constitution and by-laws of the Medal of honor legion, a military and naval order of the United States of America. Washington, D.C., Beresford, printer, 1893. 23 p. illus. 19½cm.
                CSmH   **785**

*   *   *

Military Historical Society of Massachusetts.
[Constitution, by-laws and members] Boston, Press of Rockwell and Churchill, 1892. 21, (2) p. 17cm.   CSmH   **786**
Only the name of organization, "Founded A.D. 1876. Incorporated A.D. 1891," appears on title page.
"Order of business" and list of Society's publications, (2) p.

—— [Directory, rules and list of publications] Boston, Lyman Rhodes & co., printers, 1879. 20 p. 12cm.   CSmH   **787**
Text within ruled border.
Only the name of organization and "Established A.D. 1876" appears on title page.

*   *   *

Military Order of the Loyal Legion of the United States.
Constitution and by-laws.   **788**
1877–1885, include a separately paged section, Quadrennial register.
Each issue has front. reproducing the Order's emblem.

1889–1921 are reprintings.
1868, 1870, 1877, 1881, 1885, 1889, 1897 1901, 1905, 1909, 1921.

—— Illinois Commandery.
Register of the Commandery of the State of Illinois . . . from May 8, 1879, to August 1, 1900. 238 p.   CSmH   **789**

—— —— from August 1, 1911, to July 1, 1916. 147 p.   CSmH   **790**

—— Massachusetts Commandery.
Register of the Military order of the loyal legion of the United States, compiled from the registers and circulars of the various commanderies, by J. Harris Aubin. Boston, Published under the auspices of the Commandery of the State of Massachusetts, 1906. 253 p. 24½cm.   NHi   **791**

—— Nebraska Commandery.
. . . Addresses delivered at fourth annual reunion, Monday evening, December 16th, 1889. Omaha, Neb. Omaha, Gibson, Miller & Richardson, printers, 1890. 30 p. 23cm.
                                    CSmH   **792**

—— —— History and membership from date of organization. *MOLLUS-Neb* 269–77.
                                            792A

—— Ohio Commandery.
. . . Catalogue of the library, prepared under the direction of Brevet Major A. M. Van Dyke, Recorder, by Captain William Holden, Ass't Quartermaster. Cincinnati, 1901. 115 p. 22cm.
                                    CSmH   **793**

—— —— . . . Report of the after-dinner speeches at the annual dinner of the Commandery of Ohio. . . .   **794**
1–3, 1884–1886, entitled: Proceedings of the . . . annual dinner.
A record of the 4th, 5th and 7th annual dinner was not published.
CSmH 1–28 (1884–1911); 34–36 (1917–1919).

—— Pennsylvania Commandery.
Circular no. . . . Philadelphia, 1866–1920. 883 nos. 20cm. 1 (June 7, 1866).   **795**
The CSmH file includes unnumbered [Circulars] August 3, 1865, to June 2, 1866.

Orahood, Harper M
The Loyal legion, address of Harper M. Orahood, at a meeting of the Military order loyal legion of the United States, held in Denver, May 1, 1900. [4] p. 24cm. CSmH   **796**
Caption title.

*   *   *

National Soldiers Historical Association.
Plan of organization of National soldiers historical association, 1865. . . . [Cincinnati,

Caleb Clark, printer, 1865] 14 p. 15½cm.
                            OMC   **797**
"Honorary President, Hon. Abraham Lincoln."

*   *   *

Nebraska. State Secretary.
Roster of soldiers, sailors, and marines of the War of the rebellion residing in Nebraska. . . . Lincoln, 1895–98. 3 v. 22½cm.   NN   **798**
June 1, 1893. 525, (2), xx p.
June 1, 1895. 538, xxi p.
December 1, 1897. 426, vi p.

*   *   *

Society of the Army and Navy of the Confederate States in the State of Maryland.
Roster of officers and members of the . . with constitution and by-laws. Baltimore, Press of the Sun print. office, 1883. 43 p.
                            CSmH   **799**

—— —— Baltimore, Sun print. office, 1888. 36 p. 21cm.   CSmH   **800**

*   *   *

Society of the Army and Navy of the Gulf.
First annual report of the . . . held at Long Branch, New Jersey, July 8th, 1869. New York, J. W. Pratt, printer, 1870. 24 p. 22cm.
                            CSmH   **801**

—— Report of the second annual reunion . . . , Boston, August 5, 1870. New York, S. W. Green, printer, 1871. 59 p. 23cm. NN   **802**

—— —— third annual reunion, Newport, July 7th, 1871. New York, George F. Nesbit & co., printers, 1872. 49, (1) p. 22cm.
                            CSmH   **803**

*   *   *

Society of California Volunteers.
Register of the . . . compiled from the latest data, by J. B. Whittemore . . . San Francisco, C. W. Nevin & co., printers, 1887. 27, (1) p. 13½cm.   CSmH   **804**
Title and imprint from cover.

*   *   *

Union Veteran League
Proceedings of seventh national encampment of the . . . of the United States, held at Indianapolis, Indiana, October 12th and 13th, 1892 . . . Indianapolis [H. P. Callow, printer] 1893. 136 p. 22cm.   NjJ   **805**

*   *   *

Veteran Association of the South and the South Atlantic Blockading Squadron.
Journal of the proceedings . . . State of New York, from 1892 to 1896, prepared by the

Veterans and Their Organizations, Individual Organizations, continued

Secretary, at the request of the Association, from its archives and minutes of its meetings, with an Appendix containing the names, organizations and addresses of the members and other information. New York, C. G. Burgoyne, 1897. 72 p. 22½cm.   NN   *806*

*   *   *

Survivors' Association of the State of South Carolina.

Proceedings of the first and second annual meetings of the . . . and oration of General John S. Preston, delivered before the Association, November 10th, 1870. Charleston, Walker, Evans & Cogswell, printers, 1870. 63 p. 23cm.   CSmH   *807*

—— Proceedings of the third annual meeting of the . . . and the annual address by General Jubal A. Early, delivered before the Association, November 10, 1871. Charleston, Walker, Evans & Cogswell, printers, 1872. 38 p. 23cm.   CSmH   *808*

*   *   *

Union Society of the Civil War.

The Union Society of the Civil war, organized in the City of New York on January

thirtieth, 1909. . . . 30 p. front. (illus.). 22cm.
                                      MoU   *809*
Constitution, by laws, officers and members.
"To perpetuate the memory of those loyal officials who, outside the military and naval service, rendered invaluable aid and assistance to the National government and Union cause during the Civil war."

*   *   *

United Confederate Veterans.

Constitution and by-laws for the. . . . [New Orleans, 1896] 8 p. 22½cm.   CSmH   *810*
Caption title.
Text in double columns.

VOTING

Benton, Josiah Henry, 1843–1917.

Voting in the field, a forgotten chapter of the Civil war, by Josiah Henry Benton. Privately printed. Boston [Norwood, Plimpton press] 1915. vi, (1) 332 p. front. (maps), plates (ports.). 26cm.   NbU   *811*

Williams, Thomas Harry, 1909–

Voters in Blue, the citizen soldiers of the Civil war. *MVHR* xxxi (1944) 187-204.   *812*

Winther, Oscar Osburn

The soldier vote in the election of 1864. *New York history* xxv (1944) 440-58.   *813*

Armed Forces

Armed Forces

GENERAL REFERENCES

ADMINISTRATION

Shannon, Fred Albert, 1893–1963.
The organization and administration of the Union army, 1861–1865, by Fred Albert Shannon. Cleveland, Arthur H. Clark co., 1928. 2 v. I plates (illus.); II front. (port.). 25cm.
NbU **814**

United States. Adjutant General's Office.
. . . Military departments, &c., of the United States, in which the several states and territories were embraced during the war of 1861–'65. Compiled from the records of the Adjutant General's office. Washington, Adjutant General's print. office, 1876. 33, (1) p. 20½cm. CSmH **815**
"Index of States and Territories," (1) p.
At head of title: Memoranda.

United States. Army.
Telegrams received by Major Gen. H. W. Halleck while General-in-chief and Chief of staff. Washington, War Department print. office, 1877. 5 v. 23½cm.
CSmH DLC **816**
Printed in a very limited edition.
Contents: I Abercrombie-Dwyer; II Ellet-King; III Launsbury-Rowley; IV Sanford-Sykes; V Taggart-Zeigler.
Separate indexes of names and subjects in each volume.
Each page contains a single telegram.

ARTILLERY

Alexander, Edward Porter, 1835–1910.
Confederate artillery service. *SHST* II (1875) 27–41. **817**

—— —— *SHSP* XI (1883) 98–113. **818**

Barr, Alwyn
Confederate artillery in the Trans-Mississippi. *Military affairs* XXVII (1963) 77–83. **819**

Confederate States of America. Army.
Artillery officers, C.S.A. [Washington, D.C., 188–] 186, 37 p. 21½cm. CSmH **820**
Contents: Organizations; Artillery battalions; Memorandum of artillery officers, C.S. army; List of officers Corps of artillery, C.S. army on U.S. register of 1861; Index.
Binder's title.

—— Memorandum of artillery officers in the Confederate states service. [Washington, D.C., War Records office, 1883] 146 p. 22½cm. CSmH **821**
A list of officers and organizations.

The alphabetical list of officers identifies state, organization, and date of appointment.
The alphabetical list of organizations includes the states under which all of their artillery units are listed.

Hunt, Henry Jackson, 1819–1889.
Artillery. *PMHSM* XIII (1888) 88–125. **822**

Morton, John Watson
The artillery of Nathan Bedford Forrest's cavalry, "the wizard of the saddle," by John Watson Morton, Chief of artillery. Nashville, Pub. house of the M. E. Church, South, 1909. 374 p. plates (facsims.; illus., 1 fold.; ports.). 23½cm. CSmH DLC NN **823**
"List of Confederate prisoners at Johnson's island, 1862, taken from Captain Morton's notebook," 363–74.
Coulter 334.

Naisawald, L   Van Loan
Grape and canister, the story of the field artillery of the Army of the Potomac, 1861–1865 [by] L. Van Loan Naisawald. New York, Oxford University press, 1960. xiv, 593 p. illus., maps. 21½cm. NN **824**
"Area of operations Army of the Potomac, 1862–1865," map, endpaper.
"Appendix I. Technical data," 537–52.

United States. Adjutant General's Office.
Names of Captains of light artillery (with command) in the volunteer service of the United States, 1861–1865. [Washington, 1881] 16 p. 22½cm. CSmH **825**
An alphabetical list with name of unit.

—— —— [Washington, Adjutant General's office, 1883] 16 p. 24cm. CSmH **826**

United States. War Records Bureau.
Artillery in the Army of Northern Virginia "after Gettysburg." [Washington, 1884] 4 p. 23½cm. CSmH **827**

Wise, Jennings Cropper, 1881–
The boy gunners of Lee, an address delivered before R. E. Lee camp, no. 1, Confederate veterans, Richmond, Va., December 1, 1916. *SHSP* XLII (1917) 152–73. **828**

—— The long arm of Lee; or, the history of the artillery of the Army of Northern Virginia. With a brief account of the Confederate Bureau of ordnance. By Jennings Cropper Wise. Lynchburg, J. P. Bell, 1915. 2 v. (995, (1) p.) plates (1 illus., ports.). 24cm. CSmH **829**
"Battery index," 980–91, a two part index, the first with page references are batteries arranged by place of recruitment; the second part are the batteries arranged by the names of their commanders.

Artillery, continued

"Battalion index," 992–5.
"Errata," (1) p.

—— —— With a foreword by L. Van Naisawald. New York, Oxford University press, 1959. 995 p. 21½cm.   DLC NcD   *830*
On cover: The history of the artillery of the Army of Northern Virginia.
A photographic reproduction.

BALLOONS

Captain Langdon Cheeves, Jr., and the Confederate silk dress balloon. Edited by J. H. Easterby. *SCHM* XLV (1944) 1–11, 99–110.
831

Bryan, John Randolph
Balloon used for scout duty in C.S.A. *SHSP* XXXIII (1905) 32–42.   *832*

Cornish, Jenkins
The air arm of the Confederacy [by] Jenkins Cornish III, a history of the origins and usages of war balloons by the Southern armies during the American Civil war. . . . [Richmond] 1963. 48 p. facsim., illus., maps, ports. 23cm. (Official publication no. 11 Richmond Civil war centennial committee).   *833*
"Editing and layout: Robert W. Waitt Jr."

Glassford, William Alexander, 1853–
The balloon in the Civil war. *JMSIUS* XVIII (1896) 255–66.   *834*

Williams, Jones Rhees
Reminiscences of ballooning. *Chautauquan* XXVII (1898) 257–62. ports   *835*

CAVALRY

Brackett, Albert Gallatin, 1829–1896.
History of the United States cavalry from the formation of the Federal government to the 1st of June, 1863, to which is added a list of all cavalry regiments, with the names of their commanders which have been in the United States service since the breaking out of the rebellion, by Albert C. Gallatin, Colonel Ninth Illinois volunteer cavalry. New York, Harper & Brothers, 1865. xii, [13]–337 p. plates (illus., 2 maps). 19½cm.
Civil war, 211–337. CSmH NHi NN   *836*
Plates are included in pagination.

—— —— Argonaut press, 1965. xii, [13]–337 p. plates (illus., 2 maps). 22½cm.   *837*
A photographic reproduction.

Dyer, John Percy, 1902–
Some aspects of cavalry operations in the Army of the Tennessee. *JSH* VIII (1942) 210–25.   *837A*

Harbord, James Guthrie, 1866–
. . . The history of the cavalry of the Army of Northern Virginia. *JUSCA* XIV (1904) 423–503.   *837B*
At head of title: Prize essay.

Johnson, James Ralph
Horsemen Blue and Gray, a pictorial history. Pictures by Hirst Dillion Milhollen. Text by James Ralph Johnson and Alfred Hoyt Beel. New York, Oxford University press, 1960. 236 p. illus., plans, ports. 29cm. TxU   *837C*
Facsims. of front cover and words and music: Riding a raid, 27–9; Sheridan's ride from Winchester, 180–3.

Jones, Virgil Carrington, 1906–
Gray ghosts and Rebel raiders [by] Virgil Carrington Jones, with an introduction by Bruce Catton. New York, Henry Holt and co. [1956] xiv, 431 p. plates (illus., ports.), map on endpaper. 22cm.   NN   *838*

Kniffen, Gilbert Crawford, 1832–1917.
"The cavalry of the Army of the Cumberland in 1863." 1896. 15 p. *MOLLUS-DC* 24.
839

Oates, Stephen Berry, 1936–
Confederate cavalry west of the River, by Stephen B. Oates. Austin, University of Texas press [c1961] xviii, 234 p. front. (illus.), maps and plans, plates (ports.). 23½cm.
TxU   *840*

—— Confederate cavalrymen of the Trans-Mississippi. *CWH* VII (1961) 13–19.   *841*

—— Recruiting Confederate cavalry in Texas. *SWHQ* LXIV (1960/61) 463–77.   *842*
"Confederate cavalry units raised in Texas during 1861," 477.

Rhodes, Charles Dudley, 1865–1948.
History of the cavalry of the Army of the Potomac, including that of the cavalry of the Army of Virginia (Pope's), and also the history of the operations of the Federal cavalry in West Virginia during the war, by Charles D. Rhodes . . . Kansas City, Mo., Hudson-Kimberley pub. co., 1900. 200 p. 17½cm.
CSmH DLC NHi   *843*
"Appendix," 175–92, includes organization tables.

Ryan, John Paul, 1867?–1936.
Some cavalry lessons from the Civil war. *JUSCA* VIII (1895) 268–82.   *844*

Wilson, James Harrison, 1837–1925.
The cavalry of the Army of the Potomac. *PMHSM* XIII (1880) 33–88.   *845*

Young, Bennett H
Confederate wizards of the saddle, being reminiscences and observations of one who

rode with Morgan, by Bennett H. Young. Boston, Chapple pub. co., 1914. xxii, 633 p. plates (illus., maps, ports.). 23½cm.   NN   *846*

—— —— Kennesaw, Ga., Continental Book co., 1958.   *847*

A photographic reproduction.

COMMUNICATIONS
Mail Service

Hecht, Arthur
Union military mail service. *FCHQ* xxxvii (1963) 227–48.   *848*

Telegraph Service

Harlow, Alvin F
Brass-pounder, young telegraphers of the Civil war [by] Alvin F. Harlow. Denver, Sage Books [c1962] 159 p. plates (illus.). 22cm.
                                    CSmH   *849*
Fuller, William Greenlief
The corps of telegraphers under General Anson Stager during the War of the rebellion. *MOLLUS-Ohio* ii 392–404.   *850*

O'Brien, John Emmet
Telegraphing in battle, reminiscences of the Civil war, by John Emmet O'Brien, operator and cipher operator U. S. military telegraph, 1862–1866. Scranton [Wilkes-Barre, Raeder press] 1910. xi, 312 p. plates (illus., maps, ports.). 21½cm.   CSmH NN   *851*

Plum, William Rattle
The military telegraph during the Civil war in the United States, with an exposition of ancient and modern means of communication, and of the Federal and Confederate cipher systems. Also, a running account of the War between the States. By William R. Plum. Chicago, Jansen, McClurg & co., 1882. 2 v. fronts. (ports.), facsim., illus., ports., plates (maps). 23½cm.   CSmH DLC   *852*

DEFENSIVE WORKS

Dodge, Grenville Mellen, 1831–1916.
Use of block houses during the Civil war. *Annals of Iowa*, s 3 vi (1904) 297–301.   *853*

Merrill, William Emery, 1837–1891.
Block-houses for railroad defense in the Department of Cumberland. *MOLLUS-Ohio* iii 389–421.   *854*

Wagner, Arthur Lockwood, 1849?–1905.
Hasty intrenchments in the War of secession, by Major Arthur L. Wagner. *PMHSM* xiii (1897) 127–53.   *855*

—— —— *JMSIUS* xxii (1898) 225–46. *856*

DESERTION

Dodge, David
The cave-dwellers of the Confederacy. *Atlantic monthly* lxviii (1891) 514–21.   *858*

Lonn, Ella, 1879–1962.
. . . Desertion during the Civil war, by Ella Lonn. New York, century co. [1928] vii, 251 p. fold., front. (map). 23cm.   NN   *859*
"Bibliography," 237–42.
At head of title: The American historical association.

—— —— Gloucester, Peter Smith, 1966. vii, 251 p. fold. front. (map). 21cm.   *860*
A photographic reprinting.

DISCIPLINE

United States.
. . . List of U. S. soldiers executed by United States military authorities during the late war. [Washington, DC., 1892] 11 p. 22½cm.
                                    CSmH   *861*

ENGINEERS

Confederate States of America. Army.
Memorandum of engineer officers of the regular and provisional corps for August, 1864. [Washington, D.C., 1882] 8 p. 23cm.
                                    CSmH   *862*

Hickenlooper, Andrew, 1837–1904.
Our volunteer engineers. *MOLLUS-Ohio* iii 301–18.   *863*

Nichols, James Lynn, 1919–
Confederate engineers, by James L. Nichols. Tuscaloosa, Confederate pub. co., 1957. 122 p. front. (port.). 22cm.   *864*
Half-title: Confederate centennial studies, number 5.
"Bibliography," [111]–17.

Thienel, Phillip M
Engineers in the Union army, 1861–1865. *Military engineer* xlvii (1955) 36–41, 110–15. illus., maps.   *865*
Contents: I Engineer organization; II Army of the Potomac; III Department of the South and Army of the James; Engineers in the West.

Thompson, Gilbert, 1839–1909.
Report of the reunion of the veterans of the U. S. engineer battalion, at St. Louis, Mo., September 26–29, 1887. [Washington] Byron S. Adams, printer [1887] 14 p. front. (mounted photograph, group port.). 23cm. DLC   *866*
Text signed: Gilbert Thompson, Secretary and historian.
Title and imprint from cover.

ESPIONAGE

GENERAL

Beymer, William Gilmore, 1881–
On hazardous service, scouts and spies of the North and South, by William Gilmore Beymer. Illustrated by Howard Pyle and others. New York, Harper & Brothers, 1912. xii, (2), 286, (1) p. plates (illus., partly col.; ports.). 22½cm.   CSmH DLC   867

Dana, Charles Anderson, 1819–1897.
The war, some unpublished history. *North American review* CLIII (1891) 240–5.   868

Davis, Curtis Carroll
A catalog of Civil war spy memoirs separately published. In his edition of Belle Boyd in camp and prison, 1968, 401–14.   868A
See Title 878A.

Denison, Charles Wheeler, 1809–1881.
The spy of the Shenandoah. *Potter's American monthly* XIII (1879) 284–90. illus.   869

Kurtz, Wilbur G   1882–
A Federal spy [J. Milton Glass] in Atlanta. *Atlanta historical bulletin* no 38 (December 1957) 13–20.   870

Stern, Philip Van Doren, 1900–
Secret missions of the Civil war, first-hand accounts by men and women who risked their lives in underground activities for the North and South. Woven into a continuous narrative by Philip Van Doren Stern. Chicago, Rand McNally & co. [1959] 320 p. 22cm.
NN   871

LAFAYETTE C. BAKER

Baker, Lafayette Curry, 1826–1868.
History of the United States secret service, by General L. C. Baker. Philadelphia, L. C. Baker, 1867. 704 p. front. (port.), plates (illus.). 24cm.   GEU   872

—— The secret service in the late war, comprising the author's introduction to the leading men at Washington, with the origin and organization of the detective police, and a graphic history of his rich experiences, North and South, his perilous adventures, hair-breadth escapes and valuable services, etc., by General L. C. Baker. Philadelphia, John E. Potter and co. [c1874] 398 p. illus. 20½cm. NcD   873

—— Daring exploits of scouts and spies, a graphic history of rich and exciting experiences, perilous adventures, hairbreadth escapes, and valuable services rendered by the national secret service bureau of the United States, including the origin and organization of the Department of detective police, by General La Fayette C. Baker. Illustrated by F. B. Schell, E. B. Bensell and J. M. Butler. Chicago, Thompson & Thomson [c1894] 398 p. illus. 23cm.   NcD   874

—— Spies, traitors and conspirators of the late Civil war, by General La Fayette C. Baker, organizer and first chief of the Secret service of the United States. Philadelphia, John E. Potter & co., 1894. 398 p. illus. 22cm.
Plates are paged.   LNHT   875

Mogelever, Jacob
Death to traitors, the story of General Lafayette C. Baker, Lincoln's forgotten secret service chief [by] Jacob Mogelever. Garden City, Doubleday & co., 1960. 429 p. 21½cm.
NN   876
Facsim., illus., ports. are on endpapers.

BELLE BOYD *

Boyd, Belle, 1844–1900.
Belle Boyd in camp and prison, written by herself, with an introduction by George Augusta Sala. New York, Blelock & co., 1865. 464 p. 19½cm.   TxU   877
"Introduction by a friend of the South," 13–43 dated: London, May 17th, 1865.

—— —— With an introduction by a friend of the South. London, Saunders, Otley, and co., 1865. 2 v. I front. (port.). 20½cm.
GEU   878
"Introduction," by George Augusta Sala, I 1–32. Lieutenant Sam Wylde Hardinge's journal II 117–280.

—— —— A new edition prepared from new materials, by Curtis Carroll Davis. South Brunswick, N. J., Thomas Yoseloff [c1968] 448 p. front. (port.), facsim., 1 illus., 3 ports. 21½cm.
878A
"A catalog of Civil war spy memoirs separately published," 401–14.

Sigaud, Louis A
Belle Boyd, Confederate spy, by Louis A. Sigaud. Richmond, Dietz press [c1944] xii, (1), 254 p. plates (facsim., 1 illus., ports.). 23½cm.   TxU   879

PAULINE CUSHMAN

An inside view of the army police. The thrilling adventures of Pauline Cushman, the distinguished American actress, and famous Federal spy of the Department of the Cumber-

---

* We have used the better known maiden name rather than her three names by marriage, Hardinge, Hammond, and High, or her stage name, Nina Benjamin.

land . . . Cincinnati, Rickey & Carroll, 1864. 50 p. port. 20½cm. CSmH 880
"To the public" signed: Pauline Cushman.

Sarmiento, Ferdinand L
Life of Pauline Cushman, the celebrated Union spy and scout, comprising her early history, her entry in the Secret service of the Army of the Cumberland, and exciting adventures with the Rebel chieftains and others while within the enemy lines, together with her capture and sentence to death by General Bragg and final rescue by the Union army under General Rosecrans. The whole carefully prepared from her notes and memoranda, by F. L. Sarmiento. Philadelphia, John E. Potter, 1865. 374 p. front. (port.), plates (illus.). 17½cm. CSmH 881

—— —— New York, United States Book co. [n. d.] 374 p. front. (port.). 19cm.
NcD 882

GENERAL ORDERS

Confederate States of America. Army.
Official army intelligence. Appointments and promotions in the Provisional army of the Confederate states since the adjournment of Congress, February 18th, 1864. *Smith & Barrow's monthly magazine* I (May 1864) 78–96.
883

—— Army of Tennessee. Cavalry Corps.
Official orders. [n. p., 1865] 16 p. 22cm.
CSmH 884
"The following orders [1863, no. 4–16; 1864, no. 1–5] are re-published."
CSmH has original printings of General orders, 1863, no. 12, 15–16 and 1864, no. 1–6, *Crandall* 675–76.
Dated: January 1st, 1865.
Crandall 680.

Confederate States of America. War Department.
General orders from Adjutant and Inspector general's office, Confederate states army, from January, 1862, to December, 1863, (both inclusive). In two series. Prepared from the files of Head-quarters Department of S. C., Ga., and Fla. With full indexes. Columbia, Presses of Evans & Cogswell, 1864. xlvii, 159, lix, 276 p. 18½cm. DLC NN NcD 885
Roman pagination the "Analytical index (es)."
Crandall 1343.

—— —— from July 1, 1864, to December 31, 1864, inclusive. Prepared from the files of Head-quarters, Department of South Carolina, Georgia and Florida, by Captain R. C. Gilchrist. With full index, explanatory notes, and such decisions of the War department as could be collected touching matters of general con-

cern to the service. Columbia, Evans and Cogswell, 1865. xii, 147 p. 18cm.
Crandall 1346. DLC MWA NcD 886

—— Special orders from Adjutant and Inspector general's office. [Washington, D. C., 1885–87] [5] v. 24cm. CSmH 887
I 1861. (March 7–October 25): 1–314.
II 1862. 1–306.
III 1863. 1–310.
IV 1864. 1–310.
V 1865. (January–April 1): 1–78.

Sherman, William Tecumseh, 1820–1891.
Military orders of General William T. Sherman, 1861–'65. [1869] lxxix, 375 p. 20cm.
"Index of subjects," xv–lxxix. DLC 888

United States. Adjutant General's Office.
General orders. NN 889
1861. 1–111.
1862. 1–217.
1863. 1–400.
1864. 1–308.
1865. 1–175.
Annual name and subject index.

—— General orders affecting the volunteer force . . . 1861. Washington, Govt. print. office, 1862. 60 p. 19½cm. RP 890
P. 48a, folding table.

United States. Army.
General and field orders. Campaign of the Armies of the Tennessee, Ohio and Cumberland, Maj. Gen. W. T. Sherman, commanding, 1864–5. St. Louis, R. P. Studley and co., printers, 1865. 250 p. 21cm. CSmH NN 891
General orders: no. 1–32 (March 18–December 19, 1864); no. 2 (May 9, 1865). Special field orders: no. 1–148 (May 3–December 31, 1864); no 1–76 (January 2–May 30, 1865).
Issued by Headquarters Military Division of the Mississippi.

—— Army of Virginia. General order no . . . 1862. 22 nos. 19cm. CSmH 892
1 dated: Washington, June 27, 1862; 22 dated: Cedar mountain, Virginia, August 18, 1862.

—— Corps of Observation. General orders . . . 1862. 36 p. 18½cm. NN 893
1–36 (August 12–December 31, 1861); 1–6 (January 2–22, 1862).
Headquarters: August 12, 1861, Rockville, Md.; August 16, 1861, camp near Poolesville, Md.; August 19, 1861 to January 22, 1862, Poolesville, Md. Title from cover.
Brigadier Charles P. Stone, commanding officer.

United States. War Department.
General orders of the War department, embracing the years 1861, 1862 & 1863, adopted especially for the use of the Army & Navy of the United States. Chronologically arranged in two volumes, with a full alphabetical index. By Thos. M. O'Brien & Oliver Diefendorf. New York, Derby & Miller, 1864. 2 v. 24cm.
CSmH 894

LOGISTICS

Ashcraft, Allan C   1928–
Staff functions in the Confederate district
of Texas. *TMH* III (1963) 114–19.   **895**

Bruce, Robert Vance, 1923–
Lincoln and the tools of war, by Robert V.
Bruce. Foreword by Benjamin P. Thomas. Indianapolis, Bobbs-Merrill co. [c1956] xi, (2),
368 p. front. (facsim.), plates (illus., ports.).
22½cm.   DLC NcD   **896**

Coddington, Edwin Broughton, 1925–
Soldiers' relief in the Seaboard states of the
Southern Confederacy. *MVHR* XXXVII (1950)
17–38.   **897**

Confederate States of America. War Depart-
ment.
Memorandum of officers in the Commissary-
General's department, June 6 and July 14,
1864. [Washington, D.C., 1882] 13 p. 23cm.
                          CSmH   **898**
Felt, Jeremy P
Lucius B. Northrop and the Confederacy's
Subsistence department. *VMHB* LXIX (1961)
181–93.   **899**

Huse, Caleb, 1831–1905.
The supplies for the Confederate army, how
they were obtained in Europe and how paid
for, personal reminiscences and unpublished
history, by Caleb Huse, Major and purchasing
agent, C.S.A. Boston, Press of T. R. Marvin &
Son, 1904. 36 p. front. (port.), plate (facsim.).
23cm.   CSmH NN   **900**
c1904 by James S. Rogers.

Huston, James Alvin, 1918–
Logistical support of Federal armies in the
field. *CWH* VII (1961) 36–47.   **901**

Leary, Peter
. . . A series of tables showing the allowances
of transportation required for an army corps
and its principal sub-divisions, compiled from
S.O. no. 37, Headquarters Armies of the United
States, City Point, Va., February 23rd, 1865,
by 1st Lieut. Peter Leary. Fort Monroe, Va.,
1880. 6 p. 21cm.   CSmH   **902**
At head of title: United States artillery school,
Fort Monroe, Va., 1880. Department of military history, &c.

Ruffin, F   G
A chapter of Confederate history. *North
American review* CXXXIV (1882) 97–110.
The Subsistence department.   **903**

Sharpe, Henry Granville, 1858?–1947.
The art of supplying armies in the field as
exemplified during the Civil war. *JMSIUS*
XVIII (1896) 45–95.   **904**

United States. Subsistence Department.
Circulars from the Commissary general of
subsistence. Washington, 1865. 62 p. 18cm.
                          NN   **905**
NN's copy is preceeded by leaf captioned "Index"
listing seven publications of which this title is no. 2.

Vandiver, Frank Everson, 1925–
The food supply of the Confederate armies,
1865. *Tyler's quarterly historical and genealogical magazine* XXVI (1944/45) 77–89.   **906**

—— Texas and the Confederate army's meat
problem. *SWHQ* XLVII (1943/44) 225–33. **907**

Windham, William T
The problem of supply in the Trans-Mississippi Confederacy. *JSH* XXVII (1961) 149–68.
                                              908

MANUALS

Zouave drill book. French bayonet exercise and
skirmisher's drill, as used by Col. Ellsworth's
zouaves, with over thirty illustrations. To which
is added a portrait and biography of the late
Col. Elmer E. Ellsworth. Philadelphia, King
& Baird, printers, 1861. 72 p. illus. 17cm.
                     CSmH DLC   **909**
"Life of Colonel Ellsworth," 65–72.
Cover illus. in color with port. of Ellsworth.

Butterfield, Daniel, 1831–1901.
Camp and outpost duty for infantry, with
standing orders, extracts from the revised Regulations for the army, rules for health, maxims
for soldiers, and duties of officers, by Daniel
Butterfield. New York, Harper & Brothers,
1863. 124 p. front. (illus.), 4 plans. 14½cm.
                          DLC   **910**

—— Extracts from Army regulations. Standing orders for the march and in camp, rules for
heath, &c. Compiled and printed for the use
of the Third brigade (Gen'l Butterfield's,) Porter's division, Army of the Potomac. Camp at
Hall's hill, Va., March 1862. Washington, Henry Polkinhorn, printer, 1862. 104 p. 13cm.
                          CSmH   **911**
On cover: Washington, Philip & Solomons, 1862.
Roster [officers] Third brigade (General Butterfield's), 96–102.

Confederate States of America. Army.
Regulations for General Hindman's division
in camp. Montgomery, Memphis Appeal print
[1863] 8 p. 22cm.   CSmH   **912**
Dated: McFarland's Spring, Sept. 4, 1863.
Crandall 674 supplies at head of title: [General
orders, no. 8]

Confederate States of America. War Depart-
ment.
Articles of war for the government of the
armies of the Confederate states. Charleston,
Presses of Evans & Cogswell, 1861. 24 p. 22cm.
Crandall 1224.   CSmH DLC   **913**

—— Regulations for the Army of the Confederate states, authorized edition, 1862. Richmond, West & Johnston, 1862. xxii, 420 p. 20cm.   CSmH RP   *914*
Crandall 1391.

—— Regulations for the Army of the Confederate states, 1863, corrected and enlarged, with a revised index. . . . Richmond, J. W. Randolph, 1863. xii, 420 p. 19cm.
Crandall 1392.   CSmH RP   *915*

—— Regulations for the Army of the Confederate states, with a full index, by authority of the War department . . . Richmond, West & Johnston, 1864. xxx, 432 p. 19cm.
Crandall 1396.   DLC NN RP   *916*

—— Regulations for the Army of the Confederate states, and for the Quartermaster's and Pay departments. The uniform and dress of the army. As published by authority of the Secretary of war. The articles of war, as amended by Act of Congress. Also, all the laws appertaining to the army. Revised edition. New Orleans, Bloomfield & Steel, 1861. 262, 100 p. 19cm.   CSmH DLC NN RP   *917*
"Forms" and "Index," 100 p.
Crandall 1399.

Curry, John P
Volunteers' camp and field book, containing useful and general information on the art and science of war, for the leisure moments of the soldier, by John P. Curry. Richmond, West & Johnston, 1862. 144 p. 14½cm.
Crandall 2408.   CSmH DLC   *918*

Lord, Francis Alfred, 1911–
Army and navy textbooks and manuals used by the North during the Civil war. *MC&H* IX (1957) 61–7, 95–102.   *919*
Contents: I Text; II Bibliography.

Marmont, Auguste Frederic Louis Viesse de, duc de Raguse, 1774–1852.
The spirit of military institutions, by Marshal Marmont, Duke of Ragusa. Translated from the last Paris edition (1859), and augmented by biographical, historical, topographical, and military notes. With a new version of General Jomini's celebrated thirty-fifth chapter, of part I, of treatise on grand military operations. By Frank Schaller, Colonel 22d regiment Mississippi infantry, Confederate army. Columbia, Evans & Cogswell, 1864. 278 p. 18cm.   CSmH DLC   *920*
"A review of the life and character of the late General Albert Sidney Johnston," 237–59.
Crandall 2462.

United States. War Department.
Regulations for the Army of the United States, 1861. New York, Harper & Brothers 1861 xxv, 457, 21 p. 19½cm.   MWA   *921*
Contents of 21 p.: Articles of war, 1–18; Extracts from Acts of Congress, 19–21.
Dated, May 1, 1861.

Virginia.
Rules and articles for the government of the Army of Virginia. Richmond, Wyatt M. Elliott, printer, 1861. 29 p. 22cm.   CSmH   *922*

Wells, John G
Wells' army and navy handy book; or, every soldier and marine his own counsellor. Being a full and complete guide to the soldier and marine in all matters pertaining to his duties, his obligations, and his rights, and how to obtain his rights without legal assistance. Together with everything of interest to the Army and Navy departments and a complete historical record of events connected with the war. New York, John G. Wells, 1864. ix, [11]– 191 p. 17½cm.   CSmH   *923*

Wheeler, Joseph, 1836–1906.
A revised system of cavalry tactics, for the use of the cavalry and mounted infantry, C.S.A., by Major Joseph Wheeler. Mobile, S. H. Goetel & co., 1863. ii, 220, 104, 47, 97– 108, xiv p. plates (illus.; plans, partly fold.), music. 14cm.   CSmH DLC   *924*
"Bugle signals," 97–108 p.
"Table of contents," xiv p.
Crandall 2491.

MEDICAL SERVICES

Armory square hospital [Washington, D.C.] *Northern monthly* I (1864) 688–95.   *925*

Adams, George Worthington, 1905–
Confederate medicine. *JSH* VI (1940) 151– 66.   *926*

—— Doctors in Blue, the medical history of the Union army in the Civil war [by] George Worthington Adams. New York, Henry Schuman [c1952] xii, 253 p. plates (illus.). 21½cm.
"Sources," 231–8.   CSmH   *927*

Anderson, Galusha
The story of Aunt Lizzie Aiken, by Mrs. Galusha Anderson. Fourth edition. Chicago, Ellen M. Sprague [c1880] 226 p. front. (port.). 18cm.   *928*
Civil war, 69–134.
Copyright 1880 Jansen, McClurg & co.

Baxter, Jedediah Hyde,   –1890.
Statistics, medical and anthropological, of the Provost-marshal-general's bureau, derived

Medical Services, continued

from records of the examination for military
service in the armies of the United States during the late War of the rebellion, of over a
million recruits, drafted men, substitutes, and
enrolled men. Compiled under direction of the
Secretary of war, by J. H. Baxter. Washington,
Govt. print. office. 1875. 2 v. plates (charts,
fold. maps). 30cm.   NN   **929**

Bowditch, Henry Ingersoll, 1808–1892.
A brief plea for an ambulance system for the
army of the United States, as drawn from the
extra sufferings of the late Lieut. Bowditch
and a wounded comrade, by Henry I. Bowditch. Boston, Ticknor and Fields, 1863. 28 p.
23½cm.   TxU   **930**

Bryce, Campbell
Reminiscences of the hospitals of Columbia,
S. C., during the four years of the Civil war,
by Mrs. Campbell Bryce. Philadelphia, Printed
by J. B. Lippincott co., 1897. 31 p. 18½cm.
Title from cover, p [1]   NcD ScU   **931**

Caskey, Thomas W   1816–1896.
The Oxford [Miss.] hospital, 1862. Edited
by Willie D. Halsell. *JMH* viii (1946) 36–44.
932

Clark, Eudora
Hospital memories. *Atlantic monthly* xx
(1867) 144–56, 324–36.   **933**

Cunningham, Horace Herndon, 1913–
Confederate general hospitals, establishment
and organization. *JSH* xx (1954) 376–94.
934

—— Doctors in Gray, the Confederate medical service, by H. H. Cunningham. Baton
Rouge, Louisiana State University press
[c1958] xi, 338, (1) p. plates (facsims., 1
illus., ports.). 23½cm.   CSmH DLC   **935**
"Bibliography," 291–321.

—— Edmund Burke Haywood and Raleigh's
Confederate hospitals. *NCHR* xxxv (1958)
152–66. 4 plates (illus., port.).   **936**

—— Organization and administration of the
Confederate Medical department. *NCHR* xxxi
(1954) 385–409.   **937**

Curtis, Edward, 1838–1912.
Glimpses of hospital life in war times.
MOLLUS-NY iv 54–65.   **938**

Donald, William J
Alabama Confederate hospitals. *AR* xv
(1962) 271–81; xvi (1963) 64–78.   **939**

Drum, William Findlay,   -1892.
The Fifth corps ambulance train, 1864.
JMSIUS xi (1890) 566–72.   **940**

—— Work of the Fifth corps ambulance train,
Spring and Summer of 1864. *MOLLUS-Minn*
iii 77–86.   **941**

Duncan, Louis Caspar, 1869–
The Medical department of the United
States army in the Civil war, by Captain
Louis C. Duncan. [Washington, D.C., 191–]
[327] p. illus., maps and plans, ports. 23½cm.
CSmH DLC NN   **942**
Contents: The battle of Bull Run; Pope's Virginia
campaign; Evolution of the ambulance corps and field
hospital; The bloodiest day in American history —
Antietam; The campaign of Fredericksburg, December,
1862; The greatest battle of the war, Gettysburg; The
great battle of the West, Chickamauga; Battle of the
Wilderness; When Sherman marched down to the sea.
"The chapters comprising the volume appeared
originally as separate articles in the Military surgeon.
Upon their compilation a limited number of copies
of reprints were obtained by this office and bound
together for the use of the Medical corps of the army.
The work was never published as a book," letter from
the Office of the Surgeon general, October 19, 1916,
cited from the Library of Congress entry.
Appended "Seaman prize essay. The comparative
mortality of disease and battle casualties in the historic wars of the world, by Capt. Louis C. Duncan,"
37 p.

Eastwood, Bruce S
Confederate medical problems in the Atlanta campaign. *GHQ* xlvii (1963) 276–92.
943

Fay, Frank Brigham, 1821–1904.
War papers of Frank B. Fay, with reminiscences of service in the camps and hospitals of
the Army of the Potomac, 1861–1865. Edited
by William Howell Reed. Privately printed.
[Boston, Press of Geo. H. Ellis] 1911. vii,
161 p. front. (port.), plate (illus.). 24½cm.
DLC GEU NcD TxU   **944**

Frink, Charles S   -1893.
Organization of the Surgical department in
the field, and the experience of its officers in
the battle of Franklin. *MOLLUS-Ohio* iv 418–
28.   **945**

Gaillard, Edward Samuel, 1827–1885.
The medical and surgical lessons of the late
war. *New eclectic magazine* iv (1869) 705–18.
946

Jones, Joseph, 1833–1896.
Roster of the medical officers of the Army
of Tennessee, during the Civil war. *SHSP* xxii
(1893) 165–80.   **947**

King, Joseph Edward
Shoulder straps for Aesculpius. The Vicksburg campaign, 1863. *Military surgeon* cxiv
(1954) 216–26.   **948**

Letterman, Jonathan, 1824–1872.
Medical recollections of the Army of the
Potomac, by Jonathan Letterman, late Surgeon
United States army and Medical director of the

Army of the Potomac. New York, D. Appleton and co., 1866. 194 p. 23cm.

Blank forms, 186–94. CSmH DLC **949**

Louisiana Soldiers' Relief Association.
Louisiana soldiers' relief association, and hospital in the City of Richmond, Virginia. Established August 21st and 23d, 1861. Richmond, Enquirer press, 1862. 38 p. 21½cm.

DLC LNHT **950**

"List of officers of Louisiana regiments in Virginia," 32–8.
Crandall 4965.

Lyman, George Hinckley, 1819–1891.
Some aspects of the medical service in the armies of the United States during the War of the rebellion. *MHSMP* xiii (1890) 175–228.
951

Nagle, John T
The status of acting assistant surgeons of the United States army who served in the late Civil war, being a reply to the ruling of the War department in a communication sent by L. A. Grant, Assistant Secretary of war, to E. J. Dunphy, member of Congress, March 28th, 1892, by John T. Nagle. New York, Martin B. Brown, printer, 1893. 90 p. front. (port.). 23cm.

CSmH **952**

Parker, William Thornton, 1849–
Records of the Association of acting assistant surgeons of the United States army. Edited by W. Thornton Parker. Salem, Salem Press print. co., 1891. viii, 149 p. col. plate (illus.). 25cm.

CSmH **953**

"Edition limited to two hundred copies."
Includes sketches of individual members.
"Errata" slip inserted.

Pye, Edward Arell, 1818–1873.
Letters from the Confederate medical service in Texas, 1863–1865. Introduction by Eugene C. Barker. Notes by Frank E. Vandiver. *SWHQ* lv (1951/52) 378–93, 459–74. **954**

Reed, William Howell
Hospital life in the Army of the Potomac, by William Howell Reed. Boston, William V. Spencer, 1866. 199 p. 17½cm. NN **955**
Coulter 390.

Riley, Harris D
Medicine in the Confederacy. *Military medicine* cxviii (1956) 53–63, 145–53. **956**

Severin, John Powers and Frederick Porter Todd
Medical department, U. S. army, 1861–1865. *MC&H* viii (1956) col. plate (illus.). **957**

Shippen, Edward, 1826–1911.
Memoir of John Neill, M.D., read before the College of physicians of Philadelphia, Oct. 6,

1880, by Edward Shippen, M.D. . . . Philadelphia [Collins, printer] 1880. 18 p. 24cm.

CSmH **958**

"Extracted from the Transactions, 3d series, vol. v."

Simkins, Francis B and James W. Patton
The work of Southern women among the sick and wounded of the Confederate armies. *JSH* i (1935) 474–96. **959**

Steiner, Paul Eby, 1902–
Disease in the Civil war, natural biological warfare in 1861–1865, by Paul E. Steiner. Springfield, Charles C. Thomas [1968] xv, 243 p. 23½cm. IHi NcD **959A**

Stout, S H 1822–1903.
Outline of the organization of the Medical department of the Confederate army and Department of Tennessee. Edited by Sam L. Clark and H. D. Riley, Jr. *THQ* xvi (1957) 55–82. **960**

Strait, Newton Allan
Roster of all regimental surgeons and assistant surgeons in the late war, with their service, and last-known post-office address. Compiled from official records by N. A. Strait, for use of United States Pension office. [Washington, Govt. print. office] 1882. 320 p. 23½cm.

CSmH NHi **961**

Swinburne, John, 1820–1889.
Reports on the Peninsular campaign, surgical experience, &c. [by] John Swinburne. Albany, Press of C. Van Benthuysen, 1863. 67 p. 23cm.

NN **962**

United States. Surgeon General's Office.
Annual report. War department, Surgeon general's office. [Washington, 1865] 7 p. 21cm.

Caption title. NN **963**
Dated: Washington, D.C., October 20, 1865.

—— The medical and surgical history of the War of the rebellion (1861–65). Prepared, in accordance with Acts of Congress under the direction of Surgeon general Joseph K. Barnes. Washington, Govt. print. office, 1870–88. 3 v. in 6. illus., plates (partly col. and mounted illus., fold. maps). 29½cm.

CSmH DLC **964**

Appeared in two issues and so identified on the title pages except the first issue of i 1 and ii 1.
The Medical history i 1 and ii 1 were prepared by Joseph J. Woodward, 1870–79; iii 1 by Charles Smart, 1888. Vol i 1 of the Medical history contains an Appendix with reports of medical directors and other documents, by J. J. Woodward and George A. Otis, with separate title page and pagination. The Surgical history i 2 and ii 2 were prepared by George A. Otis, 1870–76; iii 2 by George A. Otis and David L. Huntington, 1883.

Medical Services, continued

Waitt, Robert W
Confederate military hospitals in Richmond [by] Robert W. Waitt, Jr. Richmond, 1964. 40 p. illus. 22½cm. (Richmond Civil war centennial committee Official publication No. 22).
965

West, Nathaniel, 1794–1864.
History of the Satterlee, U.S.A. gen. hospital, at West Philadelphia, Pa., from October 8, 1862, to October 8, 1863, by the Rev. Nathaniel West, Chaplain to the Hospital. [Philadelphia] Printed by the Hospital press, 1863. 36 p. 19cm.   CSmH DLC   966
Title and imprint from cover.

Western Sanitary Commission.
The Western sanitary commission, a sketch of its origin, history, labors for the sick and wounded of the Western armies, and aid given to freedman and Union refugees, with incidents of hospital life. St. Louis, Published for the Mississippi Valley Sanitary Fair [by] R. P. Studley & co., 1864. 144 p. front. (illus.), plates (illus.). 22½cm.   NcD   966A

White, James Lowery, 1833–1909.
History of the Confederate general hospital, located at Farmville, Va., 1862–65, by Dr. Jas. L. White. [1897] 15 p. 2 plates (illus., port.). 16cm.   Vi   967
Title from cover.
Text dated: June 10, 1897.

—— —— [Farmville, Martin print. co., 1916] 15 p. 2 plates (illus., port.). 15½cm.
Vi   968
"Published by the Farmville chapter, U.D.C., April 7th, 1916."

State Medical Reports

Illinois. Sanitary Agent.
Report of the State sanitary agent, Col. Thomas P. Robb. [Springfield, 1864] 34 p. 21cm.   CSmH   969
At head of text: Department of the Cumberland.
Dated: Nashville, Tenn., Nov. 4, 1864.
Also paged [455]–76 as an excerpt from the Public documents.

Illinois. Sanitary Commission.
Report of transactions of the Illinois state sanitary bureau, from its organization, December 18th, 1862, to September 12th, 1863. And also of the Illinois state sanitary commission, from September 12th, 1863, to January 1st, 1864. Springfield, Press of Baker & Phillips, 1864. 98 p. 20½cm.   CSmH   970

—— Second annual report of the Illinois state sanitary commission, from January 1, 1864, to January 1, 1865. [Springfield, Baker & Phillips, printers, 1865] 116 p. 20½cm.
CSmH NN   971

—— Military and Sanitary Agent, Department of the Gulf. Report of Owen M. Long, M.D. . . . [New Orleans, 1864] 8, (1) p. 21cm.
Caption title.   CSmH   972
Issued as a Legislative document "v. 1–44" and is also paged [477]–484 without inclusion of the supplementary page.
Includes a list of deaths from Illinois regiments.
"List of regiments, &c., Illinois organizations, Department of the Gulf, 1864," (1) p.
Report dated: Dec. 10th, 1864.

Iowa.
Reports of Mrs. Annie Wittenmyer, State sanitary agent. Also, special message of Governor Wm. M. Stone, relative to sanitary matters. Des Moines, F. W. Palmer, State printer, 1864. 41 p. 22cm.   CSmH   973
For the period September 25, 1862, to June 13, 1864.

Massachusetts.
Report to Wm. J. Dale, Surgeon General, Massachusetts [by John S. Blatchford, Secretary, of a group of physicians and surgeons who left for Washington on August 31, 1862] [Boston, Printed at the Boston Post, 1862] 36 p. 21cm.   NHi TxU   974
Caption title.
Inspection reports of government hospitals with a list of Massachusetts soldiers, their wounds, and their regiments.

New York State.
Report of the General agent of the State of New York, for the relief of sick, wounded, furloughed and discharged soldiers. Albany, Comstock & Cassidy, printers, 1864. 134 p. fold. plates (illus., map, 2 plans). 22½cm.
CSmH   975

—— Annual report of the General agent for the relief of sick and wounded soldiers of the State of New York. Transmitted to the Legislature, April 14, 1865. Albany, C. Wendell, Legislative printer, 1865. 144 p. 23cm.
Title and imprint from cover.   CSmH   976

Pennsylvania. Surgeon General.
Report . . . 1862. [Harrisburg, Singerly & Myers, State printers, 1863] 19 p. 23½cm.
CSmH   977

Rhode Island
Report upon the disabled Rhode Island soldiers, their names, condition, and in what hospital they are. Made to Gov. Sprague, and presented to the General assembly of Rhode Island, January session, 1863, by Mrs. Charlotte F. Dailey, commissioned by the Governor to visit the hospitals, etc. Providence, Alfred

Anthony, Printer to the State, 1863. 24 p. 24½cm.   CSmH   **978**

Report dated: Feb. 2d, 1863.
Includes alphabetical list of soldiers with hospital, regiment and company, and description of wound.

—— . . . Report on the physical condition of the Rhode Island regiments, now in the field in Virginia and in the vicinity of Washington, D.C. Also, on the condition of the hospitals in and around Washington. Made to the General assembly of Rhode Island, January session, A.D. 1863, by Lloyd Morton, Commissioner. Providence, Alfred Anthony, Printer to the State, 1863. 21 p. 24½cm.
                    CSmH DLC   **979**
At head of title: Public document. Appendix. No. 2.

Nursing

In honor of the National association of Civil war army nurses. Atlantic City, Citizens' Executive Committee [1910] [72] p. ports. 15½ x 23½cm.   NbHi   **980**

Portraits of nurses with biographical information. Title and imprint from cover.

Chase, Julia A   (Houghton), 1842–
Mary A. Bickerdyke, "Mother," the life story of one who, as wife, mother, army nurse, pension agent and city missionary, has touched the heights and depths of human life. Written by Julia A. Chase. Published under the auspices of the Woman's relief corps (Department of Kansas). Lawrence, Journal pub. house, 1896. viii, 145 p. front. (port.). 23cm.
                    CSmH   **981**

Fischer, Le Roy Henry, 1917–
Cairo's Civil war angel, Mary Jane Safford. *Journal of the Illinois state historical society* LIV (1961) 229–45. illus., ports.   **982**

Holland, Mary A   Gardner
Our army nurses, interesting sketches, addresses and photographs of nearly one hundred of the noble women who served in hospitals and on battle fields during our Civil war. Compiled by Mary A. Gardner Holland. Sold by subscription only. Boston, B. Wilkins & co., 1895. 548 p. front. (port.), illus., ports. 23cm.   CSmH   **983**

Plates are paged.

—— Our army nurses, interesting sketches and photographs of over one hundred of the noble women who served in hospitals and on battle fields during our late Civil war, 1861–1865. Compiled by Mary A. Gardner Holland. Published in the interests of the army nurses. Sold by subscription. Boston, Press of Lounsbery, Nichols & Worth, 1897. 600 p. front. (port.), illus., ports. 23cm.   CSmH   **984**

A reprinting with the addition of eight biographies, [549]–600. The entries for these biographies in "List of illustrations" are on an inserted slip.

McKay, Charlotte Elizabeth
Stories of hospital and camp, by Mrs. C. E. McKay. Philadelphia, Claxton, Remsen & Haffelfinger, 1876. xii, 13–230 p. 19½cm.
                    CSmH DLC   **985**
"Record of incidents connected with forty months' service in our military hospitals."
Contents: I [Personal experiences in military hospitals March 1861–July 1861]; II With the freedmen [Poplar Springs and Petersburgh, Virginia, 1865–1867]

Marshall, Mary Louise
Nurse heroines of the Confederacy. *Bulletin of the Medical library association* XLV (1957/58) 319–36. facsim., ports.   **986**

Smith, S   E   D   1817–
The soldier's friend, being a thrilling narrative of Grandma Smith's four years' experience and observation, as matron, in the hospitals of the South, during the late disastrous conflict in America, by Mrs. S. E. D. Smith. Revised by Rev. John Little, and dedicated to the Rebel soldiers. Memphis, Printed by Bulletin pub. co., 1867. 300 p. front. (port.). 19cm.
                    CSmH DLC Ms-Ar TxU   **987**

MILITARY GOVERNMENT

Freidel, Frank Burt
General orders 100 and military government. *MVHR* XXXII (1946) 541–6.   **988**

MUSTERING OUT

Jones, James P
Farewell to arms, Union troops muster out at Louisville, June – August, 1865. *FCHQ* XXXVI (1962) 272–82.   **989**

Trenerry, Walter
When the boys came home. *Minnesota history* XXXVIII (1962/63) 287–97. illus.   **990**

ORDNANCE *

Albaugh, William Archibald, 1908–
Tyler, Texas, by William A. Albaugh, III. Harrisburg, Stackpole co. [c1958] 235 p. 2 maps, plates (illus.). 23cm.   NN   **995**
"Story of the Confederate states ordnance works, Tyler, Texas."

Allan, William, 1837–1889.
Reminiscences of field ordnance service with the Army of Northern Virginia, 1863–'5. *SHSP* XIV (1886) 137–46.   **996**

---

* References to administration and supply. For references to ammunition and individual weapons, see subsection "Weapons" under "Armed Forces; General References."

Ordnance, continued

Confederate States of America. Ordnance
Bureau.
. . . Names of officers of the Ordnance bureau of the Confederate states, serving under
orders of the Chief of ordnance. [n. p., n. d.]
4 p. 23cm.   CSmH   **997**
At head of title: Memoranda.

Felgar, Robert Pattison, 1882–
The Ordnance department of the Confederate state's army. *AHQ* VIII (1946) 159–232.
plate (port.).   **998**

Gorgas, Josiah, 1818–1883.
Notes on the Ordnance department of the
Confederate government. *SHSP* XII (1884)
66–94.   **999**

Mallet, John William, 1832–1912.
Work of the Ordnance bureau. *SHSP* XXXVII
(1909) 1–20.   **1000**

Rains, George Washington, 1817–1898.
History of the Confederate powder works,
by Col. (General) Geo. W. Rains, late of the
Confederate army, an address delivered by
invitation before the Confederate survivors' association, at its fourth annual meeting, on Memorial day, April 26th, 1882. Augusta, Chronicle & Constitutionalist print, 1882. 30 p. 22cm.
NN   **1001**

—— —— Newburgh, N. Y., Newburgh Daily
News print, 1882. [190–] 29 p. 22cm.
NN   **1002**

Vandiver, Frank Everson, 1925–
Makeshifts of Confederate ordnance. *JSH*
XVII (1951) 180–93.   **1003**

—— Ploughshares into swords, Josiah Gorgas
and Confederate ordnance, by Frank E. Vandiver. Austin, University of Texas press, 1952.
xiv, 349 p. 21½cm.   NN   **1004**

—— A sketch of efforts abroad to equip the
Confederate armory at Macon. *GHQ* XXVIII
(1944) 34–40. plate (illus.).   **1005**

PAYMASTER GENERAL

Pay Department, United States army. *United
States service magazine,* IV (1865) 430–43.
1006
United States. Paymaster General.
Annual report. Washington, 1865. 8 p. 21cm.
Caption title.   NN   **1007**
Dated: Washington, October 31, 1865.

PROVOST MARSHAL

Moore, Wilton P
The Provost marshal goes to war. *CWH* v
(1959) 62–71.   **1008**

—— Union army Provost marshals in the
Eastern theater. *Military affairs* XXVI (1962)
120–26.   **1009**

United States. Provost Marshal General's Bureau.
Circular no . . . Washington, 1863–65. 157
nos. 18½cm.   CSmH   **1010**
1–106 (May–December 1863)
1–43 and Index (1864)
1–9 (January–March 1865)
The unnumbered Circulars of April 29 and May 6
and 11, 1863 and the Circular letters of 1865 are
found in the collected edition.

—— Final report . . . from the commencement
of the business of the Bureau, March 17, 1863,
to March 17, 1866. The Bureau terminating by
law, August 28, 1866. [Washington, Govt.
print. office, 1866] 2 v. (748, 376 p.). 24cm.
CSmH   **1011**

—— . . . Regulations for the government of
the Bureau of the Provost marshal general of
the United States . . . April 21, 1863. Washington, Govt. print. office, 1863. xii, 57 p.
23cm.   CSmH   **1012**
At head of title: War department.
Includes Forms 1–39 and an act for enrolling and
calling out the national forces.

—— Report. Washington, 1863–65. 4 nos.
fold. tables.. 22/23cm.   CSmH   **1013**
1863 (March–October), 23 p; with Appendix, 27 p.
1863/64, p. 49–66.
1864/65, p. 77–82.
1863/64 and 1864/65 are excerpts from the Report
of the Secretary of war.

QUARTERMASTER

Boeger, Palmer H
General Burnside's Knoxville packing project. *East Tennessee historical society Publication* 35 (1963) 76–84.   **1014**

Case, Theodore S
The Quartermaster's guide, being a summary of those portions of the Army regulations
of 1863, and General orders from the War department, from May 1, 1861, to April 10, 1865,
which affect the Quartermaster's department,
with full instructions for making returns, &c.
Also, all General orders from the Q.M. general's office file to April 10, 1865. By Col. Theo.
S. Case. Saint Louis, P. M. Pinckard, 1865.
vii, [9]–339 p. 22½cm.   NcD   **1015**

Confederate States of America.
Memorandum of officers in the Quartermaster's department for June 30, 1864. [Washington, D.C., 1882] 28 p. 23cm.   CSmH   *1016*

Lee, James Grafton Carleton
The Alexandria Quartermaster's depot during the Civil war. *JMSIUS* xxxix (1906) 11–17.   *1017*

Nichols, James L
The Confederate Quartermaster in the Trans-Mississippi, by James L. Nichols. Austin, University of Texas press [1964] 126 p. 23½cm.   NN   *1018*

Rusling, James Fowler, 1834–1918.
A word for the Quartermaster's department. *United States service magazine* iii (1865) 57–67, 133–43, 255–9, 446–55.   *1019*

Weigley, Russell Frank, 1930–
Quartermaster General of the Union army, a biography of M. C. Meigs, by Russell F. Weigley. New York, Columbia University press, 1959. x, 396 p. port. 22½cm.   NN   *1020*
Title and imprint on two leaves.

RANK

McKim, William Walker,   –1895.
A brief dissertation on military titles and brevet rank, by an ex-army officer. [Boston, 1886] 7 p. 23cm.   CSmH   *1021*
Title from cover.
Text signed: W. W. M., Boston, August, 1886.

RECRUITMENT

Castel, Albert E   1928–
Enlistment and conscription in Civil war Kansas. *Kansas historical quarterly* xxvii (1961) 31–9.   *1022*

Clark, Charles Branch, 1913–
Recruitment of Union troops in Maryland, 1861–1865. *MHM* liii (1958) 153–76.   *1023*

Confederate States of America. War Department.
Troops tendered to the Confederate War department, 1861. Washington, War Department print. office, 1876. 103 p. 23½cm.
CSmH   *1024*
Alphabetical list of individuals offering troops, and their disposition by the War department.

Cox, Jacob Dolson, 1828–1900.
War preparations in the North. *B&L* i [1884–87] 84–98.   *1025*

Imholte, John Quinn, 1930–
The legality of Civil war recruiting. U. S. versus Gorman. *CWH* ix (1963) 422–9. *1026*

Moore, Albert Burton
Conscription and conflict in the Confederacy, by Albert Burton Moore. New York, Macmillan co., 1924. ix, (1), 367 p. 22½cm.
1027

Peterson, Robert L   1927–   and John A. Hudson
Foreign recruitment for the Union forces. *CWH* vii (1961) 176–89.   *1028*

Raney, William F
Recruiting and crimping in Canada for the Northern forces, 1861–1865. *MVHR* x (1923) 21–33.   *1029*

Shannon, Frederick Albert, 1893–1963.
The mercenary factor in the creation of the Union army. *MVHR* xii (1926) 523–49. *1030*

—— State rights and the Union army. *MVHR* xii (1925) 51–71.   *1031*

United States.
Miscellaneous tender of troops to the United States, 1861. [Washington, D.C., n.d.] 30 p. 23½cm.   CSmH NN   *1032*

—— Statement of number of men called for by the President of the United States, and number furnished by each State, Territory, and the District of Columbia, from April 15, 1861, to close of War of rebellion. [Washington, Adjutant General's office, 1879] broadside, 25 x 77cm.   CSmH   *1033*

—— —— [Washington, Adjutant General's office, 1880] 8 p. 20cm.   CSmH   *1034*

United States. Provost Marshal General's Office.
Calls for troops made by the President during the years 1861, 1862, 1863, and 1864. [Washington, Govt. print. office, 1898] 30 p. 23cm.   CSmH   *1035*

United States. Record and Pension Division.
Statement of number of men called for by the President of the United States, and number furnished by each State, Territory, and District of Columbia, from April 15, 1861, to close of the War of the rebellion. [Washington, 1892] 8 p. 18cm.   CSmH   *1036*
Text signed: War department, Record and pension division, January, 1892.

REGIMENTAL NAMES

Confederate States of America.
Local designations of Confederate organizations. [Washington, 1876] 169 p. 22½cm.
Caption title.   CSmH NB   *1037*
A photographic reproduction in *Personnel of the Civil war*, William F. Amann, ed, New York, T. Yoseloff, 1961, i 3–169.

Regimental Names, continued

United States. Adjutant-General's Office.

List of synonyms of organizations in the volunteer service of the United States during the years 1861, '62, '63, '64 and '65. Compiled under the direction of Brigadier General Richard C. Drum, Adjutant General United States army, by John T. Fallon. Washington, Govt. print office, 1885. 301 p. 23½cm.

    "Errata" slip inserted.   DLC NN   ***1038***
    A photographic reproduction in *Personnel of the Civil war,* William F. Amann, ed, New York, T. Yoseloff, 1961, II [75]–373.

—— Memorandum for office use. Local designations of volunteer organizations in the United States army during the rebellion, 1860–1865. [Washington, 1875] 14 p. 20½cm.

    Caption title.   CSmH   ***1039***
    Text signed: Adjutant general's office, August 9, 1875.

REGULAR ARMY

White, John Chester

A review of the services of the regular army during the Civil war. *JMSIUS* XLV (1909) 207–30, 366–96; XLVI (1910) 50–77, 277–301, 463–78; XLVII (1910) 81–96, 260–72, 417–30; XLVIII (1912) 76–85, 237–46, 401–12; XLIX (1912) 64–69, 248–56.   ***1040***

Zogbaum, Rufus Fairchild, 1849–1925.

The regulars in the Civil war. *North American review* CLXVII (1898) 16–26.   ***1041***

ROSTERS

Alphabetical army register, giving the names, date of present and original commissions, rank, place of nativity, and from whence appointed, of all the officers of the U.S. army, as shown by the Official army register, May, 1863. New York, D. Van Nostrand, 1863. 64 p. 23cm.

                          CSmH   ***1042***

Surviving Confederate pensioners. *AHQ* II (1940) 208–16.   ***1042A***

Bidgood, Joseph V

List of general officers and their staffs in the Confederate army, furnished by Virginia, as far as I have been able to get them. *SHSP* XXXVIII (1910) 156–83.   ***1043***

Booker, John A

A record of Confederate Generals, giving the States of each and rank, with a full list of the battles and the dates of each, from 1861 to 1865. Alphabetically arranged by John A. Booker, late Captain Co. D, 21st regt. Va. Richmond, Everett Waddey co., printers, 1897. 42 p. 22½cm. CSmH In NcD   ***1044***

The author was President of the Confederate diploma company whose advertisement appears on p. 41–2.

Confederate States of America.

. . . Paroles of the Army of Northern Virginia, R. E. Lee commanding, surrendered at Appomattox C. H., Va., April 9, 1865, to Lieutenant-General U. S. Grant, commanding Armies of the United States, now first printed from the duplicate originals in the archives of the Southern historical society. Edited, with introduction by R. A. Brock. Richmond, 1887. XXVII, 508 p. 22½cm.   NN   ***1045***

    At head of title: Southern historical society papers, volume xv.

—— The Appomattox roster. A list of the paroles of the Army of Northern Virginia issued at Appomattox Court House on April 9, 1865. A photographic reprint of the edition of 1887, containing the original introduction by R. A. Brock, and a foreword written for this edition, by Philip Van Doren Stern. New York, Antiquarian press, 1962. xxxiii, 508 p. plates (facs., illus., ports.). 24cm.   NN   ***1046***

Conference of Confederate Roster Commissioners.

Proceedings and memorial of a conference of Confederate roster commissioners at Atlanta, Ga., July 20–21, 1903. Montgomery, Alabama print. co., 1903. 23½cm.

                          NcD   ***1047***

Estes, Claud

List of field officers, regiments and battalions in the Confederate states army, 1861–1865. Macon J. W. Burke co., 1912. 137, 76 p. 24cm.   DLC ScU NN   ***1048***

    "List of regiments and battalions. . . ," 76 p.
    "Introduction" signed Claud Estes.

Hall, Charles Bryan, 1840–

. . . Military records of general officers of the Confederate states of America, Commander-in-chief, Generals, Lieutenant Generals and Major Generals, arranged in order of their rank, with their military records in the Confederate army and previous records in the United States army, of all those who graduated from the United States Military academy at West Point or were appointed from civil life . . . Compiled and illustrated by Charles B. Hall. New York [Lockwood press] 1898. ix, 108 p. 108 plates (ports.). 41cm.

                CSmH NN P   ***1049***

—— —— Austin, Steck co. [1963] xiii, 108, (2) p. ports. 31cm.   NcD   ***1050***
    At head of title: 1861 A facsimile reproduction 1865.

Henry, Guy Vernor, 1839–1899.
Military record of civilian appointments in the United States army, by Guy V. Henry. New York, D. Van Nostrand, 1873. 2 v. 22½cm.   CSmH DLC NN   *1051*

Jones, Charles Colcock, 1831–1893.
A roster of general officers, heads of departments, Senators, Representatives, military organizations, &c., in Confederate service during the War between the States, by Charles C. Jones, Jr., late Lieut. Colonel of artillery. Richmond, Southern Historical Society, 1876 [–77] 130 p. 22½cm.   NHi *1052*
Published in 3 sections with Southern historical society papers.

McCabe, William Gordon, 1841–1920.
Graduates of the United States Military academy at West Point, N. Y., who served in the Confederate states army, with the highest commission and highest command attained. *SHSP* xxx (1902) 34–76.   *1053*

Poland, Charles A
Army register of Ohio volunteers in the service of the United States, comprising the general staff of state, staff of the various departments, list of Brigadiers, roll of field, staff and commissioned officers of each regiment, present place of service, rank of each officer, date of commission, and a complete list of casualties, compiled from official records in the Adjutant General's office, Columbus, Ohio, for April, 1862, by Charles A. Poland. Columbus, Ohio State Journal print. co., 1862. 74 p. 21cm.   RP *1054*

—— July, 1862. Columbus, Ohio State Journal print. co., 1862. 85 p. 21cm.
"the second edition."   NcD *1055*

Smith, George B
Official army list of the volunteers of Illinois, Indiana, Wisconsin, Minnesota, Michigan, Iowa, Missouri, Kansas, Nebraska and Colorado. Compiled and published by George B. Smith. Chicago, Tribune book print. estab., 1862. 176 p. 18cm.   CSmH DLC *1056*
Officers' roster arranged by regiments.

United States.
Commanders of the armies, military divisions, departments, and corps, during the War of the rebellion. [Washington, Adjutant General's office, 1875] 15 p. 20½cm.
Caption title.   CSmH *1057*

—— List of State, Ter'y, and District of Columbia troops in the service of the United States, January 1, 1862. [Washington, D.C., 1882] 38, 18 p. 23½cm.
     CSmH DLC   *1058*
List of units by States with term of enlistment, commanders and stations.
"Index of commanders," 18 p.

—— Memorandum of field officers of volunteers, U.S. army, 1861–1865. [Washington, 188–] 180, (1) p. 23cm.   CSmH   *1059*
"Errata," p. [1]
"Addenda," (1) p.
Title from cover.

United States. Adjutant General's Office.
Official army register for . . . Washington, 1861–66. 9 v. 20/21cm.   CSmH   *1060*
January 1, 1861, 60 p.
September 1, 1861, 87 p.
January 1, 1862, 108 p., 3 fold. tables.
August 1862, 118 p., 3 fold. tables.
January 1, 1863, 141 p., "Only one hundred copies of this register were printed."
April 1, 1863, 151, (1) p., 2 fold. tables, "Errata," (1) p., and inserted slip.
January 1, 1864, 153, (1) p., 2 fold. tables, "Errata," (1) p.
January 1, 1865, 152, (1) p., 2 fold. tables, "Errata," (1) p.
August 1, 1866, 180, (1) p., 3 fold. tables, "Errata and addenda," (1) p.

—— Official army register of the volunteer force of the United States army for the years 1861, '62, '63, '64, '65 . . . Washington, Adjutant General's office, 1865–67. 8 v. 20cm.
     CSmH NN   *1061*
Vols i–iv are continuously paged, to 1299. Indexes of iv are separately paged.
Record of State troops is detailed as an Appendix to the roster of Federal troops.

United States. War Department.
. . . Memorandum relative to the general officers in the Armies of the United States during the Civil war, 1861–1865. (Compiled from official records.) [Washington, Govt. print. office] 1906. 73 p. 23cm.   NHi *1062*
At head of title: The Military secretary's office, War department.

—— . . . Memorandum relative to the general officers appointed by the President in the armies of the Confederate states, 1861–1865 . . . [Washington, Govt. print. office] 1905. 41 p. 23cm.   NN *1063*
At head of title: The Military secretary's office, War Department.

United States. War Records Office.
List of field officers, regiments, and battalions in the Confederate states army, 1861–1865. [Washington, 1881] 131, 91 p. 22cm.
     CSmH NB   *1064*

Rosters, continued

—— Roster of regular and volunteer forces in the service of the United States, June 30, 1862. [Washington, War Records office, 1884] 39 p. 23cm.   CSmH   **1065**

Roster of units with their commanders, stations, and army or department.

SIGNAL CORPS

Alms, Frederick H
With the Signal corps. G.A.R. war papers, papers read before Fred C. Jones post, no. 401, Department of Ohio, G.A.R., 1891. 284–92.
                                                 1066
Bachtell, Samuel
The Signal corps, U. S. army. G.A.R. war papers, papers read before Fred C. Jones post, no. 401, Department of Ohio, G.A.R., 1891. 23–9.   **1067**

Brown, Joseph Willard
The Signal corps, U.S.A. in the War of the rebellion, by J. Willard Brown, during four years Private, Sergeant and Lieutenant in the Corps. Boston, Published by the U. S. Veteran Signal Corps Association [Press of B. Wilkins & co.] 1896. 916 p. facsim., illus., maps, plates (illus., ports.). 25cm   NN   **1068**
Unit roster, [715]–902.

Cummins, Edmund H
The Signal corps in the Confederate States army. *SHSP* xvi (1888) 91–107.   **1069**

Fuller, Frederick
Frederick Fuller, late Lieutenant in Civil war, 52d reg't P.V. and Signal officer U.S.A., 1861–1865. [Philadelphia, 191–] 15 p. 23½cm.
                                                 PPLL   **1070**

Glassford, William Alexander, 1853–
Historical sketch of the Signal corps, U.S. army. *JMSIUS* xii (1891) 1325–38.   **1071**

Greely, Adolphus Washington, 1844–1935.
The Signal corps in the Civil war. *American review of reviews* xliv (1911) 55–63.   **1072**

Myer, Albert James, 1827–1880.
I have the honor to submit the following report of the operations and duties of the Signal department of the Army, from the date of its organization up to the termination of the late War of the rebellion. [Washington, 1865] 258 p. 22cm.   NN(M)   **1073**
Caption title.
Original publication is in the Signal corps museum at Fort Monmouth, New Jersey.

Scheips, Paul Joseph, 1914–
Union signal communications, innovation and conflict. *CWH* ix (1963) 399–421.   **1074**

Tafft, Henry Spurr,   –1909.
Reminiscences of the Signal service in the Civil war . . . 1899–1903. 41, 27 p. fold. plan. *PNRISSHS* s 5 no. 9; s 6 no. 3.   **1075**

Taylor, Charles E
. . . The signal and secret service of the Confederate states, by Dr. Chas. E. Taylor. Hamlet, N. C., Capital print. co., 1903. 24 p. 18cm.   CSmH   **1076**
At head of title: North Carolina booklet, vol. ii, no. 11, March, 1903.

United States. Signal Department.
Annual report of the Signal officer of the Army to the Secretary of war. Washington, 1862. 13 p. 21½cm.   NN   **1077**
Dated: November 10, 1862.
The Annual reports are found in the War of the rebellion, a compilation of the official records . . . s 3: i (1861) 694–7; ii (1862) 754–80; iii (1863) 948–61; iv (1864) 818–41; v (1865) 152–6.

—— . . . Annual report of the Acting signal officer of the Army to the Secretary of war. . . . Washington, Signal printing press, 1864. 35 p. 23½cm.   NN   **1078**
At head of title: War department.
Dated: October 31, 1864.
Signed: W. J. L. Nicodemus, Acting signal officer. Nicodemus was dismissed by GO 304 December 26, 1864, because he had published the Report "without the knowledge or sanction of the Secretary of war."

United States. Signal Service.
. . . Preliminary list of officers and enlisted men who served on signal duty during the War of the rebellion, 1861 to 1866. Washington, Signal office, 1891. 32 p. 19½cm.
                                                 CSmH   **1079**

United States Veteran Signal Corps Association.
Fifteenth annual reunion of the . . . held at Boston, Mass., August 11th to 16th, 1890. [Albany, Taylor & Roberts, printers, 1890] 15 p. 22½cm.   DNW   **1080**

—— The U.S. veterans signal corps association, including a partial roster of the Corps during the war, with a brief resume of its operations, from Aug. 14, 1861, to March 14, 1862. West Medford, Mass., 1884. 52 p. 18cm.
                                              CSmH DLC   **1081**
Introduction signed: J. Willard Brown, Historian of the Association.

—— A revised roster of the Signal corps, U.S.A., during the War of the rebellion, with personal records of service in the corps. [West Medford, Mass.] U.S. Veteran Signal Corps Association, 1886. 56 p. 24½cm.
                                              CSmH WHi   **1082**
"Personal memoranda of service," two narratives by Capt. Bradford R. Wood and Private Albert H. Cook, 48–56.

"Introductory note," p. 47, signed: J. Willard Brown, West Medford, Mass., July 21, 1886.

—— Roster of the Signal corps, 1861–1865 . . . Compiled by the Secretary, U.S. veteran signal corps association, July, 1901. Albany, Van Benthuysen print. house, 1901. 46 p. 23cm.   TxU   *1083*

—— Roster of Signal corps, U.S.A., 1861–1865, issued by the U.S. veteran signal corps association, Civil war division. [Stoneham, Mass.] 1910. 48 p. 23cm.
                          CSmH DLC   *1084*

—— Roster of members of the Signal corps, U.S.A., 1861–1865, comprising all whose addresses are known, arranged alphabetically and by States and Cities or Towns, April 1913. [Boston, 1913] 19 p. 22½cm.
                                  DLC   *1085*
Charles D'W. Marcy, Boston, Secretary.

THE SOLDIER

Catton, Bruce, 1899–
    Mr. Lincoln's army [by] Bruce Catton. Garden City, Doubleday & co., 1951. vi, 372 p. 22cm.   NN   *1086*
    Map on endpaper.

Cox, Jacob Dolson, 1828–1900.
    Why the men of '61 fought for the Union. *Atlantic monthly* LXIX (1892) 382–94.
                                         1087
Dodge, Theodore Ayrault, 1842–1909.
    Valor and skill in the Civil war. *Century magazine.* XL (1890) 144–50.   *1088*
    Contents: I Was either the better soldier?, by Theodore Ayrault Dodge, 144–8. II Which was the better army, by Charles A. Patch, 148–50.
    Comment by Joseph T. Derry, 1st and 63d Georgia. *Century magazine* XLII (1891) 634–5.

Donald, David Herbert, 1920–
    The Confederate as a fighting man. *JSH* XXV (1959) 178–93.   *1089*

Furness, Helen Kate (Rogers), 1837–1883.
    Our soldiers. *Atlantic monthly* XIII (1864) 364–71.   *1090*

Hill, Daniel Harvey, 1821–1889.
    The Confederate soldier in the ranks, an address by Major-General D. H. Hill, before the Virginia division of the Association of the Army of Northern Virginia, at Richmond, Virginia, on Thursday evening, October 22d, 1885, also some account of the banquet, including the response of D. B. Lucas, to the toast "our dead. . . ." Richmond, Wm. Ellis Jones, printer, 1885. 28 p. 23½cm.   CSmH NN   *1091*

Jones, John William, 1836–1909.
    The morale of General Lee's army. *AW* 191–204.   *1092*

King, Charles, 1844–1903.
    The volunteer soldier of 1861. *American review of reviews* XLIII (1911) 709–20.
                                         1093
McDonald, William Naylor, 1834–1908.
    Cavalry versus infantry. *SB* I (1882/83) 160–7.   *1094*

Parker, William Watts
    How the Southern soldiers kept house during the war, the experience of Dr. W. W. Parker, Major of artillery. *SHSP* XXIII (1895) 318–28.
                                         1095
Rusling, James Fowler, 1834–1918.
    The Yankee as a fighter. *United States service magazine* IV (1865) 27–43.   *1096*

Shannon, Frederick Albert, 1893–1963.
    The life of the common soldier in the Union army, 1861–1865. *MVHR* XIII (1927) 465–82.
                                         1097
Stern, Philip Van Doren, 1900–   editor
    Soldier life in the Union and Confederate armies. Edited with an introduction and notes, by Philip Van Doren Stern, from Hardtack and coffee, by John D. Billings and Detailed minutiae of soldier life in the Army of Northern Virginia, by Carlton McCarthy. Original sketches by Charles W. Reed and William L. Sheppard. Bloomington, Indiana University press [1961] ix, 13–400 p. illus. 21cm.
                          DLC NNC   *1098*
    "Civil war centennial series."

Waddell, Alfred Moore, 1834–1912.
    The Confederate soldier, an address delivered at the written request of 5,000 ex-Union soldiers, at Steinway hall, New York city, Friday evening, May 3d, 1878, for the benefit of the 47th N. Y. veteran volunteers (Miles O'Reilly's regiment), by Alfred M. Waddell. Washington, D.C., Joseph L. Pearson, printer, 1878. 23 p. 22½cm.
                          CSmH NcD WHi   *1099*

Wiley, Bell Irvin, 1906–
    The life on Johnny Reb, the common soldier of the Confederacy, by Bell Irvin Wiley. Indianapolis, Bobbs-Merrill co. [c1943] 444 p. plates (illus., ports.). 24cm.   *1100*

—— The life of Billy Yank, the common soldier of the Union, by Bell Irvin Wiley. Indianapolis, Bobbs-Merrill co. [c1952] 454 p. plates (illus., ports.). 24½cm.   *1101*

STATISTICAL DATA

Anderson, Charles Carter, 1867–
Fighting by Southern Federals, in which the author places the numerical strength of the armies that fought for the Confederacy at approximately 1,000,000 men, and shows that 296,579 white soldiers living in the South, and 137,676 colored soldiers, and approximately 200,000 men living in the North that were born in the South, making 634,255 Southern soldiers, fought for the preservation of the Union. By Charles C. Anderson. New York, Neale pub. co., 1912. 408 p. front. (map). 21cm.   DLC NN   *1102*

Badeau, Adam, 1831–1895.
The relative strength of the two armies, in Virginia, 1864–65. *Historical magazine* s 2 IX (Morrisania 1871) 102–11.   *1103*
Letter of General Badeau to the London Standard occasioned by an editorial on General Lee together with General Early's reply to Badeau.

Barter, George W
The War department and the Union army. *Overland monthly* XII (1874) 60–5.   *1104*

Casselman, A   B
The numerical strength of the Confederate army. *Century magazine* XLIII (1892) 792–6.
1105

—— Mr. Casselman's rejoinder. *Century magazine* XLIV (1892) 957–9.   *1106*
Reply to A Southern view of the question, by Joseph T. Derry. See Title 1107.

Derry, Joseph Tyrone, 1841–1926.
A Southern view of the question. *Century magazine* XLIV (1892) 956–7   *1107*

Fox, William Freeman, 1840–1909.
Regimental losses in the American Civil war, 1861–1865, a treatise on the extent and nature of the mortuary losses in the Union regiments, with full and extensive statistics compiled from the official records on file in the State military bureaus and at Washington, by William F. Fox. Albany, Albany pub. co., 1889. vi, 595 p. 29½cm.   CSmH NHi   *1108*
"Errata" slip inserted.

Humphreys, Andrew Atkinson, 1810–1883.
The relative strength of the two armies, in the War of secession. *Historical magazine* s 2 III (Morrisania 1875) 294–6.   *1109*

Kniffen, Gilbert Crawford, 1832–1917.
Estimated effective strength of the Union and Confederate armies and their respective losses during the War of the rebellion. 1911. 24 p. front. (port.). *MOLLUS-DC* no. 84.
1110

Livermore, Thomas Leonard, 1844–1918.
Numbers and losses in the Civil war in America, by Thomas L. Livermore. Boston, Houghton, Mifflin and co., 1901. iv, (1), 150 p. 24½cm.   DLC   *1111*
"Preface" dated: June 1, 1900.

—— —— ["second edition"] Boston, Houghton, Mifflin and co., 1901. viii, 150 p. 24½cm.
CSmH   *1112*
"Preface" dated: December 1, 1900.
"Errata" sheet inserted.

—— —— July 1, 1909. Errata in and additions to . . . [3] p. 18½cm.   CSmH   *1113*

—— —— Introduction by Edward E. Barthell, Jr. Bloomington, Indiana University press, 1957. xi, 150 p. 21cm.   NN   *1114*
At head of title: By Thomas L. Livermore.
"Civil war centennial series."

McKim, Randolph Harrison, 1842–1920.
The numerical strength of the Confederate army, an examination of the argument of the Hon. Charles Francis Adams and others, by Randolph H. McKim, late 1st Lieut. and A.D.C. 3d brigade, Army of Northern Virginia. . . . New York, Neale pub. co, 1912. 71, (1) p. 19cm.   CSmH NN   *1115*

Phisterer, Frederick, 1836–1909.
. . . Statistical record of the Armies of the United States, by Frederick Phisterer. New York, Charles Scribner's Sons, 1886. viii, 343 p. 19cm.   CSmH NN   *1116*
At head of title: Campaigns of the Civil war supplementary volume.
See Title 1362.

Thruston, Gates Phillips, 1835–1912.
The numbers and roster of the two armies in the Civil war, by Gen. Gates P. Thruston. [Philadelphia, 1909] 13 p. 25½cm.
NN   *1117*
"This article is reprinted from the Olympian magazine. The first edition of this address being now out of print, a new edition with additional data has been reprinted by my friend Clarence B. Moore of Philadelphia," inserted slip.

United States. Adjutant General's Office.
Comparative statement of the number of men furnished and of the deaths in the United States army during the late war. [Washington, 1886] 4 p. 23cm.   CSmH   *1118*

—— Statistical exhibit of deaths in the United States army during the late war. Compiled under the direction of Brigadier General Richard C. Drum, Adjutant General U.S. army, by Joseph W. Kirkley. Washington, 1885. 17 p. 23cm.   CSmH   *1119*

United States Sanitary Commission. Statistical Bureau.
. . . Ages of U.S. volunteer soldiery. New York [Cambridge University press] 18666. 43 p. 7 fold. charts. 24cm.
CSmH NN   1121
Transmitting message signed: B. A. Gould, actuary U. S. sanitary commission.
"Corrigenda" slip inserted.

SUTLERS

Hibbs, Waldo Campbell
The sutler. *B&G* III (1894) 207–09.   1122

Lord, Francis Alfred, 1911–
Civil war sutlers and their wares, by Francis A. Lord. New York, Thomas Yoseloff [1969] 162 p. plates (illus., port.). 26cm.   1122A

TRAINING CAMPS

Georgia

Wadsworth, George
. . . Camp McDonald, the school of instruction of the Fourth brigade of Georgia volunteers, organized June 11th, 1861. Atlanta, Franklin print. house [1861] 29, (3) p. 21½cm.
NjP RP   1123
Includes rosters of the 1st and 2nd regiments, rifle battalion, artillery battalion and cadets Georgia military institute.
At head of title: First edition.
Notice of publication and price, p. [32] signed: George Wadsworth.
To accompany a lithographic picture of the encampment.
Crandall 2556.

Illinois

Eisendrath, Joseph L
Chicago's Camp Douglas, 1861–1865. *Journal of the Illinois state historical society* LIII (1960) 37–63. illus., port.   1124

Indiana

Civil war camps in Indiana. *Indiana history bulletin* XXXVII (1960) 31–2.   1125
"Prepared by the Indianapolis Civil war round table."

Iowa

Site of Civil war camp in Henry county. *Annals of Iowa* s 3 XXXV (1960/61) 467–8.   1126
Camp Harlan until August 2, 1862, when it became Camp McKean. The Iowa 4th cavalry and 25th infantry used the barracks which were burned late in 1862.

McCormack, Charles B
Contemporary description of Camp McClellan and vicinity. *Annals of Iowa* s 3 XXXV (1960/61) 308–09.   1127

Temple, Seth J
Camp McClellan during the Civil war, a paper read before the Contemporary club, Davenport, Iowa, October 22, 1927, by Seth J. Temple. Published with the co-operation of the Davenport public museum. Davenport, Contemporary Club, 1928. 50 p. 23½cm.
Title and imprint from cover.   NbHi   1128

Pennsylvania

Borkowski, Joseph A
Camp Wilkins military post, 1861. *Western Penn historical magazine* XLV (1962) 229–39. plate (illus.).   1129

TRANSPORTATION
Military Railroads

Haupt, Herman, 1817–1905.
Reminiscences of General Herman Haupt . . . giving hitherto unpublished official orders, personal narratives of important military operations . . . written by himself. With notes and a personal sketch by Frank Abial Flower. [Milwaukee, Wright & Joys co., printers] 1901. xl, 43–331 p. illus., 2 plates (ports.). 25cm.
CSmH NHi   1130

—— [A report on "the most expeditious and effectual mode of destroying a railway communication"] [Washington, 1863] 4 p. 21cm.
NN   1131
At head of report: War department, Office of construction and transportation, United States military rail roads, Washington, May 16, 1863.
Text signed: H. Haupt, Brig. Gen. in charge of U.S. military railroads.

Sylvester, Robert Bruce
The U.S. military railroad and the siege of Petersburg. *CWH* x (1964) 309–16.   1132

United States. Military Railroads Department.
United States military railroads. Report of Bvt. Brig. Gen. D. C. McCallum, Director and General manager, from 1861 to 1866. [Washington, 1866] 39 p. fold. map. 22½cm.
CSmH   1132A

Weidensall, Robert
The Construction corps, U.S.M.R.R. Second edition. Robert Weidensall. [Nashville, September 1864] broadside, 37 x 53½cm.
DLC   1132B
Author's ms. annotations on DLC copy supplies imprint.

Water Transport

Loper, Richard F
Steamboat chartering. R. F. Loper in self-defence against the aspersions of the Senate committee. [Philadelphia?, 1863] 40 p. 21cm.
Caption title.   CSmH   1133

Transportation, continued

Tucker, John
Reply to the Report of the Select committee of the Senate on transports for the War department, by John Tucker, (late Assistant secretary of war), February 27, 1863. Philadelphia, Moss & co., 1863. 57 p. 22½cm.
CSmH   **1134**

WAR DEPARTMENT

Ingersoll, Lurton Dunham
A history of the War department of the United States, with biographical sketches of the Secretaries, by L. D. Ingersoll. Washington, D.C. Francis B. Mohun, 1879. xiii, 17–613 p. front. (illus.), plates (illus.). 22cm.
CSmH   **1135**
"Departmental history from the Mexican war to 1879," 320–85.

Meneely, Alexander Howard, 1899–
The War department, a study in mobilization and administration, by A. Howard Meneely. New York, Columbia University press, 1928. 400 p. front. (port.). 23cm.
NbU   **1136**
Half-title: Studies in history, economics and public law, edited by the Faculty of political science of Columbia university, number 300.

United States. War Department.
Report of the Secretary of war, 1865. [Washington, 1865] 48 p. 21cm. NN   **1137**
Caption title.
Dated: Washington city, November 22, 1865. [181]–98.

WEAPONS

Albaugh, William Archibald, 1908–
Confederate arms, by William A. Albaugh III and Edward N. Simmons. Harrisburg, Stackpole co. [1957] xvii, 278 p. illus. 29cm.
NN   **1138**
"Directory of makers, gunsmiths, dealers and those men, places and items connected with Confederate ordnance," 195–277.

—— The Confederate brass-framed Colt & Whitney, by William A. Albaugh, 3rd. Falls Church, Published privately by William A. Albaugh and Edward N. Simmons [1955] 105 p. illus., map. 26cm. NN   **1139**
Title and imprint from cover.

—— Confederate edged weapons, by William A. Albaugh III. Illustrated by Carl J. Pugliese. New York, Harper & Brothers [1960] xxiv, 198 p. illus. 28½cm. NN   **1140**
"Directory of persons and places connected with the manufacture of Confederate edged weapons," [181]–98.
Also with imprint of Bonanza Books, New York.

—— Confederate handguns, concerning the guns, the men who made them, and the times of their use. By William A. Albaugh, III, Hugh Benet, Jr. [and] Edward N. Simmons. Philadelphia, Riling and Lentz, 1963. xix, 250 p. front. (port.), illus. 28½cm.
NN   **1141**

Coggins, Jack
. . . Arms and equipment of the Civil war. Illustrated by the author. Garden City, Doubleday & co., 1962. 160 p. illus. 28½cm.
CSmH   **1142**
At head of title: Jack Coggins.
Col. illus. of insignia and corps badges, endpaper.

Edwards, William B
Civil war guns, the complete story of Federal and Confederate small arms, design, manufacture, identification, procurement, issue, employment, effectiveness, and postwar disposal, by W. B. Edwards. Harrisburg, Stackpole co. [1962] 444 p. illus. 29cm.
DLC NN   **1143**

Hinkle, Frederick Wallis
Army rifles, a paper read before the Ohio commandery of the Loyal legion, February 5, 1908, by Frederick W. Hinkle. 20 p. 23cm.
Title from cover.   NHi   **1144**

Lewis, Berkeley Read, 1904–
Notes on ammunition of the American Civil war, 1861–1865 . . . The text was prepared by Colonel Berkeley R. Lewis. Washington, American Ordnance Association, 1959. [31] p. illus. 25½cm.   **1145**
This precis . . . is the second in a series to be published by the American ordnance association in observance of the forthcoming centennial of the War between the States."

Michigan. Civil War Centennial Observance Commission.
Small arms used by Michigan troops in the Civil war. [Lansing, 1966] xiv, 133 p. front. (illus.), illus., plate (illus.). 23cm.   **1146**

Peterson, Harold Leslie, 1922–
Notes on ordnance of the American Civil war, 1861–1865 . . . The text and the tables were prepared by Harold L. Peterson . . . Drawings were made for this study by Robert L. Miller. Washington, American Ordnance Association, 1959. [20] p. illus. 26cm.   **1147**

Weller, Jac, 1913–
The Confederate use of British cannon. *CWH* III (1957) 135–52. plates (illus.).
1148

—— Imported Confederate shoulder weapons. *CWH* v (1959) 157–81. plates (illus.).
1149

CONFEDERATE ARMY

REFERENCE WORKS

Organization of the Confederate armies, 1863–'64. [Washington, D.C., 1881] 18 p. 22½cm.
CSmH   **1150**

Estes, Claud
    List of regiments and battalions in the Confederate states army, 1861–1865. *In his* List of field officers, regiments and battalions in the Confederate states Army, 1861–1865, Macon, Ga., J. W. Burke Co., 1912, a separately paged section of 76 p.   NN
    See Title 1048.

DEPARTMENT OF MISSISSIPPI
AND EAST LOUISIANA

Organization of the troops in the Department of Mississippi and E. Louisiana, (Lieutenant-General J. C. Pemberton, commanding), April, 1863. [Washington, D.C., 1881] 7 p. 23cm.
CSmH   **1151**

Organization of the Army of the Department of Mississippi and East Louisiana (Lieutenant-General W. J. Hardee, C.S. army, commanding), July 30, 1863. [Washington, War Records Office, 1885] 4 p. 23cm.   CSmH   **1152**

Organization of the troops in the Department of Mississippi and E. Louisiana (General Joseph E. Johnston commanding), November 20, 1863. [Washington, D.C., 1881] 5 p. 23cm.
CSmH   **1153**

ARMY OF THE MISSISSIPPI

. . . Organization of the Army of the Mississippi, April 6th and 7th [1862] [Washington, 1881] 4 p. 24cm.   CSmH   **1154**

    Caption title.
    At head of title: Inclosure-Exhibit B.
    Text signed: Braxton Bragg, General, Commanding, HDQRS. Department no. 2, Tupelo, Miss., June 30, 1862.

ARMY OF NORTHERN VIRGINIA

Lee's General order number nine. . . . [Chicago, Lakeside press, 1954] folder. 38cm.
CU-SB   **1155**

    Title from paste-on slip of front cover.
    Contents: Farewell to the Army of Northern Virginia. [7] p. 35½ × 12½cm.
    Facsimile of General order no. 9. 32½ × 20cm.

Monthly return of the Department of Northern Virginia, Commanded by General Robert E. Lee, March 31, 1863. [Washington, D. C., 1878] broadside, 22½cm x 72cm.
CSmH   **1156**

Monthly return of the Army of Northern Virginia commanded by General Robert E. Lee, May 31, 1863. [Washington, D.C., 1878] broadside, 23½ x 70cm.   CSmH   **1157**

Organization of the Army of Northern Virginia, July 23, 1862. [Washington, D.C., 1881] 7 p. 24cm.   CSmH   **1158**

—— (General R. E. Lee commanding), August 28 to September 1, 1862. [Washington, War Records office, 1882] 6 p. 23cm.
CSmH   **1159**

—— Organization of the Second army corps of the Army of Northern Virginia, December 20, 1862. [Washington, D.C., 1881] 6 p. 23cm.   CSmH   **1160**

Organization of the First and Second army corps of Army of Northern Virginia, June 22, 1863. [Washington, D.C., 1881] 5 p. 23½cm.
CSmH   **1161**

Organization of the Army of Northern Virginia, (commanded by General Robert E. Lee) July 31, 1863. [Washington, D.C., 1882] 7 p. 24cm.   CSmH   **1162**

—— August 31, 1863. [Washington, D.C., 1882] 7 p. 24cm.   CSmH   **1163**

—— January 31, 1864. [Washington, D.C., 1881] 8 p. 23cm.   CSmH   **1164**

—— and forces in the Richmond and Petersburg lines (under General G. T. Beauregard) early in May, 1864. [Washington, D.C., War Records office, 1888] 12 p. 22½cm.
CSmH   **1165**

—— August, 1864. [Washington, D.C., 1881] 7 p. 23½cm.   CSmH   **1166**

—— August 31, 1864. [Washington, War Records office, 1883] 8 p. 23cm.
CSmH   **1167**

—— (commanded by General Robert E. Lee) January, 1865. [Washington, D.C., 1881] 9 p. 23½cm.   CSmH   **1168**

Organization of the army of the Valley district, August 20, 1864. [Washington, War Records Bureau, 1883] [3] p. 23cm.   CSmH   **1169**

Strength of the infantry and cavalry Army of Northern Virginia as shown by the inspection reports, February 24–28, 1865. [Washington, D.C., 1886] 5 p. 23cm.   CSmH   **1170**

Jones, John William, 1836–1909.
    Army of Northern Virginia memorial volume, compiled by Rev. J. William Jones, at the

Army of Northern Virginia, continued

request of the Virginia division of the Army
of Northern Virginia association. Richmond,
J. W. Randolph & English, 1880. 347 p.
24½cm.   CSmH DLC NHi   *1171*

Includes the proceedings of the Lee memorial meeting and of the annual meetings and reunions (1st–
9th) of the Virginia division of the Army of Northern
Virginia association.
"Roster of the Army of Northern Virginia," [334]–
42.

—— Reminiscences of the Army of Northern
Virginia, or the boys in Gray, as I saw them
from Harper's ferry in 1861 to Appomattox
Courthouse in 1865. *SHSP* IX (1880) 90–5,
129–34, 185–9, 233–7, 273–80, 426–9, 557–
70; x (1881) 81–90.   *1172*

Jones, Thomas Goode, 1844–1914.
Last days of the Army of Northern Virginia,
an address delivered by Gov. Thos. G. Jones,
before the Virginia division of the Association
of the Army of Northern Virginia at the annual
meeting, Richmond, Va., October 12th, 1893.
46 p. 23cm.   DLC NN   *1173*

Also published in *SHSP* XXI (1893) 57–103.

DEPARTMENT OF THE PENINSULA

Douglas, Henry Thompson,   –1926.
A famous army and its commander. Sketch
of the Army of the Peninsula and General
Magruder. *SHSP* XLII (1917) 189–98.
                                            1174

ARMY OF TENNESSEE

Organization of the Army of Tennessee (commanded by General Braxton Bragg) August 31,
1863. [Washington, 1881] 6 p. 23cm.
                    CSmH   *1175*

—— November 20, 1863. [Washington, 1884]
9 p. 23cm.   CSmH   *1176*

Organization of the Army of Tennessee, November 23, 1863. [Washington, 1881] 6 p.
23cm.   CSmH   *1177*

Organization of the Army of Tennessee (commanded by General John B. Hood) for the
period ending December 10, 1864. [Washing-
ton, 1885] 6 p. 23½cm.   CSmH   *1178*

Organization of the cavalry Army of Tennessee
August 15, 1863. [Washington, 1881] [3] p.
23cm.   CSmH   *1179*

Hay, Thomas Robson
The Davis-Hood-Johnston controversy of
1864. *MVHR* XI (1924) 54–84.   *1180*

Ridley, Bromfield Lewis, 1804–1869.
Battles and sketches of the Army of the
Tennessee, by Bromfield L. Ridley, Lieut.-Gen.
A. P. Stewart's staff. Mexico, Mo., Missouri
print. & pub. co., 1906. xvi, [17]–662, (10) p.
illus., 2 maps, ports., plates (maps, ports.).
22½cm.   CSmH DLC NN   *1181*

On cover: Journal of B. L. Ridley . . .
"Index," (10) p.
"Errata" slip inserted.

NAMED UNITS OF THE ARMY *

List of officers and men of the cavalry brigade
of Brig.-Gen. R. L. T. Beale, C.S. army, surrendered at Appomattox C.H., Virginia, April
9th, 1865. *Collections of the Virginia historical
society,* ns VI (1887) 347–55.   *1182*

Signed: S. H. Burt, Captain commanding Beale's
brigade.

. . . Resolutions adopted by Bratton's brigade,
South Carolina volunteers, January 30th, 1865.
[Richmond, 1865] 3 p. 24cm.   DLC   *1183*

At head of title: [House] House of representatives,
Feb. 6, 1865. Ordered to be laid on the table and
printed. [Presented by Mr. Simpson.] Signed: John B.
Erwin, chairman; J. C. G. Wardlaw, Secretary.
Caption title.
Crandall 535.

Martin, Vincent F
Story of Brook's battalion. In Stories of the
Confederacy, edited by U. R. Brooks, Colum-
bia, S. C., The State Company, 1912, 313–27.
                    NN   *1184*

Buck, Irving Ashby, 1840–1912.
Cleburne and his command, by Irving A.
Buck, former Captain in A. A. G. Cleburne's
division. New York, Neale pub. co., 1908. xii,
(2), [17]–382 p. front. (port.), plates (1
illus., 5 maps). 22½cm.
                    CSmH DLC   *1185*

—— —— by Capt. Irving A. Buck and Pat
Cleburne. Thomas Robson Hay, editor. Foreword by Bell Irvin Wiley. Jackson, Tenn.,
McCowat-Mercer press, 1959. 378 p. front.
(port.), facsim., illus., maps, ports. 24cm.
                    NN   *1186*

Thomas, Henry Walter, 1842–
History of the Doles-Cook brigade, Army of
Northern Virginia, C.S.A., containing muster
rolls of each company of the Fourth, Twelfth,
Twenty-first and Forty-fourth Georgia regiments, with a short sketch of the services of
each member, and a complete history of each
regiment, by one of its own members, and
other matters of interest, by Henry W. Thomas,

---

* Entries in this section are listed alphabetically by
the most common name of the fighting unit — usually
the name of the commanding officer or in some cases
the state of origin.

Twelfth Georgia regiment. Atlanta, Franklin print. and pub. co., 1903. x, 632 p. plates (1 illus., ports.). 22½cm. DLC NN **1187**
"The author is indebted to Charles Tim Furlow of the Fourth, Charles D. Camp and B. F. Jones of the Twenty-first, and M. V. B. Estes of the Forty-fourth Georgia regiments for their services in writing the histories of their respective regiments."

Chalmers, James Ronald, 1831–1898.
Forrest and his campaigns. *SHSP* VII (1879) 451–86. **1188**

Jordan, Thomas, 1819–1895.
The campaigns of Lieut.-Gen. N. B. Forrest and of Forrest's cavalry, by General Thomas Jordan and J. P. Pryor. New Orleans, Blelock & co., 1868. xv, [17]–704 p. plans, plates (maps, partly fold.; ports.). 22½cm.
CSmH NHi TxU **1189**
"Staff and regimental rosters," [685]–703.

Lytle, Andrew Nelson, 1902–
Bedford Forrest and his critter company, by Andrew Nelson Lytle. New York, Minton, Balch & co., 1931. ix, 402 p. maps, plates (illus., ports.). 24½cm. NN **1190**

Resolutions of Forsberg's brigade, Wharton's division. [1865] 2 p. 24½cm.
CSmH DLC TxU **1191**
Signed: Committee. The four members of the Committee are not identified, only their rank and unit is supplied.
A transmitting document to Hon. F. M. Waller signed: Peter J. Otey.
Not dated.
Caption title.
Crandall 697.

Hagood, Johnson, 1829–1898.
Memoirs of the War of secession, from the original manuscripts of Johnson Hagood. . . . Columbia, State co., 1910. 2 v. (496 p.) illus., maps, fold. map. 24cm.
DLC NN TxU **1192**
Contents: I 1–193, Hagood's 1st 12 months S.C.V.; II 195–496, Hagood's brigade, Editor's Appendix, Index.
Unit rosters: 21st regiment, 398–411; 1st regiment, 411–24; 25th regiment, 424–36; 7th battalion, 436–48; 27th regiment, 448–60; 11th regiment, 460–72.
"Preface" signed: E. R. Brooks, editor.

Minutes of the proceedings of the reunion of Hampton legion survivors, held in Columbia, S. C., on the 21st day of July, A.D. 1875. Charleston, Walker, Evans & Cogswell, printers, 1875. 47 p. 23½cm. CSmH **1193**

Logan, Thomas Muldrup, 1840–1914.
Oration delivered by Gen T. M. Logan at the reunion of the Hampton legion, in Columbia, S. C., 21st July, 1875. . . . Charleston, Walker, Evans & Cogswell, printers, 1875. 28 p. 22½cm. WHi **1194**

Todd, Frederick Porter, 1903–
Hampton legion, South Carolina volunteers, 1861. *MC&H* III (1951) 68–71. col. plate (illus.). **1195**

Wells, Edward Laight, 1839–
Hampton and his cavalry, by Edward L. Wells. Richmond, B. F. Johnson pub. co., 1899. 429, xiv p. illus., ports. 21cm.
CSmH DLC NN TxU **1196**
"Index," xiv p.

Archer, G   W
A few papers of the Army of the Tennessee. *SM* XIII (1873) 194–99, 313–20. **1197**
Based on the headquarters papers of Hardee's corps which had been abandoned in the field.

The old Texas brigade, memorial stone to their heroism erected in the Wilderness. . . . *SHSP* XIX (1891) 122–4. **1198**

Resolutions of the Texas brigade. [1865] 4 p. 24½cm. CSmH DLC TxU **1198A**
Caption title.
Dated: Camp Texas brigade, January 24th, 1865.
Signed: B. S. Fitzgerald, Chairman. Heywood Brahan, Secretary.
Crandall 699.

Chilton, Frank B   1845–
Unveiling and dedication of monument to Hood's Texas brigade on the Capitol grounds at Austin, Texas, Thursday, October twenty-seven, nineteen hundred and ten, and minutes of the thirty-ninth annual reunion of Hood's Texas brigade association held in Senate chamber at Austin, Texas, October twenty-six and twenty-seven, nineteen hundred and ten, together with a short monument and Brigade association history and Confederate scrap book . . . Compiled and published by F. B. Chilton. Houston [Press of Rein & Sons co.] 1911. 372, (1) p. plates (illus., ports.). 28½cm.
Text in double columns. DLC **1199**
Plates accompanied by guard sheets.
"Battle flags of the Confederacy" reproduced in color on heavy gray paper and accompanied by text.
"Insert," additions to roll of survivors, (1) p.

Henderson, Don E
General Hood's brigade, address of Judge Don E. Henderson at the Galveston reunion. . . . *SHSP* XXIX (1901) 297–310. **1200**
Reprinted in *SHSP* XXXV (1907) 185–300.

Henderson, Harry McCorry, 1895–
Hood's Texas brigade. *In his* Texas in the Confederacy, San Antonio, Naylor co., 1955, 1–50. NN **1201**

Hutchison, John Russell, 1807–1878.
The Texas dead of Hood's brigade, battle of Franklin. *In his* Reminiscences, sketches and

addresses, Houston, Tex., E. H. Cushing, 1874, 216–18.   NN   *1202*

Polley, Joseph Benjamin, 1840–
Hood's Texas brigade, its marches, its battles, its achievements, by J. B. Polley. New York, Neale pub. co., 1910. 347 p. plates (1 illus., ports.). 21½cm.
                    CSmH DLC NN   *1203*
     Unit rosters: 1st Texas, 302–15; 4th Texas, 315–31; 5th Texas, 331–47.
     Coulter 375.

Robertson, Jerome Bonaparte, 1815–1890.
Touched with valor, Civil war papers and casualty reports of Hood's Texas brigade, written and collected by General Jerome B. Robertson, Commander of Hood's Texas brigade, 1862–1864. Edited and with a biography of General Robertson, by Colonel Harold B. Simpson. Hillsboro, Hill Junior College press [c1964] xv, 126 p. plates (1 illus., ports.). 24cm.   NcD   *1204*
     Partial contents: Jerome Bonaparte Robertson, soldier, public servant and physician, 1–24; The Civil war papers of General Jerome B. Robertson, 25–66; Casualty lists of the Texas regiments of Hood's Texas brigade, 67–98.

Winkler, Angelina Virginia (Walton), 1842–
The Confederate capital and Hood's Texas brigade, by Mrs. A. V. Winkler. . . . Austin, Eugene Von Boeckmann, 1894. xvi, 312 p. plates (2 illus., ports.). 23cm.
               CSmH NNC TxU NN   *1205*

. . . Resolutions adopted by Humphrey's Mississippi brigade, Army of Northern Virginia, February 3, 1865. [1865] broadside, 23 x 15cm.
                    DLC GEU TxU   *1206*
     At head of title: House of representatives, Feb. 6, 1865. Ordered to be laid on the table and printed.
     Resolutions signed: R. E. Yarborough, Secretary.
     Crandall 537.

Hodge, George Baird, 1828–1892.
Sketch of the First Kentucky brigade by its Adjutant general, G. B. Hodge. Frankfort, Printed at the Kentucky Yeoman office, 1874. 31 p. 22cm.   CSmH DLC NHi   *1207*

—— —— *LWL* IV (1867/68) 97–104, 177–81, 265–8, 393–401, plate (map).   *1208*

Thompson, Edwin Porter, 1834–
History of the First Kentucky brigade, by Ed. Porter Thompson. Cincinnati, Caxton pub. house, 1868. ix, [13]–931 p. plates (ports.). 24cm.   CSmH DLC   *1209*

—— History of the Orphan brigade, by Ed Porter Thompson. Louisville, Lewis N. Thomp-

son, 1898. 1104 p. col. front. (illus.), plates (1 illus., ports.). 24cm. DLC NHi   *1210*

Dickert, D   Augustus
History of Kershaw's brigade, with complete roll of companies, biographical sketches, incidents, anecdotes, etc., by D. Augustus Dickert. Introduction by Associate Justice Y. J. Pope. Newberry, Elbert H. Aull co., 1899. 583, 5, 2 p. plates (ports.). 23cm.
                    CSmH DLC NN   *1211*
     Unit rosters: 2nd, 3rd, 7th, 8th South Carolina regiments; 3rd battalion (James); and 20th South Carolina regiment, p. 545–83.
     "Index," 5 p.
     "Errata," 2 p.
     Coulter 126.

Elliott, Charles Grice, 1840–
Kirkland's brigade, Hoke's division, 1864–'65, *SHSP* XXIII (1895) 165–74.   *1212*

Lane, James Henry, 1833–1907.
History of Lane's North Carolina brigade. *SHSP* VII (1879) 513–22; VIII (1880) 1–8, 67–76, 97–104, 145–54, 193–202, 241–8, 396–403, 489–96; IX (1881) 29–35, 71–3, 124–9, 145–56, 241–6, 353–61, 489–96; X (1882) 57–9, 206–13, 241–8.   *1213*

McDonald, William Naylor, 1834–1898.
A history of the Laurel brigade, originally the Ashby cavalry of the Army of Northern Virginia and Chew's battery, by the late Captain William N. McDonald, Ordnance officer of the Brigade, edited by Bushrod C. Washington. Published by Mrs. Kate S. Macdonald. [Baltimore, Sun job print. office] 1907. 499 p. plates (illus., ports.). 23cm.
                         DLC NN   *1214*
     Unit rosters: 7th Va. cavalry, [382]–419; 11th Va. cavalry, [420]–49; 12th Va. cavalry, [450]–79; 35th Va. cavalry, [480]–95; Chew's battery, [496]–9.

Resolutions of Lewis' brigade. [n.p.] 1865. 2 p. 25cm.   DLC   *1215*
     Caption title.
     Dated: Camp Lewis' Ky. brigade, Green's Cut, Ga., Feb. 11, 1865.
     Signed: Lt. Col George W. Connor, Chairman.
     Crandall 1612.

Schenck, Martin, 1912–
Up came Hill, the story of the Light division and its leaders, by Martin Schenck. Harrisburg, Stackpole co. [1958] vi, (1), 344 p. maps, plates (ports.). 23cm.
                         DLC NN   *1216*

Alexander, Edward Porter, 1835–1910.
Longstreet's brigade. *SHST* II (1875) 53–62.   *1217*

—— —— Letter from General Early. *SHST*, II (1875) 71–4.   *1218*

Moore, Alison
The Louisiana Tigers; or, the two Louisiana brigades of the Army of Northern Virginia, 1861–1865, by Alison Moore. Baton Rouge, Ortlieb press, 1961. 183 p. fold. map, illus., ports. 23cm.   TxU   *1219*
Typed "errata" sheet included in TxU's copy.

Resolutions adopted by McGowan's brigade, South Carolina volunteers. [1865] broadside, 22½ x 15cm.   CSmH   *1220*
At head of title: House of representatives, Feb. 6, 1865.– Ordered to be laid on the table and printed. [Presented by Mr. Simpson]
    Caption title.
    Crandall 538

Caldwell, James Fitz James, 1837–
The history of a Brigade of South Carolinians, known first as "Gregg's," and subsequently as "McGowan's brigade," by J. F. J. Caldwell, lately an officer of the First regiment. Philadelphia, King & Baird, printers, 1866. 247, (1) p. 19½cm.
                    CSmH DLC NHi NN   *1221*
"Addenda, casualties among officers," (1) p.
Coulter 67.

Dunlop, William S
. . . Lee's sharpshooters; or, the forefront of battle, a story of Southern valor that never has been told [by] Major W. S. Dunlop. Little Rock, Tunnah & Pittard, printers, 1899. 488 p. front. (port.). 20½cm.
                    CSmH DLC NN   *1222*
"A story of Mississippi sharpshooters, by their commander, Capt. Robert F. Ward, interpolated by an exhaustive description of the battles of the Wilderness and Spottsylvania Court House by the correspondent of the London Morning herald," [359]–475.

Second re-union of Mahone's brigade, held on the anniversary of the battle of the Crater, in the Opera house, Norfolk, July 31, 1876. (Report of the Norfolk Landmark.) Printed on resolution of Adjutant W. A. S. Taylor. Norfolk, Printed at the Landmark office, 1876. 13 p. 22cm.   CSmH OMC   *1223*
Text in double columns.

Laughton, John E
The sharpshooters of Mahone's brigade, some account of this gallant organization. . . .
SHSP xxii (1894) 98–105.   *1224*

Elliott, Charles Grice, 1840–
Martin's brigade, of Hoke's division, 1863–64. *SHSP* xxiii (1895) 189–98.   *1225*

Dinkins, James, 1845–1939.
Griffith-Barksdale-Humphrey Mississippi brigade and its campaigns *SHSP* xxxii (1904) 250–74.   *1226*

McCaleb, E   Howard
Featherstone-Posey-Harris Mississippi brigade, by Captain E. Howard McCaleb. *SHSP* xxxii (1904) 329–37.   *1227*

Bevier, Robert S
History of the First and Second Missouri Confederate brigades, 1861–1865, and from Wakarusa to Appomattox, a military anagraph, by R. S. Bevier. St. Louis, Bryan, Brand & co., 1879. xii, [13]–480, 27 p. 4 plates (ports.). 21½cm.   CSmH DLC NN   *1228*
"List of survivors," 27 p.
Part II. Personal reminiscences, "from Wakarusa to Appomattox," a version of part of his diary of the war, was "published in Ware's valley monthly and several newspapers and is herein gathered together and reproduced without any alterations besides typographical corrections."

Duke, Basil Wilson, 1838–1916.
History of Morgan's cavalry, by Basil W. Duke. Cincinnati, Miami print. and pub. co., 1867. viii, [9]–578 p. front. (port.), maps. 22½cm.   CSmH DLC NN   *1229*

—— —— Edited with an introduction and notes by Cecil Fletcher Holland. Bloomington, Indiana University press [1960] xvii, (1), [9]–595 p. front. (port.), maps. 21cm.
                    NN   *1230*
A photographic reproduction with the addition of the editor's introduction, notes and an index.
"Civil war centennial series."

—— Morgan's cavalry, by Basil W. Duke. New York, Neale pub. co., 1906. x, [11]–441 p. plates (maps, ports.). 22½cm.
                    CSmH DLC NN   *1230A*

—— A romance of Morgan's rough-riders, the raid, the capture, and the escape. *In* Famous adventures and prison escapes of the Civil war, New York, The Century co., 1894. 116–83.   *1231*
NN has copies of the 1898 and 1915 reprintings.

Quisenberry, Anderson Chenault, 1850–1921.
History of Morgan's men. *RKHS* xv (1912) 23–46. 2 plates (ports.).   *1232*

Swiggett, Howard
The Rebel raider, a life of John Hunt Morgan, by Howard Swiggett. Indianapolis, Bobbs-Merrill co. [1934] 341 p. plates (facsims., illus., ports.). 22½cm.   DLC   *1233*
"Raids of John Hunt Morgan, Rebel raider," map endpaper.

—— —— Garden City, Garden City pub. co. [1937] 341 p. 21½cm.   *1234*
A reprinting which omits the illustrations but includes the endpaper map.

Named Units of the Army, continued

Parsons, W   H
Condensed history of Parsons Texas cavalry brigade, 1861–1865. Together with inside history and heretofore unwritten chapters of the Red river campaign of 1864. By Gen. W. H. Parsons. Corsicana [Sun-light pub. co.,] 1903. 106 p. 22cm.   CSmH   *1235*
Unit roster Texas cavalry: 12th, 41–50; 19th, 50–7; 21st, 58–9; Morgan's battalion, 59–60.
"Inside history . . . Red river campaign of 1864 . . . Washington, D.C." [65]–104 has a separate title page.

Parsons' Texas Brigade Association.
A brief and condensed history of Parson's Texas cavalry brigade, composed of Twelfth, Ninetenth, Twenty-first, Morgan's battalion, and Pratt's battery of artillery of the Confederate states. Together with roster of the several commands, as far as obtainable, some historical sketches, General orders and a memoranda of Parson's brigade association. Waxahachie, J. M. Fleming, printer, 1892. 96 p. 21cm.
Unit rosters, 48–92.   Tx   *1236*

———— ———— Waco, W. M. Morrison, 1962. 96 folios. 27½cm.   TxU   *1236A*
Mimeographed.
"Only 100 copies were run."

Report of the proceedings of Ross' Texas brigade association, at its sixth annual reunion, held in the city of Greenville, Texas, in conjunction with Ector's and Granbury's brigades, Maxey's brigade, Eleventh Texas, and many unattached ex-Confederates, Wednesday and Thursday, Aug. 5 and 6, 1885. Dallas, Carter & Gibson print. co., 1886. 57 p. 14 x 22cm.
                                                         TxU   *1237*
Rose, Victor M   –1893.
Ross' Texas brigade, being a narrative of events connected with its service in the late war between the States, by Victor M. Rose. . . . Louisville, Printed at the Courier-Journal book and job rooms, 1881. 185 p. plates (ports.). 20½cm.   CSmH DLC NN   *1238*
Coulter 398.

———— ———— Kenesaw, Ga., 1960. 185 p. plates (ports.). 22cm.   NcD   *1239*
A photographic reprinting.

Davis, Edwin Adams, 1904–
Fallen guidon, the forgotten saga of General Jo Shelby's Confederate command, the brigade that never surrendered, and its expedition to Mexico, by Edwin Adams Davis. Sante Fe, Stagecoach press, 1962. xiii, 173, (2) p. front. (port.), illus., 2 maps, port. 23½cm.
                                                         NN   *1240*

Hall, Martin Hardwick
The formation of Sibley's brigade and the march to New Mexico. *SWHQ* LXI (1957/58) 383–405. map.   *1241*

Harris, Gertrude
A tale of men who knew not fear. Dedicated to the memory of the brave men who went with Sibley's brigade and to the lonely trench graves in New Mexico where Texas boys lie buried. By Gertrude Harris. [San Antonio, Alamo print. co., 1935] 97, (2) p. illus., port. 22½cm.   NcD NN TxU   *1242*
Cover title adds: Sibley's campaign of 1862 and Robert E. Lee in Texas.
"Notes," (2) p.

A message from the Army of the valley of Virginia. [1865] broadside, 23 x 15½cm.
                                    CSmH DLC GEU RP   *1243*
Caption title.
Dated: Camp of Smith's brigade, Feb. 10, 1865.
Crandall 698.

Robertson, James Irvin, 1930–
The Stonewall brigade [by] James I. Robertson, Jr. Baton Rouge, Louisiana State University press [c1963] xiii, 271 p. plates (illus., ports.). 23½cm.   NN   *1244*

Blessington, Joseph Palmer, 1841–1918.
The campaigns of Walker's Texas division, by a private soldier, containing a complete record of the campaigns in Texas, Louisiana and Arkansas, the skirmish at Perkins' landing and the battles of Milliken's bend, bayou Bourbeux, Mansfield, Pleasant hill, Jenkins' ferry &c, including the Federal's report of the battles, names of the officers of the Division, diary of marches, camp scenery, anecdotes, description of the country through which the Division marched, &c . . . Published for the author. New York, Lange, Little & co., 1875. 314 p. 23cm.   CSmH DLC NN   *1245*
Acknowledgement, p. 312, signed: J. P. Blessington.
Coulter 41.

———— . . . The campaigns of Walker's Texas division. Bresada reprint series [XIII] Introduction by Alwyn Barr. Austin, Pemberton press, 1968. 314, (14) p. front. (port.). 22½cm.
                                                                  1246
A photographic reprinting with new material, the "Introduction" and "Index" (14) p.
At head of title: J. P. Blessington.

Henderson, Harry McCorry, 1895–
Walker's Texas division. *In his* Texas in the Confederacy, San Antonio, Naylor co., 1955, 51–68.   NN   *1247*

Gen. E. C. Walthall's Mississippi brigade. [Memphis?, 1901] 12 p. port. on cover. 23cm.
Title from cover.   MsHa   **1248**
Presentation of the Brigade flag to the survivors.

Smith, Edward A
Records of Walthall's brigade of Mississippians, compiled by Rev. E. A. Smith, Company A, 29th Miss. Brewton, Ala., 1904. 89, (1) p. 22cm.   CSmH DLC MsHa   **1249**
Officers' roster and list of survivors, 14–65.
"Errata," (1) p. "Errata additional," inserted slip.

Sykes, Edward Turner
Walthall's brigade, a cursory sketch with personal experiences of Walthall's brigade, Army of Tennessee, C.S.A., 1862–1865, by E. T. Sykes, late Adjutant-General Walthall's brigade. *PMHS* Centennary series, ɪ (1916) 477–623. plate (port.).   NN   **1250**

Dodson, William Carey, 1846–
Campaigns of Wheeler and his cavalry, 1862–1865, from material furnished by Gen. Joseph Wheeler, to which is added his concise and graphic account of the Santiago campaign of 1898. Published under the auspices of Wheeler's Confederate cavalry association and edited by W. C. Dodson. Atlanta, Hudgins pub. co., 1899. xxiv, 431, vi, 78 p. plates (illus., ports.). 24½cm.
               DLC GEU NHi   **1251**
"The Santiago campaign of Major-General Joseph Wheeler," vi, 78 p.

Resolutions of Wise's brigade. [1865] 3 p. 25cm.   CSmH DLC   **1252**
Caption title.
Dated: Headquarters Wise's brigade, trenches near Petersburg, Va., February 1st, 1865.
Crandall 2377

Wise, Henry Alexander, 1806–1876.
The career of Wise's brigade, 1861–5, an address delivered by General Henry A. Wise, near Cappahoosic, Gloucester county, Virginia, about 1870. *SHSP* xxv (1897) 1–22.   **1253**

UNION ARMY

ARMY OF THE CUMBERLAND

Legends of the Army of the Cumberland. Washington, Govt. print. office, 1869. 45 p. fold. map. 28cm.   NB   *1254*

Bickham, William Denison, 1827–1894.
Rosecran's campaign with the Fourteenth army corps; or, the Army of the Cumberland. A narrative of personal observations, with an appendix consisting of official reports of the battle of Stone river, by "W. D. B.," correspondent of the Cincinnati commercial. Cincinnati, Moore, Wilstach, Keys & co., 1863. viii, 9–476 p. front. (map). 18cm.
                               CSmH NN   *1255*

Cist, Henry Martyn, 1839–1902.
. . . The army of the Cumberland, by Henry M. Cist. New York, Charles Scribner's Sons, 1882. viii, (1), 289 p. maps, fold. map. 18½cm.   NN   *1256*
At head of title: Campaigns of the Civil war — VII. See Title 1362.

Fitch, John
Annals of the Army of the Cumberland, comprising biographies, descriptions of departments, accounts of expeditions, skirmishes, and battles. Also its police record of spies, smugglers, and prominent Rebel emissaries. Together with anecdotes, incidents, poetry, reminiscences, etc., and official reports of the battle of Stone river. By an officer. Philadelphia, J. B. Lippincott & co., 1863. 671 p. plates (illus., double map, ports.). 24cm.   NN   *1257*

—— —— By John Fitch. Fifth edition. Philadelphia, J. B. Lippincott & co., 1864. 716 p. plates (illus., 2 double maps, ports.). 24cm.
                                      NN   *1258*
A reprinting with additional text, p. 451–82 and 704–16, which also appeared as a separate publication.

Ruger, Edward
Legend of the operations of the Army of the Cumberland, during the War of the rebellion . . . With an Appendix. Louisville, Govt. print. office, 1868. 48, 192 p. 2 plates, 1 fold.; charts. 21cm.   DLC   *1259*
"Appendix," 192 p., 306 numbered "Document(s)" relating to the Army of the Cumberland.
Transmission note to Head-quarters Department of the Cumberland, Topographical engineer office signed: Edward Ruger, Supt. Topog'l engineer office. "Compiled by me, in connection with, and as explanatory of the series of maps designed to illustrate the operations of the Army of the Cumberland."

Society of the Army of the Cumberland.
. . . Reunion. 1868–1922. plates (illus., ports.). 23½cm.   CSmH DLC NN   *1260*

CSmH Nos. 1–33, 35–47.   DLC Nos. 1–49. NN Nos. 1–30, 32.
Two meetings were held in 1868, February and December. For the report of the December meeting, see the Army reunion. No meetings were held in 1877–1878, 1886, 1915 and 1918. Though the 1915 meeting was not held, it was numbered 43. The 44/45 (1916–17) and 46/47 (1919–20) meetings were published in combined volumes.

Van Horne, Thomas Budd
History of the Army of the Cumberland, its organization, campaigns, and battles, written at the request of Major-General George H. Thomas, chiefly from his private military journal and official and other documents, by Thomas B. Van Horne. Illustrated with campaign and battle maps, compiled by Edward Ruger. Cincinnati, Robert Clarke & co., 1875. 2 v. 23½cm.   CSmH DLC   *1261*

—— —— [Atlas] Cincinnati, Robert Clarke & co., 1875. 22 maps, partly fold. 24cm.
                                      NjJ   *1262*

—— —— Illustrated with a map of all its campaigns, compiled by Edward Ruger. Cincinnati, Robert Clarke & co., 1876. 2 v. fold. map. 24cm.   CSmH NHi   *1263*
"Block houses, etc., the Engineer service in the Army of the Cumberland, by Brevet-Colonel W. E. Merrill," illus., II 439–58.
At head of title: Popular edition.

ARMY OF THE JAMES

A visit to General Butler and the Army of the James. *Fraser's magazine* LXXI (1865) 434–48.   *1264*
"Part the first."

Butler, Benjamin Franklin, 1818–1893.
[Address to the Army of the James, October 11, 1864] 16 p. 19½cm.   DLC   *1265*
Captioned: Head quarters, Department of Virginia and North Carolina, Army of the James. Before Richmond, Oct. 11th, 1864.
A review of operations.

—— [Address to the Army of the James, January 8, 1865] 2 p. 19½cm.   DLC   *1266*
Captioned: Head quarters. Department of Virginia and North Carolina, Army of the James, Jan. 8th, 1865.
Text in two sections captioned respectively: Soldiers of the Army of the James!; To the colored troops of the Army of the James.

Society of the Army of the James.
Report of the proceedings of the . . . at the . . . triennial reunion . . . :

Boston, September 2, 1868. 56 p.
                       CSmH TxU MWA NN   *1267*

New York, July 19, 1871. 93, (1) p.
    CSmH TxU MWA   **1268**

New York, October 21, 1874. 83, (1) p.
    CSmH NN TxU MWA   **1269**

ARMY OF THE OHIO

United States. Army.
    Extract from consolidated tri-monthly report of the Department of the Ohio, commanded by Major-General A. E. Burnside, November 30, 1863. [Washington, D.C., 1879] broadside, 21 x 68½cm.   CSmH   **1270**

—— Organization of the Army of the Ohio, October 8, 1862. [Washington, D.C., 1882] 6 p. 23½cm.   CSmH   **1271**

    Text signed: R. C. Drum, Adjutant general, Adjutant general's office, Washington, November 18, 1882.

ARMY OF THE POTOMAC

Barnard, John Gross, 1815–1882.
    Report of the engineer and artillery operations of the Army of the Potomac, from its organization to the close of the Peninsular campaign, by Brig.-Gen. J. G. Barnard, and Brig.-Gen. W. F. Barry. New York, D. Van Nostrand, 1863. 230 p. col. front. (illus.), 18 partly fold. plates (illus., maps, plans). 24cm.
    NN   **1272**

Cochrane, John, 1813–1898.
    The Army of the Potomac, a paper read by General John Cochrane. *MOLLUS-NY* I 54–7.
    1273

French, Samuel Livingston
    The Army of the Potomac, from 1861 to 1863, an inside view of the history of the Army of the Potomac and its leaders as told in the official despatches, reports and secret correspondence, from the date of organization under General George B. McClellan in 1861, until the supersedure of General Hooker, and the assignment of General Meade to its command in 1863. By Samuel Livingston French. New York, Publishing Society, 1906. 375 p. map, plates (ports.). 23½cm.
    CSmH DLC NN   **1274**

Hassler, Warren W   1926–
    Commanders of the Army of the Potomac [by] Warren W. Hassler, Jr. Baton Rouge, Louisiana State University press [c1962] xxi, 281 p. maps, plates (1 illus., ports.). 23½cm.
    TxU   **1275**

Hay, Thomas Robson
    President Lincoln and the Army of the Potomac. *GHQ* x (1926) 277–301.   **1276**

McClellan, George Brinton, 1826–1885.
    [Farewell message to the Army of the Potomac] broadside, 17½ x 14cm.
    CSmH   **1277**
    Dated: Camp near Rectortown, Va., Nov. 7, 1862.

Society of the Army of the Potomac.
    Reunion of the. . . . New York, 1870–1927. plates (illus., ports.). 23/24cm.
    CSmH DLC NN   **1278**
    CSmH Nos. 1–43. DLC Nos. 1–46. NN Nos. 1–3, 5, 8–30, 32–43.
    Title varies: Nos. 1–7 (1869–1876) Record of proceedings at the . . . annual re-union; Nos. 8–41 (1877–1913) Report of the . . . annual re-union.
    No meetings were held in 1875, 1906, 1909, 1912, 1914, 1917–1921, 1923, 1925–1926. A business meeting was held in 1875 and reported in the 1874 Record.
    The reunions of 1915–1916 included the Military order of the Medal of honor.
    Volumes through 1904 are not illustrated.

Stine, James Henry
    History of the Army of the Potomac, by J. H. Stine, Historian of the First army corps. Philadelphia, J. B. Rodgers print. co., 1892. xiii, 751 p. plates (ports.). 24½cm.
    CSmH DLC NHi   **1279**

Swinton, William, 1833–1892.
    Campaigns of the Army of the Potomac, a critical history of operations in Virginia, Maryland and Pennsylvania, from the commencement to the close of the war, 1861–5, by William Swinton. New York, Charles B. Richardson, 1866. 640 p. maps, plates (maps, ports.). 22½cm.   CSmH DLC NN   **1280**

—— —— Revision and re-issue. New York, Charles Scribner's Sons, 1882. 660 p. maps, plates (maps, ports.). 24cm.
    DLC NNC   **1281**
    "Appendix, additional notes," 625–44.
    The "index" of the first printing, 624–40, has been placed after the Appendix and is paged 645–60.

United States. Army.
    The "battle order" of the Army of the Potomac. General order no. 10, Headquarters Army of the Potomac, March 7, 1865. This Order contains the names of two hundred and sixty-three regiments, and the names of battles each regiment is entitled to bear on its colors. Published by the First Maine cavalry association. . . . Rockland [1887] p. [695]–716. 22½cm.   DLC   **1282**
    Title from cover.
    Reprinted from History of the First Maine cavalry, by E. P. Tobie, 1887.

—— Consolidated morning report of the Army of the Potomac (commanded by . . .). [Washington, D.C., 1878–79] 8 broadsides, 21½ x 69cm.   CSmH   **1283**

Army of the Potomac, continued

Major-General Joseph Hooker: April 30, May 10,
June 10, 20, 1863.
Major-General George G. Meade: June 30, July 10,
20, 31, 1863.

—— . . . Composition and effective strength
of the Army of the Potomac at the several
dates specified. [Washington, Adjutant Gen-
eral's office, 1882] 2 p. 23½cm.
                                       CSmH   *1284*
At head of title: <Memorandum>.
Caption title.
March 31, 1862; April 30, 1863; April 30, 1864.
Department of the Rappahannock, April 30, 1862.

—— Organization of the Union forces operating against Richmond, Va., on December 31,
1864, and general summary of casualties during November and December, 1864. [Wash-
ington, War Records office, 1888] 20 p. 22½cm.
                                       CSmH   *1285*

ARMY OF THE SHENANDOAH

Sheridan, Philip Henry, 1831–1888.
Report of operations of the Army of the
Shenandoah, Major General P. H. Sheridan,
commanding, from August 4th, 1864, to February 27th, 1865. [New Orleans, 1866] 27,
(2) p. fold. table. 20½cm.   CSmH   *1286*
Dated: New Orleans, February 3, 1866.
"Grant's order to General D. Hunter, dated Aug 5,
1862; List of casualties" — (2) p.

—— Report of operations of the 1st and 3d
divisions cavalry, Army of the Shenandoah,
Major General P. H. Sheridan, commanding,
from February 27th to March 28th, 1865.
[New Orleans, 1865] 10 p. fold. table. 20½cm.
                                       CSmH   *1287*
Dated: New Orleans, La., July 16, 1865.

ARMY OF THE TENNESSEE

First reunion of the survivors of the Army of
the Tennessee and its four corps. Report of
proceedings, rosters, etc. Washington, D.C.
[Logansport, Press of Wilson, Humphrey & co.]
1892. 214 p. ports. 22½cm.   NB NN   *1288*

Horn, Stanley Fitzgerald, 1889–
The army of the Tennessee, a military his-
tory, by Stanley F. Horn. Indianapolis, Bobbs-
Merrill co. [1941] xiii, 15–503 p. plans, plates
(facsims., illus., ports.). 24½cm.
                                       DLC NN   *1289*
Society of the Army of the Tennessee.
Report of the . . . reunion(s) of the . . .
1866–1922. plates, partly col. (illus., ports.).
24cm.   CSmH NN   *1290*
CSmH Nos. 1–45. NN Nos. 1–43.
Nos. 1–4 (1866–1869) have title: Report of the
proceedings of the. . . .

The first meeting is not numbered. Combined volumes: 34/35 (1903, 05), 39/41 (1909–11), 42/43
(1912, 14), 44–45 (1916, 1922). No meetings were
held in 1870, 1890, 1902, 1904, 1913, 1917–1921.
A business meeting was held in 1921 and reported in
the volume of 1916–22.

—— Reunions of . . . Cincinnati, 1877–93. 6 v.
24cm.   CSmH   *1291*
Title from spine.
A reprinting of the annual proceedings: I/V, VI/X,
XI/XIII, XIV/XVI, XVII–XX. Each meeting has its
own title page but each volume is paged continuously.
In the earlier volumes the type has been reset but in
the later volumes the type of the annual volumes has
been used.

United States. Army.
Abstract from returns of the Dept. of the
Tennessee (Major-General U. S. Grant, com-
manding), from April 30 to July 31, 1863.
[Washington, War Records office, 1885] 8 p.
23cm.   CSmH   *1292*

—— Consolidated statement of prisoners of
war captured and paroled, and of prisoners of
war captured and sent North, by the Army of
the Tennessee (Major-General U. S. Grant
commanding) during the month of July, 1863.
[Washington, War Records office, 1885] 3 p.
23cm.   CSmH   *1293*

—— Memorandum of staff officers in the Army
of the Tennessee for February, 1864. [Wash-
ington, D.C., 1882] 10 p. 23cm.
                                       CSmH   *1295*

—— Organization of the Army of the Tennes-
see (Major-General U. S. Grant, commanding)
January 31, 1863. [Washington, War Records
Bureau, 1885] 12 p. 23cm.   CSmH   *1296*

—— Organization of the Dept. of the Tennessee (Major-General U. S. Grant, commanding), April 30, 1865. [Washington, War Records office, 1885] 15 p. 23cm. CSmH   *1297*

ARMY OF VIRGINIA

United States. Army.
Northern Virginia campaign. Organization
of the Army of Virginia during the operations
from the Rapidan to Centreville, Va., August
16 to 31, 1862. [Washington, Adjutant General's office, 1882] 6 p. 23½cm.
                                       CSmH   *1298*

ARMY OF WEST VIRGINIA

Proceedings of the . . . annual reunion of
the . . .

September 22–23, 1870; October 19–20,
1871; September 19, 1879. 56 p.
                                       DLC PHi   *1299*

September 22–23, 1880. 60 p.
           CSmH ICN   **1300**

1883 was not published.

September 2–4, 1884. 56 p. CSmH   **1301**

September 16–18, 1885. 121 p.
           CSmH   **1302**

September 7–10, 1886. 163 p.
           CSmH MWA RPB   **1303**

August 23–26, 1887. 112 p.
           Private Collection   **1304**

September 12–13, 1888. 78 p. OHi   **1305**

September 4–5, 1889. 44 p.   OHi   **1306**

I CORPS

Reunion of the Association of the First army corps.
Washington, D.C., May 16, 1883. [4] p. 23cm.   CSmH   **1307**

Brooklyn, June 11, 1884. 4, (1) p. 23cm.
           CSmH   **1308**

Baltimore, May 6, 1885. 9, (1) p. 23cm.
           CSmH   **1309**

II CORPS

Walker, Francis Amasa, 1840–1897.
General Gibbon in the Second corps. *MOLLUS-NY* 302–15.   **1310**

——— History of the Second army corps in the Army of the Potomac, by Francis A. Walker. New York, Charles Scribner's Sons, 1886. xiv, 737 p. plans, plates (fold. maps, ports.). 22cm.
           CSmH NHi   **1311**

——— ——— Second edition. New York, Charles Scribner's Sons, 1891. xx, 737 p. maps and plans, plates (fold. maps, ports.). 21cm.
           DLC   **1312**

III CORPS

Benjamin, Charles Frederick, 1842–1915.
Historical sketch of the Third army corps, a souvenir from the survivors at Washington to their visiting comrades at the thirty-sixth national encampment of the Grand army of the Republic. Washington, D.C., Published at Corps Headquarters, Camp Roosevelt, 1902. 12 p. 17 x 10½cm.   DLC   **1313**
"By Charles F. Benjamin," ms. note in DLC's copy, a gift from the author, November 19, 1902.

De Peyster, John Watts, 1821–1907.
. . . . The anniversary address delivered before the Third army corps union, 5th May,

1875, the glorious old fighting Third corps, as we understand it, by Maj.-Gen. John Watts De Peyster. New York, Atlantic pub. co. [1875] 36 p. 28cm.   CSmH NB   **1314**
Title and imprint from cover.

——— The last ten days of service of the old Third corps ("as we understand it") with the Army of the Potomac. Address delivered after the anniversary dinner of the Third corps union, 5th May, 1887, at the hotel Windsor, New York [New York, 1887]. 16 p. 23½cm.
           CSmH NN   **1315**
Caption title: Text signed: J. Watts De Peyster.

Shreve, William Price
The story of the Third army corps union, compiled from the original records, by William P. Shreve. Privately printed. Boston [Hooper print. co.] 1910. 96 p. front. (port.). 22½cm.
           CSmH DLC NHi   **1316**

Stevenson, James
History of the Excelsior or Sickles' brigade, by Jas. Stevenson. Peterson, N. J., Derhoven & Holmes, printers, 1863. 40 p. 22cm.
           CSmH DLC   **1317**

Third Army Corps Union.
Constitution and by-laws of the . . . with amendments and alterations made since the war. And the Secretary's and Treasurer's report, for the year ending May 5th, 1867. . . . Trenton, Murphy & Bechtel, printers, 1867. 24 p. 13cm.   DLC   **1318**

——— Constitution of the . . . revised and adopted at the annual meeting held at Portland, Maine, in 1896. Also, roster of members, revised to March, 1897. Boston, Printed by Wallace Spooner, 1897. 57 p. 16½cm.
           DLC   **1319**

——— Reports of Secretary and Treasurer of the . . . with constitution, by-laws, and a list of members of the Association, May 5th, 1880. Trenton, MacCrellish & Quigley, printers, 1880. 32 p. 23cm.   CSmH   **1320**

——— Roll of the Third corps union. [Princeton, 1873] 17 p. 22½cm.   NHi   **1321**
Title from cover.

IV CORPS

The Fourth army corps. *United States service magazine* v (1866).   **1322**
Contents: From the Chickamauga to the Chattahoochie, 396–410; From Atlanta to Nashville, 491–502.

Keyes, Erasmus Darwin, 1810–1895.
[Correspondence in relation to the service of the Fourth corps, Army of the Potomac. New York, 1877] 7 p. 23cm.   CSmH   **1323**

IV Corps, continued

Letter of General Keyes dated December 24, 1877, to Colonel Charles C. Suydam, and his reply dated December 29, 1877.

V CORPS

Proceedings of the Third brigade association, First division, Fifth army corps, Army of the Potomac, held at the time of the national encampment, Grand army of the republic, Washington, D.C., 21 September 1892, together with papers and addresses. New York, Rider and Driver pub. co. [1893] 74 p. plates (illus., map, ports.). 25½cm.   NN   *1324*

—— Indianapolis, Indiana, 6 September 1893, together with papers and addresses. Record no. II. New York, Exchange print. co. [1894] 160, (3) p. plates (illus., map, ports.). 25½cm.
                                          NB   *1325*

P. 142–60, (3) are printed from plates of the Report annual reunion and dinner of the Old guard association Twelfth regiment N.G.S.N.Y.

Report of the proceedings in connection with the monument erected by Maj.-Gen. Daniel Butterfield, at Fredericksburg, Va., in honor of the Fifth corps, Army of the Potomac. . . . [n.p., 1900] 39 p. 3 plates (illus., 2 ports.). 23cm.   NN   *1326*

Powell, William Henry, 1838–1901.
The Fifth army corps (Army of the Potomac), a record of operations during the Civil war in the United States of America, 1861–1865, by William H. Powell. . . . New York, G. P. Putnam's Sons, 1896. xi, 900 p. plates (maps and plans, partly fold.; ports.). 24½cm.
                                   CSmH DLC   *1327*

VI CORPS

Shaler's brigade, survivors of the Sixth corps, re-union and monument dedications at Gettysburg, June 12th, 13th and 14th, 1888. . . . [Philadelphia, W. W. Mayberry, printer] 1888. 179, (1) p. front. (port.), illus. 22cm.
                                    CSmH NHi   *1328*

Hyde, Thomas Worcester, 1841–1899.
Following the Greek cross; or, memories of the Sixth army corps, by Thomas W. Hyde. Boston, Houghton, Mifflin and co., 1894. xi, 269 p. plates (ports.). 18½cm.
                                 CSmH DLC NN   *1329*

McMahon, Martin Thomas, 1838–1906.
The Sixth army corps. *United States service magazine* v (1866).   *1330*

Contents: From Yorktown to Gettysburg, 204–14; From Gettysburg to the end, 289–300.

Society of the Sixth Army Corps.
Constitution and bye-laws of the . . . together with its organization. 1869. 8, (1) p. 20½cm.   CSmH   *1331*

"Erratum.-Bye-laws," (1) p.

—— Third annual report of the . . . with the proceedings of the meeting in Philadelphia, Pa., April 8th, 1870. New York, 1871. 5 p. 20cm.   CSmH   *1332*

Title from cover.

—— . . . Fourth [-fifth] annual report. Proceedings of the fourth annual reunion, Boston, Mass., May 12th, 1871, and fifth annual reunion, Cleveland, Ohio, May 7th, 1872. New York, Slote & James, 1873. 19 p. 22½cm.
Title from cover.   CSmH   *1333*
Each annual report has its own title page.

—— . . . Sixth annual report. Proceedings of the sixth annual reunion, New Haven, Ct., May 14, 1873 . . . and eighth annual reunion, Philadelphia, June 6, 1876. New York, De Lacy & Willson, printers, 1877. 32 p. 22½cm.
Title from cover.   CSmH   *1334*

—— . . . Seventh report. Proceedings of the ninth annual reunion, Providence, R. I., June 27th, 1877 . . . eleventh annual reunion, Albany, N. Y., June 18th, 1879. New York, De Lacy & Willson, printers, 1880. 32 p. 22½cm.
Title from cover.   CSmH   *1335*

—— . . . Eighth report. Proceedings of the twelfth annual reunion, Burlington, Vt., June 16th, 1880 . . . twenty-first annual reunion, Orange, N. J., June 12th & 13th, 1889. 56 p. 21cm.   NB NjJ   *1336*
Title from cover.

IX CORPS

Proceedings of the reunion of the Third division, Ninth corps, Army of the Potomac, held at York, Pa., March 25, 1891. Harrisburg, Harrisburg pub. co., 1892. 137 p. plates (ports.). 24cm.   DLC NB   *1337*

On cover: History of the Third division, Ninth corps, Army of the Potomac.

Embick, Milton A
Military history of the Third division, Ninth corps, Army of the Potomac. With a record of the Division association, organized Harrisburg, March 25, 1890, and dedication of equestrian statue to General John F. Hartranft, Commander Division May 12, 1899, and the dedication of the monuments at Fort Stedman and Mahone on Petersburg battle field, May 19th, 1909, with the addresses delivered there by President Taft and others. Compiled and edited by Milton A. Embick. By authority of

Battlefield commission, July, 1910. [Harrisburg] C. E. Aughinbaugh, Printer to the State, 1913. 100 p. plates (illus., ports.). 22½cm.
CSmH DLC **1338**

United States. Army.
Organization of the Ninth army corps (commanded by Major-General Ambrose E. Burnside). [Washington, D.C., 1882] 4 p. 23½cm.
CSmH **1339**

Woodbury, Augustus, 1825–1895.
Major General Ambrose E. Burnside and the Ninth army corps, a narrative of campaigns in North Carolina, Maryland, Virginia, Ohio, Kentucky, Mississippi and Tennessee, during the War for the preservation of the Union, by Augustus Woodbury. . . . Providence, S. S. Rider & Brother, 1867. vii, 554 p. plates (1 illus., maps, ports.). 23cm.
CSmH DLC **1340**

XII CORPS

. . . 30th anniversary, 1863–1893. Souvenir of the reunion, July 1st to 3rd, 1893, of Greene's brigade, 3rd brigade, 2nd div., 12th corps, the 60th, 78th, 102nd, 137th, and 149th N. Y. vols., who, alone, at Culp's hill, in the 2nd day's battle saved the right at Gettysburg. A brief sketch of the fight. . . . Syracuse, Acme pub. bureau [1893] 15, (2) p. illus., music, ports. 17cm. CSmH **1341**
Title and imprint from cover.
At head of title: (Supplement to the Acme haversack of patriotism and song.)

Greene, George Sears, 1801–1899.
Story of a brigade. *United States service magazine* iv (1865) 301–13. **1342**
XII Corps, 3d brigade, 2d division.

XIV CORPS

Association of survivors regular brigade, Fourteenth corps, Army of the Cumberland. Proceedings of reunions held at: Pittsburgh, Pa., Sept. 11–12, 1894; Crawfish Springs, Ga., Sept. 18–19, 1895; St. Paul, Minn., Sept. 1–2, 1896; Columbus, Ohio, Sept. 22–23, 1897. Historical sketch, by Capt. Frederick Phisterer. Roster of membership and death roll of Brigade during the war. Official reports of the battle of Stone river, Tenn. Columbus, Ohio, Press of John L. Trauger, 1895. 203 p. plates (illus., fold. plan, ports.). 25½cm.
On cover: Historical souvenir. NN **1343**

Re-union of Col. Dan McCook's Third brigade, Second division, Fourteenth A. C., "Army of the Cumberland." Assault of Col. Dan McCook's brigade on Kenesaw mountain, Ga., June 27, 1864. August 27th and 29th, 1900,

room 206, Court house, Chicago, Ill. 142, (2) p. 2 fronts. (fold, map, illus.), ports. 23½cm. DLC OHi **1344**

Dodge, William Sumner
History of the old Second division, Army of the Cumberland. Commanders: M'Cook, Sill, and Johnson. By Wm. Sumner Dodge. Chicago, Church & Goodman, 1864. x, [11]–582, 51 p. plates (fold. maps, ports.). 22cm.
IHi **1345**
A "second edition," 1864, DLC and NN, is a reprinting.
"Appendix. History of the regimental organizations constituting the Second division," 51 p.

XIX CORPS

Cleveland, Mather
New Hampshire infantry regiments in the 19th army corps, Department of the Gulf, 1862–1865. [Concord, 1964] [25] p. (New Hampshire and the Civil war, I 3). **1346**

Irwin, Richard Bache, 1829–1892.
History of the Nineteenth army corps, by Richard B. Irwin. New York, G. P. Putnam's Sons, 1893. vi, (1), 528 p. plates (maps). 25cm. CSmH DLC **1347**

United States. Army.
Organization of the troops in the Department of the Gulf, Nineteenth army corps, (Major-General Nathaniel P. Banks, comdg.), May 31, 1863. [Washington, War Records office, 1885] 6 p. 23½cm. CSmH **1348**

—— Organization of the Department of the Gulf (Major-General Nathaniel P. Banks, comdg.), August 31, 1863. [Washington, D.C., n.d.] 8 p. 23½cm. CSmH **1349**

XX CORPS

White Star Union.
Constitution and by-laws of the. . . . Philadelphia, King & Baird, printers, 1865. 27 p. 12cm. CSmH **1350**
Veterans of the 2nd division, 20th corps.

HOOKER BRIGADE

Hooker Brigade Committee.
Roster of the petitioners to the Massachusetts Legislature of 1904, for correction of errors on the tablet of the Hooker statue. [Boston] Hooker Brigade Committee [1904] 56 p. illus. on cover. 22½cm. NB **1351**
Title and publisher from cover.

—— Report of the hearing before the Committee on the State house on bill to authorize the Governor and Council to recast the Hooker statue tablet and the Hooker Brigade committee's reply to Secretary Olin. . . . [Boston] Hooker Brigade Committee [Alfred Mudge &

Hooker Brigade, continued

Sons, printers, 1904] 38 p. illus., on cover.
22½cm.   NB NN   *1352*
  Title and publisher from cover.

MEAGHER BRIGADE

Garland, John Lewis
  The formation of Meagher's Irish brigade.
Irish sword III (Summer 1958) 162–65. *1353*

SHERMAN BRIGADE

Minutes and register of the . . . annual Sherman brigade reunion. . . . 20cm.

Canton, Ohio, August 13–16, 1889. 23 p.
                          O   *1354*

Mansfield, Ohio, August 19–22, 1890. 24 p.
                          O   *1355*

Campaigns and Battles

Campaigns and Battles
GENERAL REFERENCES

Battle-fields of the South, from Bull run to Fredericksburg, with sketches of the Confederate commanders and gossip of the camps, by an English combatant (Lieutenant of artillery on the field staff). London, Smith, Elder and co., 1863. 2 v. 2 maps, 1 double, 1 fold. 19½cm.

    Dedication signed: T. E. C.   NN   ***1356***
    The author served in a Mississippi regiment in the Virginian campaigns. Interspersed in the narrative are letters from correspondents giving their experiences in Missouri and the Mississippi valley.
    Coulter 20.

—— —— New York, John Bradburn, 1864. xxvii, 517 p. 2 fold. maps. 22½cm.
    NN   ***1357***

Battles and leaders of the Civil war . . . being for the most part contributions by Union and Confederate officers based upon "The Century war series." Edited by Robert Underwood Johnson and Clarence Clough Buel. . . . New York, Century co. [c1887–88] 4 v. illus., maps, ports. 28cm.   DLC NN   ***1358***

—— —— New introduction, by Roy F. Nichols. New York, Thomas Yoseloff [c1956] 4 v. illus., maps, ports. 24cm. DLC   ***1359***
    A photographic reprinting.

—— —— Edited by Ned Bradford. New York, Appleton, Century Crofts [c1956] xiii, 626 p. illus., maps, ports. 26cm.   DLC   ***1360***
    Title on two leaves.
    "This [is a] new one-volume edition."

Battles and leaders of the Civil war. People's pictorial edition, being for the most part contributions by Union and Confederate officers condensed and arranged for popular reading. New York, Century co. [c1894] 324 p. facsims., illus., maps, ports. 28 x 33cm. CSmH   ***1361***
    Published weekly, March 26 to August 6, 1894, in 20 numbered parts.
    Text in four columns and within border lines.

Campaigns of the Civil war. . . . New York, Charles Scribner's Sons, 1882. 13 v.   ***1362***
    Only the titles and authors of individual volumes are supplied below; the full citation (including location) is supplied in the separate entries.
    I The outbreak of the rebellion, by John G. Nicolay. See Title 1407.
    II From Fort Henry to Corinth, by M. F. Force. See Title 2816A.
    III The Peninsula, McClellan's campaign of 1862, by Alexander S. Webb. See Title 1559.
    IV The army under Pope, by John C. Ropes. See Title 1605.
    V The Antietam and Fredericksburg, by Francis W. Palfrey. See Title 1970.
    VI Chancellorsville and Gettysburg, by Abner Doubleday. See Title 1673.

    VII The Army of the Cumberland, by Henry M. Cist. See Title 1256.
    VIII The Mississippi, by Francis V. Greene. See Title 2541.
    IX Atlanta, by Jacob D. Cox. See Title 2697.
    X The march to the sea, Franklin and Nashville, by Jacob D. Cox. See Title 2728.
    XI The Shenandoah valley in 1864, by George E. Pond. See Title 1827.
    XII The Virginia campaign of '64 and '65, the Army of the Potomac and the Army of the James, by Andrew A. Humphreys. See Title 1713.
    Supplementary volume. Statistical record of the armies of the United States, by Frederick Phisterer, 1886. See Title 1116.
    The work was reprinted in 1885 with title: The army in the Civil war . . . "subscription edition."
    The work was reproduced by photo offset in 1959, by Jack Brussel, New York, The Blue & the Gray press, distributors. This reprint does not mention the series title, nor is there a publication date.

The rebellion record, a diary of American events with documents, narratives, illustrative incidents, poetry, etc. Edited by Frank Moore. . . . With an introductory address on the causes of the struggle, and the great issues before the country, by Edward Everett. New York, G. P. Putnam, 1861–63; D. V. Nostrand, 1864–69. 11 v. maps and plans, plates (I–II fold. maps, ports.). 25cm.   CSmH DLC   ***1363***
    Vols I–VIII each contain three divisions, separately paged: I Diary of events; II Documents and narratives; III Poetry, rumors and incidents.
    Vol IX has two divisions, omitting "Diary of events."
    Vols X–XI "Documents" only.
    Published in monthly parts.
    Contents "Diary of events":
    I December 17 1860–June 18 1861.
    II June 19–August 21 1861.
    III August 22–December 1861.
    IV January–April 1862.
    V May–October 9 1862.
    VI October 10 1862–May 1863.
    VII June–October 1863.
    VIII November 1863–April 1864.
    The "Documents" continue through the close of the war.
    Each volume is indexed.

—— Supplement. First volume. New York, G. P. Putnam, 1864. vi, 759, iv p. 2 plans, plates (maps, 1 fold.; ports.). 25cm.
    CSmH DLC   ***1364***
    "Contains important official reports, narratives and state papers, both National and Rebel, which the Editor was unable to obtain for publication in the regular issues."
    Published in parts with title: Companion to the Rebellion record.

Abbot, Willis John, 1863–1934.
    Battle-fields of '61, a narrative of the military operations of the War for the Union up to the end of the Peninsular campaign, by Willis J. Abbot. With illustrations by W. C.

General References, continued

Jackson. New York, Dodd, Mead and co. [c1889] xii, 356 p. illus., maps. 23½cm.

Plates are paged.   CSmH NN   *1365*

—— Battle fields and camp fires, a narrative of the principal military operations of the Civil war, from the removal of McClellan to the accession of Grant (1862–1863), by Willis J. Abbot. Illustrated by W. C. Jackson. New York, Dodd, Mead & co. [c1890] xii, 349 p. illus., maps. 23½cm.

Plates are paged. CSmH DLC NN   *1366*

—— Battle-fields and victory, a narrative of the principal military operations of the Civil war, from the accession of Grant to the command of the Union armies to the end of the war, by Willis J. Abbot. Illustrated by W. C. Jackson. New York, Dodd, Mead and co. [c1891] x, [3]–329 p. illus. 23½cm.

Plates are paged.   CSmH   *1367*

Angle, Paul McClelland, 1900–
Tragic years, 1860–1865 . . . a documentary history of the American Civil war, by Paul M. Angle and Earl Schenck Miers. New York, Simon and Schuster, 1960. 2 v. maps and plans. 24cm.   NN   *1368*

Bishop, John Spast, 1834–1915.
A concise history of the war designed to accompany Perrine's new war map of the Southern states with an introduction and statistical appendix, compiled from authentic sources by Capt. John S. Bishop. Indianapolis, Charles O. Perrine [1864] x, 11–32 p., xi p. fold. map. 15cm.   CSmH DLC   *1369*

On cover: Perrine's new topographical map of the Southern states, with a chronology of the great rebellion. . . .

Blythe, Vernon, 1876–
A history of the Civil war in the United States, by Vernon Blythe. . . . New York, Neale pub. co., 1914. 411 p. plates (maps). 21cm.
          TxU   *1370*

Catton, Bruce, 1899–
This hallowed ground, the story of the Union side of the Civil war, by Bruce Catton. Garden City, Doubleday & co., 1956. ix, 437 p. maps. 24cm.   DLC NN   *1371*

"The Western theater" and "The Eastern theater," maps on endpapers.

Coffin, Charles Carleton, 1823–1896.
Drum-beat of the Nation, the first period of the War of the rebellion, from its outbreak to the close of 1862, by Charles Carleton Coffin. New York, Harper & Brothers, 1888. xiv, 478 p. front. (illus.), facsim., illus., maps and plans, ports. 23½cm.   CSmH NN   *1372*

Plates are paged.

—— Freedom triumphant, the fourth period of the War of the rebellion, from September, 1864, to its close, by Charles Carleton Coffin. New York, Harper & Brothers, 1891. xv, 506 p. front. (port.), illus., maps and plans, ports. 23½cm.   CSmH NN   *1373*

Plates are paged.

—— Marching to victory, the second period of the War of the rebellion including the year 1863, by Charles Carleton Coffin. New York, Harper & Brothers, 1889. xv, 491 p. front. (port.), illus., maps and plans, ports. 23½cm.

Plates are paged.   CSmH NN   *1374*

—— Redeeming the Republic, the third period of the War of the rebellion in the year 1864, by Charles Carleton Coffin. New York, Harper & Brothers, 1890. xv, 478 p. front. (illus.), illus., maps and plans, ports. 23½cm.

Plates are paged.   CSmH NN   *1375*

Davis, Burke
Gray, Fox, Robert E. Lee and the Civil war, by Burke Davis. New York, Rinehart & co. [1956] xi, 466 p. maps, 4 plates (illus., ports.). 23½cm.   NcD   *1376*

Deaderick, John Barron, 1886–
Strategy in the Civil war, by Barron Deaderick. . . . Harrisburg, Military Service pub. co., 1946. 200 p. maps and plans, ports. 21½cm.   CSmH NcD   *1377*

"To show how these axioms [of war] were observed, or were disregarded, by Northern and Southern commanders."

"Appendix [biographical] sketches," 155–93.

De Peyster, John Watts, 1821–1907.
. . . The decisive conflicts of the late Civil war, or slaveholders' rebellion, battles morally, territorially, and militarily decisive . . . by J. Watts De Peyster. New York, MacDonald & co., printers, 1867. 2 v. 23cm.
          CSmH DLC NN WHi   *1378*

Title and imprint from cover.

Contents: 1. The Maryland campaign of September, 1862, the battles of the South mountain and of the Antietam. 76 p. Title page adds: First class. Shiloh, or Pittsburgh Landing — Antietam or Sharpsburg — Stone river, or Murfreesborough — Gettysburg — Nashville. Second class. Baltimore, Md. — Rich mountain, W. Va. — Springfield, Mo. — Williamsburgh, Va. — Munfordsville, Ky.

Contents: 3. The Pennsylvania-Maryland campaign of July, 1863. 163 p. Title page adds: Battle of Oak Ridge at Gettysburg, Thursday, Friday, July 2d and 3d, 1863. After Gettysburg and at Williamsport and Falling Water, July 4th to 14th, 1863.

This transcription of the title pages does not include poetical tags.

No. 2 not published.

No. 3. "Three hundred copies printed as manuscript."

CSmH has a 28cm. copy of no. 3.

Dodge, Theodore Ayrault, 1842–1909.

A bird's-eye view of our Civil war, by Theodore Ayrault Dodge. Boston, James R. Osgood and co., 1883. xi, 346 p. plans, fold. maps. 22cm.   DLC NN   *1379*

—— —— New and revised edition. Boston, Houghton, Mifflin and co., 1897. xiii, 348 p. plans, double maps. 20cm.   CSmH   *1380*

"General map of the theatre of war," endpaper. On spine: Student's edition.

Dupuy, Richard Ernest, 1887–

. . . The compact history of the Civil war. With battlefield maps designed by T. N. Dupuy and C. G. Dupuy. New York, Hawthorn Books [1960] 445, (2) p. maps. 23½cm.
                                                      NN   *1381*

At head of title: Colonel Ernest R. Dupuy [and] Colonel Trevor N. Dupuy.
"Area of operations American Civil war," map on endpaper.
"The authors and their book," (2) p.
Title on two leaves.

Eisenschiml, Otto, 1880–

The Civil war . . . by Otto Eisenschiml and Ralph Newman. New York, Grosset & Dunlap [1956] 2 v. I maps and plans; II facsims., illus., ports. 23½cm.   NN   *1382*

Contents: I The American Iliad as told by those who lived it.
II The picture chronicle of the events, leaders and battlefields of the war.

Esposito, Vincent Joseph, 1934–

The West Point Atlas of the Civil war (adapted from the West Point atlas of American wars: volume I). Compiled by the Department of military art and engineering, the United States military academy. Chief editor, Colonel Vincent J. Esposito. New York, Frederick A. Praeger [1962] 154 numbered maps on rectos with text on facing versos. 28 x 36½cm.   *1383*

"Recommended reading list," (4) p.

Evans, Clement Anselm, 1833–1911, editor.

Confederate military history, a library of Confederate states history . . . written by distinguished men of the South, and edited by Gen. Clement A. Evans. Atlanta, Confederate pub. co., 1899. 13 v. plates (illus., maps, partly fold. and double; ports.). 24cm.

Contents: CSmH DLC NN   *1384*

I Legal justification of the South in secession, by J. L. M. Curry, 1–58; The South as a factor in the territorial expansion of the United States, by William R. Garrett, 59–246; The civil history of the Confederate states, by Clement A. Evans, 247–570; Biographical, officers of civil and military organizations, 571–737.
II–XI The States' monographs are analyzed and their collation appears in the individual entries.
XII The Confederate states navy, by Capt. William H. Parker, 1–115; The morale of the Confederate

army, by J. William Jones, 117–93; An outline of Confederate military history, by Clement A. Evans, 195–265; The South since the war, by Stephen D. Lee, 267–368; Documental and statistical appendix, 369–512; General index, 513–51.
XIII Biographies of Confederate soldiers residing in the North.
A photographic reprinting of the standard edition volumes I–XII was published by Thomas Yoseloff, New York, 1962.
The only located copy of XIII is held by CSmH.
The work was issued in two editions, the commonly held standard edition and the scarce extended edition.
Vol I and each state narrative of vol II–X include a "Biographical section." limited to general officers. The extended edition added to each state narrative "Additional sketches illustrating the services of officers and patriotic citizens." For a discussion of the extended edition, see The South to posterity, by Douglas S. Freeman, 1939, 186–7.
The collation of the "Additional sketches . . ." and location of copies:
II Maryland, p. 185–447. DLC NHi West Virginia, p. 139–296. DLC NHi
III Virginia, p. 693–1295. DLC NHi Vi
IV North Carolina, p. 355–813. DLC
V South Carolina, p. 425–931. DLC
VI Georgia, p. 463–1069. GEU NcD
VII Alabama, p. 453–865. GEU NcD Mississippi, p. 279–515. MsAr.
VIII Tennessee, p. 350–487. Collection of Bell I. Wiley
IX Kentucky, p. 259–592. KyU Missouri, p. 227–451. MoHi
X Louisiana, p. 323–631. LU Arkansas, p. 421–605. ArL
XI Texas, p. 269–713. T Florida, p. 213–367. FDU FU FMU

Fiebeger, Gustav Joseph, 1858–1939.

Campaigns of the American Civil war, by G. J. Fiebeger. West Point, United States Military Academy print. office, 1914. 432 p. 23½cm.   DLC   *1385*

—— —— Atlas. [1914] 1 v. 17½ x 25½cm.
Title from cover.   DLC   *1386*
46 maps and plans.
"Principal operations of American Civil war," 7 p.

Fleming, Vivian Minor, 1844–1930.

Campaigns of the Army of Northern Virginia, including the Jackson Valley campaign, 1861–1865, by Vivian Minor Fleming. Richmond, William Byrd press [1928] 167 p. 2 fold. maps. 19½cm.   DLC   *1387*

Foote, Shelby

The Civil war, a narrative, Fort Sumter to Perryville, by Shelby Foote. New York, Random House [1959] 840 p. maps. 25cm.
                                                      NN   *1388*

"Theater of war, 1861–1862"; "Virginia theater, 1861–1862," maps on endpapers.

Foster, Eli Greenawalt

The Civil war by campaigns, by Eli G. Foster. Topeka, Crane & co., 1899. 286 p. maps (3 double). 19½cm.   CSmH DLC   *1389*

General References, continued

Freeman, Douglas Southall, 1886–1953.
Lee's Lieutenants, a study in command, by Douglas Southall Freeman. . . . New York, Charles Scribner's Sons, 1942–44. 3 v. maps and plans, plates (2 fold. maps, ports.). 24cm.
        CSmH DLC *1390*

Geer, Walter, 1857–1937.
Campaigns of the Civil war, by Walter Geer. New York, Brentano's, 1926. xxii, 490 p. maps and plans, plates (maps, partly fold.). 24cm.   DLC Vi *1391*

Greene, Francis Vinton, 1850–1921.
The United States army. *Scribner's magazine* xxx (1901) 286–311, 446–62, 593–613. illus., ports.   *1392*
  Civil war, 593–601.

Holmes, Prescott
The battles of the War for the Union, being the story of the great Civil War from the election of Abraham Lincoln to the surrender at Appomattox, by Prescott Holmes. Philadelphia, Henry Altemus [c1897] front. (port.), illus., ports. 19½cm.   NN *1393*

Hull, Augustus Longstreet
The campaigns of the Confederate army, by Augustus Longstreet Hull. Atlanta, Foote & Davies co., printers, 1901. 107 p. 3 plates (2 maps, 1 fold.; port.). 19½cm.
       CSmH DLC NN *1394*

Jennings, Janet
The Blue and Gray, by Janet Jennings. . . . [Madison, Cantwell print. co., c1910] 204, (1) p. plates (2 illus., ports.). 15½cm.
           Vi *1395*

Johnson, Clifton, 1865–1940.
Battleground adventures, the stories of dwellers on the scenes of conflict in some of the most notable battles of the Civil war. Collected in personal interviews, by Clifton Johnson. Illustrated by Rodney Thomson. Boston, Houghton Mifflin co., 1915. ix, (1), 422 p. plates (illus.). 22cm.   TxU DLC *1396*

Johnson, Edwin Rossiter, 1840–1931.
Campfire and battle-field, history of the conflicts and campaigns of the great Civil war in the United States, by Rossiter Johnson. With special contributions by . . . [6 names] And an introduction by John Clark Ridpath. Sold by subscription only. New York, Knight & Brown [c1894] 551 p. facsims., illus., map, ports. 34cm.   CSmH *1397*
  Text in double columns.

—— The fight for the Republic, a narrative of the more noteworthy events of the War of secession, presenting the great contest in its

dramatic aspects, by Rossiter Johnson. . . . New York, G. P. Putnam's Sons, 1917. xii, 404 p. plates (illus.; maps, partly fold.; ports.). 23½cm.   DLC NN *1398*

Johnston, Joseph Eggleston, 1807–1891.
Narrative of the military operations, directed during the late War between the States, by Joseph E. Johnston. New York, D. Appleton and co., 1874. 602 p. plates (maps, ports.). 24cm.   NN *1399*

—— —— Introduction by Frank E. Vandiver. Bloomington, Indiana University press, 1959. xxxi, 621 p. plates (maps, ports.). 21cm.
  "Civil war centennial series."   NN *1400*

Jones, Archer, 1916–
 . . . Confederate strategy from Shiloh to Vicksburg. Baton Rouge, Louisiana State University press [1961] xxi, 258 p. 3 maps at end. 22½cm.   DLC NN *1401*
  At head of title: Archer Jones.

[Latrobe, John Hazlehurst Boneval] 1803–1891.
Three great battles. Baltimore, Printed (not published) by John D. Toy [1863?] 35 p. 23cm.
          DLC NN *1402*
  Contents: Buena Vista, the Seven days battle, and Gettysburg.
  First article reprinted from *Baltimore American*, January 17, 1849; second from *Germantown telegraph*, October 29, 1862; third from *Baltimore American*, August 6, 1863.

Livermore, William Roscoe, 1843–1919.
The story of the Civil war, a concise account of the war in the United States of America between 1861 and 1865, in continuation of the story by John Codman Ropes, by William Roscoe Livermore. New York, G. P. Putnam's Sons, 1913. 2 v. plates (maps), fold. maps in pocket. 23½cm.   CSmH *1403*
  Contents: III [I and II: See Title 1413] The campaigns of 1863 to July 10th together with the operations on the Mississippi from April, 1862; Book I. Chancellorsville, operations against Vicksburg, etc.; Book II. Vicksburg, Port Hudson, Tullahoma, and Gettysburg.
  "Errata" slip in II.

Mahan, Asa, 1799–1889.
A critical history of the late American war, by A. Mahan. With an introductory letter by Lieut.-General M. W. Smith. New York, A. S. Barnes & co., 1877. viii, 461 p. 22cm.
       CSmH DLC TxU *1404*

Military Historical Society of Massachusetts.
Papers, Boston, 1881–1918. 16 v. [See below] 23–24½cm.   *1405*
  Contents:
  I The Peninsular campaign of General McClellan in 1862. 1881. xvii, (1), 249 p. 3 fold. maps.

I [Second edition] Campaigns in Virginia, 1861–1862. Edited by Theodore F. Dwight. 1895. li, 369 p. 5 fold. maps. "Errata" slip inserted. "A revised and enlarged edition of The Peninsular campaign of General McClellan in 1862." Pages 1–240 of the 1881 edition are pages 59–300 in this edition.

II The Virginia campaign of General Pope in 1862. 1886. xxvi, (1), 394 p. 8 fold. maps.

II [Second edition] The Virginia campaign of 1862 under General Pope. Edited by Theodore F. Dwight. 1895. xxi, 541 p. 8 fold. maps. "A revised and enlarged edition." Pages 1–385 are unchanged from the earlier edition.

III Campaigns in Virginia, Maryland and Pennsylvania, 1862–1863. 1903. 509 p. fold. map.

IV The Wilderness campaign, May–June 1864. 1905. vi, 471 p. 6 fold. maps. "Errata" slip inserted.

V Petersburg, Chancellorsville, Gettysburg. 1906. vi, 442 p. 4 fold. maps.

VI The Shenandoah campaigns of 1862 and 1864 and the Appomattox campaign, 1865, 1907. 518 p. 6 fold. maps.

VII Campaigns in Kentucky and Tennessee, including the battle of Chickamauga, 1862–1864. 1908. vi, 557 p. 9 fold. maps.

VIII The Mississippi valley, Tennessee, Georgia, Alabama, 1861–1864. 1910. vi, 619 p. 8 fold. maps.

IX Operations on the Atlantic coast, 1861–1865, Virginia, 1862, 1864. 1912. vi, 585 p. 13 fold. maps.

X Critical sketches of some of the Federal and Confederate commanders. Edited by Theodore F. Dwight. 1895. x, 348 p.

XI Naval actions and operations against Cuba and Puerto Rico, 1593–1815. 1901. 205 p.

XII Naval actions actions and history, 1799–1898. 1902. 398 p.

XIII Civil and Mexican wars, 1861, 1846. 1913. vi, 660 p. 6 fold. maps. "Erratom" slip inserted.

XIV Civil war and miscellaneous papers. 1918. vi, (2), 474 p. illus., plates (illus., maps, ports.).

Mitchell, Joseph Brady, 1915–
Decisive battles of the Civil war, by Lt. Col. Joseph B. Mitchell. New York, G. P. Putnam's Sons [c1955] 226 p. maps and plans, partly double. 21½cm.   DLC   *1406*

Nicolay, John George, 1832–1901.
. . . The outbreak of rebellion, by John G. Nicolay. New York, Charles G. Scribner's Sons, 1881. vii, (1), 220 p. maps and plans. 18½cm.
                                          NN   *1407*
At head of title: Campaigns of the Civil war — I.
See Title 1362.

Petersen, Frederick A
A military review of the campaign in Virginia & Maryland, under General John C. Fremont, N. P. Banks, Irwin McDowell, Franz Siegel, John Pope, James S. Wadsworth, Wm. H. Halleck and George B. McClellan in 1862, by Fred'k A. Petersen. Part [1]-II. A contribution to the future history of the United States. New York [1862] 2 v. (55, 69 p.) 22cm.
Title and imprint from cover. CSmH   *1408*
"Wholesale agents, Sinclair Tousey . . . H. Dexter."

Pratt, Fletcher
. . . Ordeal by fire, an informal history of the Civil war. Illustrated by Merritt Cutler.

New York, Harrison Smith and Robert Haas, 1935. 481 p. illus., maps, ports. 21½cm.
At head of title: Fletcher Pratt.   NN   *1409*

——— ——— Maps by Rafael Palacios. New York, William Sloane Associates [1948] xvi, 426 p. maps and plans. 21½cm.   *1410*
At head of title: Fletcher Pratt.
"Revised edition."

Ramsay, T   N
Sketches of the great battles in 1861, in the Confederate states of America. Sumter, Bethel, Manassas, Springfield, Hatteras, Lexington, Leesburg, Port Royal, Columbia or Belmont. Also, sketches of Jefferson Davis and A. H. Stephens. By T. N. Ramsey, North Carolina. Salisbury, J. J. Bruner, printer, 1861. 32 p. 21½cm.   CSmH DLC NcD   *1411*
Text within ruled border.
Crandall 2657.

Redfield, Horace V
Characteristics of the armies. AW 357–71.
                                                 1412

Ropes, John Codman, 1836–1899.
The story of the Civil war, a concise account of the War in the United States of America between 1861 and 1865, by John Codman Ropes. New York, G. P. Putnam's Sons, 1894–[98] 2 v. fold. maps (one at end of volume; another in pocket). 23cm.   CSmH   *1413*
Contents: I To the opening of the campaigns of 1862; II The campaigns of 1862.
Continued by William R. Livermore [see Title 1403].

Schalk, Emil, 1832–
Campaigns of 1862 and 1863, illustrating the principles of strategy, by Emil Schalk. Philadelphia, J. B. Lippincott & co., 1863. viii, 252 p. maps and plans, 2 fold. maps. 21cm.
                                          CSmH DLC   *1414*
Contents: Chap I Principles of strategy; II Geography of the Southern Confederacy; III Applications of the maxims laid down in chapter I to the theater of war constituted by the Southern confederacy; IV Campaign of 1862; V Campaign of 1863.

Simpson, Harold Brown, 1917–
Brawling brass, North and South, the most famous quarrels involving: Stonewall Jackson and A. P. Hill; Jos. E. Johnston and John B. Hood; Robert E. Lee and James Longstreet; George Meade and Dan Sickles; Phil Sheridan and Gouverneur K. Warren; John Pope and Fitz-John Porter. By Harold B. Simpson. [Waco, Texian press, c1960] 78 p. 23cm. *1415*

Steele, Matthew Forney, 1861–1953.
. . . American campaigns, by Matthew Forney Steele. Washington, Byron S. Adams, 1909. 2 v. 22½cm.   NN   *1416*

General References, continued

At head of title: War department. Office of the Chief of staff: Second section, General staff, no. 13.
Contents: I Text; II Maps.
Civil war, I 127–587.

Stern, Philip Van Doren, 1900–
Prologue to Sumter, the beginnings of the Civil war, from the John Brown raid to the surrender of Fort Sumter, woven into a continuous narrative, by Philip Van Doren Stern. Bloomington, Indiana University press [1961] xvi, (1), 17–576 p. 5 maps, plates (illus., ports.). 21cm.   *1417*
"Civil war centennial series."

Swinton, William, 1833–1892.
The twelve decisive battles of the war, a history of the Eastern and Western campaigns, in relation to the actions that decided their issue, by William Swinton. New York, Dick & Fitzgerald, 1867. 520 p. plates (maps, ports.). 23cm.   CSmH DLC   *1418*

Threlkeld, Hansford Lee, 1868–1949.
The equipment and tactics of our infantry 1861–1865 compared with that of today. *JMSIUS* XLIX (1911) 173–87.   *1419*

Tilley, John Shipley, 1880–
Lincoln takes command, by John Shipley Tilley. Chapel Hill, University of North Carolina press, 1941. xxxvii, 334 p. 22cm.
                                      DLC NN   *1420*

Todd, Albert, 1854–1913.
The campaigns of the rebellion, by Albert Todd, First Lieutenant First U. S. artillery. Manhattan, Print. dept., State Agricultural College, 1884. vi, (1), 130 p. 2 fold. maps. 22cm.   CSmH DLC NN   *1421*

Vandiver, Frank Everson, 1925–
Jefferson Davis and unified army command. *LHQ* XXXVIII (1955) 26–38.   *1422*

Williams, Kenneth Powers, 1887–1958.
. . . Lincoln finds a General, a military study of the Civil war. With maps by Clark Ray. New York, Macmillan co., 1949–59. 5 v. maps and plans, plates (ports.). 21½cm.
                                      CSmH DLC   *1423*
At head of title: Kenneth P. Williams.
Facsims., maps, on endpapers.
I–II paged continuously.

Williams, Thomas Harry, 1909–
Lincoln and his Generals [by] T. Harry Williams. New York, Alfred A. Knopf, 1952. viii, (2), 363, iv p. 22cm.   NN   *1424*
"The story of Abraham Lincoln the Commander in Chief."

Wise, George
Campaigns and battles of the Army of Northern Virginia, by George Wise. New York, Neale pub. co., 1916. 432 p. 2 plates (ports.). 23½cm.   DLC   *1425*

OFFICIAL REPORTING OF MILITARY OPERATIONS

Confederate States of America. War Department.
Official reports of battles. Published by order of Congress. Richmond, Enquirer press, 1862. 571 p. 23cm.   CSmH DLC NN   *1426*
Crandall 1374.

—— —— Richmond, R. M. Smith, Public printer, 1864. 562 p. 23cm.
Crandall 1375.   CSmH DLC   *1427*

—— —— Richmond, R. M. Smith, Public printer, 1864. 96, (2) p. 23cm.
CSmH DLC NN   *1428*
Transmitted to Congress, January 7, 1864.
Crandall 1376.

—— —— Richmond, R. M. Smith, public printer, 1864. 98 p. 23cm.
CSmH DLC NN   *1429*
Enemy attack on Fort McAllister, Feb. 1, 1863; reports engagements at Fayette Court House, Cotton Hill, Gauley, Charleston, and pursuit of the enemy to the Ohio; General Bragg's reports of the battles of Richmond, Munfordsville & Perryville; report of Rhode's brigade at Seven Pines; capture of the gunboat J. P. Smith at Stone river.
Crandall 1377.

—— Official reports of battles; embracing Colonel Wm. L. Jackson's report of expedition to Beverly; Major General Price's report of evacuation of Little Rock; Major General Stevenson's report of battle of Lookout mountain; and Lieutenant Colonel M. A. Haynes' reports of engagements at Knoxville, Limestone creek and Carter station. Published by order of Congress. Richmond, R. M. Smith, public printer, 1864. 72 p. 22½cm.
Crandall 1378.   CSmH DLC NN   *1430*

—— —— embracing the defence of Vicksburg, by Major General Earl Van Dorn; and the attack upon Baton Rouge, by Major Geneal [sic] Breckinridge; together with the reports of the battles of Corinth and Hatchie Bridge; the expedition to Hartsville, Tennessee; the affair at Pocotaligo and Yemassee; the action near Coffeeville, Mississippi; the action and casualties of the brigade of Colonel Simonton at Fort Donelson. Richmond, Smith, Bailey & co., printers, 1863. 170 p. 21½cm.
Crandall 1379.   DLC NN   *1431*

—— Official reports of Generals Johnson and Beauregard of the battle of Manassas, July 21st, 1861. Also official reports of the battle of 10th Sept., Brig. Gen. Floyd commanding; engagement at Oak Hill, Mo., Brig. Gen. Ben McCulloch commanding; engagement at Lewinsville Sept. 11th, Col. J. E. B. Stuart com-

manding; engagement on Greenbrier river, Oct. 3d, Brig. Gen. H. R. Jackson commanding; engagement at Santa Rosa island, Oct. 8th, Maj. Gen. Braxton Bragg commanding; engagement at Leesburg, Oct. 21st and 22d, Brig. Gen. N. G. Evans commanding; bombardment of Forts Walker and Beauregard, Nov. 7th, Brig. Gen. Thomas F. Dayton commanding; engagement at Piketon, Ky., Col. John S. Williams commanding; battle in Alleghany mountains, Dec, 13th, Col. Edward Johnston commanding; battle of Chustenahlah, which took place in the Cherokee nation, on the 26th of Dec. 1861, Col. James McIntosh commanding; battle of Belmont, Nov. 7th, Leonidas Polk, Major-General commanding. Richmond, Enquirer press, 1862. 144 p. 21cm.
Crandall 1381.   CSmH DLC NN   *1432*

—— Report of General Robert E. Lee, and subordinate reports of the battle of Chancellorsville. Also reports of Major General J. E. B. Stuart and Brigadier General Fitz Lee, of cavalry engagements at Kelleysville. Also, report of Brigadier General W. H. F. Lee, and subordinates of cavalry operations of the 14th and 15th of April, 1863. Published by order of Congress. Richmond, R. M. Smith, Public printer, 1864. 144, (5) p. 24½cm.
CSmH DLC   *1433*
Reports of Colonel Chambliss, Colonel Beale, Captain J. W. Strange, Captain Moorman, Lieutenant Ford — (5) p.
Crandall 1419.

—— Report of General Robert E. Lee, of operations at Rappahannock bridge. Also, report of Lieut. Gen. E. K. Smith, of operations in lower Louisiana. And report of Major General Jones, of engagement at Rogersville, Tennessee. Published by order of Congress. Richmond, R. M. Smith, Public printer, 1864. 61 p. 23cm.   CSmH DLC   *1434*
Crandall 1420.

—— Report of Lieutenant General Holmes of the battle of Helena. Also, report of Lieutenant General A. P. Hill of the battle of Bristoe station. Also, report of Major General Stevenson of expedition into East Tennesse. Published by order of Congress. Richmond, R. M. Smith, Public printer, 1864. 63, (1) p. 25cm.
Crandall 1421.   CSmH DLC NN   *1435*

Grant, Ulysses Simpson, 1822–1885.
Official report of Lieut.-Gen. Ulysses S. Grant, embracing a history of the operations of the armies of the Union, from March, 1862, to

Official Reporting of Military Operations, con't

the closing scenes of the rebellion. New York, Beadle and co. [1865] 87 p. 16cm.

CSmH NN   **1436**

—— Report of Lieutenant General U. S. Grant, of the armies of the United States, 1864–'65. [Washington, 1865] 44 p. 21cm. NN   **1437**

Caption title.
Dated: Washington, D.C., July 22, 1865.

Hancock, Winfield Scott, 1824–1886.

Official reports of military operations of troops commanded by General W. S. Hancock during the Civil war, 1861–65. [New York] 1879. 1 v. 20½cm.   CSmH DLC   **1438**

A collection of 14 separately paged reports as originally published.

Ripley, Roswell Sabine, 1823–1887.

Report of Brigadier General R. S. Ripley, of operations from August 21, to September 10, 1863, with sub-reports. Published by order of Congress. Richmond, R. M. Smith, Public printer, 1864. 42 p. 25cm.

CSmH DLC   **1439**

Dated, Headquarters First military district, Department of South Carolina, Georgia and Florida, Charleston, September 22d, 1863.
Crandall 1416.

United States. War Record Publication Office.

Catalogue of written and printed battle reports on file in the Archive office, War department. Washington, War Record Publication office, 1878. liv, 133 p. 24cm. CSmH   **1440**

"Errata, Index of subjects, Index of names," liv p.

United States. War Records Office.

Reports of military operations during the rebellion, 1860–1865. Washington, War Records Publication office, 1874–1880. 15 v. 23½cm.   CSmH   **1441**

Vols. I–VII titles add: including reports of the actions of Southern state authorities in siezing U.S. forts, arsenals, etc. Arranged in chronological order in accordance with an Act of Congress approved June 23, 1874, under the direction of the Adjutant general of the army, by Mr R. S. Davis.
Printer varies: I–VII Adjutant General's print. office; VIII–X War Dept. print. office. XII has title, Supplement. . . , and is without imprint.
Indexes in each volume except XII.
"A preliminary and obsolete edition," Checklist of United States public documents, 1789–1909, 1395.

—— Reports of military operations during the rebellion, 1860–1865. [Washington, 1876–8] 20 v. 23½cm.   CSmH   **1442**

Title varies: I Confederate reports of battles during the War of the rebellion; III–IV, VI–VIII Reports of military operations (Confederate) during the rebellion, 1860–1865.
Imprint: I Adjutant General's print. office, 1876; III–IV, VI–VIII War Records Publication office, 1878–82. Other volumes are without imprint.
Numerous errata slips and additional reports identified by supplementary pagination.
Volumes usually contain an index of authors and list of events.
Fold. maps II–III.
"A preliminary and obsolete edition," Checklist of United States public documents, 1789–1909, 1395.

United States. War Records Office.

Summary of military operations, as reported on the returns of the Army of the United States, 1861–1865. Washington, War Records Publication office, 1877–83. 3 v. 23½cm.

CSmH   **1443**

I War Department print. office.

LISTING OF BATTLES

Cooper, Charles R

Chronological and alphabetical record of the engagements of the great Civil war, with the casualties on both sides, and full and exhaustive statistics and tables of the Army and Navy, military prisons, national cemeteries, etc., compiled from the official records of the War department and Confederate archives, Washington, D.C., by Charles R. Cooper, late 67th Ohio V.V. Milwaukee, Caxton press, 1904. 211 p. front. (port.). 23½cm. DLC   *1443A*

—— —— Second edition. Milwaukee, Caxton press, pub., 1904. 211 p. front. (port.). 23cm.   TxU   *1444*

Drake, Edwin L

Chronological summary of battles and engagements of the Western armies of the Confederate states, including summary of Lt. Gen. Joseph Wheeler's cavalry engagements. Nashville, Tavel, Eastman & Howell, 1879. 99, (1) p. 23½cm.   CSmH DLC   *1445*

First published with *The annals of the Army of Tennessee*, edited by Edwin L. Drake, 1878.
An order of battle.

Dresser, Horace Erastus, 1841–

The battle record of the American rebellion, by Horace E. Dresser. New York, Tribune Association [1863] 72 p. 22cm.
CSmH NN TxU   *1446*

Dyer, Frederick Henry, 1849–1917.

A complete record of the campaigns, battles, engagements, actions, combats, sieges, skirmishes, etc., in the United States connected with the War of the rebellion.

In his A compendium of the War of the rebellion, 1908, 577–991.
See Title 104.

Kremer, Wesley Potter, 1841–

100 great battles of the rebellion, a detailed account of regiments and batteries engaged, casualties, killed, wounded and missing and the number of men in action in each regiment. Also, all the battles of the Revolution, War of 1812–5, Mexican war, Indian battles, American-Spanish war, and naval battles. State rosters from the several Northern states, giving the enrollment, number killed, wounded, died and deserted from each organization during the war, by W. P. Kremer. Hoboken. 1906. 366 p. 17cm.   DLC NN   *1447*

A letter laid in NN's copy has printed letter head: W. P. Kremer, publisher.

Strait, Newton Allen

. . . An alphabetical list of the battles of the War of the rebellion, with dates, from Fort Sumter, S. C., April 12 and 13, 1861, to Kirby Smith's surrender, May 26, 1865 . . . And a chronological history of the War with Mexico, from 1845 to 1848 . . . Revised by Newton A. Strait. . . . Washington, J. H. Soulé, 1878. 94 p. 23½cm.   CSmH DLC   *1448*

—— Alphabetical list of battles, 1754–1900, War of the rebellion, Spanish-American war, Philippine insurrection, and all old wars with dates. Summary of events of the War of the rebellion, 1860–1865, Spanish-American war, Philippine insurrection, 1898–1900, troubles in China, 1900, with other valuable information in regard to the various wars. Compiled from official records, by Newton A. Strait. Washington [Govt. print. office] 1909. 252 p. 23½cm.
CSmH NHi   *1449*

Strickler, Theodore D

When and where we met each other on shore and afloat, battles, engagements, actions, skirmishes, and expeditions during the Civil war, 1861–1866, to which is added concise data concerning the army corps and legends of the army corps badges. Compiled from official and other authentic sources by Theodore D. Strickler. Philadelphia, Walter C. Strickler [1899] 279 p. 19½cm.
CSmH NN   *1450*

United States. Adjutant General's Office.

Chronological list of battles, engagements, etc., during the rebellion, 1860–1865, with the designation of troops engaged. Compiled from the records of the Adjutant General's office. Washington, Adjutant General's print. office, 1875. 136 p. 24cm.   CSmH   *1451*
Volume covers battles only through 1862, because work was suspended.

—— List of battles, engagements, skirmishes, etc., during the rebellion of 1861, with dates and designation of troops engaged. Washington, Adjutant General's office, 1873. 168 p. 24½cm.   CSmH   *1452*

United States. Surgeon General's Office.

Chronological summary of engagements and battles with maps from the Medical and surgical history of the War of the rebellion, 1861–65. Philadelphia, 1880. [xxxiii]–clv p. plates (maps). 29cm.   CSmH   *1453*

Wells, John Wesley

An alphabetical list of the battles (with dates) of the War of the rebellion, compiled by J. W. Wells, 1875. Washington, Govt. print. office, 1875. 64 p. 24½cm.   MHi   *1454*

—— —— Washington, Govt. print. office, 1875. 66 p. 23cm.   CSmH DLC   *1455*

Listing of Battles, continued

—— An alphabetical list of the battles of the War of the rebellion, with dates, from Fort Sumter, S. C., April 13, 1861, to Kirby Smith's surrender, May 26, 1865. Compiled from the official records of the offices of the Adjutant-General and the Surgeon-General, U.S.A., by J. W. Wells . . . Revised and published by N. A. Strait, giving the number killed, wounded and missing in each of the important battles, Union troops engaged, names of the Generals killed and wounded in both armies, also the total number of enlistments, number discharged, number wounded, number missing, number of deaths, number killed in battle, number of graves . . . with a complete synopsis of the Annual report of H. M. Atkinson, Commissioner of pensions. . . . Washington, D.C., Gibson Brothers, printers, 1875. 81 p. 22½cm.
NN TxU   1456

—— An alphabetical list of the battles of the War of the rebellion, with dates, compiled from official records, by J. W. Wells and N. A. Strait . . . and a roster of all regimental surgeons in the late war, with their service and last-known post-office address. Compiled from official records, for use of U. S. Pension office. Washington, D.C., N. A. Strait, 1882. 320 p. 23cm.
TxU   1457

—— An alphabetical list of the battles of the War of the rebellion, with dates . . . compiled from the official records . . . by J. W. Wells and N. A. Strait, with the addition of many incidents of the war . . . and a chronological history of the War of the rebellion . . . and a roster of all the regimental surgeons and assistant surgeons . . . Washington, D.C., G. M. Van Buren, 1883. 330, (2) p. 23½cm.
NeHi   1458
"Explanations" and an advertisement, (2) p.

Wooters, William R

An alphabetical list of the battles of the War of the rebellion with dates, from Ft. Sumter, S.C., April 12 and 13, 1861, to General Kirby Smith's surrender, May 26, 1865, compiled from official sources, giving the number killed, wounded, and missing in each of the important battles, Union troops engaged . . . A chronological history of the War of the rebellion. Philadelphia, W. R. Wooters [1889] 120 p. 19½cm.
CSmH   1459
Advertising matter, 92–120.

JOINT CONGRESSIONAL COMMITTEE
ON THE CONDUCT OF THE WAR

United States. Conduct of the War, Joint Committee on the.
    . . . Report . . . Washington, Govt. print. office, 1863. 3 v. 23cm.
                    CSmH DLC NN   **1460**

Contents: I Army of the Potomac including journal of the Committee, December 20, 1861 – April 3, 1863; II Bull run. Ball's Bluff; III Western department or Missouri. Miscellaneous.

At head of title: 37th Congress, 3d session. Senate. Rep. com. no. 108. The Report was also issued as House of representatives rep. com. and the head of title statement varies accordingly. B. F. Wade, Chairman.

—— Report . . . second session Thirty-eighth Congress. Washington, Govt. print. office, 1865. 3 v. 23cm.   CSmH DLC   **1461**

Each volume includes reports of the Committee, testimony and documentary appendices.

Contents: I Army of the Potomac. Battle of Petersburg; II Red river expedition. Fort Fisher expedition. Heavy ordnance; III Sherman-Johnston. Light-draught monitors. Massacre of the Cheyenne Indians. Ice contracts. Rosecrans campaign. Miscellaneous.

—— Supplemental report. . . . Washington, Govt. print. office, 1866. 2 v. II illus., fold. maps. 23cm.   CSmH   **1462**

Contents: I Reports Major General(s) . . . Sherman, Thomas; II Reports Major General(s) . . . Pope, J. O. Foster, Pleasonton, Hitchcock, Sheridan, Brigadier General Ricketts. Communication of Norman Wiard.

OFFICIAL RECORDS OF THE WAR OF THE REBELLION

For a detailed statement of the War of the rebellion records and the accompanying Atlas, the user is referred to the Checklist of United States public documents 1789–1909 (third edition, revised and enlarged, Washington, D.C., Gov't. print. office, 1911; New York, Kraus reprint corp, 1962) pages 1390–95. Another useful reference is the Bibliography of State participation in the Civil war, 1861–1866 (third edition, Washington, D.C., War Department Library, 1913) pages 1391–92.

Eisendrath, Joseph L
The official records, sixty-three years in the making. *CWH* i (1955) 89–94.   **1463**

Irvine, Dallas D   1904–
The genesis of the official records. *MVHR* xxiv (1937) 221–9.   **1464**

United States. War Department.
General index to series I of the official records of the War of the rebellion. Prepared by John S. Moodey. Published under the direction of Stephen B. Elkins, Secretary of war, by . . . [3 names] Board of publications. In two parts. Part I, Operations 1861, 1862, 1863, volumes i to xxxi inclusive. Washington, Govt. print. office, 1892. 128 p. 23cm.   CSmH   **1465**

United States. War Records Office.
Index to names of places mentioned in volumes 1 to 15, inclusive, Official records of the War of the rebellion. [Washington, Govt. print. office n.d.] 86 p. 22½cm. CSmH NN   **1466**

—— Report of the Office of publication of the Official records of the Union and Confederate armies.   CSmH   **1467**
Title varies.
Reports for 1878–1899 were published in Annual reports of War department and also issued separately.
The War records office was merged with the Record and pension office, July 1, 1899.
1st report dated: September 30, 1878.
Except for 1894, CSmH has a complete file of the Reports which were assembled by John P. Nicholson. With this file have been preserved printed forms and documents contributing to a knowledge of the Offices' operations.

INDIVIDUAL BATTLES LISTED BY STATE *

VIRGINIA

Long, John Sherman
The Gosport affair, 1861. *JSH* xxiii (1957)
155–72.   *1469*

Patterson, Robert, 1792–1881.
A narrative of the campaign in the Valley
of the Shenandoah in 1861, by Robert Patterson, late Major-General of volunteers. Philadelphia, Sherman & co., printers, 1865. 128 p.
front. (map). 22cm.   NN   *1470*
NN has two large paper editions ("Only six copies printed," "Only one hundred copies printed") with title printed partly in red. Another NN copy is identified by "Fifth thousand."

—— —— Philadelphia, John Campbell, 1865.
128, 194, (1) p. 2 front. (map, port.). 22cm.
"Index to editorials," (1) p. NHi NN   *1471*
"Appendix, embracing letters from men of high distinction . . . and editorials from leading journals."
"Third thousand."
On spine: Shenandoah Valley campaign of 1861, Patterson commanded the Department of Pennsylvania, April 27, 1861, to August 24, 1861, when it was merged with the Department of the Potomac.

Pilcher, John M   1841–
The early days of the war. *In* War talks of Confederate veterans, compiled and edited by Geo. S. Barnard, 1892, 1–7.   *1472*

Big Bethel
June 10, 1861

Confederate States of America. War Department.
Letter from the Secretary of war [copies of the official reports of the battle of Bethel] [Richmond, 1862] 31 p. 21cm.
                                CSmH   *1473*
Letter of transmittal dated: March 31, 1862.
Crandall 1358.

United States, Infantry School, Camp Benning, Ga.
. . . Battle of Big Bethel. [Camp Benning] Printed at the Infantry school press, 1921.
38 p. fold. plan. 25½cm.   NN   *1474*
Official reports of participants in the battle.
At head of title: Department of research. The Infantry school, Camp Benning, Ga., Course in historical research, 1920–1921. Military history pamphlet no. 3.

Blackburn's Ford
July 18, 1861

Early, Jubal Anderson, 1816–1894.
Report of the operations of Early's brigade in the affair at Blackburn's ford on Bull

run, the 18th of July, 1861. *SHST* ii (1875)
74–7.   *1475*

Bull Run
July 21, 1861

Confederate cavalry at the First Manassas. *SB* ii (1883/84) 529–34. map.   *1476*
Text signed: J. S. B.

National tribune war maps no. 1. Supplement to the National tribune, Dec. 26, 1895. The first battle of Bull run. broadside, 55 x 42cm.
                                        NcD   *1477*
Map with col. illus. border, ports., and text.

Alexander, Edward Porter, 1835–1910.
The battle of Bull run. *Scribner's magazine* xli (1907) 80–94. plan.   *1478*

Barnard, John Gross, 1815–1882.
The C.S.A. and the battle of Bull run (a letter to an English friend), by J. G. Barnard.
New York, D. Van Nostrand, 1862. 136 p.
5 fold. maps. 22½cm.   NN   *1479*
"Errata" leaf inserted.
"C. S. A." of title are illus. initials.

—— —— [Revised reprinting] New York, D. Van Nostrand, 1862. 124 p. 5 fold. maps.
22½cm.   NN   *1480*

Beatie, Russel Harrison
Road to Manassas, the growth of Union command in the Eastern theater from the fall of Fort Sumter to the first battle of Bull run, by R. H. Beatie, Jr. [New York] Cooper Square, 1961. xi, 285 p. maps, plates (illus., ports.).
23½cm.   NN   *1481*

Beauregard, Pierre Gustave Toutant, 1819–1893.
A commentary on the campaign and battle of Manassas of July, 1861, together with a summary of the art of war [by] Gen. G. T. Beauregard. New York, G. P. Putnam's Sons, 1891. xiv, 187 p. 2 fold. maps. 20½cm.
                        CSmH DLC NN   *1482*

—— The first battle of Bull run, by G. T. Beauregard. *B&L* i 196–227.   *1483*

—— Gen. Beauregard's official report of the "battle of Manassas." [1861] 29 p. 19cm.
Caption title.   CSmH NN   *1484*
Dated: Headquarters First corps, Army of the Potomac, Manassas, Aug. 26, 1861.
Crandall 1341.

* Battles are listed chronologically within each state; states are listed in a geographical arrangement which takes into account the order of campaigns and the most important battles.

Bull Run, continued

Brown, Campbell, editor.
The first Manassas, correspondence between Generals R. S. Ewell and G. T. Beauregard, to which are added extracts from a letter of Gen. Fitz Lee. Nashville, Wheeler, Osborn & Duckworth M'f'g co., printers, 1885. 8 p. 23cm.
DLC LNHT NcD   **1485**
"Note," p. [2] signed: Campbell Brown.

Conrad, Daniel B
History of the first battle of Manassas and the organization of the Stonewall brigade, how it was so named. *SHSP* xix (1891) 82–92. **1486**

—— History of the first fight and organization of Stonewall brigade. How it was so named. *US* ns vii (1892) 466–75.   **1487**

—— The Stonewall brigade at Bull run. *B&G* iv (1894) 359–65. illus., port.   **1488**

—— With Stonewall Jackson before Bull run. *Magazine of history* ix (1909) 148–52. **1489**

Crockett, Cary Ingram
The battery that saved the day. *Field artillery journal* xxx (1940) 26–33. plan, 2 ports.
1490
John D. Imboden's account of the Staunton artillery retold by his stepson.

Fry, James Barnet, 1827–1914.
McDowell's advance to Bull run. *B&L* i 167–93.   **1491**

—— McDowell and Tyler and the campaign of Bull run, 1861, by James B. Fry. New York, D. Van Nostrand, 1884. 63 p. plan. 19½cm.
"Errata" slip inserted.   NN   **1492**

Hanson, Joseph Mills, 1876–
Bull run remembers, the history, traditions and landmarks of the Manassas (Bull run) campaigns before Washington, 1861–1862, by Joseph Mills Hanson, lately Superintendent Manassas National battlefield park. Manassas, National Capitol publishers, 1953. ix, 194 p. plates (illus., 3 maps, 1 double). 23cm.
NN   **1493**

Henry, Hugh Fauntleroy
Souvenir of the battlefield of Bull run, battles of July 21, 1861, and August 28, 29 and 30, 1862, by Hugh F. Fauntleroy. [Manassas] Manassas Journal press, c1900. 29, (1) p. illus., map, ports. 24cm.   CSmH DLC   **1494**
Text in double columns.

Johnson, Joseph E
The battle of Bull run, an important letter from. . . . *Historical magazine* s 2 ii (1867) 232–7.   **1495**

Johnston, Joseph Egleston, 1807–1891.
Gen. Johnston's report of the battle of Manassas. *LWL* ii (1866/67) 155–63. **1496**

—— —— Suppressed part. . . . *LWL* ii (1866/67) 259–60.   **1497**

Johnston, Robert Matteson, 1867–1920.
Bull run, its strategy and tactics, by R. M. Johnston. Boston, Houghton Mifflin co., 1913. xiv, (1), 293 p. plates (maps and plans, 1 double). 22cm.   NN   **1498**

—— The significance of Bull run, by R. M. Johnston. . . . Washington, D.C., 1913. [7] p. 23cm.   NcD   **1499**
"Reprinted from Infantry journal, September–October 1913."

Putnam, George Palmer, 1814–1872.
Before and after the battle, a day and night in Dixie, by G. P. Putnam. [New York, 1861] 20 p. 23cm.   CSmH   **1500**
"Re-printed from the Knickerbocker magazine," September 1861.

Russell, Sir William Howard, 1820–1897.
Mr. Russell on Bull run, with a note from the Rebellion record. New York, G. P. Putnam, 1861. 12 p. 25½cm.   CSmH NN   **1501**
Dated: Washington, July 19, 1861.
Text in double columns.
Running title: Rebellion record, 1860–61. Documents.

Smith, Gustavus Woodson, 1822–1896.
General J. E. Johnston and G. T. Beauregard at the battle of Manassas, July, 1861. By Gustavus W. Smith. New York, C. G. Crawford, printer, 1892. 48 p. fold. map. 23cm.
CSmH DLC NN   **1502**

Stedman, Edmund Clarence, 1833–1908.
The battle of Bull run, by Edmund C. Stedman, army correspondent of the New York World. New York, Rudd & Carleton, 1861. 42, (1) p. 19cm.   NN   **1503**
"The publishers . . . have chosen to reprint it just as it came to 'The World.' "

Steele, Matthew Forney, 1861–1953.
. . . The first battle of Bull run, by Captain M. F. Steele, [Fort Leavenworth] Department of Military Art, Infantry and Cavalry School, 1907. 28 p. 19½cm.   NN   **1504**
At head of title: Department of military art. Infantry and cavalry school. Course in strategy, 1906–1907. Lecture no. VII.
Title and imprint from cover.

Swift, Eben, 1854–1938.
The Bull run campaign in Virginia, 1861 . . . Compiled by Captain Eben Swift, Fifth cavalry. [n.p., n.d.] 4 p. 19½cm.
Caption title.   CSmH   **1505**

United States. Army

Organization of the Union army (Brigadier-General Irvin MacDowell commanding) at the battle of Bull run, Va., July 21, 1861. [Washington, 1882] 4 p. 23½cm.   CSmH   *1506*

United States. Conduct of the War, Joint Committee on the.

. . . How Bull run battle was lost. The Ball's Bluff massacre. Department of the West – Fremont. [New York, 1863] 8 p. 22cm.

NN   *1507*

At head of title: The Tribune war tracts, no. 3.
Reprinted from Report of the Joint committee on the conduct of the war, parts 2–3, Washington, 1863.

Vincent, Thomas MacCurdy, 1832–1909.

The battle of Bull run, July 21, 1861, by Brigadier-General Thomas M. Vincent. [1905] 35 p. 2 plans. *MOLLUS-DC* no 58.   *1508*

Warder, T   B

Battle of Young's branch; or, Manassas plain, fought July 21, 1861, with maps of the battle field made by actual survey, and the various positions of the regiments and artillery companies placed thereon, with an account of the movements in each, procured from the Commanding officer, or an officer of the regiment. Also, an account of the battle. Also, the battle ground of the 18th July, 1861, with General Beauregard's report of said battle. By T. B. Warder & Jas. M. Catlett. Richmond, Enquirer press, 1862. 156, (1) p. fold. map. 16cm.   CSmH NN   *1509*

"Errata," (1) p.
Crandall 2662.

Wilkes, George, 1820–1855.

The great battle, fought at Manassas, between the Federal forces, under General McDowell, and the Rebels under Gen. Beauregard, Sunday, July 21, 1861. From notes taken on the spot, by George Wilkes. New York, Brown & Ryan, 1861. 36 p. front. (double map). 15½cm.   NB   *1510*

Wilshin, Francis F

Manassas (Bull run) National battlefield park, Virginia, by Francis F. Wilshin. . . . Washington, D.C., 1953 (revised 1957). 47 p. illus., plans, ports. 23cm.   NN   *1511*

"National park service historical handbook series no. 15."

Ball's Bluff

October 21, 1861

Irwin, Richard Bache

Ball's Bluff and the arrest of General Stone. *B&L* II 123–34.   *1512*

Patch, Joseph Dorst

The battle of Ball's Bluff, by Joseph Dorst Patch . . . Edited by Fitzhugh Turner, with an introduction by Virgil Carrington Jones. Photographs from the Library of Congress; illustrations and maps by Majorie Keen. Leesburg, Potomac press [1958] 123 p. plates (illus., plan, ports.). 23cm.   NN   *1513*

Plans p. [2–3] of cover.

White, Elijah Veirs, 1832–1907.

History of the battle of Ball's Bluff, fought on the 21st of October, 1861. Written by Col. E. V. White, Dedicated by him to the Loudon chapter of U.D.C., Leesburg, Va. for benefit of monument to be erected in Leesburg to the Confederate soldiers of Loudon. Leesburg, "The Washingtonian" print [1902] 24 p. front. (port.), fold. map. 22cm.

CSmH NN NcD   *1514*

Jackson's Valley Campaign

March 23 – June 9, 1862

The Valley campaign of 1862. Correspondence of Generals Lee, Jackson, and others with General Ewell. *SHST* I (1874) 91–101.   *1515*

Allan, William, 1837–1889.

History of the campaign of Gen. T. K. (Stonewall) Jackson in the Shenandoah valley of Virginia, from November 4, 1861, to June 17, 1862. By William Allan, with full maps of the region and of the battlefields by Jed. Hotchkiss. Philadelphia, J. B. Lippincott & co., 1880. 175 p. 7 maps, 6 fold. 24cm.

NN   *1516*

—— Jackson's valley campaign, address of Col. William Allan . . . before the Virginia division of the Army of Northern Virginia, at their annual meeting, held in the Capitol in Richmond, Va., Oct. 30th, 1878. Richmond, G. W. Gary & co., printers, 1878. 30 p. 23½cm.

CSmH   *1517*

Also published in *SHSP* VII (1879) 1–30.

—— Stonewall Jackson's Valley campaign. *AW* 724–49.   *1518*

Boteler, A   R

Stonewall Jackson in campaign of 1862. *SHSP* XL (1915) 162–82; XLII (1917) 174–80.   *1519*

Deems, Clarence

General Jackson's Shenandoah valley campaign, May and June, 1862. *Coast artillery journal* LXV (1926) 215–38. map.   *1520*

Goldthorpe, George Weimer

The battle of McDowell, Virginia. *WVH* XIII (1952) 159–215.   *1521*

Jackson's Valley Campaign, continued

Imboden, John Daniel, 1832–1895.
Stonewall Jackson in the Shenandoah. *B&L*
I 282–98.   **1522**

Kellogg, Sanford Cobb, 1842–
The Shenandoah Valley and Virginia, 1861
to 1865, a war study, by Sanford C. Kellogg.
New York, Neale pub. co. [1903] 247 p.
20½cm.   CSmH   **1523**

Kelly, Henry B
Port Republic, by Henry B. Kelly, Colonel
C.S.A. [8th Louisiana] Philadelphia, Printed
by J. B. Lippincott co., 1886. 27 p. front.
(map). 23½cm.   LNHT   **1524**

King, Horatio Collins, 1837–1918.
The Shenandoah Valley in the great war.
MOLLUS-NY III 167–76.   **1525**

—— The Shenandoah Valley as a military
race-course. *JMSIUS* VI (1885) 400–09.
                                             1526

Munford, Thomas Taylor
Reminiscences of Jackson's valley campaign.
SHSP VII (1879) 523–34.   **1527**

Pilsen, John
[A letter] to Mr. Emil Schalk, author of
"Summary of the art of war." [New York,
1863] 13 p. 22cm.   CSmH NN   **1528**
Signed: John Pilsen, Lt.-Col., A.D.C. on General
Fremont's staff.
Caption title.
Battle of Cross Keys, June 8, 1862.

Taylor, Richard, 1826–1879.
Stonewall Jackson and the Valley campaign.
North American review LXXVI (1878) 238–61.
                                             1529

Tracy, Albert, 1818–1893.
Fremont's pursuit of Jackson in the Shenan-
doah valley, the journal of Colonel . . .March–
July 1862. Edited by Francis F. Wayland.
VMHB LXX (1962) 165–93, 332–54. plate
(map, port.).   **1530**

The Peninsular Campaign

March 17 – September 2, 1862

The defence of Richmond against the Federal
army under General McClellan, by a Prussian
officer in the Confederate service. Translated
from the Koelnische Zeitung. New York,
George F. Nesbitt & co., printers, 1863. 16 p.
23cm.   NN   **1531**

General McClellan's change of base. *North
American review* CXLI (1885) 335–45.   **1532**
"No name essays."

McClellan's campaign, reprinted from the
World of August 7, 1862. "There is justice in
history." New York, Anson D. F. Randolph,
1862. 12 p. 19cm.   NN   **1533**

Allan, William, 1837–1889.
The Army of Northern Virginia in 1862, by
William Allan. With an introduction by John
C. Ropes. Boston, Houghton, Mifflin and co.,
1892. x, 537 p. front. (port.), fold. map. 22cm.
                                   NN   **1534**

Barnard, John Gross, 1815–1882.
The Peninsular campaign and its antec-
edents, as developed by the report of Maj.-Gen.
Geo. B. McClellan, and other published docu-
ments, by J. G. Barnard. New York, D. Van
Nostrand, 1864. 96 p. fold. map. 19cm.
"Errata" slip inserted.   NN   **1535**

—— —— Washington, D.C., Union Congressional Committee, 1864. 15, (1) p. 23½cm.
An abridgement.   NN   **1536**

Churchill, Frederick A
An answer to "The first six weeks of Mc-
Clellan's Peninsula campaign" [by James F.
Rhodes] *US* ns XVI (1896) 101–09.   **1537**

Cook, Joel, 1842–1910.
The siege of Richmond, a narrative of the
military operations of Major-General George
B. McClellan, during the months of May and
June, 1862, by Joel Cook, special correspondent
of the Philadelphia press. Philadelphia, George
W. Shields, 1862. viii, 7–358 p. 18½cm.
                             CSmH   **1538**

Cooke, Phillip St. George, 1809–1895.
Army of the Potomac before Richmond, a
correspondence with General McClellan, and
touching Fitz-John Porter. *US* XIII (1885)
654–9.   **1539**

Franklin, William Buel, 1823–1903.
The first great crime of the war. *AW* 72–81.
                                             1540
Detachment of McDowell's corps from the Army
of the Potomac to the Department of the Rappahannock, April 4, 1862.

—— Rear-guard fighting during the change
of base. *B&L* II 366–82.   **1541**

Irwin, Richard Bache
The administration of the Peninsular campaign. *B&L* II 435–8.   **1542**

James, C   Rosser, 1854–1937.
An untold incident of McClellan's Peninsular
campaign. *Western Penn. historical magazine*,
XLIV (1961) 151–7.   **1543**

Joinville, Francois Ferdinand Philippe Louis Marie d'Orleans, prince de, 1818–1900.

. . . The army of the Potomac: its organization, its commander, and its campaign, by the Prince de Joinville. Translated from the French, with notes, by William Henry Hurlbert. New York, Anson D. F. Randolph, 1862. 118 p. front. (fold. map). 23cm.

                                DLC NN   **1544**

At head of title: Copyright edition.
First appeared in Reveux des deux mondes, October 15, 1862.

—— Campagne de l'armee du Potomac, mars–juillet 1862, par M. A. Trognon [pseud.] Paris, Imprimerie de J. Claye, 1862. 72 p. fold. map. 24cm.   **1545**

"Extrait de la Revue des deux mondes, livraison du 15 octobre 1862."

—— Campagne de l'Armée du Potomac, (mars–juillet 1862), par A. Trognon (le Prince de Joinville). New York, Librairie de F. W. Christern, 1862. 64 p. front. (fold. map). 23½cm.   DLC NN   **1546**

—— Feldzug der Potomac-armee, vom März bis Juli 1862. (Vom Grafen von Paris, Prinzen von Orleans.) Aus dem Französischen. Naumburg, Druck und Verlag von G. Pätz/Leipzig, Wolfgang Gerhard, 1863. 83 p. fold. map. 22½cm.   NN   **1547**

Ketchum, Hiram
General McClellan's Peninsula campaign. Review of the Report of the Committee on the conduct of the war relative to the Peninsula campaign. By Hiram Ketchum. [New York] 1864. 72 p. 22cm.   CSmH DLC   **1548**

Text in double columns.
"The following numbers were published in the Journal of commerce through several successive months, ending in May 1864." Another issue of same year has "Watchwords for patriots" on p. 72.

Law, Evander McIvor, 1836–1920.
The fight for Richmond in 1862. SB ns II (1886/87) 649–60, 713–23. maps.   **1549**

[Lunt, George] 1803–1885.
Review of McClellan's campaign, as Commander of the Army of the Potomac. Boston, Press of the Daily Courier, 1863. 21 p. 23½cm.
                            CSmH DLC   **1550**

McClellan, George Brinton, 1826–1885.
The complete report of the organization and campaigns of the Army of the Potomac, by George B. McClellan . . . with his last revision. [n.p., 1863] 142 p. 23½cm.   NN   **1551**

Title from cover.
Text in double columns.
Dated: August 4th, 1863.

—— Letter from the Secretary of war, transmitting report on the organization of the Army of the Potomac and of its campaigns in Virginia and Maryland, under the command of Maj. Gen. George B. McClellan, from July 26, 1861, to November 7, 1862. Washington, Govt. print. office, 1864. 242 p. 23cm.   NN   **1552**

At head of title: 38th Congress, 1st session. Senate. Ex. doc. no. 15.
"Without accompanying maps and documents."

—— The Peninsular campaign. B&L II 160–87.   **1553**

——Report of Maj. Gen. George B. McClellan upon the organization of the Army of the Potomac, and its campaigns in Virginia and Maryland, from July 26, 1861, to November 7, 1862. Re-printed entire from the copy transmitted by the Secretary of war to the House of representatives, with the addition of a complete index and several maps. [New York] American News co. [1863] 64 p. 3 maps. 26cm.
                                NN   **1554**

Title and imprint from cover. Text in double columns.

—— Report on the organization and campaigns of the Army of the Potomac, to which is added an account of the campaign in West Virginia . . . by George B. McClellan. New York, Sheldon & co., 1864. 480 p. front. (fold. map), plates (maps). 23cm.
                            CSmH DLC   **1555**

"The campaigns in West Virginia," 5–36.

Magruder, John Bankhead, 1810–1871.
Major-General Magruder's report of his operations on the Peninsula, and of the battles of "Savage station" and "Malvern hill," near Richmond. Richmond, Chas. W. Wynne, printer, 1862. 46 p. 22½cm.   NN   **1555A**

Crandall 1367.

Naglee, Henry Morris, 1815–1886.
. . . The secret history of the Peninsular campaign. Letter of General H. M. Naglee about General McClellan. A message from old soldiers to the army. The address to the army and navy, adopted at Hope chapel, on Wednesday evening, September 28th, 1864, by the McClellan legion. [New York, 1864] 8 p. 22cm.
                          CSmH NN   **1556**

At head of title: Document 21.
Naglee's letter dated: Sept. 27, 1864, p. 3–6.
"McClellan song, by Major Sidney Herbert," p. 8.

Rhodes, James Ford, 1848–1927.
The first six weeks of McClellan's Peninsular campaign. American historical review I (1896) 464–72.   **1557**

The Peninsular Campaign, continued

Ropes, John Codman, 1836–1899.
General McClellan's plans for the campaign of 1862, and the alleged interference of the government with them. *PMHSM* I (1876) 59–87.   **1558**

Webb, Alexander Stewart, 1835–1911.
. . . The Peninsula, McClellan's campaign of 1862, by Alexander S. Webb. New York, Charles Scribner's Sons, 1881. x, (1), 219 p. maps, fold. map. 19½cm.
                   CSmH DLC NN   **1559**
At head of title: Campaigns of the Civil war — III.
See Title 1362.

Whittier, Charles Albert
Comments on the Peninsular campaign of General McClellan. *PMHSM* I (1878) 277–300.   **1560**

Yorktown
April 5 – May 4, 1862

Arthur, Robert, 1886–
The sieges of Yorktown, 1781 and 1862, by Robert Arthur. . . . Fort Monroe, Va., The Bookshop [Coast Artillery School press, 1927] 63 p. front. (port.), illus., maps. 23½cm.
                              NN   **1561**

Confederate Survivors' Association.
Address delivered before the Confederate survivors' association of Augusta, Georgia, upon the occasion of its seventeenth annual reunion, on Memorial day, April 26th, 1895. By Captain F. Edgeworth Eve, and the Historian's report, submitted by Charles Edgeworth Jones. . . . Augusta, Chronicle job print. co., 1895. 33, (1) p. 23cm.   NN   **1562**
"General Butler's narrative . . . descriptive of an event during the evacuation of Yorktown by the Confederates in May 1862," 18–30.

Edge, Frederick Milnes
Major-General McClellan and the campaign on the Yorktown peninsula, by Frederick Milnes Edge. New York, Loyal Publication Society, 1865. iv, 201 p. 22½cm.
                        DLC NN   **1563**
On cover: [Pamphlet] no. 81.

Palfrey, John Carver, 1833–1906.
The siege of Yorktown. *PMHSM* I (1878) 89–152.   **1564**

*   *   *

Palfrey, Francis Winthrop, 1831–1889.
The period which elapsed between the fall of Yorktown and the beginning of the seven days' battle. *PMHSM* I (1880) 153–215.
                                         1565

Naglee, Henry Morris, 1815–1886.
Reconnaissance from Bottom's bridge to Seven Pines, May 24, 25, and 26, 1862, made by Naglee's brigade. Philadelphia, Collins, printer, 1863. 12 p. 23cm.   CSmH   **1566**

Porter, Fitz John, 1822–1901.
Hanover court house and Gaines' Mill. *B&L* II 319–43.   **1567**

Fair Oaks (Seven Pines)
May 31 – June 1, 1862

Harmon, George Dewey, 1896–
General Silas Casey and the battle of Fair Oaks. *Historian Phi alpha theta* IV 1 (Autumn 1941) 84–102. fold. map.   **1568**

Johnston, Joseph Eggleston, 1807–1891.
Manassas to Seven Pines. *B&L* II 202–18.
                                         1569
A consideration of Jefferson Davis' statements in The rise and fall of the Confederacy upon the operations following the withdrawal from Manassas and including the battle of Seven Pines.

Kearny, Philip, 1814–1862.
Official reports of General Kearny and General Birney of the battle of Seven Pines, May 31st, 1862. Philadelphia, Steampower print. office, 1863. 16 p. 19½cm.   NN   **1570**
Kearny's report dated: Head-quarters, Third div., Heintzelman's corps, entrenched camp, near Savage's June 2d, 1862; General Birney's Head-quarters Birney's brigade, First division, Third corps, Harrison's landing, July 8th, 1862.

Lowe, Thadeus Sobieski Coulincourt, 1832–1913.
Observation balloons in the battle of Fair Oaks. *American review of reviews* XLIII (1911) 186–90.   **1571**

Naglee, Henry Morris, 1815–1886.
Report of Brig. Gen. Henry M. Naglee, commanding First brigade, Casey's division, Army of the Potomac, of the part taken by his brigade in the battle of Seven Pines, May 31, 1862. With an appendix containing the official report of Gen. Casey. Philadelphia, Collins, printer, 1862. 24 p. 23cm.   NN   **1572**

Smith, Gustavus Woodson, 1822–1896.
The battle of Seven Pines, by Gustavus W. Smith. New York, C. G. Crawford, printer, 1891. 202 p. facsims., 2 maps. 23½cm.
                           CSmH NN   **1573**

——— Two days of battle at Seven Pines (Fair Oaks). *B&L* II 220–63.   **1574**

Seven Days' Battle
June 26 – July 2, 1862

How the Seven days' battle around Richmond began. *SHSP* xxviii (1900) 90–7.   **1575**
Text signed: J. B. M.

What I saw of the battle of Chickahominy. *SM* x (1872) 1–15.   **1576**

Alexander, Edward Porter, 1835–1910.
Records of Longstreet's corps, A.N.V., by General E. P. Alexander, Chief of artillery. The "Seven days battles." *SHSP* i (1876) 61–76.   **1577**

—— Seven days' battles. *SHST* ii (1875) 99–116.   **1578**

Dowdey, Clifford
The seven days, the emergence of Lee, by Clifford Dowdey. With maps by Samuel H. Bryant. Boston, Little, Brown and co. [1964] 380 p. maps. 22cm.   NN   **1579**

Hill, Daniel Harvey, 1842–1889.
Lee's attack north of the Chickahominy. *B&L* ii 347–62.   **1580**

—— McClellan's change of base and Malvern hill. *B&L* ii 383–95.   **1581**

Law, Evander McIvor, 1836–1928?.
On the Confederate right at Gaines's Mill. *B&L* ii 363–5.   **1582**

Longstreet, James, 1821–1904.
"The Seven days," including Frayser's farm. *B&L* ii 396–405.   **1583**

McCall, George Archibald, 1802–1868.
Pennsylvania reserves in the Peninsula. General McCall's official reports of the part taken by his division in the battles of Mechanicsville, Gaines' Mills, and New Market crossroads, together with statements of General Meade and Porter, and Colonels . . . [7 names] and others. [n.p., 1862] 10 p. 23cm.
Title from cover.   NNC   **1584**

—— The Seven days' contest. Pennsylvania reserves. General McCall's report, and accompanying documents. New York, Rebellion record, 1864. p. [663]–75. 23cm.
Title from cover.   CSmH NNC   **1585**
Text in double columns.

—— Sequel to General McCall's report on the Pennsylvania reserves in the Peninsula. [Belair, Penn., 1862] 4 p. 23cm.
          CSmH DLC NNC   **1586**
Title from cover.
Text signed: George A. McCall, Belair, October 22, 1862.

McClellan, Carswell, 1835–1892.
General Andrew A. Humphreys at Malvern hill, Va., July 1, 1862, and Fredericksburg, Va., December 13, 1862, a memoir, by Carswell McClellan. Privately printed. St. Paul, 1888. 34 p. 21cm.   CSmH NN   **1587**

Magruder, John Bankhead, 1810–1871.
Major-General Magruder's report of his operations on the Peninsula, and of the battles of "Savage station" and "Malvern hill," near Richmond. Richmond, Chas. H. Wynne, printer, 1862. 46 p. 22½cm.   CSmH   **1588**
Crandall 1367.

Naglee, Henry Morris, 1815–1886.
Report of Henry M. Naglee, of the part taken by his Brigade in the Seven days, from June 26, to July 2, 1862. Army of Potomac. Philadelphia, Collins, printer, 1863. 15 p. 23cm.
          CSmH NN   **1589**
Dated: Hd. qrs. Naglee's brigade, January, 1863.

Phillipson, Irving J
General McClellan's intentions on 25 June 1862. *Coast artillery journal* lxv (1926) 311–23. map.   **1590**

[Pollard, Edward Alfred] 1831–1872.
The Seven days' battles in front of Richmond. An outline narrative of the series of engagements which opened at Mechanicsville, near Richmond, on Thursday, June 26, 1862, and resulted in the defeat and retreat of the Northern army under Major-General M'Clellan. Compiled from the detailed accounts of the newspaper press. Richmond, West and Johnston, 1862. 45 p. 23cm. CSmH   **1591**
"Evans & Cogswell, printers, Charleston, S.C."
Crandall 2654.

Porter, Fitz John, 1822–1901.
The battle of Malvern hill. *B&L* ii 406–27.   **1592**

Pope's Campaign
August 16 – September 2, 1862

Pope's campaign in Virginia, its policy and results and the relations of the Army of the Potomac to the campaign, exposed by a general officer, who served at the Headquarters of the Army of Virginia from the first to the last day of the campaign. [n.p., n.d.] 32 p. 21½cm.
          OMC   **1593**

Allan, William, 1837–1889.
Lee's campaign against Pope in 1862. *Magazine of American history* xii (1884) 126–47.   **1594**

—— Pope's campaign again, a noteworthy review of facts and figures. *Magazine of American history* xvi (1886) 483–9.   **1595**

Pope's Campaign, continued

—— Strength of the forces under Pope and Lee, contributed by Lieut.-Col. William Allan, late Chief of ordnance Second corps Army of Northern Virginia, C.S.A., to which is appended a note by John C. Ropes. *PMHSM* II (1886) 195–219.   **1596**

Early, Jubal Anderson, 1816–1894.
Jackson's campaign against Pope in August, 1862, an address by Lieut. Gen'l Jubal A. Early, before the first annual meeting of the Association of the Maryland line, together with the proceedings at the third annual banquet of the Society of the army and navy of the Confederate states of the State of Maryland. [1883] 52, 38 p. 2 plates (ports.). 22cm.
                         CSmH NN   **1597**
"The third annual banquet . . . February 22, 1883," 38 p.

Horton, Charles Paine and John Codman Ropes
The campaign of General Pope in Virginia, its objects and general plan. *PMHSM* II (1877) 31–97.   **1598**

Johnston, Robert Matteson, 1867–1920.
Pope's campaign in Virginia. *Military historian and economist.* II (1917) 297–8; III (1918) 39–48, 182–94.   **1599**

Lippitt, Francis James, 1812–1902.
Pope's Virginia campaign and Porter's part in it. *Atlantic monthly* XLII (1878) 349–66. maps.   **1600**

Longstreet, James, 1821–1904.
Our march against Pope. *B&L* II 512–26.
                                               1601
Mills, Lewis Este
General Pope's Virginia campaign of 1862, read before the Cincinnati literary club, February 5, 1870, by Lewis Este Mills. Cincinnati, Robert Clarke & co., 1870. 32 p. 23cm.
                         CsMh NcD WHi   **1602**

Pope, John, 1822–1892.
The campaign in Virginia of July and August 1862. Official report of Major General John Pope. Milwaukee, Jermain & Brightman, printers, 1863. 74 p. 21cm.   NN   **1603**
Dated: New York, January 27th, 1863. Title and imprint from cover.

—— Report of Major General John Pope. Letter from the Secretary of war, in answer to the resolution of the House of 18th ultimo, transmitting copy of report . . . March 3, 1863. [Washington, 1863] 256 p. fold. map. 22½cm.
                                            NN   **1604**

At head of title: 37th Congress, 3d session. House of representatives. Ex. doc. no. 81.
Caption title.

Ropes, John Codman, 1836–1899.
. . . The army under Pope, by John Codman Ropes . . . New York, Charles Scribners' Sons, 1882. xii, (1), 229 p. fold. map, plans. 19cm.   DLC NN   **1605**
At head of title: Campaigns of the Civil war — IV.
See Title 1362.

United States. Army.
Northern Virginia campaign. Organization of the Army of the Potomac and other forces co-operating with the Army of Virginia (under Major General John Pope) during the operations from the Rapidan to Centreville, Va., August 16 to 31, 1862. [Washington, Adjutant General's office, 1882] 5 p. 23cm.
                                          CSmH   **1606**

        *   *   *

Andrews, George Leonard, 1828–1899.
The battle of Cedar mountain, August 9, 1862. *PMHS* II (1895) 387–442.   **1607**

Stackpole, Edward James, 1894–
From Cedar mountain to Antietam, August – September, 1862. Cedar mountain, second Manassas, Chantilly, Harpers ferry, South mountain, Antietam. By Edward J. Stackpole. Maps by Colonel Wilbur S. Nye. Harrisburg, Stackpole co. [1959] 466 p. illus., maps and plans, ports. 23cm.   NN   **1608**
Maps on endpapers.

Wilcox, Cadmus Marcellus, 1824–1890.
Battle of Reams station. *SHST* II (1875) 63–7, 99.   **1609**

Taliaferro, William Booth, 1822–1898.
Jackson's raid around Pope. *B&L* II 501–11.
                                               1610
King, Charles, 1844–1933.
Gainesville, August 28th, 1862, by Charles King. Milwaukee, Burdick & Allen, printer, 1903. 27 p. 22cm.   CSmH   **1611**
Also published in *MOLLUS-Wis* III 259–83; *US* s3 III (1903) 1128–48.

Second Bull Run
August 29–30, 1862

A comprehensive sketch of the battle of Manassas; or, second battle of Bull run, giving a brief account of one of the most important engagements of the late Civil war. Washington, D.C., Manassas Panorama co., 1886. 24 p. illus., 2 maps. 25cm.   NN   **1612**

"Opinions of the press," 20–4.
Artist, Théophile François Henri Poilpot, 1848–1915.
NN has an 1887 reprinting.

—— Washington, D.C., Manassas Panorama co.; Judd & Detweiler, printers, 1886. 20 p. illus., 2 maps. 25cm. **1613**
A reprinting omitting the "Opinions of the press."

Second battle of Bull run, by Committee no. 1, Coast artillery school, 1926–27. *Coast artillery journal* LXVII (1927) 302–33. maps. **1614**

Ambrose, Stephen E   1936–
Henry Halleck and the second Bull run campaign. *CWH* VI (1960) 238–49. **1615**

Ames, Adelbert, 1835–1933.
The second Bull run. *Overland monthly* VIII (1872) 399–406. **1616**

Crutchfield, Stapleton
Report of Colonel Crutchfield of the second battle of Manassas. *OLOD* II (1875) 152–6. **1617**
Text signed: Colonel and Chief of artillery, Second corps.

Cussons, John, 1838–
The passage of Thoroughfare gap and the assembling of Lee's army for the second battle of Manassas, by a Confederate scout. With an introduction by Senator Daniel. York, Penn., Gazette print, 1906. 31 p. 21cm.
Title from cover.   NB NN   **1618**

Franklin, William Buel, 1823–1903.
The Sixth corps at the second Bull run. *B&L* II 539–44. **1619**

Frobel, B   W
Report of . . . second battle of Manassas. *OLOD* II (1875) 24–6. **1620**
Report dated: Camp near Frederick, Maryland, September 9, 1862.
Signed: Major and Chief of artillery.

Jones, David Rumph, 1825–1863.
Report of Major-General D. R. Jones, of second battle of Manassas and operations in Maryland. *SHST* I (1874) 56–60. **1621**

McClellan, George Brinton, 1826–1885.
"Leave Pope to get out of his scrape." McClellan's dispatches. [Washington, D.C., Printed by McGill & Witherow, 1864] 8 p. 24cm.   CSmH DLC   **1622**
Caption title.
Republican congressional committee 1863–1865 publications campaign of 1864, no. 19.

—— McClellan's dispatches from Alexandria during the 2d battle of Bull run. [n.p., n.d.] 3 p. 25½cm.   CSmH   **1623**
Caption title.
"I [John Pope] ask no better testimony to refute this statement than the dispatches and letters which passed between the President, the General-in-chief, and General McClellan."

Mason, W   Roy
Marching on Manassas. *B&L* II 528–9. **1624**

Mayo, Robert M
The second battle of Manassas, by Colonel Robert M. Mayo. *SHSP* VII (1879) 122–5. **1625**

Pollard, Edward Alfred, 1831–1872.
The second battle of Manassas, with sketches of the recent campaign in Northern Virginia and on the upper Potomac. Prepared from special materials, by the author of "The first year of the war." Richmond, West & Johnston, 1862. 48 p. 22½cm.   CSmH   **1626**
Crandall 2649.

Pope, John, 1822–1892.
Correspondence between General Pope and the Comte de Paris, concerning the second battle of Bull run. 1876. 3, 3, 3 p. 24½cm.
       CSmH OMC   **1627**
Pope's letters have at head of title: Headquarters Department of the Missouri. Fort Leavenworth, Kas.
Pope's first letter is dated, May 29, 1876; the second, in ms., December 21, 1876. CSmH has a further letter to the Comte de Paris from John Pope dated, April 19, 1877, broadside, 25 × 20cm.

—— The second battle of Bull run. *B&L* II 449–94. **1628**

Stevens, Hazard, 1842–1918.
The second battle of Bull run. *PMHSM* IX (1898) 449–95. **1629**

Chantilly
September 1, 1862

Moore, John G
The battle of Chantilly. *MA* XXVII (1964) 49–63. maps. **1630**

Fredericksburg
December 12–13, 1862

Map of the battle field of Fredericksburg, explained by extracts from official reports. Also, Gen. Ro. E. Lee's report of the battle. Lynchburg, Virginian Power-press book and job office, 1866. 44 p. fold. map. 22cm.
       CSmH DLC NN   **1631**
Copyright by Carter M. Braxton, civil engineer.
"All communications respecting this map and pamphlet should be addressed to M. B. Anderson."
Advertising matter, 36–44.
"Errata" slip inserted.

Allan, William, 1837–1889.
Fredericksburg, by Lieutenant-Colonel William Allan. *PMHSM* III (1899) 122–49. **1632**

Fredericksburg, continued

Catton, Bruce, 1899–
Glory road, the bloody route from Fredericksburg to Gettysburg [by] Bruce Catton. Garden City, Doubleday & co., 1952. 416 p. 3 maps and endpaper map. 21½cm.
CSmH NN   **1633**

Colston, Raleigh Edward, 1825–1896.
Lee's knowledge of Hooker's movements. *B&L* III 233.   **1634**

Couch, Darius Nash, 1822–1897.
Sumner's "right grand division." *B&L* III 105–20.   **1635**

[De Peyster, John Watts] 1821–1907.
Fredericksburg. Who was responsible for the repulse? *Onward* Vol 2, no 3 (September 1869) 199–208.   **1636**

Dinkins, James, 1845–1939.
Barksdale's Mississippi brigade at Fredericksburg, read at seventeenth annual reunion Lousiana division U.C.V., Monroe, October 15, 1908. *SHSP* xxxvi (1908) 17–25.
               1637

Early, Jubal Anderson, 1816–1894.
Stonewall Jackson at Fredericksburg, a letter from . . . *Historical magazine* s 2 VIII (Morrisania 1870) 32–5.   **1638**

Fleming, Vivian Minor, 1844–1930.
Battles of Fredericksburg and Chancellorsville, Virginia, by V. M. Fleming. Richmond, W. C. Hill print. co., 1921. 30 p. 23cm.
NN   **1639**

Franklin, William Buel, 1823–1903.
A reply of Maj.-Gen. William B. Franklin, to the Report of the Joint committee of Congress on the conduct of the war, submitted to the public on the 6th April, 1863. New York, D. Van Nostrand, 1863. 31 p. fold. map. 22½cm.   NN   **1640**

—— Reply of Major-General W. B. Franklin to the Joint committee of Congress on the conduct of the war, on the first battle of Fredericksburg. Second edition, with notes and correspondence. (From the Rebellion record). New York, D. Van Nostrand, 1867. 14 p. map. 24½cm.   CSmH DLC   **1641**
    Text in double columns.

Greene, Jacob Lyman, 1837–1908.
Gen. William B. Franklin and the operations of the left wing at the battle of Fredericksburg, December 13, 1862, by Jacob L. Greene. Hartford, Belknap and Warfield, 1900. 38 p. front. (port.), fold. map in pocket. 21½cm.
NN CtHi CSmH   **1642**

Hotchkiss, Jedediah, 1827–1899.
The battle-fields of Virginia. Chancellorsville, embracing the operations of the Army of Northern Virginia, from the first battle of Fredericksburg to the death of Lieutenant-General Jackson, by Jed. Hotchkiss and William Allan. New York, D. Van Nostrand, 1867. 152 p. front. (port.), fold. maps. 23½cm.
CSmH NHi   **1643**

Humphreys, Andrew Atkinson, 1810–1883.
The army of the Potomac. General Humphreys at Fredericksburg. Communicated by General J. Watts de Peyster. *Historical magazine* s 2 v (Morrisania 1869) 353–6.   **1644**

Humphreys, Henry Hollingsworth, 1840–
Major General Andrew Atkinson Humphreys at Fredericksburg, Va., December 13th, 1862, and Farmville, Va., April 7th, 1865, by Henry H. Humphreys. Chicago, Press of R. R. McCabe & co. [c1896] 60 p. 22cm.
CSmH   **1645**

Longstreet, James, 1821–1904.
The battle of Fredericksburg. *B&L* III 70–85.   **1646**

—— Battle of Fredericksburg. Report of Lieutenant-General Longstreet. *SHST* I (1874) 42–8.   **1647**

McLaws, Lafayette, 1821–1897.
The battle of Fredericksburg. *In* Addresses delivered before the Confederate veterans of Savannah, Ga., 1895, 71–93.   **1648**
    See Title 419A.

—— The Confederate left at Fredericksburg. *B&L* III 86–94.   **1649**

Moore, J   H
Fredericksburg. *SB* ns II (1886/87) 179–84. map.   **1650**

Ransom, Robert, 1828–1892.
Ransom's division at Fredericksburg. *B&L* III 94–5.   **1650A**

—— —— Kershaw's brigade at Fredericksburg, by Joseph Brevard Kershaw. *B&L* III 95.
               1651
    "General J. B. Kershaw writes to the editor . . . December 6th, 1887," correcting an error of Ransom's narrative.

Scales, Alfred Moore, 1827–1892.
The battle of Fredericksburg, an address by Alfred M. Scales, before the Association of the Virginia division of the Army of Northern Virginia, at Richmond . . . November 1, 1883. . . . Washington, D.C., R. O. Polkinhorn & Son, printer, 1884. 23 p. 22½cm.
CSmH NHi NcD   **1652**
    Also published in *SHSP* XL (1915) 195–223.

Smith, William Farrar, 1824–1903.
Franklin's "left grand division." *B&L* III 128–38.   **1653**

—— The military situation in Northern Virginia, from the 1st to the 14th of November, 1862. *PMHSM* III (1889) 104–21.   **1654**

Stackpole, Edward James, 1894–
Drama on the Rappahannock, the Fredericksburg campaign, by Edward J. Stackpole. Harrisburg, Military Service pub. co. [1957] xx, 297 p. front. (illus.), illus., maps and plans, ports. 23cm.   NN   **1655**

United States. Army.
Organization of the Army of the Potomac (commanded by Major-General Ambrose E. Burnside) December 11–15, 1862. [Washington, War Records bureau, 1882] 10 p. 23cm.
CSmH   **1656**

—— Organization of the Union forces at the battle of Fredericksburg, Va., December 11–15, 1862. [Washington, D.C., 1883] 16 p. 22½cm.   CSmH   **1657**

United States. Conduct of the War, Joint Committee on the.
. . . Report [on the battle of Fredericksburg] [Washington, D.C., 1863] 40 p. 22cm.
NN   **1658**

At head of title: 37th congress, 3d session. Senate. Rep. com. no. 71. . . .
Caption title

Whan, Vorin E
Fiasco at Fredericksburg [by] Vorin E. Whan, Jr. [State College] Pennsylvania State University press [1961] xii, 159 p. maps and plans. 23½cm.   NN   **1659**
"View of the battlefield looking northeast from the southern end of Willis hill," illus. endpaper.

Fredericksburg Memorials

Fredericksburg and Adjacent National Battlefields Memorial Park Association of Virginia.
A few among the many reasons why there should be established at or near Fredericksburg, in the State of Virginia, a national battlefield park, embracing the battlefields of Fredericksburg, Chancellorsville, Salem Church, Todd's Tavern, the Wilderness and Spotsylvania Court-house. [Fredericksburg, Star print, n.d.] 11 p. fold. map. 18cm. CSmH   **1660**

Pennsylvania. Fredericksburg Battlefield Memorial Commission.
Dedication of monument erected by Pennsylvania to commemorate the charge of General Humphreys' division, Fifth army corps,

Army of the Potomac, on Marye's heights, Fredericksburg, Virginia, December 13th, 1862. Dedicatory ceremonies, November 11th, 1908. Philadelphia, Press of J. B. Lippincott co., 1908. 29, (1) p. 24½cm. CSmH   **1661**

*   *   *

Bigelow, John, 1854–1936.
The battle of Kelly's ford. *JUSCA* XXI (1910) 5–28. 2 plans, fold. map.   **1662**

Stevens, Hazard, 1842–1918.
The siege of Suffolk, April 11 – May 3, 1863. *PMHSM* IX (1906) 195–231.   **1663**

Chancellorsville

April 27 – May 6, 1863

The battle of Chancellorsville and the Eleventh army corps. New York, G. B. Teubner, printer, 1863. 48 p. 22cm.   DLC   **1664**

Bates, Samuel Penniman, 1827–1902.
The battle of Chancellorsville, by Samuel P. Bates. . . . Meadville, Penn., Edward T. Bates, 1882. 261 p. 2 maps, 2 plates (ports.). 23½cm.
CSmH NN   **1665**

—— Hooker's comments on Chancellorsville. *B&L* III 215–23.   **1666**

Bigelow, John, 1854–1936.
The campaign of Chancellorsville, a strategical and tactical study, by John Bigelow, Jr. New Haven, Yale University press [1910] xvi, 528 p. 42 fold. maps (9 in pocket). 29½cm.
"Errata" slip inserted.   CSmH NN   **1667**

Bisset, Johnson
The mysteries of Chancellorsville. Who killed Stonewall Jackson, by Johnson Bisset. New York, Hobson book press [1945] ix-xi, (1), 37 p. 21cm.   NN   **1668**

Colston, Raleigh Edward, 1825–1896.
Official report of the operations of General Colston's division during the battle of Chancellorsville, May 2 and 3, 1863. *SM* XI (1872) 57–63.   **1669**

Couch, Darius Nash, 1822–1897.
The Chancellorsville campaign. *B&L* III 154–71.   **1670**

[De Peyster, John Watts] 1821–1907.
Chancellorsville, a critical review of the battle. *Onward* vol 2, nos 1–6 (July – December, 1869) 35–46, 155–64, 336–41, 411–22, 471–85; [February, 1870] xxi-xxiii.   **1671**

Chancellorsville, continued

Dodge, Theodore Ayrault, 1842–1909.
   The campaign of Chancellorsville, by Theodore A. Dodge. Boston, James R. Osgood and co., 1881. vi, (1), 261 p. 4 fold. maps. 23½cm.
                              CSmH   *1672*
Doubleday, Abner, 1819–1893.
   . . . Chancellorsville and Gettysburg, by Abner Doubleday. New York, Charles Scribner's Sons, 1882. xi, (1), 243 p. maps and plans. 19cm.   CSmH NN   *1673*
   For an appraisal, see Doubleday's Chancellorsville and Gettysburg, by John A. Carpenter, *MA* xxvii (1963) 84–8.
   At head of title: Campaigns of the Civil war — vi. See Title 1362.

Hamlin, Augustus Choate, 1829–1905.
   . . . The battle of Chancellorsville, the attack of Stonewall Jackson and his army upon the right flank of the Army of the Potomac at Chancellorsville, Virginia, on Saturday afternoon, May 2, 1863, by Augustus Choate Hamlin. Published by the author. Bangor, 1896. 196 p. plates (maps). 22cm.
                              CSmH NN   *1674*
Hancock, Winfield Scott, 1824–1886.
   Chancellorsville and Gettysburg, extracts from General Doubleday's monograph, with General Hancock's autograph notes thereon. Introduction by General Webb. *JMSIUS* xlviii (1911) 101–17. facsims., ports.   *1675*

Howard, Oliver Otis, 1830–1909.
   The Eleventh corps at Chancellorsville. *B&L* iii 189–202.   *1676*
—— Jackson's attack on the right at Chancellorsville. *MOLLUS-Nebr* i 6–20.   *1677*

Humphreys, Benjamin Grubb, 1808–1882.
   Recollections of Fredericksburg, from the morning of the 29th of April to the 6th of May, 1863. *LWL* iii (1867) 443–60. plate (map).   *1678*

Lane, James Henry, 1833–1907.
   Gen. Lane's report of the battle of Chancellorsville. *OLOD* iii (1875) 183–7.   *1679*

Lee, Fitzhugh, 1835–1905.
   Chancellorsville, address of Gen. Fitzhugh Lee, before the Virginia division, of the Army of Northern Virginia, at their annual meeting, held in the Capitol in Richmond, Va., Oct. 29th, 1879. Richmond, Geo. W. Cary, printer, 1879. 44 p. 23cm.   CSmH   *1680*
   Also published in *SHSP* vii (1879) 545–85.

McGlashan, Peter Alexander Selkirk
   Battle of Salem Church, May 3, 1863. *In* Addresses delivered before the Confederate association of Savannah, Ga., 1893, 89–94.
   See Title 419A.   *1681*

McIntosh, David Gregg, 1836–1916.
   The campaign of Chancellorsville, by David Gregg McIntosh, Colonel of artillery, C.S.A. Richmond, Wm. Ellis Jones' Sons, printers, 1915. 59 p. 23cm.   DLC ScU   *1682*
   Also published in *SHSP* xl (1915) 44–100.

Meysenburg, Theodore August,   –1901.
   Reminiscences of Chancellorsville, by Major T. A. Meysenburg. *MOLLUS-Mo* i 295–307.
                                            1683
Pleasonton, Alfred, 1824–1897.
   The successes and failures of Chancellorsville. *B&L* iii 172–82.   *1684*

Randolph, William Fitzhugh
   Chancellorsville, the flank movement that routed the Yankees, General Jackson's mortal wound, description of how he received it, by Captain W. F. Randolph. *SHSP* xxix (1901) 329–37.   *1685*
—— With Stonewall Jackson at Chancellorsville, by W. F. Randolph, Captain of Jackson's bodyguard. [n.p., n.d.] [12] p. 19cm.
                              NcD   *1686*
Richardson, Charles
   The Chancellorsville campaign, Fredericksburg to Salem Church, by Charles Richardson. New York, Neale pub. co., 1907. 124 p. 19cm.
                              CSmH NN   *1687*
Rodes, Robert Emmett, 1829–1864
   General R. E. Rodes' report of the battle of Chancellorsville. *SHSP* ii (1876) 161–72. *1688*

Smith, James Power, 1837–
   Stonewall Jackson and Chancellorsville, by Rev. James Power Smith, formerly Captain and A.D.C. to General Jackson. *PMHSM* v (1904) 351–76.   *1689*
—— Stonewall Jackson's last battle. *B&L* iii 203–14.   *1690*

Stackpole, Edward James, 1894–
   Chancellorsville, Lee's greatest battle, by Edward J. Stackpole. Harrisburg, Stackpole co. [1958] 384 p. illus., maps and plans, ports. 23cm.   NN   *1691*
   Maps on endpapers.

United States. Army.
   The Chancellorsville campaign. Organization of the Army of the Potomac (commanded by Major-General Joseph Hooker) May 1–5, 1863. [Washington, D.C., n.d.] 18 p. 23cm.
                              CSmH   *1692*
—— Chancellorsville campaign. Organization of the Army of the Potomac commanded by Major-General Joseph Hooker, May 1–5, 1863. [Washington, Adjutant General's office, 1882] 12 p. 23½cm.   CSmH   *1693*

Webb, Alexander Stewart, 1835–1911.
[Correspondence with General Meade occasioned by an article "Chancellorsville, by a staff officer," published in the New York Times of June 3, 1867] [4] folios. 21cm.
CSmH   **1694**

—— Meade at Chancellorsville. *PMHSM* III (1888) 219–39.   **1695**

Wilson, James Harrison, 1837–1925.
The campaign of Chancellorsville <April 27 – May 5, 1863> by Major John Bigelow, Jr. A critical review . . . by James Harrison Wilson. Wilmington, C. L. Stoey, printer, 1911. 77 p. fold. map. 23cm.
CSmH DLC   **1696**
"Reprinted by permission from the Sun of November 6th, 13th and 20th, 1910."

Brandy Station
June 9, 1863

Beck, Robert McCandless
General J. E. B. Stuart at Brandy Station, June 9, 1863. *Cavalry journal* XLIV (May/June 1935) 5–10. port., 2 plans.   **1697**

Borcke, Heros von, 1835–1895.
Die grosse Reiterschlacht bei Brandy Station, 9. Juni 1863., bearbeitet von Heros von Borcke, damals Stabchef des General Stuart [und] Justus Scheibert, damals Captain. Berlin, Paul Kittel, 1893. 179 p. illus., ports, plates (maps). 24cm.   DLC NN   **1698**
Illus. and ports. are paged plates.

Downey, Fairfax Davis, 1893–
Clash of cavalry, the battle of Brandy Station, June 9, 1863, by Fairfax Downey. New York, David McKay co. [1959] xv, 238 p. illus., music, plates (illus., ports.). 22cm.
Maps on endpapers.   NN   **1699**

Fleetwood
June 9, 1863

McClellan, Henry Brainerd, 1840–1914.
The battle of Fleetwood. *AW* 392–402. **1700**

Winchester
June 15, 1863

Keifer, Joseph Warren, 1836–1932.
Official reports of J. Warren Keifer, detailing movements and operations of his command in the battles of Winchester (1863). . . . Springfield, Ohio, Daily Republican office, 1866. 50 p. 21cm.   OHi   **1701**

Milroy, Robert Huston, 1816–1890.
Letter to the President of the United States, explanatory of the evidence before the Court of inquiry relative to the evacuation of Winchester by the command of Maj. Gen. R. H. Milroy. Washington, Gideon & Pearson, printers [1863] 14 p. 23cm.   DLC NN   **1702**
Title and imprint from cover.

*   *   *

McMahon, Martin Thomas, 1838–1906.
From Gettysburg to the coming of Grant. *B&L* IV 81–94.   **1703**

United States. Army.
The Bristoe (Va.) campaign. Organization of the Army of the Potomac (commanded by Major-General George G. Meade), October 10, 1863. [Washington, D.C., n.d.] 12 p. 23cm.
CSmH   **1704**

Hathaway, John Livingston,   –1891.
The Mine Run movement, by Bvt. Lieut. Col. John L. Hathaway. *MOLLUS-Wis* I 120–4.   **1705**

1864–1865

Catton, Bruce, 1899–
A stillness at Appomattox, by Bruce Catton. Garden City, Doubleday & co., 1954. viii, 438 p. 21½cm.   CSmH   **1706**
Map on t.p. spread and on endpaper.

Dowdey, Clifford, 1904–
Lee's last campaign, the story of Lee and his men against Grant, 1864, by Clifford Dowdey. With maps by Samuel H. Bryant. Boston, Little, Brown and co. [1960] 415 p. maps. 22cm.   NN   **1707**
"The Wilderness to Petersburg," map on endpaper.

Early, Jubal Anderson, 1816–1894.
A memoir of the last year of the war for independence in the Confederate states of America, containing an account of the operations of his commands in the years 1864 and 1865, by Lieutenant-General Jubal A. Early. . . . Toronto, Printed by Lovell & Gibson, 1866. x, (2) [13]–144 p. 20½cm.
CSmH NN   **1708**

—— —— Lynchburg, Charles W. Button, 1867. xii, [13]–135, (1) p. 21½cm.
CSmH DLC NN   **1709**
"Contents," (1) p.

—— —— New Orleans, 1867. x, (1), [13]–112 p. 22cm.   NcD   **1710**
On cover: Southern edition.
"Preface" dated: November 1866.
Advertisement of Blelock & co., publishers, p. [4] of cover.

Campaigns of 1864–1865, continued

Field, Charles William, 1828–1892.
Campaigns of 1864 and 1865, narrative of Major-General C. W. Field. *SHSP* xiv (1886) 542–63.   *1711*

Howard, McHenry
Notes and recollections of opening the campaign of 1864, by First Lieutenant McHenry Howard, C.S.A. *PMHSM* iv (1883) 81–116.
1712

Humphreys, Andrew Atkinson, 1810–1883.
. . . The Virginia campaign of '64 and '65, the Army of the Potomac and the Army of the James, by Andrew A. Humphreys. New York, Charles Scribner's Sons, 1883. x, (1), 451 p. fold. maps. 18½cm.   CSmH NN   *1713*
At head of title: Campaigns of the Civil war — xii.
See Title 1362.

Longstreet, James, 1821–1904.
Plan of campaign for 1864 extract. *LWL* i (1868) 170–1.   *1714*
Dated: Headquarters Petersburg, en route to E. T., March 15, 1864.

Meade, George Gordon, 1815–1872.
General Meade's report of the Rapidan campaign, May 4th to November 1st, 1864. Communicated by William Swinton. *Historical magazine* s 2 v (Morrisania 1869) 161–70.
1715

Perry, William Flake, 1823–1901.
Reminiscences of the campaign of 1864 in Virginia, by General William F. Perry. *SHSP* vii (1879) 49–63.   *1716*

Ropes, John Codman, 1836–1899.
Grant's campaign in Virginia in 1864. *PMHSM* iv (1884) 363–405.   *1717*

Vogdes, Israel,   –1889.
Observations on the military operations in Virginia in 1864. *Historical magazine* s 2 v (Morrisania 1869) 309–13.   *1718*

Kilpatrick's Raid
February 28 – March 4, 1864

The cavalry raid by Custer, Kilpatrick and Dahlgren. *SHST* i (1874) 155–75.   *1719*
Text signed: G. W. M.

What is the truth of Dahlgren's raid? *Tyler's quarterly historical and genealogical magazine* xxviii (1946/47) 65–90.   *1720*

Hampton, Wade, 1818–1892.
Attempt of Kilpatrick and Dahlgren to capture Richmond, from report of Lieutenant-General Wade Hampton. *SHST* i (1874) 150–4.   *1721*

James, G   Watson
Dahlgren's raid. . . . *SHSP* xxxix (1914) 63–72.   *1722*

Jones, John William, 1836–1909.
The Kilpatrick-Dahlgren raid against Richmond. *SHSP* xiii (1885) 515–60.   *1723*

Jones, Virgil Carrington, 1906–
. . . Eight hours before Richmond. Introduction by Colonel Robert Selph Henry. New York, Henry Holt and co. [1957] x, 180 p. plates (facsims., illus., map, ports.). 21½cm.
NN   *1724*
At head of title: By Virgil Carrington Jones.
Title on two leaves.
Map on endpaper.

Pond, George Edward, 1837–1899.
Kilpatrick's and Dahlgren's raid to Richmond. *B&L* iv 95–6.   *1725*

*   *   *

A night in the Wilderness [March 12, 1864] *Galaxy* xi (1871) 687–93.   *1726*

Sheridan, Philip Henry, 1831–1888.
Report of operations of the Cavalry corps, Army of the Potomac, Major General P. H. Sheridan, commanding, from April 6th to August 4th, 1864. 24 p. 20½cm.
CSmH NN   *1727*
Dated: New Orleans, La., May 13, 1866.

*   *   *

Notes on the May campaign on the James river. *United States service magazine* iii (1865) 23–8, 245–54.   *1728*

Hannum, Warren T
The crossing of the James river in 1864. *Military engineer* xv (1923) 229–37. illus., map.   *1729*

Kautz, August Valentine, 1828–1895.
Operations south of the James river. *B&L* iv 533–5.   *1730*

Wilderness
May 5–7, 1864

Gen. Lee at the "Wilderness," by R. C. of "Hood's Texas brigade." *LWL* v (1868) 481–6.
1731

Alexander, Edward Porter, 1835–1910.
The Wilderness campaign. Grant's conduct of the Wilderness campaign. *Annual report of the American historical association* 1908 i 225–34.   *1732*

Coffin, Charles Carleton, 1823–1896.
The May campaign in Virginia. *Atlantic monthly* XIV (1864) 124–32. plans.   **1733**

Livermore, William Roscoe, 1843–1919.
The Wilderness campaign. Lee's conduct of the Wilderness campaign. *Annual report of the American historical association* 1908 I 235–43.
1734

Long, Armistead Lindsay, 1825–1891.
Report of Brigadier-General A. L. Long, artillery, Second corps, from 4th to 31st May, 1864. *SHST* I (1874) 113–18.   **1735**

McClernand, Edward John, 1849?–1926.
Cavalry operations, the Wilderness to the James river. *JMSIUS* XXX (1902) 321–43. 2 illus., map.   **1736**

Ramseur, Stephen Dodson, 1837–1864.
Maj.-Gen. S. D. Ramseere's [sic] report of operations, from 4th to 27th May, 1864. *SHST* I (1874) 138–40.   **1737**

Robinson, Leigh
The South before and at the battle of the Wilderness. Address of Leigh Robinson (formerly of the Richmond Howitzers) of Washington, D.C., before the Virginia division of the Army of Northern Virginia at their annual meeting, held in the Capitol in Richmond, Va., Nov. 1, 1877. Richmond, James E. Goode, printer, 1878. 111 p. 23cm.   CSmH   **1738**

Schaff, Morris, 1840–1929.
The battle of the Wilderness, by Morris Schaff. Boston, Houghton, Mifflin co., 1910. 345 p. 5 plates (maps, 2 double). 21½cm.
CSmH NN   **1739**
First published in *Atlantic monthly* CIII–V.

Spalding, Branch
Eyes that saw not. *Infantry journal* XLVII (1940) 249–59. illus., plans.   **1740**

Steere, Edward, 1908–
The Wilderness campaign, by Edward Steere. Harrisburg, Stackpole co. [1960] 522 p. maps and plans. 23cm.   NN   **1741**
Maps on endpapers.

Stevens, Hazard, 1842–1918.
The Sixth corps in the Wilderness. *PMHSM* IV (1887) 175–203.   **1742**

Swift, Eben, 1854–1938.
The Wilderness campaign. The Wilderness campaign from our present point of view. *Annual report of the American historical association* 1908 I 244–7.   **1743**

United States. Army.
Organization of the Army of the Potomac (commanded by Major General George G.
Meade), on May 4, 1864. [Washington, D.C., 1882] 9 p. 23½cm.   CSmH   **1744**

—— The Wilderness campaign. Organization of the Army of the Potomac (commanded by Major-General George G. Meade) on the morning of May 5, 1864. [Washington, War Records office, 1883] 13 p. 23cm.   CSmH   **1745**

—— Organization of the Union forces operating against Richmond, Va., (under the command of Lieutenant-General U. S. Grant,) on the morning of May 5, 1864. [Washington, War Records office, 1888] 16 p. 22½cm.
CSmH   **1746**

—— Return of casualties in the Union forces from the Wilderness to the James river, May–June, 1864. [Washington, War Records office, 1888] 120 p. 22½cm.   CSmH   **1747**

Venable, Charles Scott, 1827–1900.
The campaign from the Wilderness to Petersburg. Address of Col. C. S. Venable, (formerly of Gen. R. E. Lee's staff) . . . before the Virginia division of the Army of Northern Virginia, at their annual meeting, held in the Virginia state capitol, at Richmond, Thursday evening, Oct. 30th, 1873. Richmond, Geo. W. Gary, printer, 1879. 20 p. 23cm.
CSmH DLC GEU   **1748**
Also in *SHSP* XIV (1886) 522–42.

—— General Lee in the Wilderness campaign. *B&L* IV 240–6.   **1749**

Webb, Alexander Stewart, 1835–1911.
Through the Wilderness. *B&L* IV 152–69.
1750

White, Henry Alexander, 1861–
Lee's wrestle with Grant in the Wilderness 1864. *PMHSM* I (1897) 25–75.   **1751**

Wilcox, Cadmus Marcellus, 1826–1890.
Lee and Grant in the Wilderness. *AW* 485–501.   **1752**

Spottsylvania
May 8–21, 1864

"The bloody angle." The Confederate disaster at Spotsylvania [sic] Court-house, May 12, 1864, by which the "Stonewall brigade" was annihilated . . . accounts by General James A. Walker, Colonel Thomas H. Carter, Lieutenant Wm. S. Archer, M. S. Stringfellow and Major D. W. Anderson. *SHSP* XXI (1893) 228–54.   **1753**

Barlow, Francis Channing, 1834–1896.
Capture of the salient, May 12, 1864. *PMHSM* IV (1879) 243–62.   **1754**

Spottsylvania, continued

Cutshaw, Wilfred E
The battle near Spottsylvania Courthouse on May 18th, 1864. An address delivered before R. E. Lee camp no. 1, C. V., on the night of January 20, 1905, by W. E. Cutshaw. Richmond, R. E. Lee Camp No. 1, Confederate Veterans [1905] 17 p. 23cm.
              DLC NN   **1755**
Also in *SHSP* xxxix (1914) 195–212.

Driver, William Raymond
The capture of the salient at Spottsylvania, May 12, 1864. *PMHSM* iv (1882) 273–85.
                                1756
"Reviewing the papers of General F. C. Barlow, of Captain McHenry Howard, C.S.A., and of General Lewis A. Grant."

Ewell, Richard Stoddert, 1817–1872.
Battle of Spottsylvania. Report of General Ewell. *SHST* i (1874) 107–13.   **1757**

Grant, Lewis Addison, 1829–1918.
Review of Major-General Barlow's paper on the capture of the salient at Spottsylvania, May 12, 1864. *PMHS* iv (1881) 263–71.   **1758**

Johnson, Edward, 1816–1873.
Major-Gen. E. Johnson's report of operations at Spottsylvania C. H. *SHST* i (1874) 140–1.
                                1759

Patch, Charles A
At the "death angle," May 12, 1864. *Magazine of American history* xvi (1886) 176–9.
                                1760

New Market

May 15, 1864

Cocke, Preston
The battle of New Market and the cadets of the Virginia military institute, May 15, 1864. Salient features of the battle in connection with the part taken by the cadets. With a map of the battle-field and key. By a V. M. I. New Market cadet. [Richmond] 1914. 11 p. double map. 23½cm.   DLC NN   **1761**
"Prefatory note" signed: Preston Cocke.

Colonna, B   A
The battle of New Market. *JMSIUS* li (1912) 343–9. map.   **1762**

Couper, William, 1884–
The V.M.I. New Market cadets. Biographical sketches of all members of the Virginia military institute corps of cadets who fought in the battle of New Market, May 15, 1864, by Wm. Couper. Charlottesville, Michie co., 1933. xi, 272 p. plates (illus., fold. map). 23½cm.
              DLC NN   **1763**

Imboden, John Daniel, 1823–1895.
The battle of New Market, May 15th, 1864. *B&L* iv 480–6.   **1764**

Salyards, Joseph
Memorial elegy on the battle of New Market, May 15th, 1864, and a eulogy on the life and character of Gen. John C. Breckinridge, delivered at New Market, May the 15th, 1877. New Market, Henkel & co. [1877] 13 p. 24cm.
                    CSmH   **1765**
Address, 5–9, is in double columns.

Short, James R
Field of honor. At New Market Confederate forces repulsed a Yankee invasion, and a battalion of boys became men. *Virginia cavalcade* iii 4 (Spring 1954) 30–5. illus. (1 col.), 2 plans, ports.   **1766**

Stanard, Beverly, 1845–1864.
Letters of a New Market cadet, Beverly Stanard. Edited by John G. Barnett and Robert K. Turner, Jr. Chapel Hill, University of North Carolina press [c1961] xxiv, 70 p. front. (illus.). 23½cm.   DLC   **1767**

Strother, David Hunter, 1816–1888
With Sigel at New Market, the diary of Colonel D. H. Strother. Edited by Cecil D. Eby, Jr. *CWH* vi (1960) 73–83.   **1768**

Turner, Edward Raymond, 1881–1929.
The New Market campaign, May, 1864, by Edward Raymond Turner. Richmond, Whittet & Shepperson, 1912. xiv, 203 p. plates (illus., 2 double maps, ports.). 23cm.
              DLC NN   **1769**
Roster of the Cadet battalion, 163–71.

Virginia.
. . . Official report of the Commandant of cadets [Virginia military institute] of the battle of New Market. [Richmond, 1865] 14 p. 24½cm.   CSmH   **1770**
At head of title and running title: Doc. no. XXV [Documents called session, 1864–5]
Message of transmittal, dated January 11, 1865, by Superintendent Francis H. Smith reports the faculty casualties of the war.
The Report, dated July 4, 1864, is by Lieut. Col. S. Ship, Commandant of cadets.
Also published in Memorial address of John S. Wise, 189–. (See Title 1772.)

Wise, John Sergeant, 1846–1913.
Battle of New Market, Va., May 15th, 1864, an address repeated by John S. Wise, a cadet in the corps of 1864, before the professors, officers and cadets of the Virginia military institute . . . May 13th, 1882. 72 p. 18½cm.
      CSmH WHi NN NcD   **1771**

—— Memorial address of John S. Wise, delivered at the unveiling of a monument to the memory of the Southern soldiers and V.M.I. cadets, who fell in the battle of New Market, May 15th, 1864. Also, rolls of officers and cadets engaged, with official lists of casualties, orders, and official report of the battles, from volume xxxvii, Part I, Series I, of Records of Union and Confederate armies. . . . [Roanoke, Stone print. co., 189–] 62, (1) p. 19cm.

DLC NcD **1772**

Drewry's Bluff

May 16, 1864

Beauregard, Pierre Gustave Toutant, 1819–1893.
The defense of Drewry's Bluff. *B&L* iv 195–205. **1773**

—— Drury's Bluff and Petersburg. *North American review* cxliv (1887) 244–60. **1774**

—— Gen. Beauregard's report of the battle of Drury's Bluff. *LWL* iii (1867) 1–8. **1775**

Smith, William Farrar, 1824–1903.
Butler's attack on Drewry's Bluff. *B&L* iv 206–12. **1776**

Jericho's Ford

May 23, 1864

Lane, James Henry, 1833–1907.
Gen. Lane's report of the battle of Jericho's Ford. *OLOD* iv (1876) 19–21. **1777**

Cold Harbor

May 31 – June 12, 1864

Clingman, Thomas Lanier, 1815–1868.
Clingman's brigade at Cold Harbor. *OLOD* ii (1875) 291–2. **1778**
A letter dated, June 5, 1864, to the Richmond papers correcting the impression that "Clingman's brigade gave way for a time."

Law, Evander McIvor, 1836–1920.
From the Wilderness to Cold Harbor. *B&L* iv 118–44. **1779**

McMahon, Martin Thomas, 1838–1906.
Cold Harbor. *B&L* iv 213–20. **1780**

Ropes, John Codman, 1836–1899.
The battle of Cold Harbor. *PMHSM* iv (1883) 341–62. **1781**

Smith, William Farrar, 1824–1903.
The Eighteenth corps at Cold Harbor. *B&L* iv 221–30. **1782**

—— General W. F. Smith's report of the battle of Cold Harbor, from the original draft, now first printed. Communicated by William

Swinton. *Historical magazine* s 2 v (Morrisania 1869) 240–8. **1783**

United States. Army.
Organization of the Army of the Potomac (commanded by Major-General George G. Meade), May 31, 1864. [Washington, D.C., 1886] 13 p. 23cm. CSmH **1784**

Pennsylvania. Cold Harbor Battle-field Commission.
. . . Pennsylvania at Cold Harbor, Virginia. Ceremonies at the dedication of the monument, erected by the Commonwealth of Pennsylvania in the National cemetery at Cold Harbor, Virginia. To mark the positions as well as in memory of the Pennsylvania commands, engaged in the battle of Cold Harbor, of June, A.D. 1864. . . . [Harrisburg] C. E. Aughinbaugh, Printer to the State, 1912 [i.e. 1913] 60 p. front. (5 ports.), 3 plates (2 illus., port.). 22cm. DLC NN **1785**
At head of title: 1864–1910.

* * *

Hampton, Wade, 1818–1892.
Gen. Hampton's report of operations of 1st and 2nd divisions of cavalry, from the 8th to the 26th June, 1864. *LWL* ii (1866/67) 1–4. **1786**

Trevilian Station

June 11, 1864

Butler, Matthew Calbraith, 1836–1909.
The cavalry fight at Trevilian Station. *B&L* iv 237–9. **1787**

Monaghan, James, 1891–
Custer's "last stand," Trevilian station, 1864. *CWH* viii (1962) 245–58. **1788**

Lynchburg

June 17–18, 1864

Blackford, Charles Minor, 1833–1903.
The campaign and battle of Lynchburg, an address delivered before the Garland-Rodes camp of Confederate veterans at Lynchburg, Va., July 18, 1901. *SHSP* xxx (1902) 279–314. **1789**

—— Campaign and battle of Lynchburg, Va., by Charles M. Blackford, Delivered by request of the Garland-Rodes camp of Confederate veterans of Lynchburg, Virginia, June 18th, 1901. [Lynchburg, Press of J. P. Bell co., 1901] 72 p. front. (port.). 19½cm.

DLC NN **1790**
"Lynchburg companies in the service of the Confederacy, 1861–'65," 61–72.

Lynchburg, continued

Humphreys, Milton Wylie, 1844–
A history of the Lynchburg campaign, by Milton W. Humphreys, member of King's artillery, C.S.A. Charlottesville, Michie co., printers, 1924. 74 p. 23cm.   Vi   *1791*

Walker, Francis Amasa, 1840–1907.
Ream's station [June 22, 1864] *PMHSM* v (1884) 267–305.   *1792*

Willcox, Orlando Bolivar, 1823–1903.
Actions on the Weldon railroad. *B&L* iv 568–73.   *1793*

Staunton River Bridge
June 25, 1864

Confederate States of America. War Department.
Report of the engagement at Staunton river, June 25th, 1864. [n.p., 1864] 3 p. 24½cm.
Caption title.   MBAt Vi   *1794*
Page 3 numbered 4.
Crandall 1424.

Farinholt, B   S
The gallant defence of Staunton river bridge. *SHSP* xxxvii (1909) 321–5.   *1795*

Sappony Church
June 27, 1864

Hampton, Wade, 1818–1892.
Gen. Hampton's report of the engagement at Sappony church. *LWL* ii (1866/67) 78–9.
                                                      1796

Petersburg
June 4, 1864 – April 3, 1865

A guide to the fortifications and battlefields around Petersburg . . . Prepared and published as a hand-book, by the proprietor of Jarratt's hotel. Petersburg, John B. Ege's print. house, 1869. 26 p. fold. map. 22½cm.
Title from cover.   WHi NN   *1797*

Alexander, Edward Porter, 1835–1910.
The movement against Petersburg. *Scribner's magazine* xli (1907) 180–94. 2 plans.
                                                      1798

Archer, Fletcher H
The defense of Petersburg on the 9th June, 1864. *In* War talks of Confederate veterans, compiled and edited by Geo S. Bernard, Petersburg, Va., 1892, 107–48.
                                        NN   *1799*

Beauregard, Pierre Gustave Toutant, 1819–1893.
The battle of Petersburg. *North American review* cxlv (1887) 367–77, 506–15.   *1800*

—— Defence of Petersburg in June, 1864, letter of General Beauregard. *SHST* i (1874) 134–7.   *1801*

—— Letter of General G. T. Beauregard to General C. M. Wilcox. *PMHSM* v (1906) 119–23.   *1802*
Dated, June 9, 1874, and concerned with his recollections of the defence of Petersburg, from the 15th to 18th June, 1864.

Driver, William Raymond
The siege of Petersburg after the capture of the Weldon railroad. *PMHSM* v (1883) 307–17.   *1803*

Hagood, Johnson, 1829–1898.
Hagood's brigade, its services in the trenches of Petersburg, Virginia, 1864, an address by General Johnson Hagood before the survivors association of Charleston district, South Carolina, April 12, 1887. *SHSP* xvi (1888) 395–415.   *1804*

Lyman, Theodore, 1833–1897.
Crossing of the James and advance on Petersburg, June 13–16, 1864. *PMHSM* v (1878) 25–31.   *1805*

—— Operations of the Army of the Potomac, June 5–15, 1864. *PMHSM* v (1882) 1–24.
                                                      1806

McGlashan, Peter Alexander Selkirk
Recollections of Petersburg, Va., June, 1864. *In* Addresses delivered before the Confederate veterans association of Savannah, Ga., 1895, 67–9.   *1807*
See Title 419A.

Peabody, Frank Everett
Crossing of the James and first assault upon Petersburg, June 12–15, 1864. *PMHSM* v (1900) 125–45.   *1808*

—— Some observations concerning the opposing forces at Petersburg on June 15, 1864. *PMHSM* v (1896) 147–56.   *1809*

Pleasants, Henry, 1884–
Inferno at Petersburg, by Henry Pleasants, Jr. and George H. Straley. Philadelphia, Chilton co. [c1961] vii, 181 p. plates (illus., 2 double maps, port.). 21cm.   DLC NcD   *1810*

Ropes, John Codman, 1836–1899.
The failure to take Petersburg on June 16–18, 1864. *PMHSM* v (1879) 157–86.   *1811*

Scott, John, 1820–1907.
A ruse of war. *AW* 380–3.   *1812*

Smith, William Farrar, 1824–1903.
General W. F. Smith at Petersburg. *Century magazine* liv (1897) 318.   *1813*

—— The movement against Petersburg, June, 1864. *PMHSM* v (1887) 75–115. **1814**

Stevens, Hazard, 1842–1918.
The storming of the lines of Petersburg by the Sixth corps, April 2, 1865. *PMHSM* vi (1884) 409–35. **1815**

Thomas, William M
The slaughter at Petersburg, June 18, 1864 . . . some interesting personal reminiscences of the fatal day, and those which immediately preceded and succeeded it, by Wm. M. Thomas, then an officer of Rion's battalion in Hagood's brigade. *SHSP* xxv (1897) 222–30. **1816**

United States. Army.
Return of casualties in the Union forces at the Crater, near Petersburg, Va., July 30, 1864. [Washington, War Records office, 1888] 8 p. 23cm. CSmH **1817**

United States. Conduct of the War, Joint Committee on the.
Report . . . on the attack on Petersburg, on the 30th day of July, 1864. Washington, Govt. print. office, 1865. 272 p. 22½cm.
CSmH **1818**
Reports of committees no. 114, Senate 38th Congress, 2d session.

Petersburg Memorials

Lykes, Richard Wayne
Petersburg National military park, Virginia, by Richard Wayne Lykes. . . . Washington, D.C., 1951 (revised 1956) 56 p. illus., plans, ports. 24cm. NN **1819**
"National park service historical handbook series no. 13."
On cover: Petersburg battlefields.

Roe, Alfred Seelye, 1844–1917.
Address of Alfred S. Roe [dedication of the Massachusetts monument at the Crater, Petersburg, November 13, 1911] 10 p. front. (illus.). 23cm. NB **1820**
Caption title.
Portion of title supplied from cover.

Shenandoah Valley

June – July, 1864

Snicker's gap. *United States service magazine* iv (1865) 323–8. **1821**

Imboden, John Daniel, 1823–1895.
Fire, sword, and the halter. *AW* 169–83. **1822**

Kennon, Lyman Walter Vere, 1858?–1918.
The Valley campaign of 1864, a military study. *PMHSM* vi (1891) 31–57. **1823**

Long, Armistead Lindsay, 1827–1891.
General Early's valley campaign. *SHSP* iii (1877) 112–22. **1824**

—— —— [ammended] *SHSP* xviii (1890) 80–91. **1825**

Merritt, Wesley, 1836–1910.
Sheridan in the Shenandoah valley. *B&L* iv 500–21. **1826**

Pond, George Edward, 1837–1899.
. . . The Shenandoah valley in 1864, by George E. Pond. New York, Charles Scribner's Sons, 1883. ix, (2), 287 p. maps, 2 fold. maps. 19cm. CSmH DLC NN **1827**
At head of title: Campaigns of the Civil war — xi.
See Title 1362.

Sigel, Franz, 1824–1902.
Sigel in the Shenandoah valley. *B&L* iv 487–91. **1828**

Stackpole, Edward James, 1894–
Sheridan in the Shenandoah, Jubal Early's nemesis, by Edward J. Stackpole. Maps by Col. Wilbur S. Nye. Illustrations from the Kean archives. Harrisburg, Stackpole co. [c1961] xvii, 413 p. illus., maps, ports. 22½cm.
NcD **1829**
"The lower [upper] Shenandoah in 1864," maps on endpapers.

United States. Army.
General summary of the casualties in the Union forces operating against Richmond, Va., July 1–31, 1864. [Washington, War Records office, 1888] 36 p. 22½cm. CSmH **1830**

*　　　*　　　*

—— Casualties in the Union forces operating against Richmond, Va., during August 1864. Deep Bottom, August 13–20. Weldon's railroad, August 18–21. Ream's station, August 25. [Washington, War Records office, 1888] 28 p. 23cm. CSmH **1831**

Powell, Junius Levert
A memory of our great war. *JMSIUS* xlviii (1911) 87–99. illus., map, port. **1832**
Battle of Deep Bottom, August 16, 1864.

United States. Army.
Casualties of the Union forces operating against Richmond, Va., during September, 1864. [Washington, War Records office, 1888] 20 p. 23cm. CSmH **1833**

Hampton, Wade, 1818–1892.
Extract from General Wade Hampton's report of cavalry operations in the Fall of 1864. *SHST* i (1874) 72–80. **1834**

Virginia, 1864, continued

Boykin, Edward

Beefstake raid [by] Edward Boykin. New York, Funk & Wagnalls co. [1960] 305 p. maps, plates (illus., ports.). 21½cm.
                                    NN   **1835**
Hampton's raid, September 16, 1864.

Winchester
September 19, 1864

Briggs, John Ely

In the battle of Winchester. *Palimpsest* VI (1925) 394–402.   **1836**

United States. Army.

Organization of the Union forces (commanded by Major-General Philip H. Sheridan) at the battle of Winchester, or the Opequon, Va., September 19, 1864, and return of casualties. [Washington, War Records office, 1888] 20 p. 23cm.   CSmH   **1837**

*   *   *

Wilcox, Cadmus Marcellus, 1824–1890.

Battle of Jones's farm, Sept, 20, 1864. *SHST* II (1875) 67–71.   **1838**

Fisher's Hill
September 22, 1864

Lane, John H

The battle of Fisher's hill. . . . *SHSP* XIX (1891) 289–95.   **1839**

United States. Army.

Return of casualties in the Union forces, commanded by Major-General Philip H. Sheridan, at Fisher's hill, Va., September 21–22, 1864. [Washington, War Records Office, 1888] 11 p. 23cm.   CSmH   **1840**

*   *   *

Moon, William Arthur, 1902–

Historical significance of Brown's gap in the War between the States [by] William Arthur Moon. . . . Waynesboro, Va., 1937. 18 p. 21cm.
Title and imprint from cover.   Vi   **1841**
"Reprinted from Waynesboro-news-Virginian (January 13, 14, 15 and 16, 1937)."

Lane, James Henry, 1833–1907.

[Report of engagement, September 30, 1864. Casualties in Lane's brigade, campaigns 1862–1864] *Southern historical monthly* I (1876) 247–52.   **1842**

Saltville
October 2, 1864

Burnet, T   L

The battle of Saltville. *SB* II (1883/84) 20–2.   **1843**

Cedar Creek
October 19, 1864

"It's Sheridan — hooray!, a note from the knapsack of a soldier in the Sixth. *Onward* Vol 3 no 1 (January 1870) 1–12. plate (illus.).   **1844**

Dennis, Truman B

The two roads with a vivid description of Sheridan's ride and the battle of Cedar creek, by Truman B. Dennis. [Brooklyn, 1889] 20, (2) p. front. (illus.). 25½cm.
                            CSmH DLC   **1845**

Grant, Lewis Addison, 1829–1918.

The Second division of the Sixth corps at Cedar creek. *MOLLUS-Minn* VI 9–27.   **1846**

Hamlin, Augustus Choate, 1829–1905.

Who recaptured the guns at Cedar Creek, October 19, 1864? *PMHSM* VI (1903) 183–208.   **1847**

King, Horatio Collins, 1837–1918.

The battle of Cedar Creek. *MOLLUS-NY* I 33–9.   **1848**

McGlashan, Peter Alexander Selkirk

The Battle of Cedar Creek. *In* Addresses delivered before the Confederate veterans association of Savannah, Ga., 1893, 49–55.
See Title 419A.   **1849**

Stevens, Hazard, 1842–1918.

The battle of Cedar Creek. *PMHSM* VI (1894) 83–151. Also *MOLLUS-Mass* I 183–246. double plate (map).   **1850**

United States. Army.

Organization of the Union forces (commanded by Major-General Philip H. Sheridan) at the battle of Cedar Creek, Va., October 19, 1864, and return of casualties. [Washington, War Records office, 1888] 20 p. 23cm.
                                    CSmH   **1851**

Wright, Horatio Gouverneur, 1820–1899.

The battle of Cedar Creek. General Wright's report. *Historical magazine* s 2 VI (1869) 279–82.   **1852**

Boydton Plank Road
October, 1864

United States. Army.

Casualties in the Union forces operating against Richmond, Va., during October, 1864. Darbytown and New Markets roads, October 7.

Darbytown road, October 27–28. Boydton Plank road, or Hatcher's run, October 27–28. [Washington, War Records office, 1888] 31 p. 22½cm. CSmH **1853**

Walker, Francis Amasa, 1840–1897.
The expedition to Boydton Plank road, October, 1864. *PMHSM* v (1885) 319–50.
1854

Appomattox
March 28 – April 9, 1865

A Confederate diary of the retreat from Petersburg, April 3–20, 1865. Edited by Richard Barksdale Harwell. Atlanta, The Library, Emory University, 1953. 23 p. 22½cm.
NcD **1855**
Half-title: Emory University publications. Sources & reprints. Series VIII, number 1.

Custer at the surrender. *SB* ns I (1885/86) 76–7. **1856**

Barringer, Rufus, 1821–1895.
Cavalry sketches [Chamberlain run, March 27, 1865] *LWL* IV (1867/68) 1–6. **1857**

Beauregard, Pierre Gustave Toutant, 1819–1893.
Sketch of operations for the Spring campaign of 1865. *LWL* I (1866) 188–9. **1858**

Campbell, John Archibald, 1811–1889.
Recollections of the evacuation of Richmond, April 2d, 1865, by John A. Campbell. Baltimore, John Murphy & co., 1880. 27 p. 22cm.
CSmH NN **1859**
Caption title adds: by the Confederate army and government, in April, 1865, and of incidents that followed it.

Catton, Bruce, 1899–
Sheridan at Five Forks. *JSH* XXI (1955) 305–15. **1860**

Chamberlain, Joshua Lawrence, 1828–1914.
Appomattox. *MOLLUS-NY* III 260–80. **1861**

Colston, Frederick M
Recollections of the last months in the Army of Northern Virginia. *SHSP* XXXVIII (1910) 1–15. **1862**

Cooke, Giles Buckner, 1838–1937.
Just before and after Lee surrendered to Grant. [Houston, Houston Chronicle, 1922] [10] p. 23cm. NcD **1863**
"The personal experiences of Major Giles B. Cooke, as related by himself . . . reproduced by H. T. Staiti of Houston, Texas."
Title from cover.
"From the Houston chronicle, Sunday, October 8, 1922."

Davis, Burke
To Appomattox, nine April days, 1865 [by] Burke Davis. New York, Rinehart & co. [c1959] 433 p. 3 maps, plates (illus., ports.). 23½cm.
NN **1864**

De Peyster, John Watts, 1821–1907.
La Royale parts I, II, III, IV, V, & VI. The grand hunt of the Army of the Potomac, on the 3d-7th (a.m.) April, Petersburg to High bridge . . . by Anchor. . . . New York, Julius R. Huth, printer, 1872. v, (1) 70 p. front. (port.), fold. map. 24½cm. CSmH **1865**
Title from cover.
"One hundred copies printed as manuscript for private circulation."
"An epitome of a series of articles which appeared weekly in the New York Citizen and round table between the 9th September, 1871, and the 23d March, 1872."

—— La Royale part VII. Cumberland church; or the heights of Farmville: the last stricken field of the Army of Northern Virginia, 7th April, 1865 . . . by Anchor. . . . New York, Julius R. Huth, printer, 1874. xii, 150 p. front. (port.), 2 fold. maps. 24½cm.
Title from cover. CSmH **1866**
"Two hundred copies printed as manuscript for private circulation, but not revised nor corrected."

Driscoll, Frederick, 1830–
The twelve days' campaign, by Frederick Driscoll, an impartial account of the final campaign of the late war. Montreal, Printed by H. Longmoore & co., 1866. 103 p. fold. map. 22cm. CSmH NN NcD **1867**
"The defense of the [Canadian] provinces," 70–103.

Duke, Basil Wilson, 1838–1916.
After the fall of Richmond. *SB* ns II (1886/87) 156–66. **1867A**

—— Last days of the Confederacy. *B&L* IV 762–7. **1868**

Dwight, Charles Stevens
A South Carolina Rebel's recollections, personal reminiscences of the evacuation of Richmond and the battle of Sailor's creek, April, 1865. Read before Camp Hampton's, U.C.V., Columbia, S. C., By Charles Stevens Dwight, Captain Corps of engineers, Staff of Major General J. B. Kershaw. . . . Columbia, State co. [1917] 18 p. 23cm. NcD ScU **1869**
"One hundred and fifty copies printed."

Ewell, Richard Stoddert, 1817–1872.
Evacuation of Richmond. Reports of Gens. Ewell and Kershaw. *SHST* I (1874) 101–06.
1870

Gardiner, Asa Bird, 1839–1919.
The battle of "Gravelly run," "Dinwiddie Court-House," and "Five Forks," Va., 1865.

Appomattox, continued

Argument in behalf of Lieut. Gen. Philip H. Sheridan, U.S.A. respondent, by Asa Bird Gardner [sic] Judge Advocate, U.S.A. of counsel, before the Court of inquiry convened by the President of the United States (S.O. 277, ex. 6 army hd qrs, A.G.O. 9 Dec., 1879) in the case of Lieut. Col. and Bvt. Major-General Gouverneur K. Warren, Corps of engineers, formerly Major-General commanding 5 army corps, applicant. Delivered July 27, 28 and 30, 1881. Washington, Govt. print. office, 1881. 126 p. 2 maps. 23cm.   CSmH NN   *1871*

Gorman, John C
    Lee's last campaign, by Captain J. C. G. Raleigh, Wm. B. Smith & co., 1866. 59 p. 14cm.   NN NcU   *1872*

—— Lee's last campaign, with an accurate history of Stonewall Jackson's last wound, by Capt. J. C. Gorman. Second edition — tenth thousand. Raleigh, Wm. B. Smith & co., 1866. iv, [5]–71 p. 14cm.   CSmH DLC   *1873*
    "Jackson's last wound," 53–71.

Hartranft, John Frederic, 1830–1889.
    The recapture of Fort Stedman. *B&L* IV 584–9.   *1874*

Hatcher, Edmond Neuson, 1849–
    The last four weeks of the war, by Edmond N. Hatcher. Columbus, Ohio, Co-operative pub. co., 1892. xvi, [17]–416 p. plates (illus.). 20cm.   CSmH   *1875*
    "The contents are from the war correspondents and editorials of the following papers [18 North and South] . . . , as well as from files of many papers of less prominence."

Howard, McHenry, 1838–
    Retreat of Custis Lee's division, and battle of Sailor's creek. *SHST* I (1874) 61–72.   *1876*
    Text signed: McHenry Howard, A.A.I.G. Custis Lee's division, Baltimore, Oct. 1865.

Humphreys, Andrew Atkinson, 1810–1883.
    Report of operations of the Second army corps, from March 29, to April 9, 1865. [Washington, D.C., n.d.] 13 p. 24cm.
                                        CSmH   *1877*

Jones, John William, 1836–1909.
    Appomattox, the true story of the surrender. *Historical magazine* XXXI (Morrisania 1873) 235–9.   *1878*

Keifer, Joseph Warren, 1836–1932.
    The battle of Sailor's creek. *MOLLUS-Ohio* III 1–20.   *1879*

—— A forgotten battle, Sailor's creek, April 6, 1865, by J. Warren Keifer. [n.p., n.d.] 7 p. 22cm.   CSmH NN   *1880*
    Caption title.

King, Horatio Collins, 1837–1918.
    Lee's last great stand. *B&G* I (1893) 273–8.
                                              1881

Lee, Fitzhugh, 1835–1905.
    Report of Major-General Fitzhugh Lee of the operations of the Cavalry corps A.N.V., from March 28th to April 9th, 1865 (both inclusive). *SHST* II (1875) 77–85.   *1882*

Lee, George Washington Custis, 1832–1913.
    Report of General G. W. C. Lee, from 2d to 6th April, 1865. *SHST* I (1874) 118–21. *1883*

McDonald, William Naylor, 1834–1898.
    Lee's retreat. *SB* I (1882/83) 28–34. *1884*

McGlashan, Peter Alexander Selkirk
    Our last retreat. *In* Addresses delivered before the Confederates veterans association of Savannah, Ga., 1895, 57–65.   *1885*
    See Title 419A.

Merritt, Wesley, 1836–1910.
    The Appomatox [sic] campaign. *MOLLUS-Mo* I 108–31.   *1886*

Packard, Joseph
    The retreat from Petersburg to Appomattox, personal recollections. *MHM* XIII (1915) 1–19.
                                              1887

Patrick, Rembert Wallace, 1909–
    . . . The fall of Richmond. Baton Rouge, Louisiana State University press [1960] ix, 144 p. illus., map, plates (illus., ports.). 22½cm.   NN   *1888*
    At head of title: Rembert W. Patrick.
    Title on two leaves.
    "The Walter Lynwood Fleming lectures in Southern history."

Perry, Herman H
    Appomattox courthouse, account of the surrender of the Confederate states army, April 9, 1865, by Colonel Herman H. Perry. *SHSP* XX (1892) 56–61.   *1889*

Pollard, Edward Albert, 1828–1872.
    Recollections of Appomattox's Court-house. *Old and new* IV (1871/72) 166–75.   *1890*

Porter, Horace, 1837–1924.
    Five Forts and the pursuit of Lee. *B&L* IV 708–22.   *1891*

—— Lee's surrender at Appomattox. *Outlook* LXXXIV (1906) 970–6. 2 ports.   *1892*

—— The surrender at Appomattox Court House. *B&L* IV 729–46.   *1893*

Potts, Frank, 1835–1890.
    The death of the Confederacy, the last week of the Army of Northern Virginia as set forth in a letter of April, 1865, by Frank Potts, Captain Confederate states army, staff of Lieut.-

General James Longstreet. Edited with a foreword by Douglas Southall Freeman. Privately printed for Allen Potts of Happy Creek. Richmond, 1928. 15 p. 23cm.   NcD   *1894*

Rodick, Burleigh Cushing, 1889–
Appomattox, the last campaign, by Burleigh Cushing Rodick. New York, Philosophical Library [1965] 220 p. 21½cm.   NN   *1895*
"Map showing roads used by General Lee in his retreat from Richmond and Petersburg and General Grant's advance on Appomattox," endpaper.

Schaff, Morris, 1840–1929.
The sunset of the Confederacy, by Morris Schaff. Boston, John W. Luce and co. [c1912] 302 p. front. (fold. map), 2 plates (maps, 1 double). 21cm.   DLC NN   *1896*

Shepley, George Foster, 1819–1878.
Incidents of the capture of Richmond. *Atlantic monthly* XLVI (1880) 18–28.   *1897*

Sheridan, Philip Henry, 1831–1888.
Appendix to reports of operations in the Appomattox campaign. Statements relative to the battle of Five Forks, made before the Warren Court of inquiry, and additional despatches referring to operations during the campaign. [n.p., n.d.] 7 p. 24½cm.
CSmH   *1898*
—— The last days of the rebellion. *North American review* CXLVII (1888) 279–80. plate (map).   *1899*

—— Report of operations of the 1st and 3d divisions cavalry, Army of the Shenandoah, Major General P. H. Sheridan commanding, from Feb. 27th to March 28th, 1865. [New Orleans, 1865] 11 p. 21½cm.   NN   *1900*
Dated: New Orleans, La., July 16, 1865.

—— Report of operations of the United States forces under command of Major General P. H. Sheridan, from March 29, 1865, to April 9, 1865, including the Appomattox campaign, and the subsequent march from Petersburg to the Dan river, and the return. [n.p., 1865] 17, 4 p. 20½cm.   CSmH   *1901*
Dated: Cavalry headquarters, May 16, 1865. "Appendix," 4 p.

—— —— [another edition] 16 p. 24½cm.
CSmH   *1901A*

Stern, Philip Van Doren, 1900–
. . . An end to valor, the last days of the Civil war. Boston, Houghton Mifflin co., 1958. x, (2), 418 p. maps, plates (illus., ports.). 22cm.   CSmH   *1902*
At head of title: Philip Van Doren Stern.
"The Appomattox campaign," map on endpaper.

Stevens, Hazard, 1842–1918.
The battle of Sailor's creek. *PMHSM* VI (1884) 437–48.   *1903*

Stribling, Robert Mackey, 1833–1914.
Story of the battle of Five Forks and other events of the last days of the Confederacy. The Appomattox surrender. *SHSP* XXXVII (1909) 172–8.   *1904*

Sulivane, Clement
The fall of Richmond. The evacuation. *B&L* IV 725–6.   *1905*

Tremain, Henry Edwin, 1841–1910.
The closing days about Richmond; or, the last days of Sheridan's cavalry, by H. Edwin Tremain, Major and A.D.C. New York, Waldron & Payne [1873] 66 p. 17½cm.
CSmH   *1906*
"25 copies printed," Nicholson Catalogue.

—— —— Privately printed for the Clarendon historical society. [1884] 58/[293]–350 p. 23cm.   NN   *1907*

—— Last hours of Sheridan's cavalry, a reprint of war memoranda, by Henry Edwin Tremain, late Brevet Brigadier-General, Major, and aide-de-camp. New York, Bonnell, Silver & Bowers, 1904. 568 p. front. (port.). 2 plates (illus., fold. map). 19cm. CSmH NN   *1908*
"To John Watts de Peyster who rescued, edited and published (1871–72) these notes. this reprint. . . ."

—— Sailors' Creek to Appomattox Court House, 7th, 8th, 9th April, 1865; or, the last hours of Sheridan's cavalry. War-memoranda of Henry Edwin Tremain. Edited, with notes and chapters on Farmville, fording, &c., by J. Watts de Peyster. New York, Charles H. Ludwig, printer, 1885. 75, civ p. plates (maps), front. (port.). 25cm.
CSmH DLC   *1909*
Cover title adds: La royale (part VIII, amended edition). The last twenty-four hours of the Army of Northern Virginia, with memoranda relating to Farmville, fording and bridging, by J. Watts de Peyster.

United States. Army.
The Appomattox campaign. Organization of the Union forces (commanded by Lieutenant-General U. S. Grant) March 28 – April 9, 1865. [Washington, War Records Office, 1883] 21 p. 23cm.   CSmH   *1910*

—— The Appomattox campaign. Organization of the Union forces operating against Richmond, Va., under the immediate command of Lieut. Gen. U. S. Grant, on the morning of March 31, 1865. [Washington, War Records office, n.d.] 23cm.   CSmH   *1911*

Appomattox, continued

—— Casualties in the Union forces at Fort Stedman, near Petersburg, Va., March 25, 1865. [Washington, War Records office, n.d.] 6 p. 22½cm.   CSmH   *1912*

—— Casualties in the Union forces in the Appomattox campaign, March 28 – April 9, 1865, and general summary of casualties in the armies operating against Richmond, January 1 – April 9, 1865. [Washington, n.d.] 35 p. 22½cm.   CSmH   *1913*

—— Casualties in the Union forces at Hatcher's run, Va., (otherwise Dabney's Mill, Armstrong's Mill, Rowanty creek, and Vaughan road), February 5–7, 1865. [Washington, n.d.] 12 p. 22½cm.   CSmH   *1914*

Warren, Gouverneur Kemble, 1830–1882.
An account of the operations of the Fifth army corps, commanded by Maj.-Gen. G. K. Warren, at the battle of Five Forks, April 1, 1865, and the battles and movements preliminary to it. New York, William M. Franklin, printer, 1866. 53 p. front. (fold. map). 24cm.
CSmH DLC NHi NcD   *1915*

Watson, Walter C
Sailor's creek. *SHSP* XLII (1917) 136–51.
1916

DISTRICT OF COLUMBIA
General References

The Frontier guard at the White house, Washington, 1861. *Transactions of the Kansas state historical society* x (1908) 419–21. plate (facsim.).   *1917*

Barnard, John Gross, 1815–1882.
. . . A report of the defenses of Washington to the Chief of engineers, U. S. army, by Brevet Major-General J. G. Barnard. Washington, Govt. print. office, 1871. 152 p. 30 fold. plates (maps, plans, tables). 30cm.
CSmH NN   *1918*
At head of title: Professional papers of the Corps of engineers, U. S. army no. 20.
Added engraved t. p.
"Errata" slip inserted.

Benjamin, Marcus, 1857–1932.
Washington during war time, a series of papers showing the military, political, and social phases, during 1861 to 1865. Official souvenir of the thirty-sixth annual encampment of the Grand army of the Republic. Collected and edited by Marcus Benjamin, under the direction of the Committee on literature for the encampment. Washington, Byron S. Adams

[1902] xv, 215 p. front. (port.), illus., ports., 3 fold. plates (facsim., maps). 23cm.
NN   *1919*

Donn, John W
With the Army of the Potomac from the defences of Washington to Harrison s Landing, prepared by Captain John W. Donn, "at large." 1895. 22 p. *MOLLUS-DC* no 22.   *1920*

Fernald, Granville, 1828–
The story of the first defenders, District of Columbia, Pennsylvania, Massachusetts. Written and compiled by Granville Fernald. Washington, Clarence E. Davis, 1892. 24 p. 1 illus., ports. 23½cm.   CSmH DLC NHi   *1921*

Langsdorf, Edgar
Jim Lane and the Frontier guard. *Kansas historical quarterly* IX (1940) 13–25.   *1922*

Leech, Margaret
Reveille in Washington, 1860–1865, by Margaret Leech. New York, Harper & Brothers [1941] x, 483 p. facsim., 2 maps, plates (illus., fold. map). 24cm.   NN   *1923*
"Bibliography," 459–66.

Stone, Charles Pomeroy, 1824–1887.
A dinner with General Scott in 1861. *Magazine of American history* XI (1884) 528–32.
1924

—— Washington on the eve of the war. *B&L* I 7–25.   *1925*

—— Washington in March and April, 1861. *Magazine of American history* XIV (1885) 1–24. facsims., ports.   *1926*

Wilson, John Moulder, 1837–1919.
The defenses of Washington, 1861–1865. 1901. 24 p. *MOLLUS-DC* no 38.   *1927*

Woodruff, Thomas Mayhew,   –1899.
Early war days in the Nation's capital. *MOLLUS-Minn* III 87–105.   *1928*

Early's Raid
July 11–12, 1864

Cox, William Van Zandt, 1852–1923.
The Baltimore & Ohio railroad during the Civil war, the important part taken by President John W. Garrett in saving Washington from capture by General Jubal Early, the battle at Monocacy and at Fort Stevens. *Book of the royal blue* IV 10 (July 1901) 9–13. illus.
1929

—— The defenses of Washington. General Early's advance on the Capital and the battle of Fort Stevens, July 11 and 12, 1864, by

William V. Cox. [Washington, D.C., 1901]
31 p. 2 paste-on illus. p. [1] and [4] of cover.
24cm.　　　　　　　　　　　NcD　*1930*
Title from cover.
Also published in *Records of the Columbia historical society* IV (1901) 135–65.

Early, Jubal Anderson, 1816–1894.
The advance upon Washington in July,
1864. *SM* VIII (1871) 750–63.　　*1931*

—— General Barnard's report on the defences
of Washington, in July 1864. *SM* X (1872)
716–24.　　　　　　　　　　　*1932*

Hicks, Frederick C
Lincoln, Wright, and Holmes at Fort
Stevens. *Journal of the Illinois historical
society* XXXIX (1946) 323–32.　　*1933*

Vandiver, Frank Everson, 1925–
Jubal's raid, General Early's famous attack
on Washington in 1864 [by] Frank E. Vandiver. New York, McGraw-Hill book co. [c1960]
xiii, 198 p. maps, 2 plates (illus., ports.).
22cm.　　　　　　DLC NcD　*1934*

MARYLAND

April 1861

Baltimore and the crisis of 1861. Introduction
by Charles McHenry Howard. *MHM* XLI
(1946) 257–81.　　　　　　　*1935*
"From the papers of General Isaac Ridgeway
Trimble."

Brown, George William, 1812–1891.
Baltimore and the nineteenth of April, 1861,
a study of the war, by George William Brown.
Baltimore, N. Murray, Publication agent, Johns
Hopkins University, 1887. 176 p. front. (map).
23½cm.　　　　CSmH DLC NN　*1936*
Half-title: Johns Hopkins university studies in historical and political science . . . extra volume III.

Emory, Frederic, 1853–1908.
The Baltimore riots. *AW* 775–93.　*1937*

Everett, Edward G
The Baltimore riots, April, 1861. *Pennsylvania history* XXIV (1957) 331–42.　*1938*

Harris, James Morrison
A reminiscence of the troublous times of
April, 1861, based upon interviews with the
authorities at Washington, touching the movements of troops through Baltimore, a paper
read before the Maryland historical society,
March 9th, 1891, by J. Morrison Harris. Baltimore, 1891. 25 p. 23cm. CSmH NN　*1939*

Nicholson, Isaac F　　　1836–1923.
The Maryland guard battalion, 1860–61.
MHM VI (1911) 117–31.　　　*1940*

Robinson, Edward Ayrault, 1836/37–1900.
Some recollections of April 19, 1861. *MHM*
XXVII (1932) 274–9.　　　　　*1941*

Robinson, John Cleveland,　　　–1897.
Baltimore in 1861. *Magazine of American
history* XIV (1885) 257–68. illus., plan.　*1942*

Antietam

September, 1862

The lost dispatch. Galesburg, Ill., Galesburg
print. and pub. co., 1889. 115 p. 17½cm.
　　　　　　　　　　　　NHi　*1943*
Allan, William, 1837–1889.
First Maryland campaign, review of General
Longstreet.　　*SHSP* XIV (1886) 102–18.
　　　　　　　　　　　　　　1944

—— The invasion of Maryland. *SB* ns II
(1886/87) 300–06. map.　　　*1945*

—— Strategy of the campaign of Sharpsburg
or Antietam, September, 1862. *PMHSM* III
(1888) 73–103.　　　　　　　*1946*

—— Strategy of the Sharpsburg campaign.
MHM I (1906) 247–71.　　　*1947*

Cobb, Clarence F
The Maryland campaign, 1862, an address
delivered before the Maryland historical society, March 12th, 1883, by Clarence F. Cobb,
late Private, 9th corps, U.S. Army. Washington,
D.C., Judd & Detweiler, printers, 1891. 30 p.
22cm.　　　　　　CSmH NN　*1948*
Title and imprint from cover.

Cox, Jacob Dolson, 1828–1900.
The battle of Antietam. *B&L* II 630–60.
　　　　　　　　　　　　　　1949

—— Forcing Fox's gap and Turner's gap.
B&L II 583–90.　　　　　　*1950*

De Peyster, John Watts, 1821–1907.
. . . The decisive conflicts of the late Civil
war, or slave-holders' rebellion, battles morally,
territorially, and militarily decisive . . . by J.
Watts de Peyster. New York, MacDonald & co.,
printers, 1867. 2 v. 23cm. CSmH WHi　*1951*
Contents: vol. 1. The Maryland campaign of September, 1862, the battles of South Mountain and of
the Antietam. . . . 76 p.
See Title 1378 for full listing.

Douglas, Henry Kyd, 1840–1903.
Stonewall Jackson in Maryland. *B&L* II
620–9.　　　　　　　　　　　*1952*

Antietam, continued

Franklin, William Buel, 1823–1893.
Note's on Crampton's gap and Antietam.
B&L II 591–7.　　　　　　　　　　*1953*

Frobel, B　　　　W
Report of . . . battle of Sharpsburg. *OLOD*
II (1875) 26–9.　　　　　　　　　*1954*
Report dated, October 1, 1862, and signed, Major of artillery.

Frothingham, Thomas Goddard
The crisis of the Civil war, Antietam. *Mass historical society proceedings* LVI (1922/23) 173–208.　　　　　　　　　　　*1955*

Grattan, George D
The battle of Boonsboro gap or South Mountain. *SHSP* XXXIX (1914) 31–44.　　*1956*

Gray, John Chipman, 1839–1915.
Report of Major John C. Gray, Jr. for the Committee on investigation of the alleged delay in concentration of the Army of the Potomac under McClellan at Antietam, and the causes of the delay of the Second army corps in entering into the battle of Antietam.
PMHSM XIV (1876) 1–3.　　　　　*1957*

Hassler, Warren W
The battle of South mountain. *MHM* LII (1957) 39–64. plan.　　　　　　　*1958*

Hess, George
The Maryland campaign, from Sept. 1st to Sept. 20th, 1862. History and explanation of the battles of South mountain and Antietam, Md., giving a brief account of the most important engagements of the Maryland campaign. Also, an estimate of the forces engaged, and losses in the above-named battles. Compiled, written and illustrated by Geo. Hess, Superintendent Antietam national cemetery, late of Co. I, 28th regt. Pa. vet. vol. infantry. Hagerstown, Globe job rooms print, 1890. 67, (3) p. 2 fronts. (ports.), illus., plan, ports. 22cm.　　　　　　　　CSmH NN　*1959*
On cover: Battle-field guide of the battles South mountain and Antietam, Md., September 14th to 20th, 1862.

Hill, Daniel Harvey, 1821–1889.
The battle of South mountain, or Boonsboro'. Fighting for time at Turner's and Fox's gaps. *B&L* II 559–81.　　　　　　　　*1960*

—— The lost dispatch. *LWL* IV (1867/68) 270–84.　　　　　　　　　　　*1961*

Jackson, Thomas Jonathan, 1824–1863.
Report of . . . of operations from 5th to 27th September 1862. *OLOD* I (1874/75) 22–8.　　　　　　　　　　　　　*1962*

Keidel, George C
Jeb Stuart in Maryland, June, 1863. *MHM* XXXIV (1939) 161–4.　　　　　　*1963*

Lane, James Henry, 1833–1907.
Report of . . . of the first Maryland campaign from the battle of Cedar run to Sheperdstown. *OLOD* I (1874/75) 16–21.　　　*1964*

Lee, Robert Edward, 1807–1870.
A Lee letter on the "lost dispatch," and the Maryland campaign of 1862. Edited by Hal Bridges. *VMHB* LXVI (1958) 161–6.　*1965*

Longstreet, James, 1821–1904.
The invasion of Maryland. *B&L* II 663–74.　　　　　　　　　　　　*1966*

Monroe, William Harrison
The battle of Antietam, a military study. *JMSIUS* XLIX (1911) 248–79. plans.　*1967*

Murfin, James V
The gleam of bayonets, the battle of Antietam and the Maryland campaign of 1862, by James V. Murfin. Maps by James D. Bowlby. Introduction by James I. Robertson, Jr. New York, Thomas Yoseloff [1965] 451 p. maps, plates (facsims., illus., ports.). 23½cm.
　　　　　　　　　　　　NN　*1968*

Nichols, George Ward, 1837–1885.
The General's story. *Harper's magazine* XXXV (1867) 60–74.　　　　　　　*1969*

Palfrey, Francis Winthrop, 1831–1889.
. . . The Antietam and Fredericksburg, by Francis Winthrop Palfrey. New York, Charles Scribner's Sons, 1882. x, (1), 228 p. 4 plates (maps). 18½cm.　　　　　NN　*1970*
At head of title: Campaigns of the Civil war — v. See Title 1362.

Pleasonton, Alfred, 1824–1897.
General Pleasonton's cavalry division in the Maryland campaign, September, 1862. *Historical magazine* s 2 v (Morrisania, 1869) 290–4.　　　　　　　　　　　　　*1971*

Reilly, Oliver T
The battlefield of Antietam. [Sharpsburg, Oliver T. Reilly, 1906] [32] p. illus., map. 20 x 25cm.　　　　　　　ViU　*1972*
Title from cover.
Contents: The story of Antietam from tablets erected by the Battlefield commission; Stories of Antietam as told to Mr. Reilly by veterans and eye-witnesses of the battle; History of Sharpsburg . . . by John P. Smith.
"Published by Oliver T. Reilly, Sharpsburg, Md. Copyright 1906 by O. T. Reilly, Sharpsburg, Md., . . . Hagerstown Bookbinding and Printing Co., Hagerstown, Md."
Author was a battlefield guide and operated a souvenir store.

Robertson, Don
By Antietam creek [by] Don Robertson. Englewood Cliffs, Prentice-Hall [1960] 268 p. 2 maps. 22cm.   **PGC**   *1973*
Title on two leaves.

Sanborn, John Benjamin, 1826–1904.
Battles and campaigns of September, 1862. *MOLLUS-Minn* v 208–73.   *1974*

Schenck, Martin
Burnside's bridge. *CWH* ii 4 (December 1956) 5–19. plan.   *1975*

Schildt, John W
September echoes, the Maryland campaign of 1862, the places, the battles, the results, by John W. Schildt. [Middleton, Md., Valley Register, 1960] viii, 140 p. illus., plans, ports, 22½cm.   **DLC NN**   *1976*

Smith, William Farrar, 1824–1903.
The Army of the Potomac from Antietam to Warrentown. *MOLLUS-Ohio* iv 159–79.
1977

Spear, William E
The North and the South at Antietam and Gettysburg, by William E. Spear ... Published by the author. Boston [Press of Murray and Emery co.] 1908. 171 p. 4 plates (plans). 19½cm.   **CSmH**   *1978*

United States. Army.
Maryland campaign, 1862. Organization of the Army of the Potomac (commanded by Major-General George B. McClellan), September 14, 1862. [Washington, War Records office, 1882] 10 p. 22½cm.   **CSmH NN**   *1979*
Title from cover, p. [1]

—— —— at the battle of Antietam, Md., September 16 and 17, 1862. [Washington, War Records office, 1882] 10 p. 22½cm. CSmH NN
Title from cover, p. [1]   *1980*

—— —— September 14–17, 1862. [Washington, 1883] 15 p. 23cm.   **CSmH**   *1981*

Walker, John George, 1822–1893.
Report of Brig. General Walker of the battle of Sharpsburg. *OLOD* i (1874/75) 225–8.
1982

—— Sharpsburg. *B&L* ii 675–82.   *1983*

Antietam Memorials

Anderson, Ephraim F
Memorial address delivered by Col. Ephraim F. Anderson, at Antietam National cemetery, May 30, 1870. Baltimore, John Cox, printer [1870] 20 p. 23cm. DLC NN WHi   *1984*

Antietam National Cemetery.
Antietam national cemetery, Sharpsburg, Maryland. [n.p., 186–] 14 p. 22½cm. CSmH
Caption title.   *1985*
A list of the identified dead by State and regiment, p. 3–14. A tabulation by States has 1,479 identified dead; unidentified, 598.

—— History of Antietam national cemetery, including a descriptive list of the loyal soldiers buried therein, together with the ceremonies and address on the occasion of the dedication of the grounds, September 17th, 1867. Baltimore, John W. Woods, printer, 1869. 202 p. fold. map. 22½cm.   **NHi**   *1986*

Barney, Caleb Henry
The Reno memorial, South mountain, Md., unveiled, September 14, 1889, its inception, erection and dedication. Edited by Gen. C. H. Barney, Secretary of the Burnside expedition and of the Ninth army corps. Published by order of the Society. [New York] 1891. 16 p. front. (port.). 22cm.   **NHi**   *1987*

Burgan, Martin L
Antietam, the picture and the story. Sharpsburg, Martin L. Burgan, c1928. [36] p. illus., map. 20 x 25cm.   **NN**   *1988*

Crawford, Samuel Wylie, 1829–1892.
Address delivered at Antietam national cemetery, on Decoration day, May 30, 1874, by S. W. Crawford. Washington, D.C., M'Gill & Witherow, printers, 1874. 10 p. 22cm.
CSmH NN   *1989*
Title and imprint from cover.

Fesler, James W
The commemoration of Antietam and Gettysburg. *Indiana magazine of history* xxxv (1939) 237–60.   *1990*
A report of the anniversary exercises at Antietam on September 15–17, 1937, and at Gettysburg on July 1–4, 1938.

Kennedy, Robert Paterson, 1840–1918.
An address delivered upon the occasion of the dedication of her monuments erected by the State of Ohio to the memory of the illustrious dead upon the battlefield of Antietam, September 17, 1903, by Gen. Robt. P. Kennedy. [n.p.] Index print. & pub. co. [1903] [20] p. 17cm.   **CSmH NN**   *1991*

Maryland.
A descriptive list of the burial places of the remains of Confederate soldiers, who fell in the battles of Antietam, South mountain, Monocacy, and other points in Washington and Frederick counties in the State of Maryland, published by direction of Oden Bowie Governor of Maryland. Hagerstown, "Free Press" print [1865?] 84 p. 21½cm.   **NB**   *1992*

Antietam Memorials, continued

Miller, Robert Clinton, 1871–
The battlefield of Antietam. [Gettysburg, c1906] [36] p. illus., plan. 20 x 25cm.
Title from cover.   CSmH   *1993*
"Published by R. C. Miller, custodian Jennie Wade house, Gettysburg, Pa."

New York State. Monuments Commission for the Battlefields of Gettysburg, Chattanooga and Antietam.
Dedication of the New York state monument on the battle-field of Antietam. Authorized by Chapter 582, Laws of 1920. Albany, J. B. Lyons co., printers, 1923. 171 p. front. (illus.), illus., plans, ports. 27½cm.   *1994*

Ohio. Antietam Battlefield Commission.
Antietam, report of the Ohio Antietam battlefield commission, by D. Cunningham, late Major 30th Ohio infantry and W. W. Miller, late Captain 8th Ohio infantry, President and Secretary of the Commission. [Springfield, Springfield pub. co., State printers, 1904] viii, 150 p. plates (illus., ports.). 24cm. NN   *1995*

Pennsylvania. Antietam Battlefield Memorial Commission.
Pennsylvania at Antietam, report of the Antietam battlefield memorial commission of Pennsylvania and ceremonies at the dedication of the monuments erected by the Commonwealth of Pennsylvania to mark the position of thirteen of the Pennsylvania commands engaged in the battle. . . . [Harrisburg, Harrisburg pub. co., State printer] 1906. 260 p. plates illus., fold. map, ports.). 24½cm. NN   *1996*
Compiler and editor, Colonel Oliver C. Bosbyshell, Secretary.

—— Second brigade of Pennsylvania reserves at Antietam, report of the Antietam battlefield memorial commission of Pennsylvania and ceremonies at the dedication of the monuments erected by the Commonwealth of Pennsylvania to mark the position of four regiments of the Pennsylvania reserves engaged in the battle. . . . [Harrisburg, Harrisburg pub. co., State printer] 1908. 110 p. plates (illus., fold. map. ports.). 24cm.   NN   *1997*
Compiler and editor, Alexander F. Nicholas, Secretary.

Pickerill, William N
Indiana at Antietam, report of the Indiana Antietam monument commission and ceremonies at the dedication of the monument, in commemoration of the services of her soldiers who fell there, together with history of events leading up to the battle of Antietam, the report of General George B. McClellan, of the battle, and the histories of the five Indiana regiments en-

gaged. Indianapolis [Aetna press] 1911. 153 p. plates. (illus., ports.). 23cm. DLC NN   *1998*
"Preface" signed: W. N. Pickerill, compiler and editor.

Scofield, John C
An address delivered by John C. Scofield in accepting on behalf of the United States government the monuments of the Pennsylvania reserves erected at Antietam, September 17, 1906. 8 folios. 20cm.   CSmH   *1999*
"One hundred copies privately printed."

Westminster
June 29, 1863

Pearson, I   Everett
Stuart in Westminster, a narrative of events in Westminster, Carroll county, Maryland, during the week of the war in which took place the battle of Gettysburg. *SHST* ii (1875) 17–27.   *2000*

Wilson, James Harrison, 1837–1925.
Captain Charles Corbit's charge at Westminster, an episode of the Gettysburg campaign. *USCAJ* xxiv (1914) 971–94.   *2001*

Monocacy
July 9, 1864

Cowen, Benjamin Rush
The battle of Monocacy, July 9, 1864. *MOLLUS-Ohio* v 255–74.   *2002*

Goldsborough, Edward Y
Early's great raid. He advances through Maryland, battle of Monocacy . . . by E. Y. Goldsborough. [Frederick, Md., 1898] 35 p. illus., 2 plans, fold. map. 21cm.
CSmH DLC   *2003*
On cover: The battle of Monocacy.

Gordon, John Brown, 1832–1904.
Maj. Gen. Gordon's report of the battle of Monocacy, *LWL* ii (1866/67) 311–13.   *2004*

Worthington, Glenn Howard, 1858–
Fighting for time; or, the battle that saved Washington and mayhap the Union, a story of the War between the States, showing how Washington was saved from capture by Early's army of invasion, and how that achievement contributed to the preservation of the Union, with many stories and incidents of the invasion hitherto untold, by Glenn H. Worthington. . . . [Baltimore, Day print. co.] 1907. ix, 306 p. plates (illus., map, ports.). 23½cm. NN *2005*
"Map of the terrain involved in Early's invasion," front endpaper; "Monocacy battlefield near Frederick, Maryland, July 9, 1864," map on back endpaper.

United States. Military Affairs Committee (House, 70:1).

National military park at battle field of Monocacy, Md. Hearing before the Committee on military affairs, House of representatives, Seventieth Congress, first session on H. R. 11722, April 13, 1928. Washington, Govt. print. office, 1928. 14 p. 22½cm.   NN   *2006*

PENNSYLVANIA

Gettysburg

July 1–3, 1863

Further recollections of Gettysburg, by Major-General Daniel E. Sickles, Major-General D. M. Gregg, Major-General John Newton and Major-General Daniel Butterfield. *North American review* CLII (1891) 257–86).   *2007*

General Alexander Hays at the battle of Gettysburg. Extracts from "Life and letters of Alexander Hays," by George T. Fleming, and "Under the Red patch," by Gilbert Adams Hays. Pittsburgh, 1913. 21 p. 2 illus.. port. 22½cm.
          CSmH   *2008*

Gettysburg thirty years after, by the Count of Paris, Major-General O. O. Howard, Major-General Henry W. Slocum, and Major-General Abner Doubleday. *North American review* CLII (1891) 129–47.   *2009*

Alexander, Edward Porter, 1835–1910.
The great charge and artillery fighting at Gettysburg *B&L* III 357–68.   *2010*

Allan, William, 1837–1889.
A reply to General Longstreet's Lee's invasion of Pennsylvania and Lee's right wing at Gettysburg. *B&L* III 355–6.   *2011*

—— The strategy of the Gettysburg campaign, objects, progress, results. *PMHSM* III (1887) 415–48.   *2012*

Anthony, William
Anthony's history of the battle of Hanover (York county, Pennsylvania), Tuesday, June 30, 1863, compiled from writings of George R. Prowell and others, by William Anthony, editor, printer and publisher. Hanover, Pa., 1945. 160 p. illus., double plan, ports. 23½cm.
          NN   *2013*

Ashe, Samuel A'Court, 1840–1938.
The charge at Gettysburg. [Raleigh, 1887] 15 p. plan. 27½cm.   CSmH   *2014*
Caption title.
Text in double columns.

—— —— Raleigh, Capital print. co., 1902. 28 p. 18cm.   CSmH   *2015*
At head of title: North Carolina booklet, vol. 1, no. 11, March 10, 1902.

Bachelder, John Badger, 1825–1894.
List of regiments and batteries engaged in the opening scenes of the battle of Gettysburg representing the tactical evolutions of twelve phases of battle. . . . [1894] [12] folios. 12½ x 9½cm.   CSmH NbHi   *2016*
"Notice" signed: Jn. B. Bachelder," Government historian of the battle.
"25 copies printed," *Nicholson Catalogue.*

—— Reasons why the lines of battle of the Army of Northern Virginia at Gettysburg should be marked. [Hyde Park, Mass., 1889] [3] p. 25cm.   CSmH   *2017*
Caption title.
Stationery of Gettysburg battle-field memorial association used for page [1].

—— —— [revised and amplified edition] [Hyde Park, Mass., 1889] [6] p. 25cm.
          CSmH   *2018*
The letterhead again appears as p. [1] with the addition of text.

Balch, William Ralston, 1852–
The battle of Gettysburg, an historical account. Philadelphia [Press of McLaughlin Bros. co.] 1885. 128, xv p. front. (plan), illus., plans, ports. 17cm.   CSmH   *2019*
Preface signed: William Ralston Balch.
Roster of troops engaged, xv p.
Cover illus. in color.

Bates, Samuel Penniman, 1827–1902.
The battle of Gettysburg, by Samuel P. Bates. . . . Philadelphia, T. H. Davis & co., 1875. 336 p. plates (illus.; 2 maps, 1 fold.; ports.). 23½cm.   CSmH NN   *2020*
CSmH has another issue which Nicholson describes as "first edition 100 copies printed." This issue, which is printed on thinner paper and is 21½cm., omits the Preface, p. 217–336, and the illustrative material.

Bellah, James Warner, 1899–
Soldiers' battle, Gettysburg, by James Warner Bellah. Preface by Henry Graff. New York, David MacKay co. [1962] x, (2), 204 p. 5 maps. 21cm.   NN   *2021*

Biddle, James Cornell, 1835–1898.
General Meade at Gettysburg. *AW* 205–19.
          2022

Billet, Glenn E
The Department of the Susquehanna. *Journal of the Lancaster county historical society* LXVI (1962) 1–64. illus., double plan, ports.   *2023*

Bingham, Henry Harrison, 1841–1912.
The second and third days of the battle of Gettysburg, July 2d and 3d, 1863, an address by Bvt. Brig. General Henry H. Bingham on Pennsylvania day at Gettysburg, September 12, 1889. Harrisburg, E. K. Meyers, printer, 1894. 18 p. 23cm.   CSmH NHi   *2024*

Gettysburg, continued

Bollinger, Jesse
The battle of Hanover, Pennsylvania, June 30th, 1863. Its influence on the results of the greater battle of Gettysburg, July 1st, 2nd and 3rd, 1863. By Jesse Bollinger. Hanover, n.d. [10] p. 15cm.   CSmH   2025
Text within ruled border.

Bond, William R   1839–
Pickett or Pettigrew, an historical essay, by Capt. W. R. Bond. Weldon, N.C., Hall & Sledge [1888] 40 p. 22cm. CSmH NHi   2026

—— —— (revised and enlarged), by Capt. W. R. Bond . . . second edition. Scotland, N.C. [Commonwealth print, 1900] 91 p. 21cm.
                             CSmH NN   2027
—— Pickett or Pettigrew? North Carolina at Gettysburg, a historical monograph, by Capt. W. R. Bond . . . third edition. Scotland Neck, N.C., W. L. L. Hall, 1901. 94 p. 20½cm.
                             CSmH NN   2028
Buford, John, 1826–1863.
The Pennsylvania campaign of 1863. General Buford's report. *Historical magazine* s 2 vi (Morrisania 1869) 65–8.   2029

Burrage, Henry Sweetser, 1837–1926.
Gettysburg and Lincoln, the battle, the cemetery, and the National park, by Henry Sweetser Burrage. New York, G. P. Putnam's Sons, 1906. xii, 204 p. plates (illus., 3 maps, 2 ports.). 21½cm.   2029A

Carpenter, John A   1921–
General O. O. Howard at Gettysburg. *CWH* ix (1963) 261–76.   2030

Carrington, James McDowell
First day on left at Gettysburg. . . . *SHSP* xxxvii (1909) 326–37.   2031

Clark, Walter, 1846–1924.
North Carolina at Gettysburg and Pickett's charge a misnomer. Also, sixty years afterwards and the rearguard of the Confederacy, by Chief Justice Walter Clark. [Raleigh, 1921] 31 p. 3 plans. 23cm.   NN NcU   2032
Title from cover.

Confederate States of America. Army.
Organization of the Army of Northern Virginia (General R. E. Lee commanding) during the Gettysburg campaign. [Washington, War Records office, 1882] 6 p. 23cm. CSmH   2033

—— —— [Washington, D. C., 1883] 7 p. 23cm.   CSmH   2034

Cowell, Alexander Tyng, 1859–
Tactics at Gettysburg, as described by participants in the battle. . . . Gettysburg, Compiler print, 1910. 81 p. 19cm.
                             CSmH DLC   2035
"Copyrighted by A. T. Cowell."

Crist, Robert Grant
Confederate invasion of the West shore [of the Susquehanna] 1863, by Robert Grant Crist. A paper presented before the Cumberland county historical society and Hamilton library association on March 23, 1962. Lemoyne, Lemoyne Trust co., 1963. 44 p. illus., plans. 23½cm.   NN NcD   2036

Daniel, John Warwick, 1842–1910.
The campaign and battles of Gettysburg. Address of Major John W. Daniel (formerly Asst. Adjt. Gen'l C.S.A. on the staff of Gen. Jubal A. Early), before the Virginia division of the Army of Northern Virginia, at their annual meeting, held in the Capitol in Richmond, Va., Oct. 28th, 1875. . . . Lynchburg, Bell, Browne & co., printers, 1875. 45 p. 23cm.
                             CSmH   2037
De Peyster, John Watts, 1821–1907.
Before, at, and after Gettysburg . . . by J. Watts De Peyster. New York, Charles H. Ludwig, printer, 1887. 56 p. 1 illus. 23½cm.
                             CSmH NN   2038
Title and imprint from cover.

—— Gettysburg, was it a decisive battle? *Onward* Vol. 1, nos. 5–6. (New York, May–June, 1869) 414–18, 482–4.   2039
"To be continued."

—— Lee on the Susquehanna in 1863, a military criticism, by J. Watts De Peyster. [n.p., n.d.] 16 p. 25½cm.   CSmH   2040
Caption title.

—— The Third corps at Gettysburg, July 2, 1863. General Sickles vindicated. *The volunteer* i (New York 1869) 307–12, 322–9, 354–9.   2041

—— The Third corps and Sickles at Gettysburg, an address delivered before the "Third army corps union," on the twenty-fourth anniversary of their first battle, as a Corps (Williamsburg, 5th May, 1862), on Wednesday 5th May, 1886, at the Hoffman house, N.Y. 20 p. 24½cm.   CSmH   2042
Caption title.

Devens, Charles, 1820–1891.
General Meade and the battle of Gettysburg, an oration delivered before the Society of the Army of the Potomac, at its reunion, at New Haven, Connecticut, May 14th, 1873, by Ma-

jor-General Charles Devens, Jr. Morrisania, N.Y., 1873. 30 p. 23½. CSmH In **2043**

Also published in *Historical magazine* s 3 II (Morrisania 1873) 16–25.

Ditterline, Theodore
Sketch of the battle of Gettysburg, July 1st, 2d, and 3d, 1863, with an account of the movements of the respective armies for some days previous thereto. Compiled from the personal observations of eye-witnesses of the several battles . . . by T. Ditterline. New York, C. A. Alvord, printer, 1863. 24 p. fold. map. 18½cm.
CSmH NN **2044**

Doubleday, Abner, 1819–1893.
Gettysburg made plain, a succinct account of the campaign and battles . . . by Abner Doubleday. New York, Century co. [c1888] 59 p. maps. 19½cm. CSmH **2045**

—— —— New York, Century co., c1909. 59, (2) p. fronts. (ports.), maps. 19½cm.
A reprinting. CSmH **2046**
"High tide at Gettysburg [by] Will Henry Thompson," (2) p.

—— Reports of the battles of Gettysburgh, July 1st, 2d and 3d, 1863, by A. Doubleday. Montpelier, Waltons press, 1865. 19 p. 22cm.
DLC NN **2047**

Douthat, Robert William, 1840–
Gettysburg, a battle ode descriptive of the grand charge of the third day, July 3, 1863, by Robert Wm. Douthat. . . . New York, Neale pub. co., 1905. 30 p. front. (illus.). 19cm.
CSmH **2048**

Dowdey, Clifford, 1904–
Death of a Nation, the story of Lee and his men at Gettysburg, by Clifford Dowdey. New York, Alfred A. Knopf, 1958. 383, ix, (1) p. fronts. (5 maps). 22cm. NN **2049**

"A note on sources and a selected bibliography," 353–74.
"Index," ix p.
"About the author," (1) p.

Downy, Fairfax Davis, 1893–
The guns at Gettysburg, by Fairfax Downey. New York, David McKay co. [1958] xii, 290 p. illus., 2 double plans, plates (illus., port.). 22cm. NN **2050**

Maps on endpapers.

Drake, Samuel Adams, 1833–1905.
. . . The battle of Gettysburg, 1863, by Samuel Adams Drake. . . . Boston, Lee and Shepard, 1892. 178 p. front. (port.), plans. 17½cm. CSmH DLC **2051**

At head of title: Decisive events in American history.

Driver, William Raymond
Pickett's charge at Gettysburg. *PMHSM* III (1879) 351–6. **2052**

Early, Jubal Anderson, 1816–1894.
The Gettysburg campaign, report of Major-General J. A. Early. *SM* XI (1872) 311–23, 385–93. **2053**

Fiebeger, Gustav Joseph, 1858–1939.
The campaign and battle of Gettysburg, from the Official records of the Union and Confederate armies. Prepared for the use of the Cadets of the United States Military academy, by Colonel G. J. Fieberger. West Point, United States Military Academy press, 1915. 116, (4) p. fold. maps. 24cm.
"Appendix A," (4) p. CSmH NN **2054**

—— The campaign of Gettysburg. [1902] 31, (2) p. 5 maps, 1 fold. 22cm. CSmH **2055**
Title from cover.
Order of battle, (2) p.
"Prepared for visit of Class of 1902 U. S. Military academy to field of Gettysburg, April 1902, by Lt. Col. G. J. Fieberger, Prof. Engineering," ms. note in CSmH's copy.

Finley, G   W
With Pickett at Cemetery ridge. *B&G* IV (1894) 37–40. illus. **2056**

Folsom, William R
Vermont at Gettysburg. *Vermont quarterly* ns XX (1952) 161–79. plan. **2057**

Garnett, John J
Gettysburg, a complete historical narrative of the battle of Gettysburg, and the campaign preceding it, by John J. Garnett, Colonel of artillery, C.S.A. Published for his patrons, by J. M. Hill, manager of the cyclorama of the battle of Gettysburg. New York [Press of Brooklyn Daily Eagle] 1888. 48 p. 19½cm.
CSmH NHi DLC **2058**

Gibbon, John, 1827–1896.
Another view of Gettysburg. *North American review* CLII (1891) 704–13. plan **2059**

—— The council of war on the second day. *B&L* III 313–14. **2060**

Goodyear, Samuel M
General Robert E. Lee's invasion of Carlisle 1863, a paper read before the Hamilton library association, by Samuel M. Goodyear. [Carlisle, n.d.] 7 p. 23cm. PSt **2061**
Caption title.

Gregg, David McMurtrie, 1833–1916.
. . . The Second cavalry division of the Army of the Potomac in the Gettysburg campaign. Philadelphia, 1907. 14 p. 24cm.
CSmH NHi **2062**

Gettysburg, continued

At head of title: Military order of the loyal legion of the United States, Commandery of the State of Pennsylvania.
Also published in *JUSCA* xviii (1907) 213–25.

—— The Union cavalry at Gettysburg. *AW* 372–9.   **2063**

Gross, George J
The battle-field of Gettysburg, by George J. Gross. . . . Philadelphia, Collins, printer, 1866. 32 p. 23cm.   CSmH TxU   **2064**
"From the Philadelphia Press of Nov. 27, 1865."

Hage, Anne H
The battle of Gettysburg as seen by Minnesota soldiers. *Minnesota history* xxxviii (1962/63) 245–57. illus., port.   **2065**

Halsted, Eminel Potter
"The first day of the battle of Gettysburg," prepared by Brevet Major E. P. Halstead [sic] 1887. 10 p. *MOLLUS-DC* no 1.   **2066**

Hancock, Winfield Scott, 1824–1886.
Gettysburg. Reply to General Howard. *Galaxy* xxi (1876) 821–31.   **2067**

Hanly, James Franklin, 1863–1920.
The battle of Gettysburg, from "The world disarmed," by J. Frank Hanly. Cincinnati, Jennings and Graham [c1912] 106 p. front. (illus.), plate (port.). 19cm.   CSmH   **2068**

Hanover, Penn. Chamber of Commerce. Historical Publication Committee.
Encounter at Hanover, prelude to Gettysburg, story of the invasion of Hanover and Gettysburg, June and July, 1863. With a bicentennial view of the Town founded by Colonel Richard McAllister in 1763. [Gettysburg, Printed by Times and News pub. co.] 1963 [c1962] xi, 274 p. front. (illus.), illus., ports. 24cm.   **2069**

Harsha, David Addison, 1827–1895.
The battle of Gettysburg. *Fort Orange monthly* (Albany, April, 1886) 97–110.   **2070**

Haupt, Herman, 1817–1905.
The crisis of the Civil war. *Century magazine* xliv (1892) 794–7.   **2071**

Hazlewood, Martin William
Gettysburg charge, paper as to Pickett's men. *SHSP* xxiii (1895) 229–37.   **2072**

Hill, Ambrose Powell, 1825–1865.
General A. P. Hill's report of battle of Gettysburg. *SHSP* ii (1876) 222–6.   **2073**

Hillyer, George
Battle of Gettysburg, by George Hillyer, address before the Walton county Georgia Confederate veterans, August 2nd, 1904. 16 p. 23cm.   **2074**
Title from cover.
"From the Walton Tribune."

Hoke, Jacob, 1825–1893.
The great invasion of 1863; or, General Lee in Pennsylvania, embracing an account of the strength and organization of the Armies of the Potomac and Northern Virginia . . . by Jacob Hoke. Dayton, W. J. Shuey, 1887 xxxi, 33–613 p. illus., map (fold. map at end), ports, plates (ports.). 23cm.   DLC NN   **2075**

—— —— Fiftieth anniversary edition. Dayton, Otterbein press, 1913. xxxi, 33–613 p. illus., map (fold. map at end), ports. plates (ports.). 22cm.   NN   **2076**
On cover: Gettysburg.
A reprinting.

—— —— New York, Thomas Yoselof [1959] xxi, 33–613 p. illus., map (fold. map at end), ports, plates (ports.). 22cm.   DLC   **2077**
A photographic reprinting.

—— Historical reminiscences of the war; or, incidents which transpired in and about Chambersburg during the War of the rebellion, by J. Hoke. Chambersburg, M. A. Foltz, printer, 1884. 211, (1) p. 24cm. CSmH NHi   **2078**
"Written expressly for Public opinion, by J. Hoke, appeared in that journal from week to week until completed, commencing with the issue of January 12, 1884."

Hollingsworth, Alan M
The third day at Gettysburg: Pickett's charge [by] Alan M Hollingsworth and James M. Cox. New York, Henry Holt and co. [1959] vii, 162 p. maps and plans. 24½cm.
                                          PGC   **2079**
A collection of 93 documents chiefly from the official records.
Three copies of a map for student use at end.

Hosmer, George Washington, 1846–
The battle of Gettysburg, by George W. Hosmer. Reprinted from the Sunday world of June 29, 1913. Revised by the author. New York, Press pub. co., 1913. plan on p. [2] of cover. 20½cm.   NN   **2080**

Howard, Charles Henry
First day at Gettysburg. *MOLLUS-Ill* iv 238–64.   **2081**

Humphreys, Andrew Atkinson, 1810–1883.
From Gettysburg to the Rapidan, the Army of the Potomac, July, 1863, to April, 1864, by Andrew A. Humphreys. New York, Charles Scribner's Sons, 1883. viii, 86 p. 3 fold. maps. 19cm.   CSmH DLC   **2082**

—— The Pennsylvania campaign of 1863. General Humphrey's report. *Historical magazine* s 2 vi (Morrisania 1869) 1–8.   **2083**

Hunt, Henry Jackson, 1819–1889.
The first [-third] day at Gettysburg. *B&L* iii 255–84, 290–313, 369–85.   **2084**

—— Rejoinder [to General Hancock and the artillery at Gettysburg by Francis Amasa Walker]. *B&L* iii 386–7.   **2085**
See Title 2183.

—— [Letter to Alexander S. Webb on Meade and the battle of Gettysburg. Washington, D.C., 1888] [2] p. 20½cm.   CSmH   **2086**
Dated: Soldiers' home, Washington, D.C., January 12, 1888.

Hyde, Thomas Worcester
Recollections of the battle of Gettysburg, *MOLLUS-Me* i 191–206.   **2087**

Imboden, John Daniel, 1823–1895.
The Confederate retreat from Gettysburg. *B&L* iii 420–9.   **2088**

—— Lee at Gettysburg. *Galaxy* xi (1871) 507–13.   **2089**

Jacobs, Michael William, 1850–
The Gettysburg campaign of 1863, a paper read before the Historical society of Dauphin county, Pennsylvania, by Michael William Jacobs, at its forty-fourth anniversary, Thursday, June 12, 1913. . . . Harrisburg, 1913. 20 p. 22½cm.   NN   **2090**

—— Notes on the Rebel invasion of Maryland and Pennsylvania and the battle of Gettysburg, July 1st, 2d and 3d, 1863, accompanied by an explanatory map, by Michael Jacobs. Philadelphia, J. B. Lippincott & co., 1864. iv, 5–47 p. front. (fold. map). 19cm. CSmH NN   **2091**

—— —— <Fourth edition, revised.> Gettysburg, "Star and Sentinel, printer," 1884. 43, (1) p. fold. map. 17½cm.   CSmH   **2092**

—— —— <Sixth edition, revised.> Gettysburg, Gettysburg Novelty Works, c1888. 50 p. front. (fold. map). 15cm.   **2093**

—— —— Seventh edition, revised and enlarged. Gettysburg, Times print. house, 1909. 39, (3) p. front. (fold. map). 23½cm.
                                            PGC   **2094**
Jenkins, Thomas E
The battle of Gettysburg. *Book of the royal blue* ii 10 (July 1899) 9–18. illus.   **2095**

Jones, Archer, 1916–
The Gettysburg decision. *VMHB* LXVIII (1960) 331–42.   **2096**

Kantor, MacKinlay, 1904–
Gettysburg, by MacKinlay Kantor. Illustrated by Donald McKay. New York, Random House [1952] 189 p. illus. 21½cm.
                                            DLC   **2097**
Kershaw, Joseph Brevard, 1822–1894.
Kershaw's brigade at Gettysburg. *B&L* iii 331–8.   **2098**

Klein, Frederic Shriver
Meade's Pipe creek line. *MHM* LVII (1962) 133–49. map.   **2099**

Lane, James Henry, 1833–1907.
Gen. Lane's report of the battle of Gettysburg. *OLOD* iii (1875) 321–6.   **2100**

Law, Evander McIvor, 1836–1920.
The struggle for "Round Top." *B&L* iii 318–30.   **2101**

Lee, Robert Edward, 1807–1870.
General Lee's final report of the Pennsylvania campaign, and battle of Gettysburg, from the original manuscript, now first printed. Communicated by William Swinton. *Historical magazine* s 2 v (Morrisania 1869) 97–105.   **2102**

Lewis, Frederick Worthington, 1873?–1948.
The regular infantry in Gettysburg campaign. *JMSIUS* XLIV (1909) 39–45. illus.   **2103**

Longstreet, Helen Dortch, 1863–1962.
Lee and Longstreet at high tide, Gettysburg in the light of the official records, by Helen D. Longstreet. Published by the author. Gainesville, Ga. [Philadelphia, Printed by J. B. Lippincott co.] 1904. 346 p. plates (illus., ports.). 24½cm.   NN   **2104**

—— —— ["second edition"] Gainesville, Ga. [Philadelphia, Printed by J. B. Lippincott co.] 1905. 346 p. plates (facsims., illus., ports.). 24½cm.   Vi   **2105**

Longstreet, James, 1821–1904.
General Longstreet's report on the Pennsylvania campaign. *SHST* i (1874) 49–55.   **2106**

—— Lee in Pennsylvania. *AW* 414–46.   **2107**

—— Lee's invasion of Pennsylvania. *B&L* iii 244–51.   **2108**

—— Lee's right wing at Gettysburg. *B&L* iii 339.   **2109**

—— The mistakes of Gettysburg. *AW* 619–33.   **2110**

McGlashan, Peter Alexander Selkirk
Longstreet's charge at Gettysburg, July 2, 1863. *In* Addresses delivered before the Con-

Gettysburg, continued

federate veterans' association of Savannah, Ga. 1898–1902. 20–5.   **2111**

See Title 419A.

McIntosh, David Gregg, 1836–1916.
Review of the Gettysburg campaign, by David Gregg McIntosh, Col. of artillery, C.S.A. [n.p., 1909] 83 p. 2 maps. 23½cm.
                                    DLC ScU   **2112**
Also published in *SHSP* xxxvii (1909) 74–143.

McKim, Randolph Harrison, 1842–1920.
Gen. J. E. B. Stuart in the Gettysburg campaign. A reply to Col. John S. Mosby. By Randolph Harrison McKim. . . . Richmond, Wm. Ellis Jones, printer, 1909. 24 p. 24½cm.
                                         CSmH   **2113**
"Reprint from Southern historical society papers, vol. xxxvii," 210–31.

—— The Gettysburg campaign. *SHSP* xl (1915) 253–300.   **2114**

McLaws, Lafayette, 1821–1897.
The Battle of Gettysburg. *In* Addresses delivered before the Confederate veterans' association of Savannah, Ga., 1896, 57–97.   **2115**
See Title 419A.

McMichael, William,   –1893.
An address upon Rothermel's battle of Gettysburg, by Colonel William McMichael, delivered upon the occasion of unveiling the picture at the Academy of music, Philadelphia, December 20, 1870. Privately printed. [Philadelphia] Sherman & co., printers [1870] [12] p. 23cm.   CSmH   **2116**

Marshall, Charles, 1830–1902.
Events leading up to the battle of Gettysburg, address of Colonel Charles Marshall, before the Confederate veteran association of Washington, D.C. . . . *SHSP* xxiii (1895) 205—29.   **2117**

Marye, John L
The first gun at Gettysburg, "with the Confederate advance guard." *American historical register* ii (1895) 1225–32.   **2118**

Meade, George, 1843–1897.
Did General Meade desire to retreat at the battle of Gettysburg? By George Meade. Philadelphia, Porter & Coates, 1883. 29 p. 23½cm.
                                    CSmH NN   **2119**

Meade, George Gordon, 1815–1872.
General Meade's letter on Gettysburg. Philadelphia, Collins print. house, 1886. 6 p. 23cm.
                                    CSmH NN   **2120**
Title and imprint from cover.
"Written seven years after the battle, to Colonel G. G. Benedict, of Vermont, and published for the first time by Colonel Benedict, in the "Weekly press," of Philadelphia, of August 11, 1886, in refutation of the statements made on the battlefield by General Daniel E. Sickles, on the occasion of the reunion, July 2, 1886. . . ."

Meade, George Gordon, 1877–1947.
The battle of Gettysburg from "The life and letters of George Gordon Meade," compiled by General Meade's son, George Meade, and edited by Colonel Meade's son, George Gordon Meade. . . . Ambler, Penn., Published by George Gordon Meade [1924] 109 p. maps. 23cm.   **2121**

—— With Meade at Gettysburg, by George Gordon Meade. Published under the auspices of War library and museum of the Military order of the loyal legion of the United States. Philadelphia, John C. Winston co., 1930. 205 p. plates (illus., fold. maps, ports.). 22½cm.
                                         NN   **2122**
"The narrative of the campaign and battle of Gettysburg herein has been taken from The life and letters of George Gordon Meade, 1913."

Meligakes, Nicholas Antonios
The spirit of Gettysburg, the growth of a nation, its hour of redemption and a symbolic interpretation of its preservation through the people's devotion to a cause, by N. A. Meligakes. Gettysburg, Bookmart [1950] xx, (2), 252 p. plans, plates (illus., ports.). 22½cm.
                                         NN   **2123**

Miers, Earl Schenck, 1910–
Gettysburg. Edited by Earl Schenck Miers and Richard A. Brown. Maps by Harold C. Detje. New Brunswick, Rutgers University press, 1948. xviii, 308 p. illus. chapter headings, plans. 21cm.   DLC   **2124**
Title on two leaves.

Miller, Francis Trevelyan
Gettysburg, a journey to America's greatest battleground in photographs taken by the world's first war photographers while the battle was being fought. . . . Text by Francis Trevelyan Miller. New York, Review of Reviews co., 1913. [98] p. facsim., illus., ports. 28cm.
                                    CSmH DLC   **2125**

Montgomery, James Stuart
The shaping of a battle: Gettysburg [by] James Stuart Montgomery. With official maps published by authority of the Secretary of war by the Office of the chief of engineers, U.S. army. Philadelphia, Chilton Book co. [1959] xxxi, 259 p. map, fold. maps in pocket. 24½cm.
                                         NN   **2126**

Mosby, John Singleton, 1833–1916.
Stuart in the Gettysburg campaign, a defense of the cavalry commander. *SHSP* xxxviii (1910) 184–96.   **2127**

Normoyle, James Edward
Fiftieth anniversary of the battle of Gettysburg. *JMSIUS* LIV (1914) 178–212.   *2128*
Establishment and operation of the camp for veterans attending the celebration.

Paris, Louis Philippe Albert D'Orleans, comte de, 1838–1894.
The battle of Gettysburg, from the history of the Civil war in America, by the Comte de Paris. . . . Philadelphia, Porter & Coates [c1886] ix, 315 p. 3 fold. maps. 24cm.
                                        CSmH   *2129*
A reprinting of the author's History of the Civil war in America III 450–694.
"Editor's note" signed: John P. Nicholson.

—— —— New, revised edition. Philadelphia, John C. Winston co. [c1907] ix, 315 p. 3 fold. maps. 23cm.   CSmH   *2130*
A reprinting.

—— —— New revised edition. Philadelphia, John C. Winston co. [c1912] 315 p. 3 fold. maps. 23cm.   DLC   *2131*
A reprinting.

Pearce, Haywood Jefferson, 1893–
Longstreet's responsibility on the second day at Gettysburg. *GHQ* x (1926) 26–45.   *2132*

Pierce, Francis Marshall, 1847–
The battle of Gettysburg, the crest-wave of the American Civil war, by Francis Marshall. New York, Neale pub. co., 1914. 337 p. plates (3 maps, plan, ports.). 21cm.   NN   *2133*

Pleasonton, Alfred, 1824–1897.
The campaign of Gettysburg. *AW* 447–59.
                                             2134

—— The Gettysburg campaign, 1863. General Pleasonton's report of operations of the Cavalry corps, Army of the Potomac. *Historical magazine* s 2 VII (Morrisania, 1870) 36–8.
                                             2135

Rhodes, James Ford, 1848–1927.
The battle of Gettysburg. *American historical review* IV (1899) 665–77.   *2136*

Robertson, Beverly Holcombe, 1827–1910.
The Confederate cavalry in the Gettysburg campaign. *B&L* III 253.   *2137*

—— General Robertson in the Gettysburg campaign, a re-joinder to Colonel Mosby. *Century magazine* XXXVII (1888) 150–1.   *2138*

Rockwell, Charles Kellog, 1881–
The engineer battalion in the Gettysburg campaign. *JMSIUS* XLIV (1909) 22–7. illus.
                                             2139

Rodenbough, Theophilius Francis, 1838–1912.
"To commemorate the services of the regular army in the Gettysburg campaign, June–July, 1863." *JMSIUS* XLIV (1909) 10–67. illus., maps.   *2140*
The ceremonies and speeches dedicating a monument, May 31, 1909.
Articles on the services at Gettysburg, 22–45, have been entered separately.
"Survivors of the regular commands engaged in the Gettysburg campaign," 46–50.

Rodes, Robert Emmett, 1829–1864.
General R. E. Rodes's report of the battle of Gettysburg. *SHSP* II (1876) 135–58.   *2141*

Rosengarten, Joseph George, 1835–1921.
General Reynold's last battle. *AW* 60–6.
                                             2142

Scott, James Knox Polk, 1845–
The story of the battles at Gettysburg, by James K. P. Scott, H. 1st Penna. cavalry. Harrisburg, Telegraph press, 1927. 301 p. plates (illus., ports.). 22½cm.   NN   *2143*
On spine: Book 1.
"Officers killed and mortally wounded at Gettysburg," 253–70, identifies regiment and place of death.

Sefton, James E
Gettysburg, an exercise in the evaluation of historical evidence. *Military affairs* XXVIII (1964) 64–72.   *2144*

Sickles, Daniel Edgar, 1819–1914.
"The following letters respecting the successful movements of the 3d army corps, on the afternoon of July 2, 1863, on the battlefield of Gettysburg are published by me for the information of the surviving veterans of the 3d army corps. . . ." New York, 1911. 10, (1) p. 23cm.
                                        CSmH   *2145*

Slayton, James R
The great battles of the war. Gettysburg. Paper no. 1. [Gettysburg, Compiler print, n.d.] 12 p. 22½cm.   CSmH   *2146*
Title from cover.
"By General James R. Slayton."

Smith, James Power, 1837–
General Lee at Gettysburg, by Rev. James Power Smith, formerly A.D.C. to General Ewell. *PMHSM* v (1905) 377–410.   *2147*

Stackpole, Edward James, 1894–
Harrisburg the objective of Lee's invasion of Pennsylvania, June 1863; setting the stage for the Gettysburg campaign. *Dauphin county historical review* VI (1958) 13–22.   *2148*

—— They met at Gettysburg, by Edward J. Stackpole. Harrisburg, Eagle Books [1956] xxiv, 342 p. front. (illus.), illus., maps and plans, ports. 23cm.   NN   *2149*
Map on endpaper.

Stewart, George R
Pickett's charge, a microhistory of the final attack at Gettysburg, July 3, 1863, by George R. Stewart. Boston, Houghton Mifflin co., 1959. xii, 354 p. plans, plates (illus., ports.). 22cm.
NN   **2150**

Storrick, William C
Gettysburg, the place, the battles, the outcome, by W. C. Storrick, the retired superintendent of guides. Harrisburg, J. Horace McFarland co. [1932] 167 p. plans, plates (illus., ports.). 20½cm.   NN   **2151**

Stribling, Robert Mackey, 1833–1914.
Gettysburg campaign and campaigns of 1864 and 1865 in Virginia, by Robert M. Stribling, Lieut. Col. of artillery, C.S.A. Petersburg, Franklin press co., 1905. x, [11]–308 p. 19½cm.   NN TxU   **2152**

Stuart, James Ewell Brown, 1833–1864.
General J. E. B. Stuart's report of operations after Gettysburg. *SHSP* II (1876) 65–78.
2153

Swallow, William H
From Fredericksburg to Gettysburg. *SB* ns I (1885/86) 352–66.   **2154**

—— The first [-third] day at Gettysburg. *SB* ns I (1885/86) 436–44, 490–9, 567–72. map, port.   **2155**

Swinton, William, 1833–1892.
Notes on the battle of Gettysburg. *Hours at home* III (1866) 88–98.   **2156**

Talcott, Thomas M   R
Stuart's cavalry in the Gettysburg campaign, a reply to the letter of Col. John S. Mosby, published in the Richmond, Va., Times-despatch, January 30, 1910. *SHSP* XXXVIII (1910) 197–210. plate (map).   **2157**

—— Stuart's cavalry in the Gettysburg campaign, by Col. John S. Mosby. A review by. . . . *SHSP* XXXVII (1909) 21–37.   **2158**

—— The third day at Gettysburg. *SHSP* XLI (1916) 37–48.   **2159**

Taylor, Walter Herron, 1838–1916.
The campaign in Pennsylvania. *AW* 305–18.
2160

Trimble, Isaac Ridgeway, 1802–1888.
North Carolinians at Gettysburg. *Southern historical monthly* I (1876) 56–63.   **2161**

Trowbridge, John Townsend, 1827–1916.
The field of Gettysburg. *Atlantic monthly* XVI (1865) 616–24.   **2162**

Tucker, George Wellford, 1866–1938.
Lee and the Gettysburg campaign, by G. W. Tucker. [Richmond, 1932] xix, 61 p. front. (port.). 20½cm.   NcD V   **2163**
Illus. of Virginia monument at Gettysburg, inset front. cover.

—— —— [Richmond, c1933] xix, 61 p. front. (port.), plates (illus.). 20½cm.
TxU   **2163A**

Tucker, Glenn
High tide at Gettysburg, the campaign in Pennsylvania, by Glenn Tucker. Indianapolis, Bobbs-Merrill co. [1958] viii, (2), 462 p. maps and plans. 22½cm.   NN   **2164**

—— Some aspects of North Carolina's participation in the Gettysburg campaign. *NCHR* xxxv (1958) 191–212.   **2165**

Tuttle, Joseph Farrand, 1818–1901.
Interesting reminiscences. Two papers on the battle of Gettysburg. [Crawfordsville, Ind., 1874] [3] p. 24½cm.   CSmH   **2166**
Caption title.
Text in double columns.
Addresses of Generals Rufus R. Dawes and Oliver O. Howard at Marietta, Ohio, July 1, 1868, with introductory text signed: J. F. T.

United States. Adjutant General's Department.
. . . Itinerary of the Army of the Potomac and co-operating forces in the Gettysburg campaign, June and July, 1863, and organization of the Army of the Potomac at the battle of Gettysburg. Compiled under the direction of Brigadier General Richard C. Drum, Adjutant General U.S. army, by Joseph W. Kirkley. Washington, 1882. 26 p. 23cm.
CSmH NN   **2167**
At head of title: Adjutant General's Department.

—— —— [another issue] Washington, 1882. 36 p. 23cm.   CSmH   **2168**
A reprinting through p. 17.

—— —— and return of casualties in the Union and Confederate forces. Compiled under the direction of Brigadier General Richard C. Drum, Adjutant general U.S. army, by Joseph W. Kirkley. <Second edition> Washington, 1886. 70 p. 22½cm. CSmH   **2169**
At head of title: Adjutant General's Department.

—— Itinerary of the Army of the Potomac and co-operating forces in the Gettysburg campaign, June 5 – July 31, 1863; organization of the Army of the Potomac and Army of Northern Virginia at the battle of Gettysburg; and return of casualties in the Union and Confederate forces. Compiled under the direction of Brigadier-general Richard C. Drum, Adjutant

general U.S. army. <Third edition> Washington, Govt. print. office, 1888. 69 p. 23½cm.
CSmH 2170

At head of title: Adjutant-general's department.

—— Pennsylvania volunteers and militia called into service during the Gettysburg campaign. [Washington, 1885] 9, (1) p. 23cm.
CSmH 2171

Penn militia General order no. 46, September 7, 1863, (1) p.

—— Statement showing the number of Confederate prisoners of war captured in the Gettysburg campaign with disposition. [Washington, 1878] broadside, 14½x22½cm.
CSmH 2172

Text signed: Adjutant-general's office (enlistment branch), Division of records of prisoners of war, July 19, 1878.

United States. Army.
Minutes of council, July 2, 1863. [Washington, D.C., 1881] 2 p. 19cm. CSmH 2173

Caption title.
"In pencil, and excepting indorsement, in General Meade's handwriting."

United States. War Records Office.
Official reports, order, correspondence and telegrams of the Union and Confederate armies in the Gettysburg campaign. Washington, War Record's office, 1890. 3 v. 24½cm.
CSmH 2174
Preprint of the Official records xxvii.

—— Official reports [Union] relating to the Gettysburg campaign, 1863. Washington, 1880. lv, 958 p. 2 fold. maps, 23½cm.
CSmH 2175

—— —— [Confederate] Washington, 1883. 492 p. 23½cm. CSmH 2176

Both volumes are preliminary printings of the Official records.

—— Return of casualties in the Union forces (Maj.-Gen. George G. Meade, U.S. army, comdg.) at the battle of Gettysburg, Pa., July 1–3, 1883. [Washington, War Records office, 1885] 25 p. 23cm. CSmH NN 2177

Vanderslice, John Mitchell, 1846–
Gettysburg, a history of the Gettysburg battlefield memorial association, with an account of the battle, giving movements, positions and losses of the commands engaged, by John M. Vanderslice. Philadelphia, Gettysburg Battle-field Memorial Association [Printed by J. B. Lippincott co.] 1897. 320 p. front. (fold., map). 20½cm. CSmH 2178

—— Gettysburg, where and how the regiments fought and the troops they encountered. An account of the battle giving movements,

positions, and losses of the commands engaged. By John M. Vanderslice. Philadelphia [Printed by J. B. Lippincott co.] 1897. 264 p. front. (fold. map). 20½cm. CSmH DLC 2179
A reprinting with some supplementary matter omitted.

—— Gettysburg, then and now, the field of American valor. Where and how the regiments fought . . . By John M. Vanderslice . . . New York, G. W. Dillingham co., 1899. 492, (1) p. front. (fold. map.), illus., ports. 21cm.
Plates are paged. CSmH 2180

—— A memento of the Grand army encampment at Gettysburg, 1878. The latest and most authentic history of the battle, with maps of the Antietam and Gettysburg campaigns, prepared expressly for the occasion. Philadelphia, Samuel P. Town [1878] 32 p. 2 fronts. (maps). 19cm. CSmH 2181

Vincent, Boyd
The attack and defense of Little Round Top, Gettysburg, July 2, 1863, a paper read before the Ohio commandery of the Loyal legion, February 3, 1915, by Boyd Vincent. 14 p. 21½cm. In 2182
Title from cover, p. [1].

Walker, Francis Amasa, 1840–1897.
General Hancock and the artillery at Gettysburg. B&L III 385–6. 2183
Rejoinder by Henry J. Hunt (see Title 2085).

—— Meade at Gettysburg. B&L III 406–12. 2184

Weigley, Russell Frank, 1930–
Emergency troops in the Gettysburg campaign. Penn history xxv (1958) 39–57. illus. 2185

Young, Louis Gourdin, 1833–1922.
The battle of Gettysburg, an address by Capt. Louis G. Young. [Savannah, 1900?] 8 p. 26cm. CSmH NCD 2186

Caption title.
Text in double columns.
Also published in Addresses delivered before the Confederate veterans' association of Savannah, Ga., 1898–1902, 38–48 [see Title 419A].

—— Pettigrew's brigade at Gettysburg. OLOD I (1874/75) 552–8. 2187

Gettysburg Memorials

Proceedings at the dedication of the monumental shaft, October 15th, 1884, erected upon the field of the cavalry engagement on the right flank of the Army of the Potomac, July 3d, 1863, during the battle of Gettysburg. Philadelphia, 1885. 59 p. front. (fold. map), plate (illus.). 25½cm. CSmH P 2188

Gettysburg Memorials, continued

"Historical address, by Colonel William Brooke Rawle," 13–36.

Association of the Survivors of the Sixth U.S. Cavalry.

[Correspondence concerned with the erection of a monument to the Sixth cavalry on the field of Gettysburg. n.p., 1891] [4] p. 23½cm.
                              CSmH   **2189**

Bartlett, John Russell, 1805–1886.

The soldiers' national cemetery at Gettysburg, with the proceedings at its consecration, at the laying of the cornerstone of the monument, and at its dedication, by John Russell Bartlett. Providence, Printed by the Providence press, 1874. 109 p. front. (illus.). 31½cm.
                      CSmH DLC NHi   **2190**

McClure, Alexander Kelly, 1828–1909.

The proposed equestrian statue to Lee at Gettysburg. Argument presented before the Committee of the Legislature in favor of the bill providing that Pennsylvania and Virginia shall unite to erect an equestrian statue to Lee on Seminary hill, at Gettysburg, by A. K. Mc-Clure. [1903] 13 p. 22cm.   CSmH   **2191**
Caption title.

Soldiers' National Cemetery Association.

Charter and proceedings of the Board of commissioners of the. . . . Providence, Knowles, Anthony. & co., printers, 1864. 20 p. 23cm.
                              CSmH   **2192**

—— [Names of all the officers and privates who fell in the battle of Gettysburg, and in the skirmishes incident thereto, or who died of wounds received in that battle. 1864] 153 p. 31cm.   Nh   **2193**
"Thirty copies of this volume were printed," *Bartlett* 1839.
Title taken from page of introductory text dated May, 1864, and signed by David Wills, President of the Soldiers' National Cemetery.
Additional list of Massachusetts soldiers, inserted leaf.

—— Oration of Hon. O. P. Morton. Address of Major General George G. Meade, and poem of Bayard Taylor. Together with the other exercises at the dedication of the monument in the Soldiers' national cemetery at Gettysburg, July 1st, 1869. Published by the Association. Gettysburg, J. E. Wible, printer, 1870. 47, (1) p. 22½cm.   CSmH   **2194**

Thompson, Joseph Parrish, 1819–1879.

The National cemetery at Gettysburg. *Hours at home* II (1865/66) 181–4.   **2195**

United States. Gettysburg National Military Park Commission.

Annual reports to the Secretary of war, 1893–1901. Washington, Govt. print. office, 1902. 56 p. plates (illus.). 24cm. NHi   **2196**

First report is dated, November 16, 1893, and commences with the appointment of the Commission, May 25, 1893.

—— —— 1893–1904. Washington, Govt. print. office, 1905. 107 p. plates (illus.). 24cm.
                                              2197

—— The location of the monuments, markers and tablets on the battlefield of Gettysburg. Washington, Govt. print. office, 1898–23cm.   **2198**
1898; 1903; 1907; 1912 and reprintings dated, 1914, 1915; 1916; 1918; 1921.
NN has 1912, 1915, 1916, 1921.

—— Regulations for the government of the Gettysburg national park. Gettysburg, 1895. [6] p. 21cm.   CSmH   **2199**

Delaware

Report of the Joint committee to mark the positions occupied by the 1st and 2d Delaware regiments at the battle of Gettysburg, July 2d and 3d, 1863. Dover, Printed at the Delaware-an office, 1887. 28 p. illus. on p. [1] and [4] of cover. 22½cm.   NHi   **2200**

Illinois

Illinois monuments at Gettysburg. . . . Springfield, H. W. Rokker, State printer, 1892. 37 p. plates (illus., ports.). 23½cm.   NN   **2201**

Indiana

Indiana. Governor.

Soldiers' national cemetery, at Gettysburg, Pennsylvania. To the Legislature. Indianapolis, W. R. Holloway, State printer, 1865. 35 p. 21½cm.   CSmH In   **2202**
Official correspondence, August 10, 1863, to November 30, 1864.

Pickerill, William N

Indiana at the fiftieth anniversary of the battle of Gettysburg. Report of the fiftieth anniversary commission of the battle of Gettysburg, of Indiana . . . with rosters of the Army of the Potomac and the Army of Northern Virginia, and a brief history of each of the regiments from Indiana that participated in the battle of Gettysburg. [Indianapolis, 1913] 121 p. plates (1 illus., ports.). 23cm.
                              NN   **2203**
"Preface" signed: W. N. Pickerill, compiler and editor.

Maine

Chamberlain, Joshua Lawrence, 1828–1914.

Address of Gen. Joshua L. Chamberlain at the dedication of the Maine monuments on the battlefield of Gettysburg, October 3, 1893. Augusta, Maine Farmers' Almanac press, 1895. 15 p. 21½cm.   NB   **2204**

—— —— Second edition. Portland, Lakeside press, 1898. 16 p. 24½cm.   NB   **2205**

Hamlin, Charles, 1837–1911.
Brief sketch of the battle of Gettysburg, introduction to Maine at Gettysburg, by Brevet Brig.-Gen. Charles Hamlin. [Portland, Lakeside press, 1898] 13 p. front. (illus.), 4 plates (maps). 24cm.   CSmH DLC   **2206**
A reprint of the introductory portion of "Maine at Gettysburg. Commissioners' report" (see Title 2207).

Maine. Gettysburg Commission.
Maine at Gettysburg, report of Maine commissioners, prepared by the Executive committee. [Portland, Lakeside press, 1898] viii, 602 p. maps, plates (illus., maps). 23½cm
                            NN   **2207**

Maryland

Maryland. Gettysburg Monument Commission.
Report of the . . . to E. E. Jackson, Governor of Maryland, June 17th, 1891. . . . Baltimore, Printed by William K. Boyle & Son, 1891. 144 p. plates (illus., ports.). 24cm.
                        CSmH   **2208**
"Official list of casualties," 80 A–D.

Massachusetts

Boston.
    . . . Report of the Joint special committee on the burial of Massachusetts dead at Gettysburg, together with the oration of Edward Everett, at the consecration of the National cemetery, and other matters in relation thereto. Boston, J. E. Farwell and co., printers, 1863. 93 p. 23½cm.   NN   **2209**
At head of title: City document, no. 106.
"Names of soldiers buried in the Massachusetts lot," [87]–93.

—— . . . Report of the Joint special committee on the burial of Massachusetts dead at Gettysburg, with a list of the Massachusetts soldiers buried in the National cemetery, and other matters in relation thereto. Boston, J. E. Farwell and co., Printers to the City, 1863. 29 p. fold. plan. 23½cm.   CSmH   **2210**
A reprinting omitting the Oration.

Massachusetts. Soldiers' National Cemetery at Gettysburg Commission.
    [Report] 1864. fold. map. *In* Address of John A. Andrew [Governor] . . . January 8, 1864, xxxiv–lxxxiii.   **2211**

Michigan

Boies, Albert H
Roster of the survivors of the battle of Gettysburg living in the State of Michigan, May 1913. [Hudson, Gazette print, 1913] [16] p. 17cm.   DLC   **2212**

Title from cover.
"Explanatory" signed: A. H. Boies, Co. F. 4th Mich inft'y. "In September, 1912, Governor Osborn delegated me with authority to prepare a roster."

Michigan.
Dedication of the Michigan monuments on the battlefield of Gettysburg, Pa., Wednesday, June 12, 1889, under the auspices of the Governor of Michigan and the Monument commission. Detroit, Aldine print co. [1889] 1 v. plates (illus.). 22cm.   CSmH   **2213**
On cover: Gettysburg. Michigan day, June 12th, 1889.

—— Michigan at Gettysburg, July 1st, 2nd and 3rd, 1863. June 12th, 1889. Proceedings incident to the dedication of the Michigan monuments upon the battlefield of Gettysburg June 12th, 1889, together with a full report of the Monument commission and a detailed statement of the work committed to and performed by it, and the proceedings at the various regimental reunions. Detroit, Winn & Hammond, printers, 1889. 173, iv p. plates (illus.; 3 plans, 1 fold.; ports.). 25cm.
                            NHi   **2214**
"Index. List of illustrations. Alphabetical index of names of persons mentioned in this book," iv p.

New Jersey

New Jersey. Gettysburg Battle-field Commission.
Report. . . . Trenton, Printed by the John L. Murphy pub. co., 1887–88. 2 v. 22½cm.
December 7th, 1886. 18 p.   NN   **2215**
December 15th, 1887. 20 p.

—— Final report. . . . Trenton, Printed by the John L. Murphy pub. co., 1891. 165 p. plates (illus., fold. map). 23cm. NN   **2216**

New Jersey. Gettysburg Battlefield, Commissioners to Enclose, Care for and Improve the Monuments.
    . . . Report . . . 1892. Trenton, Naar, Day & Naar, printers, 1893. 19 p. plates (illus.). 22cm.   NN   **2217**
At head of title: State of New Jersey.

Toombs, Samuel, 1844–1889.
New Jersey troops in the Gettysburg campaign, from June 5, to July 31, 1863, by Samuel Toombs. Orange, Evening Mail pub. house, 1888. xvi, 406 p. illus.; maps, 1 fold.; ports. 20½cm.   DLC NN   **2218**

New York

New York State. Battle of Gettysburg, Commissioners to Designate and Mark the positions of New York Troops in the. . . .
Circular and instructions of the New York board of commissioners, Gettysburg monuments, together with the laws of '86 and '87,

Report of the commissioners, tables of casualties, etc. . . . New York, Martin B. Brown, printer, 1887. 31 p. 25cm.   CSmH   **2219**
Second report, 21–6.

—— Report . . . and a bill accompanying the report. Transmitted to the Legislature, February 17th, 1887. Albany, Argus co., printers, 1887. 12 p. fold. map. 22½cm. DNW   **2220**

—— Third annual report . . . January 15, 1889. [New York, 1889] 16 p. 25½cm.
Title from cover.   CSmH   **2221**

New York State. Monuments Commission for the Battlefields of Gettysburg and Chattanooga.
Final report on the battlefield of Gettysburg. . . . Albany, J. B. Lyon co., printers, 1902. 3 v. (1462 p.) 5 fold. maps in pockets, plates (illus., ports.). 28cm.   DLC NN   **2222**
Copyright by William F. Fox, contributor and editor.

New York State. Monuments Commission for the Battlefields of Gettysburg, Chattanooga and Antietam.
Dedication of the New York auxiliary state monument on the battlefield of Gettysburg. Authorized by Chapter 181, Laws of 1925. Albany, J. B. Lyon co., printers, 1926. xi, 226 p. plates (illus., plan, ports.). 22½cm.
        NN   **2223**

—— . . . Report of the Commission . . . to plan and conduct a public celebration of the fiftieth anniversary of the battle of Gettysburg, transmitted to the Legislature, March 26, 1914. Albany, J. B. Lyon co., printers, 1914. 85 p. 23cm.   NN   **2224**

—— Report of the . . . for the year(s). . . . Albany, 1914–27. 13 nos. 23cm.   NN   **2225**
Issued annually.
First report covers the period from the organization of the Commission, May 22, 1913, through December 1914.

—— Fiftieth anniversary of the battle of Gettysburg, 1913. Report of the. . . . Albany, J. B. Lyon co., printers, 1916. 106 p. plates (illus., ports.). 27½cm.   NN   **2226**

New York State. Soldiers' National Cemetery at Gettysburg. Commissioner.
Report of the State commissioner relative to the Soldiers' national cemetery, at Gettysburg, Penn., accompanying documents. Transmitted to the Legislature, April 6, 1869. Albany, Argus co., printers, 1869. 132 p. 22cm.
        CSmH   **2227**

Potter, Henry Codman, 1834–1908.
The oration delivered, July 2, 1893, at the dedication of the monument commemorative of the men of New York who fell at Gettysburg, July 2, 1863, by Henry C. Potter, Bishop of New York. Published by order of the Board of Gettysburg monuments commissioners of the State of New York. 16 p. front. (illus.). 23½cm.   CSmH NHi   **2228**

North Carolina

North Carolina. Gettysburg Memorial Comission.
Ceremonies attending the presentation and unveiling of the North Carolina memorial on the battlefield of Gettysburg, Wednesday, July 3rd, 1929. 44 p. 2 plates (illus.). 24½cm.
        NcD   **2229**

Ohio

Ohio. Gettysburg Memorial Commission.
Dedication of the Ohio memorials on the battlefield at Gettysburg, Pa., Wednesday, Sept. 14, '87, under the auspices of the Gettysburg memorial commission of Ohio. [Columbus, Nitschke Bros., printers, 1887] 14 p. 22cm.   CSmH OMC   **2230**

—— Report. Columbus, Press of Nitschke Bros. [1888] 142 p. map, plates (illus.). 23½cm.   **2231**
Contents: Report of the Commission, 1–94; The battle of Gettysburg, by Alfred E. Lee, [95]–142. Both sections were also published separately without alteration of pagination.

Pennsylvania

Gobin, John Peter Shindel, 1837–1910.
Oration delivered upon the transfer of the monuments to the Governor, by J. P. S. Gobin, Brevet Brigadier General and Colonel 47th Pennsylvania veteran volunteers, at Gettysburg, Pa., September 12th, 1889, Pennsylvania day. [4] p. 27cm.   CSmH   **2232**
Caption title.

Huidekoper, Henry Shippen, 1839–1918.
Address of General H. S. Huidekoper, President of the Gettysburg battlefield memorial commission on September 27th, 1910, tendering to Governor Edwin S. Stuart the monument erected at Gettysburg to the Pennsylvania soldiers who fought there in 1863. broadside, 31 x 22½cm.   NB   **2233**

Pennsylvania. Gettysburg Battle-field Commission.
Pennsylvania at Gettysburg. Ceremonies at the dedication of the monuments erected by the Commonwealth of Pennsylvania to mark

the positions of the Pennsylvania commands engaged in the battle. . . . [Harrisburg, E. K. Meyers, State printer, 1893] 2 v. fronts. (ports.), plates (illus., maps). 25½cm.
NN **2234**

Edited and compiled by John P. Nicholson, Secretary of the Commision.

—— —— [Harrisburg, W. S. Ray, State printer, 1904] 2 v. fronts. (ports.), plates (illus., maps). 24½cm. NN **2235**

Edited and compiled by John P. Nicholson, Secretary of the Commission.
On spine: Revised edition, 1904.

—— Pennsylvania at Gettysburg. [Harrisburg, Wm. Stanley Ray, State printer (iv Gettysburg, Times & News pub. co.) 1914–39] 4 v. in 5. i–iii plates, partly fold. (illus., maps, ports.); iv illus., ports., 2 fold. plates (illus.). 24cm. NN **2236**

Contents:
i–ii Ceremonies at the dedication of the monuments erected by the State of Pennsylvania to . . . and to mark the positions of the Pennsylvania commands engaged in the battle. ii (second part) Report of the Gettysburg battlefield memorial commission, 1914.
iii Fiftieth anniversary of the battle of Gettysburg.
iv The seventy-fifth anniversary of the battle of Gettysburg.
Editors and compilers: i–ii John P. Nicholson; iii L. E. Beitler; iv Paul L. Roy.
iv published by the Seventy-fifth anniversary of the battle of Gettysburg commission.
ii (second part) adds to series title: Revised in three volumes.
iii also issued separately.

Pennsylvania. Soldiers' National Cemetery, Select Committee.
Report of the Select committee relative to the Soldiers' national cemetery, together with the accompanying documents, as reported to the House of representatives of the Commonwealth of Pennsylvania, March 31, 1864. Harrisburg, Singerly & Myers, State printers, 1864. 108, (3) p. front. (map), fold. plate (plan) 24cm. CSmH NN **2237**

Hymn composed by R. B. French; Dedicatory address of President Lincoln; Benediction by Rev. H. L. Baugher — (3) p.

—— Revised report of the . . . together with the accompanying documents, as reported to the House or representatives of the Commonwealth of Pennsylvania. . . . Harrisburg, Singerly & Myers, State printers, 1865. 212 p. 2 plates (map, fold. plan). 24cm.
CSmH NN **2238**

List of soldiers buried . . . [19]–132.

—— Revised report made to the Legislature of Pennsylvania, relative to the Soldiers' national cemetery, at Gettysburg, embracing an account of the origin of the undertaking; address of Edward Everett, at its consecration, with the dedicatory speech of President Lincoln, and the other exercises of that event. Together with the address of Maj. Gen. O. O. Howard, delivered July 4, 1866, upon the dedication of the soldiers' national monument, and the other proceedings upon that occasion. Harrisburg, Singerly & Myers, State printers, 1867. 282 p. front. (illus.), 2 plates (plans, 1 fold.). 23½cm. NN **2239**

The Revised report of 1865 has been reset and occupies p. 1–234.

Rhode Island

Rhode Island. Soldiers' National Cemetery at Gettysburg, Commissioners for Rhode Island.
Report of the . . . 1870. [Providence, 1870] 3 p. 23½cm. RP **2240**

At head of title: Public document, Appendix no. 16.
Caption title.

Vermont

Benedict, George Grenville, 1826–1907.
The battle of Gettysburg and the part taken therein by Vermont troops, by G. G. Benedict. Burlington, Free Press print, 1867. 24 p. plates (illus.). 22cm. CSmH NHi **2241**

—— Vermont at Gettysburg, a sketch of the part taken by the Vermont troops, in the battle of Gettysburg, by G. G. Benedict. Burlington, Free Press Association, 1870. 27, iv p. front. (port.), plates (illus., map). 23cm.
DLC **2242**

Vermont.
Monuments at Gettysburg, report of the Vermont commissioners, 1888, including illustrations and recommendations. Rutland, Tuttle co., printers, 1888. 16 p. plates (illus., 2 fold.). 21½cm. NN **2243**

—— Vermont at Gettysburg, July 1863, and fifty years later. Rutland, Marble City press, 1914. 53 p. front. (port.), illus., ports. 21cm. CSmH **2244**

Virginia

Dedication of the Virginia memorial at Gettysburg, Friday, June 8, 1917. SHSP xlii (1917) 83–135. **2245**

Addreess, by Leigh Robinson, 97–134.

Guide Books to Gettysburg

The battlefield. Gettysburg, 1896. 4 nos. illus. 54cm. CSmH **2246**

i 1–4; June 20–July 18, 1896.
A. P. Seilhamer, publisher.

Brevier Quad's souvenir of Gettysburg, containing names of soldiers buried in the Na-

Guide Books to Gettysburg, continued

tional and Evergreen cemeteries. Published by Warren & Milford. Cumberland, Md., Independent print, 1885. [20] p. 1 illus. 19½cm.
Title from cover.   CSmH   **2247**

Picture of the battle of Gettysburg, painted by P. F. Rothermel, now on exhibition at Tremont temple, Boston. Philadelphia, Longacre & co., printers, 1871. 37, (1) p. fold. plate (illus.). 23cm.   CSmH   **2248**

—— [another edition] Philadelphia, Longacre & co., printers, 1871. 33, (1) p. fold. plate (illus.). 23cm.   CSmH   **2249**

Bachelder, John Badger, 1825–1894.
   Descriptive key to the painting of the repulse of Longstreet's assault at the battle of Gettysburg (July 3, 1863), historically arranged by John B. Bachelder, and painted by James Walker. Embracing a brief outline of the battle, showing the relative positions of the contending forces, and explaining the points of local and military interest delineated by the artist. With an appendix containing private letters and official reports from both armies, showing the authorities for the painting. With a complete index of the officers and troops mentioned. By John Bachelder. New York, John B. Bachelder, 1870. 94 p. fold. front. (illus. with key), plates (facsims., 1 illus.). 24cm.   CSmH   **2250**

—— —— New York, John B. Bachelder, 1870. 94 p. fold. illus. with key, plates (facsims., 1 illus., ports.). 28cm.   CSmH   **2251**

—— Gettysburg. Description of the painting of the repulse of Longstreet's assault painted by James Walker. Historical arrangement and description by John B. Bachelder. Boston, John B. Bachelder, 1870. 43 p. fold. illus. with key. 23½cm.   CSmH   **2252**
   Printed from the plates of his Descriptive key.
   CSmH has a copy of another printing, 1884.

—— Gettysburg battle-field. . . . Boston, New York, Jn. B. Bachelder, c1863. col. relief map, 66 x 95cm.   CSmH   **2253**
   "Jno. B. Bachelder, del."
   "Endicott & co., lith., N.Y."

—— —— Key to Bachelder's isometrical drawing of the Gettysburg battle-field, with a brief description of the battle. New York, C. A. Alvord, 1864. 10 p. 20½cm. CSmH   **2254**
   Title from cover.

—— Gettysburg: what to see, and how to see it. Embodying full information for visiting the field. Beautifully embellished with wood-cuts. With complete index. Illustrated by the iso-

metrical drawings of the Gettysburg battle-field showing the position of every regiment and battery of both armies, by John B. Bachelder. Boston, John B. Bachelder, 1873. viii, 148 p. illus., fold. plan, plates (illus.). 20cm.
                                     CSmH   **2255**

—— —— Ninth edition. Boston, John B. Bachelder, 1889. vi, 151 p. front. (illus.), illus., map, fold. plan. 20cm.
                              CSmH IHi   **2256**
   On cover: Bachelder's new historical guide book. . . .
   NN has a copy marked "Tenth edition," 1890, a reprinting.

—— Key to the painting and engraving of the battle of Gettysburg "repulse of Longstreet's assault," July 3, 1863. Boston, Heliotype print. co. [1870] broadside, 36 x 54½cm.
                                     CSmH   **2257**

Coddington, Edwin B
   Rothermel's painting of the battle of Gettysburg. *Penn history* XXVII (1960) 1–27. plate (illus.).   **2258**

Danner, Joel Albertus, 1804–1885.
   Danner's pocket guide book of the battle-field of Gettysburg, and history of the battle. . . . Baltimore, Jno. S. Bridges & co., printers [188–] 12 p. fold. map. 15cm. CSmH   **2259**
   Title and imprint from cover.
   Danner was proprietor of a battle-field museum at 23 Baltimore street.
   No attempt has been made to record the editions of this guidebook.

Ertter, Adam
   The Blue and Gray at Gettysburg, a historical guide book. The story of the three days' battle plainly and concisely told, together with a complete roster of the two armies. Gettysburg, Adam Ertter [1898] 55 p. illus., plan, ports. 23cm.   CSmH   **2260**

Gilbert, John Warren, 1863–1954.
   Battle of Gettysburg made plain, historical guide book . . . by J. Warren Gilbert, the battlefield guide. [Gettysburg?] Miller print [n.d.] 17 p. 21cm.   CSmH   **2261**
   Title and imprint from cover.

—— —— [Harrisburg, J. Horace McFarland co. Mount Pleasant printery, n.d.] 56 p. illus., ports. 22½cm.   CSmH   **2262**
   Title from cover.
   Advertising matter included.

—— —— Third edition, revised. [Columbus, Ohio, Chas. M. Cott, printer] c1898. 55 p. illus., map, ports. 23cm.   CSmH   **2263**

—— —— Revised edition. Gettysburg, Harry J. Rhine, 1904. 55 p. 23cm.   CSmH   **2264**

—— . . . The Blue and the Gray, a history of the conflicts during Lee's invasion and battle of Gettysburg, being for the most part contributions by Union and Confederate officers, condensed and arranged for popular reading, by Prof. J. Warren Gilbert. [Chicago, Curt Teich & co.] c1922. 166 p. front. (fold. map), illus. 23cm.   CSmH   **2265**

At head of title: People's pictorial edition.
Cover illus. in color.

Hammond, Schuyler Augustus
Monumental guide to the Gettysburg battlefield, with index showing the location of every monument, marker and tablet with approaching roads and avenues. Gettysburg [1899?] 16 p. fold. map. 17cm.   CSmH   **2266**

Title and imprint from cover.
Map copyright 1899 by Schuyler A. Hammond & Edgar M. Hewitt.

Henschen, George Newton Cressy
Epitome of the battle of Gettysburg. [Harrisburg, n.d.] [4] p. 25½cm. CSmH   **2267**

Caption title.
Map [1]; facsimile of Lincoln's Gettysburg address [4]

Hoke, Jacob, 1825–1893.
A guide to the battle-field of Gettysburg . . . by Jacob Hoke. Dayton, W. J. Shuey, 1887. 24 p. illus., fold. map. 21½cm.
CSmH DLC   **2268**

Title and imprint from cover.

Jenkins, Thomas E
Gettysburg in war and in peace, a brief review of interesting historical facts and incidents relative to the famous three-days. . . . Baltimore, Passenger Department of the Western Maryland Railroad [Press of John Cox's Sons, 1890] 8, 92 p. illus., fold. illus. and map, plate (map). 23½cm. CSmH DLC   **2269**

Roster of the Army of Northern Virginia, (8) p.
"The old 'Tape worm railroad,' now the Gettysburg short line of the Western Maryland railroad," 61–80.

—— —— Baltimore, Passenger Department of the Western Maryland Railroad [Press of John Cox's Sons, 1898] 116 p. illus., fold. map, plate (map). 23½cm.   CSmH   **2270**

A reprinting.
At head of title: Second souvenir edition.

Laney, H
Laney's Gettysburg battlefield and its monuments, a guide book and souvenir. . . . Cumberland, Md., Laney Souvenir co., c1895. [53] p. illus. 18 x 23½cm. CSmH   **2271**

Long, Harry W
Gettysburg as the battle was fought, a complete story of the 16th decisive battle of the world, July 1–2–3, 1863. With complete maps of the battlefield and itinerary of both armies, by H. W. Long, guide and lecturer. Gettys-

burg, H. W. Long [c1927] 164 p. illus., plans, ports. 22½cm.   NN   **2272**

Long, James Thomas, 1843–1811.
Gettysburg: how the battle was fought, by Captain James T. Long, the guide and delineator. [Gettysburg, Barbehenn & Little, c1890] 96 p. front. (fold. map), illus., ports., plans. 20½cm.   NN   **2273**

—— —— Harrisburg, E. K. Meyers print. house, 1891. 92 p. illus., plans, ports., fold. map. 23cm.   NN   **2274**

A reprinting

—— —— Harrisburg, E. K. Meyers print. house, 1891. 99 p. illus., plans, ports., fold. map. 22½cm.   NjJ   **2275**

—— The 16th decisive battle of the world, Gettysburg, by James T. Long. Gettysburg, Compiler print [c1906] 95, (1) p. plates (illus., ports.). 19cm. CSmH DLC   **2276**

—— —— Gettysburg, Compiler print [1911] 97, (5) p. plates (illus., ports.). 19½cm.
Advertising matter, (5) p.   NN   **2277**

Minnigh, Luther William
The battlefield of Gettysburg, how to see and understand it. The tourist's guide and hand-book, with explanatory map and roster of the armies. By L. W. Minnigh. Gettysburg, J. E. Wible, printer [n.d.] 26 p. illus., fold. map. 22½cm.   CSmH   **2278**

Title and imprint from cover.
Errata slip inserted.

—— The battlefield of Gettysburg. Locations of regimental and brigade monuments and memorials, erected upon the field. Arranged by Luth W. Minnigh. [c1890] broadside, 49 x 30cm.   CSmH   **2279**

—— —— [Holly Springs, Printed by the Mt. Holly print. co., 1893] leaf, 49 x 34cm.
CSmH   **2280**

Text on recto, advertising matter on verso.

—— The battlefield of Gettysburg and National military park, the mecca for veterans, patriots and students of history, by Luther W. Minnigh. . . . Harrisburg, Keystone print, 1895. [32] p. 16½cm.   CSmH   **2281**

Title and imprint from cover.
Map on p. [2] of cover.
Advertising matter included.

—— The Gettysburg knapsack, a souvenir of useful information for veterans, patriots, tourists, and the great army of generous youth, in whose souls the stirring reminiscences of the battle of Gettysburg find a place, by Luther

Guide Books to Gettysburg, continued

W. Minnigh. Mt. Holly Springs, Mt. Holly print. co. [c1897] 32 p. 16½cm.

Map on p. [2] of cover.   **CSmH**   *2282*
Author's port. on cover.
Advertising matter included.

—— —— [n.p.] c1897. 40 p. 16½cm.

Title and imprint from cover. **CSmH**   *2283*
Map on p. [2] of cover.
Author's port. on cover.
Advertising matter included.

—— . . . Gettysburg, "what they did here," by Luther W. Minnigh, the guide and expositor. . . . Harrisburg, Keystone print [c1892] 104 p. illus., plans, ports., fold. map. 22cm.

Title and imprint from cover. **CSmH**   *2284*
At head of title: National park edition.

—— Gettysburg: "what they did here," profusely illustrated historical guide book, by Luther W. Minnigh. . . . [c1892] 150 p. front. (illus.), plans, ports., fold. map. 23½cm.

                                 CSmH   *2285*
On cover: Enlarged and revised edition.

—— —— [Gettysburg, Tipton & Blocher, c1924] 168 p. front. (fold. map), illus., plans, ports. 22½cm.   *2286*

—— 20th century Gettysburg battlefield souvenir, useful information for veterans, patriots, tourists, and the great army of generous youth, in whose souls the stirring reminiscences of the battle of Gettysburg find a place [by] Luther W. Minnigh. Gettysburg, 1901. 20 p. 15cm.

Title and imprint from cover. **CSmH**   *2287*
Map on p. [2] of cover.
Advertising matter included.

Moyer, Henry S
General Lee's headquarters at Gettysburg, Penna., by Henry S. Moyer. [Allentown, c1911] [4] p. 1 illus., 2 maps. 24cm.

Caption title.   **CSmH DLC**   *2288*

Pitzer, John Emanuel, 1839–1916.
Three days at Gettysburg, a complete handbook of the movements of both armies during Lee's invasion of Pennsylvania, and his return to Virginia. The three days' battle at Gettysburg, July 1st, 2nd and 3rd, 1863, and a guide to the position of each Federal organization marked with a monument or tablet on the Gettysburg battlefield, with casualties of both Union and Confederate forces. By John E. Pitzer. [Gettysburg, "News" press, n.d.] 100 p. maps, port. on cover. 23½cm.

                                 CSmH   *2289*
NeHi has an undated edition with 77 p.
The author operated a hotel at Gettysburg.

Scott, William A
Battle of Gettysburg, by William A. Scott. Gettysburg, c1905. 28 p. 2 plans on cover. 21cm.   **CSmH**   *2290*
Title and imprint from cover.

Stackpole, Edward James, 1894–
The battle of Gettysburg, a guided tour, by General Edward J. Stackpole and Colonel Wilbur S. Nye. . . . Harrisburg, Stackpole co., 1960. illus., plans. 22cm.   **NN**   *2291*
Text, illus. and plan on p. [2–4] of cover.

Waldron, Holman D
With pen and camera on the field of Gettysburg in war and peace. Text by Holman D. Waldron. . . . Portland, Me., Chisholm Bros., c1898. [56] p. illus., ports. 30½ x 23½cm.
                              CSmH DLC   *2292*

Wert, J   Howard
A complete handbook of the monuments and indications and guide to the positions on the Gettysburg battle-field, by J. Howard Wert. Harrisburg, R. M. Sturgeon & co., 1886. 212 p. illus., ports. 22cm.   **NN**   *2293*

Chambersburg
July 30, 1864

Gherst, M
Military situation and burning of Chambersburg. *Kittochtinny historical society papers* VIII (Chambersburg, 1915) 277–96.   *2294*

McCausland, John, 1836–1927.
The burning of Chambersburg. AW 770–4.
                                             2295

Schneck, Benjamin Schroeder, 1806–1874.
The burning of Chambersburg, Pennsylvania. By Rev. B. S. Schneck, an eye witness and a sufferer. With corroborative statements, from the Rev. Joseph Clark, Hon. A. K. McClure, J. Hoke, and Rev. S. J. Nicholls. Philadelphia, Lindsay & Blakiston, 1864. 72 p. 19½cm.   **DLC**   *2296*

—— —— With corroborative statements from the Rev. J. Clark, Hon. A. K. McClure, J. Hoke, Rev. T. G. Apple, Rev. B. Bausman, Rev. S. J. Niccols, and J. K. Shryock. In letters to a friend. Second edition, revised and improved, with a plan of the burnt portion of the town. Philadelphia, Lindsay & Blakiston, 1864. iv, 5–76 p. front. (plan). 19½cm.
                                     NN   *2297*
A "third edition, revised and enlarged," 1864, is a reprinting.

Seibert, George Carl, 1828–1902.
The burning of Chambersburg, Pa. *Pennsylvania-German* IX (1908) 291–302. illus. *2298*

—— Die Zerstörung der Stadt Chambersburg durch die Rebellen am 30. Juli 1864. Nach persönlicher Erkundigung an Ort und Stelle, sowie nach den veröffentlichten Berichten des Augenzeugen Dr. B. S. Schneck. Historisch treu dargestellt von Dr. George Seibert. Philadelphia, J. Kohler, 1865. 48 p. front. (plan). 19cm.   NN   **2299**

WEST VIRGINIA

General References

Reports of Federal and Confederate officers, including account of the battles at Lewisburg, West Virginia, May 24, 1862, and the battle of Dry creek, (White Sulpher springs) W. Va., August 26th and 27th, 1863 . . . These copies of reports were recently furnished by Col. J. M. Schoonmaker who commanded the Fourteenth Pennsylvania regiment in the battle of Dry creek. [White Sulpher Springs, 1915] 19 p. 15½cm.   NcD   **2300**

On cover: Official reports of battles of Lewisburg, W. Va., May 24th, 1862, and Dry creek (White Sulpher springs) West Virginia, August 26 and 27, 1863.

Ambler, Charles Henry, 1876–1957.
General R. E. Lee's Northwest Virginia campaign. *WVH* v (1943/44) 101–15.   **2301**

—— Romney in the Civil war. *WVH* v (1943/44) 151–20.   **2302**

Bailes, Clarice Lorene.
Jacob Dolson Cox in West Virginia. *WVH* vi (1944/45) 5–58.   **2303**

Benham, Henry Washington, 1813–1884.
Recollections of West Virginia campaign, with "the three months troops," May, June, and July, 1861, by an Engineer officer. Private copy, from the monthly magazine "Old and new," for June, 1873. Boston, 1873. p. [676]–90. 23½cm.   CSmH NHi   **2304**

Carrington, Henry Beebe, 1824–1912.
Ohio militia and West Virginia campaign, 1861. Address of General Carrington to Army of West Virginia, at Marietta, Ohio, Sept. 10, 1870. New edition. Boston, R. H. Blodgett & co., printers, 1904. 26 p. 20½cm.
CSmH NN   **2305**

Cook, Roy Bird, 1886–1961.
Battlefields of West Virginia. *In* West Virginia legislative handbook and manual and official register, 1934, 471–81.   **2306**

Cox, Jacob Dolson, 1828–1900.
McClellan in West Virginia. *B&L* i 126–48.   **2307**

—— West Virginia operations under Fremont. *B&L* ii 278–81.   **2308**

Ford, H   S
Foraging in the Kanawha valley. *B&G* iii (1895) 209–11.   **2309**

Fremont, John Charles, 1813–1890.
Report of the operations of Maj.-Gen. Fremont while in command of the Mountain department, during the Spring and Summer of 1862. New York, Baker & Godwin, printers, 1866. 40 p. 22½cm.   CSmH DLC   **2310**

Grove, Stephen Ed
Souvenir and guide book of Harper's Ferry, Antietam and South mountain battlefields, by S. Ed. Grove. Martinsburg, Press of Thompson Brothers, 1898. 104 p. illus., map, ports. 23cm.
CSmH   **2311**

Hall, Granville Davisson, 1837–1934.
Lee's invasion of Northwest Virginia in 1861, by Granville Davisson Hall. . . . [Chicago, Press of Mayer & Miller co.] 1911. 164 p. 20cm.   CSmH DLC TxU   **2312**

Hill, Charles Wesley, 1813–1881.
Comments on Maj.-Gen. McClellan's account of his West Virginia campaign. [Toledo, 1864] 4 p. 24½cm.   DLC   **2313**

Caption title.
Text signed: Chas. W. Hill.

Humphreys, Milton Wylie, 1844–1928.
Military operations, 1861–1863, Fayette county, West Virginia, by Milton W. Humphreys, Bryan's battery, Kings's artillery, C.S.A., Battle of Carnifex Ferry, by Roy Bird Cook. Fayetteville, Privately issued by Charles A. Goddard [1931] 38, (2) p. illus. 22cm.
WvU   **2314**

"Affair at Carnifex Ferry," map laid in.
"The retreat of Union forces under Lightburn from Fayetteville and Gauley bridge, September 1862, by John L. Vance, Lt. Col. Fourth West Va.," [35]–8.
The battle of Carnifex ferry, by Roy Bird Cook, is reprinted from the separate publication.

—— Military operations, 1861–1863, Fayetteville, West Virginia, by Milton W. Humphreys. Fayetteville, Privately printed by Charles A. Goddard, 1926. 31 p. illus., port. 24cm.
T Vi   **2315**

See *Shetler* 361–64A for other editions of Title.

Jones, Allen W
Military events in West Virginia during the Civil war, 1861–1865. *WVH* xxi (1959/60) 186–96.   **2316**

Kincaid, Mary Elizabeth
Fayetteville, West Virginia, during the Civil war. *WVH* xiv (1952/53) 339–64. fold. plate (illus.).   **2317**

Levering, John
Lee's advance and retreat in the Cheat mountain campaign in 1861: supplemented by the tragic death of Colonel John A. Washington of his staff, read December 12, 1889. *MOL-LUS-Ill* IV 11–35. map. **2339**

Price, William Thomas, 1830–
Guerrilla warfare, the ambush on Greenbrier river in which seven troopers were killed. *West Virginia historical magazine* IV (1904) 241–9. **2340**

Benjamin, J   W
Gray forces defeated in battle of Lexington [May 23, 1862] *WVH* XX (1958/59) 24–35. plate (port.). **2341**

Harper's Ferry
September 12–15, 1862

Douglas, Henry Kyde, 1840–1903.
Stonewall Jackson's intentions at Harper's ferry. *B&L* II 617–18. **2342**

Phelps, R   N   R
How Harper's Ferry fell, new light on the hard fight in the mountains from a Federal point of view. *Book of the royal blue* v 6 (March 1902) 15–19. **2343**

Walker, John George, 1822–1893.
Jackson's capture of Harper's ferry. *B&L* II 604–11. **2344**

White, Julius, 1816–1890.
The surrender of Harper's Ferry. *B&L* II 612–15. **2345**

*   *   *

Summers, Festus Paul, 1895–
The Jones-Imboden raid. *WVH* I (1939–40) 15–29. map. **2346**

Droop Mountain
November 6, 1863

Echols, John, 1823–1896.
Report of Brigadier General Echols of the battle of Droop mountain. Published by order of Congress. Richmond, R. M. Smith, Public printer, 1864. 16 p. 25cm.   CSmH **2347**
Dated: Headquarters First brigade, Army southwestern Virginia, Lewisburg, Nov. 19, 1863.
Crandall 1414.

McNeill, George Douglas, 1877–
The battle of Droop mountain. *Davis and Elkins historical magazine* VI (1953) 1–7.
2348

Price, Andrew, 1871–1930.
The battle of Droop mountain, fought November 6, 1863, marked the date of the supremacy of the Union forces in West Virginia

in the Civil war. *In* West Virginia legislative hand book and manual and official register, 1926, 463–8. **2349**

West Virginia. Droop Mountain Battlefield Commission.
. . . Report of . . . Charleston [Jarrett print co.] 1928. 34 p. front. (port.), fold. map, ports. 23½cm.   WvU **2350**

*   *   *

Capture of the forts at New Creek station. *SB* II (1883/84) 64–9. **2351**

Haselberger, Fritz
A synopsis of the battle of Folck's Mill, August 1, 1864, by Fritz Haselberger. [1962] 6, (1) folios. 28cm. mimeo. **2352**
Caption title. Plan of the battle area and Order of battle, (1) p.
Prepared for the Allegany county Civil war centennial commission.

VERMONT
St. Alban's Raid
1864

Benjamin, Louis N
The St. Albans raid; or, investigation into the charges against Lieut. Bennett H. Young and command, for their acts at St. Albans, Vt., on the 19th October, 1864. Being a complete and authentic report of all the proceedings on the demand of the United States for their extradition, under the Ashburton treaty, before Judge Coursol and the opinions of the Judges revised by themselves. Compiled by L. N. Benjamin. Montreal, Printed by John Lovell, 1865. 480 p. 22cm.   CSmH MoHi NN **2353**

—— —— Boston, A. Williams & co., 1865. 480 p. 22cm.   MoHi **2354**
A reprinting.

Benton, Reuben C
Personal recollections of the St. Albans raid, by Lieutenant-Colonel R. C. Benton. *MOL-LUS-Minn* III 404–21. **2355**

Borthwick, John Douglas, 1832–
History of the Montreal prison, from A.D. 1784, to A.D. 1886. . . . Montreal, A. Periard, 1886. vii, (1), 269, (1) p. 22½cm.
DLC NN **2356**
St. Alban's raid, names of the raiders, trial of the same, last remarks of Judge Smith . . . , 184–215.

Branch, John, 1852–
St. Alban's raid, St. Albans, Vermont, October 19, 1864. Compiled and distributed by John Branch, Sr. St. Albans [1936] 67 p. front. (port.), 2 ports. 22½cm.   NN **2357**

St. Alban's Raid, continued

"A chronological account of the St. Albans raid
. . . The articles and editorials are reprinted from
the files of the St. Albans Daily messenger."

Gray, Clayton, 1918–
Conspiracy in Canada, by Clayton Gray.
Montreal, L'Atelier press [1959] 145 p. fac-
sims., illus., ports. 19½cm.   NN   **2358**
"This edition is limited to two hundred and fifty
copies."

Hibbard, L   H
The St. Alban's raid, 1864. *Report of the
Missisquoi county historical society* no 2 (St.
Johns, 1907). 55–60.   **2359**

Kinchen, Oscar A
Daredevils of the Confederate army, the
story of the St. Albans raiders. Boston, Christopher pub. house [1959] 171 p. 20½cm.
                                             NN   **2360**

Sowles, Edward A
History of the St. Albans raid, annual address delivered before the Vermont historical
society, delivered at Montpelier, Vt., on Tuesday evening, October 17, 1876, by Edward A.
Sowles. St. Albans, Messenger print. works,
1876. 48 p. 22½cm.   CSmH NeHi   **2361**

[Tetu, Henri] i.e. Louis David Henri, 1849–
David Tetu et les raiders de Saint-Alban,
episode de la guerre americaine, 1864–1865.
Deuxieme edition. Quebec, N. S. Hardy, 1891.
187 p. front. (port.). 16½cm.
                              DLC NN   **2362**

Walsh, James T
Story of St. Albans raid, October 19, 1864,
by James T. Walsh. Reprinted from St. Albans
Daily messenger, Oct. 19, 1939. [St. Albans,
Messenger press, 1939] 10 p. 3 ports. 18cm.
    Caption title.   Vt   **2363**
    On cover: Compiled from material and data in
possession of John Branch, Sr.

Winks, Robin W
The St. Albans raid, a bibliography. *Vermont history* XXVII (1959) 46–51.   **2364**

—— —— An addenda. *Vermont history*
XXVII (1959) 168–9.   **2365**

FLORIDA

General References

Bearss, Edwin Cole, 1923–
Civil war operations in and around Pensacola. *FHQ* XXXVI (1957/58) 125–65; XXXIX
(1960/61) 231–55, 330–53.   **2366**

Cushman, Joseph D
The blockade and fall of Apalachicola,
1861–1862. *FHQ* XLI (1962/63) 36–46. **2367**

East, Omega G
St. Augustine during the Civil war. *FHQ*
XXXI (1952/53) 75–91.   **2368**

Holcombe, John L   and Walter J. Butt-
    genbach
Pensacola harbor, Florida, October 9, 1861–
January 1, 1862. *Journal of the United States
artillery* XXXVIII (1912) 312–17.   **2369**

Jones, Allen W
Military events in Florida during the Civil
war, 1861–1865. *FHQ* XXXIX (1960/61) 42–5.
                                             2370

Larkin, J   L
Battle of Santa Rosa island. *FHQ* XXXVII
(1958/59) 372–6. illus.   **2371**

St. John's Bluff
September 11 – October 3, 1862

Bearss, Edwin Cole, 1923–
Military operations on the St. Johns, September–October 1862. *FHQ* XLII (1963/64) 232–
47, 331–51. 2 maps.   **2372**

Davis, T   Frederick
Engagements at St. Johns Bluff, St. Johns
river, Florida, September–October, 1862. *FHQ*
XV (1936/37) 77–84.   **2373**

West, George Mortimer, 1845–
The skirmish at "Old Town," St. Andrew's,
Fla., March 20th, 1863, by G. M. West. St.
Andrews, Panama City pub. co., 1918. 7 p.
23cm.   NN   **2374**
Title and imprint from cover.

Boyd, Mark F
The Federal campaign of 1864, in East Florida, a study for the Florida state board of parks
and historic monuments. *FHQ* XXIX (1950/51)
3–37. fold. map.   **2375**

Olustee
February 20, 1864

The Florida expedition. *United States service
magazine* II (1864) 150–7.   **2376**

Baltzell, George F
The battle of Olustee (Ocean pond), Florida.
FHQ IX (1930/31) 199–223. fold. map. **2377**

Cole, Ruth H
The battle of Olustee, a description of Florida's major battle in the War between the
States, which took place near Lake city, February 20, 1864, by Ruth H. Cole, a senior in
Rollins college. [St. Augustine?] Florida Division, United Daughters of the Confederacy,
1929. 15 p. 19½cm.   DLC NN   **2378**

Title and imprint from cover, p. [1]
Title piece, 7–13.

Furness, William Eliot
The battle of Olustee, Florida, February 20, 1864. *PMHSM* IX (1904) 233–263.   **2379**

Jones, Samuel, 1819–1887.
The battle of Olustee, or Ocean pond, Florida. *B&L* IV 76–9.   **2380**

—— —— Comments on General Jones's paper, by Joseph R. Hawley, *B&L* IV 79–80.
2381

*   *   *

Bearss, Edwin Cole, 1923–
Asboth's expedition up the Alabama and Florida railroad [July 21–25, 1864] *FHQ* XXXIX (1960/61) 159–66.   **2382**

Boyd, Mark F
The battle of Marianna [September 27, 1864] *FHQ* XXIX (1950/51) 225–42.   **2383**
Roster of Home guards in the battle, 240–1.

—— The joint operations of the Federal army and navy near St. Marks, Florida, March 1865. *FHQ* XXIX (1950/51) 96–124.   **2384**
Contents: I The battle of Natural Bridge; II The cadets of the West Florida seminary in the battle of Natural Bridge.

NORTH CAROLINA
General References

Barrett, John Gilchrist
North Carolina as a Civil war battlefield, by John Gilchrist Barrett. Raleigh, State Department of Archives and History, 1960. viii, 99, (1) p. illus., ports., fold. map. 22½cm.
DLC   **2385**

Buttgenbach, Walter J
Fort Macon, Georgia [sic] *Journal of the United States Artillery* XL (1913) 306–13.
"Coast defense in the Civil war."   **2386**

Gardner, James Browne, 1842–
Massachusetts memorial to her soldiers and sailors who died in the Department of North Carolina, 1861–1865, dedicated at New Berne, No. Carolina, November 11, 1908. [Boston, Gardner & Taplin, 1909] 102 p. plates (illus., ports.). 22½cm.   NLC NN NcD   **2387**
c1909 by James B. Gardner.
Appropriated funds being insufficient "I decided to publish an account on my individual responsibility."

Hatteras Inlet
August 28–29, 1861

Holcombe, John L   and Walter J. Buttgenbach
Hatteras inlet, N.C., August 28 and 29, 1861. *Journal of the United States artillery* XXXVIII (1912) 35–41. map, plans.   **2388**

Merrill, James M
The Hatteras expedition, August, 1861. *NCHR* XXIX (1952) 204–19.   **2389**

*   *   *

Burnside, Ambrose Everett, 1842–1881.
The Burnside expedition. 1882. 33 p. *PNRI-SSHS* s2 no. 6.   **2390**

Buttgenbach, Walter J
Attack on Roanoke island, North Carolina, February 7 and 8, 1862. *Journal of the United States artillery* XL (1913) 47–58. map.   **2391**

Iobst, Richard W   1934–
Battle of New Bern, by Richard Iobst. Raleigh, North Carolina Centennial Commission [1962] 14 p. 1 illus., plan. 21cm.
CSmH   **2392**

Morris, Jerome F
The brief belligerence of Fort Macon, by Jerome F. Morris. [Raleigh, North Carolina Confederate Centennial Commission, 1962] 12 p. illus., plan. 21½cm.   CSmH   **2393**

Stackpole, Joseph Lewis
The Department of North Carolina under General Foster, July, 1862, to July, 1863, by Major J. Lewis Stackpole. *PMHS* IX (1887) 85–110.   **2394**

Goldsborough
December 11–20, 1862

Kinston, Whitehall and Goldsboro (North Carolina) expedition, December, 1862. New York, W. W. Howe, 1890. 92, xii p. 4 fold. plates (illus., port.). 17cm.
CSmH DLC NN   **2395**
Edited by W. W. Howe.
Letters written by a correspondent of the New York Herald, in December 1862, from New Berne, N.C.
"Index," xii p.
"Errata" slip included.

Clingman, Thomas Lanier, 1815–1868.
Gen. Clingman's report [Goldsboro, December 17, 1862] *OLOD* III (1875) 448–54.   **2396**

*   *   *

Correspondence, orders, etc., between Major-General David Hunter, Major-General J. G. Foster, and Brigadier-General Henry M. Naglee, and others. February and March, 1863. Philadelphia, J. B. Lippincott & co., 1863. 60 p. 22½cm.   CSmH   **2397**

Clingman, Thomas Lanier, 1815–1868.
Official report of Gen. Clingman [New Berne, N.C., January 30–February 3, 1864] *OLOD* IV (1875) 409–12.   **2398**

North Carolina, miscellaneous, continued

Naglee, Henry Morris, 1815–1866.

Report of the conduct of the advance of the column for the relief of Little Washington, N.C., April 18th–19th, 1863, by Gen. Henry M. Naglee. Also an appendix consisting of Gen. Foster's report of the siege of the same place, from March 30 to April 18, 1863. Philadelphia, Collins printer, 1863. 16 p. 22cm.

DNW NcU   *2399*

Spencer, Cornelia Phillips

The last ninety days of the War in North-Carolina, by Cornelia Phillips Spencer. New York, Watchman pub. co., 1866. 287 p. 16½cm.   NN   *2400*

Vance, Zebulon Baird, 1830–1894.

The last days of the war in North Carolina, an address, by Z. B. Vance, delivered Feb. 23, 1885, at the third annual reunion of the Maryland line. . . . Baltimore, Sun book and job print. office, 1885. 32 p. 23cm.

CSmH NN NcD   *2401*

Waddell, Alfred Moore, 1834–1912.

The last year of the war in North Carolina, including Plymouth, Fort Fisher and Bentonville, an address before the Association Army of Northern Virginia, delivered in the hall of the House of delegates, Richmond, Va., October 28, 1887, by A. M. Waddell. . . . Richmond, Wm. Ellis Jones, printer, 1888. 31 p. 21½cm.   CSmH NN   *2402*

Yates, Richard Edwin, 1910–

Governor Vance and the end of the war in North Carolina. *NCHR* xvIII (1941) 315–38.
2403

Fort Fisher
January 15, 1865

Ames, Adelbert, 1835–1933.

Capture of Fort Fisher, North Carolina, Jan. 15, 1865 [by] General Adelbert Ames. [1897] 24 p. 21½cm.   NN   *2404*

Title from cover.
Additional statement from the author, inserted slip.
Also published in *PMHSM* IX (1895) 388–416; *MOLLUS-Mass* I 271–95; *MOLLUS-NY* III 1–51.

—— The failure at Fort Fisher. *Overland monthly* IV (1870) 488–96.   *2405*

Buttgenbach, Walter J

Fort Fisher in North Carolina. *Journal of the United States artillery* XLII (1914) 68–83. map.
2406

Gordon, G   I

The battle of Fort Fisher. *OLOD* I (1874/75) 313–15.   *2407*

Report of Lieut. Col. and A.I.G., dated January 17, 1865, to the General commanding, Lieut. Col. Anderson.

Lockwood, Henry Clay,   –1902.

The capture of Fort Fisher. *Atlantic monthly* xxVII (1871) 622–36, 684–90.   *2408*

—— A man from Maine, a true history of the army at Fort Fisher. *Maine bugle* I (1894) 29–71. 2 illus., 2 plans, plate (port.).   *2409*

—— A true history of the army at Fort Fisher. *US* ns x (1893) 401–29.   *2410*

Lossing, Benson John, 1813–1891.

The first attack on Fort Fisher. *AW* 228–40.
2411

*   *   *

Wells, Edward Laight, 1839–

Hampton at Fayetteville. *SHSP* xIII (1885) 144–8.   *2412*

Bentonville
March 19–21, 1865

Barnwell, Robert W

Bentonville, the last battle of Johnston and Sherman. *Proceedings of the South Carolina historical association* 1943 42–54.   *2413*

Carlin, William Passmore, 1829–

The battle of Bentonville. *MOLLUS-Ohio* III 231–52.   *2414*

Ford, Arthur Peronneau

The last battle of Hardee's corp. *SB* ns I (1885/86) 140–3.   *2415*

Hampton, Wade, 1818–1902.

The battle of Bentonville. *B&L* IV 700–05.
2416

Luvaas, Jay

Johnston's last stand — Bentonville. *NCHR* xxxIII (1956) 332–58. 2 plans, 2 plates (illus.).
2417

McClurg, Alexander Caldwell,   –1901.

The last chance of the Confederacy. *Atlantic monthly* L (1882) 389–400.   *2418*

Also published in *MOLLUS-Ill* I 369–93.

SOUTH CAROLINA
General References

Courtenay, William Ashmead, 1831–1908.

Fragments of war history relating to the coast defense of South Carolina, 1861–'65, and the hasty preparations for the battle of Honey hill, November 30, 1864. *SHSP* xxvI (1898) 62–87.   *2419*

Davis, Nora M
Military and naval operations in South Carolina, 1860–1865; a chronological list, with references to sources of further information. Compiled by Nora M. Davis. With a foreword by W. Edwin Hemphill. Columbia, Published by the South Carolina Archives Department for the South Carolina Confederate War Centennial commission, 1959. [24] p. 23cm.
DLC   **2420**

Fort Sumter

April 12–14, 1861

The battle of Fort Sumter and first victory of the Southern troops, April 13th, 1861. Full accounts of the bombardment, with sketches of the scenes, incidents, etc., compiled chiefly from the detailed reports of the Charleston press. . . . Charleston, Presses of Evans & Cogswell, 1861. 35 p. fold. map. 22½cm.
Crandall 2616.   CSmH   **2421**

—— [another issue] Charleston, Presses of Evans & Cogswell, 1861. 32 p. fold. map. 22½cm.   CSmH NN   **2422**
Crandall 2615.

—— [Charleston, Walker, Evans & Cogswell co., 1961] 35 p. 2 plates (double map). 23cm.
A photographic reprinting.   **2422A**

The Fall of Port Royal, S.C., in 1861, with a sketch of subsequent events to the present time. *SM* xiii (1873) 553–62.   **2423**

Fort Sumter memorial. The fall of Fort Sumter, a contemporary sketch, from Heroes and martyrs, edited by Frank Moore. Replacing the flag upon Sumter, from the narrative of an eye witness [William A. Spicer] adapted by Dr. F. Milton Willis. General Robert Anderson, by Col. Edward S. Cornell. New York, Edwin C. Hill, 1915. xv, 17–65 p. plates (illus., ports.). 27cm.   NN   **2424**

Barnes, Frank
Fort Sumter national monument, South Carolina, by Frank Barnes. Washington [Govt. print. office] 1952. 48 p. illus., map, double plan. 22½cm. (National park service historical handbook series no. 12).   NN   **2425**

Carse, Robert, 1903–
Department of the South. Hilton Head island in the Civil war. By Robert Carse. Columbia, State print. co., 1961. x, 156 p. partly col. illus., plan. 27½cm.   ScU TxU   **2426**
Map on endpaper.

Crawford, Samuel Wylie, 1829–1892.
The first shot against the flag. *AW* 319–29.   **2427**

—— The genesis of the Civil war, the story of Sumter, 1860–1861, by Samuel Wylie Crawford. New York, Charles L. Webster & co., 1887. xxiv, 486 p. front. (group port.), facsims., illus., plans. 24cm.   CSmH   **2428**

—— The history of the fall of Fort Sumter, being an inside history of the affairs in South Carolina and Washington, 1860–1, and the conditions and events in the South which brought on the rebellion. The genesis of the Civil war. By Samuel W. Crawford. [n.p., c1896] xxiii, 486 p. front. (group port.), facsims., illus., plans. 23½cm.   CSmH   **2429**
Copyright Francis P. Harper.

—— —— New York, J. A. Hill & co., 1898. xxiii, 486 p. front. (group port.), facsims., illus., plans. 24cm.   CSmH   **2430**

De Fontaine, Felix Gregory, 1832–1896.
The first day of real war. *SB* ns ii (1886/87) 73–9. illus.   **2431**

—— The second day of the war. *SB* ns ii (1886/87) 200–07. illus.   **2432**

Fletcher, A.
Within Fort Sumter; or, a view of Major Anderson's garrison family for one hundred and ten days, by one of the company. New York, N. Tibbals & co., 1861. 72 p. front. (port.). 18½cm.   DLC NN   **2433**
"Widows' and orphans' edition." Published anonymously.

Foster, John Gray, 1823–1874.
The evacuation of Fort Moultrie, 1860. Edited by Frank F. White, Jr. *SCHM* liii (1952) 1–5.   **2434**

Harris, William Alexander
The record of Fort Sumter, from its occupation by Major Anderson, to its reduction by South Carolina troops, during the administration of Governor Pickens, compiled by W. A. Harris. . . . Columbia, South Carolina print. office, 1862. 50 p. 22½cm.
Crandall 2628.   CSmH NN ScU   **2435**

Holcombe, John L   and Walter J. Buttgenbach
The Port Royal expedition. Capture of Forts Walker and Beauregard. *Journal of the United States artillery* xxxviii (1912) 198–212.   **2436**

Hoogenboom, Ari
Gustavus Fox and the relief of Fort Sumter. *CWH* ix (1963) 383–98.   **2437**

Lawton, Eba (Anderson),   –1919.
Major Robert Anderson and Fort Sumter, 1861, by Eba Anderson Lawton. New York,

Fort Sumter, continued

Knickerbocker press, 1911. 19 p. front. (port.), plate (facsim.). 23½cm.

> Errata slip inserted.   CSmH DLC   **2438**

Meredith, Roy, 1908–
    Storm over Sumter, the opening engagement of the Civil war, by Roy Meredith. New York, Simon and Schuster, 1957. 214, (1) p. front. (map), plates (illus., ports.). 21½cm.

> Plan on endpaper.   NHi   **2439**
> "About the author," (1) p.

Ramsdell, Charles W
    Lincoln and Fort Sumter. *JSH* III (1937) 259–88.   **2440**

South Carolina. Governor.
    . . . Correspondence [January 1861] and other papers, relative to Fort Sumter. Charleston, Presses of Evans & Cogswell, 1861. 28 p. 23cm.   CSmH   **2441**

> At head of title: Executive documents, no. 2.
> *Crandall* 2095.

—— —— Including correspondence of Hon. Isaac W. Hayne with the President. Second edition. Charleston, Presses of Evans and Cogswell, 1861. 43 p. 23cm.   NN   **2442**

> At head of title: Executive documents, no. 2.
> *Crandall* 2096.

Spaulding, Oliver Lyman, 1875–1947.
    The bombardment of Fort Sumter, 1861. *In* Annual report of the American historical association, 1913, 177–203.   **2443**

> "Available armament at Fort Sumter, Apr. 12, 1861," 201.

Swanberg, W   A   1907–
    . . . First blood, the story of Fort Sumter. New York, Charles Scribner's Sons [1957] viii, 373 p. plan, plates (illus., ports.). 23½cm.

> At head of title: W. A. Swanberg. NN   **2444**

Viele, Egbert Ludovickus 1825–1902.
    The Port Royal expedition, 1861, the first Union victory of the Civil war. *Magazine of American history* XIV (1885) 329–40. illus., maps, ports.   **2445**

Defense of Charleston
1862–1864

Correspondence relating to fortification of Morris island and operations of engineers. [Charleston?, 1864?] 44 p. 17½ccm.

> Title from cover, p. [1]   NB   **2446**
> *Crandall* 1334.

Life in Battery Wagner. *LWL* II (1866/67) 351–5.   **2447**

Ashe, Samuel A'Court, 1840–1938.
    Life at Fort Wagner. *Confederate veteran* XXXV (1927) 254–6.   **2448**

Beauregard, Pierre Gustave Toutant, 1819–1893.
    The defense of Charleston. *B&L* IV 1–23.   **2449**

—— Defense of Charleston, South Carolina, in 1862, 1863 and 1864. *North American review* CXLII (1886) 419–36, 564–71.   **2450**

> "To be concluded."

—— General Beauregard's official report of the operations on Morris island . . . during the months of July, August, and September 1863. *SM* VIII (1871) 581–9, 679–88; IX (1871) 45–57.   **2451**

—— Report of General G. T. Beauregard of the defence of Charleston. Published by order of Congress. Richmond, R. M. Smith, Public printer, 1864. 91, (2) p. 25cm.
    CSmH NN   **2452**

> Many pages are unnumbered.
> *Crandall* 1417.

—— Torpedo service in Charleston harbor. *AW* 513–26.   **2453**

Buttgenbach, Walter J
    Fort Sumter, Charleston, S.C. (subsequent attacks). *Journal of the United States artillery.* XLII (1914) 185–213. map.   **2454**

Davis, Robert Stewart, 1839–1911.
    Three months around Charleston bar; or, the great siege as we saw it. *United States service magazine* I (1864) 169–79, 273–83, 462–74.   **2455**

Florance, John E
    Morris island, victory or blunder? *SCHM* LV (1954) 143–52.   **2456**

Furness, William Eliot
    The siege of Fort Wagner, read January 5, 1881. *MOLLUS-Ill.* 210–29. map.   **2457**

Gilchrist, Robert Cogdell, 1829–
    The Confederate defence of Morris island, Charleston harbor, by the troops of South Carolina, Georgia and North Carolina, in the late War between the States . . . Prepared from official reports and other sources, by Maj. Robert C. Gilchrist, a participant, commanding the Gist guard artillery in that defence. [From the Yearbook–1884] [Charleston, News and Courier book presses, 1884] 53 p. front. (fold. map), fold. plan. 23½cm.
    CSmH DLC NN   **2458**

Gillmore, Quincy Adams, 1825–1888.
    The army before Charleston in 1863. *B&L* IV 52–71.   **2459**

—— Engineer and artillery operations against the defences of Charleston harbor in 1863; comprising the descent upon Morris island, the demolition of Fort Sumter, the reduction of Forts Wagner and Gregg. With observations on heavy ordnance, fortifications, etc. By Q. A. Gillmore . . . With the official reports of Chief of artillery, assistant engineers, etc. . . . (Published by authority). New York, D. Van Nostrand, 1865. vi, [7]–354 p. col. front. (illus.), plates (fold. maps and plans, illus, partly col.). 24cm.   NN   **2460**

—— . . . Engineer and artillery operations against the defences of Charleston harbor in 1863; with a supplement. By Q. A. Gillmore. New York, D. Van Nostrand, 1868. viii, [7]–314, 172 p. front. (col. illus.), plates (illus., partly col.; fold. maps and plans). 24cm.
NN   **2461**
    At head of title: Professional papers, Corps of engineers, no. 16.
    "It has been deemed to use an unbound edition of the original publication, rather than incur the expense of new composition."

Hayne, Paul Hamilton
    The defense of Fort Wagner. *SB* ns I (1885/ 86) 599–608.   **2462**

Heyward, Du Bose, 1885–1940.
    Fort Sumter, by DuBose Heyward and Herbert Ravenel Sass. New York, Farrar & Rinehart [1938] xi, 109 p. 20cm.   **2463**
    On cover: 1861–1865.

Holcombe, John L   and Walter J. Buttgenbach
    Fort Sumter, Charleston, S.C. (first attack). *Journal of the United States artillery* XXXVII (1912) 169–87.   **2464**

Johnson, John, 1829–1907.
    The Confederate defense of Fort Sumter. *B&L* IV 23–6.   **2465**

—— The defense of Charleston harbor, including Fort Sumter and adjacent islands, 1863–1865, by John Johnson. . . . Charleston, Walker, Evans & Cogswell co., 1890. 276, clxxvii p. illus., map, plates (fold. illus., fold. maps, ports.). 24½cm. CSmH NN   **2466**

Jones, Charles Colcock, 1831–1893.
    Defence of battery Wagner, July 18th, 1863, addresses delivered before the Confederate survivors' association, in Augusta, Georgia, on the occasion of its fourteenth annual reunion, on Memorial day, April 26th, 1892, by Col. Charles C. Jones, Jr., by Lieut. Col. H. D. D. Twiggs, and by Captain F. Edgeworth Eve. . . . Augusta, Chronicle pub. co., 1892. 30, (1) p. 23cm.   DLC NN   **2467**

—— The evacuation of Battery Wagner and the battle of Ocean pond, an address delivered before the Confederate survivors' association, in Augusta, Georgia, on the occasion of its tenth annual reunion on Memorial day, April 26th, 1888, by Col. Charles C. Jones, Jr. . . . Augusta, Chronicle pub. co., 1888. 20 p. 23cm.
NN   **2468**

Jones, Samuel, 1819–1887.
    The siege of Charleston and the operations on the South Atlantic coast in the War among the States, by Samuel Jones, formerly Major-General, C.S.A. New York, Neale pub. co., 1911. 295 p. front. (port.). 21cm.
CSmH NN   **2469**

Jordan, Francis
    The occupation of Fort Sumter, and hoisting the old flag thereon, April 14, 1865. *US* ns XIV (1895) 406–25.   **2470**

Meynardie, Elias James
    The siege of Charleston, its history and progress, a discourse delivered in Bethel church, Charleston, S.C., November 19, 1863, (Thanksgiving day), by Rev. E. J. Meynardie. . . . Columbia, Press of Evans & Cogswell, 1864. 15 p. 22cm.   CSmH DLC   **2471**
    Crandall 2640.

Parker, Francis Le Jau, 1836–1913.
    The battle of Fort Sumter as seen from Morris island [edited by F. L. Parker] *SCHM* LXII (1961) 65–71.   **2472**

Ripley, Roswell Sabine, 1823–1887.
    Report of Brigadier General R. S. Ripley of operations, from August 21, to September 10, 1863, with sub-reports. Published by order of Congress. Richmond, R. M. Smith, Public printer, 1864. 42 p. 25cm.   CSmH   **2473**
    Dated: Headquarters First military district, Department of South Carolina, Georgia and Florida, Charleston, September 22d, 1863.
    Crandall 1416.

—— Correspondence relating to fortifications of Morris island and operations of engineers, Charleston, S.C., 1863. New York, John J. Caulon, printer, 1878. 43 p. 22½cm.
CSmH DLC   **2474**

Stryker, William Scudder, 1838–1900.
    The "swamp angel." *B&L* IV 72–4.   **2475**

—— The "swamp angel," the gun used in firing on Charleston, 1863. *Magazine of American history* XVI (1886) 553–60. illus., ports.   **2476**

Tower, Roderick
    The defense of Fort Sumter, by Roderick Tower. Publication sponsored by the Fort Sumter hotel. Charleston [Printed by Walker, Evans & Cogswell co., 1938] 39 p. illus. 17cm.
    Plates are paged.   NcD   **2477**

Defense of Charleston, 1862–1864, continued

Twiggs, Hansford Dade Duncan
Defense of Battery Wagner, July 18, 1863. *In* Addresses delivered before the Confederate veterans association of Savannah, Ga., 1898. 73–89.   **2478**
     Also published in *SHSP* xx (1892) 166–84. See Title 419A.

Wagner, Thomas W
Report of Thomas W. Wagner of the sinking of the stone fleet at the entrance of Charleston harbor. [n.p., 1862] 2 p. 21½cm.
     See Title 419A.   NcD   **2479**
     Dated: February 12th, 1862.
     Crandall 1433.

*   *   *

An account of the Fort Sumter memorial, Charleston, S.C. Published by the Commission. [Charleston, Presses of Jno. J. Furlong & Son] 1933. 37 p. plates (illus., 2 ports.). 23½cm.
               DLC NcD   **2480**
Stevens, Hazard, 1842–1918.
Military operations in South Carolina in 1862, against Charleston, Port Royal Ferry, James island, Secessionville, by Major Hazard Stevens. *PMHSM* ix (1890) 111–57.   **2481**

Honey Hill
November 30, 1864

Courtenay, William Ashmead, 1831–1908.
Heroes of Honey hill, brief sketches of Stuart's, Kanapaux's and Earle's batteries. . . . *SHSP* xxvi (1898) 232—41.   **2482**

Jones, Charles Colcock, 1831–1893.
The battle of Honey-hill, an address delivered before the Confederate survivors's association in Augusta, Georgia, at its seventh annual meeting, on Memorial day, April 27, 1885, by Col. Charles C. Jones. . . . Augusta, Chronicle print. estab., 1885. 16 p. 22cm.   NN   **2483**
     Also published in *SHSP* xiii (1885) 355–67.

*   *   *

Boylston, Raymond P
The battle of Aiken, by Raymond P. Boylston, Jr. Sketches by Samuelton L. Boylston. [Belvedere, S.C., 1960] 22 p. illus., double map. 23cm.   ScU   **2484**

Burning of Columbia
February 17, 1865

The burning of Columbia. I. Letter of Gen. Wade Hampton, June 24, 1873, with appendix.

II. Report of Committee of citizens, ex-Chancellor J. P. Carroll, Chairman, May, 1866. <From the News and courier, Charleston, S.C., January 15, and February 5, 1888.> Charleston, Walker, Evans & Cogswell co., printers, 1888. 24 p. 23cm.   CSmH   **2485**
     Text in double columns.

Who burnt Columbia? Part 1st. Official depositions of Wm. Tecumseh Sherman and Gen. O. O. Howard, for the defence, and extracts from some of the depositions for the claimants. Filed in certain claims vs. United States, pending before "the Mixed commission on British and American claims in Washington, D.C. . . . Charleston, Walker, Evans & Cogswell, printers, 1873. 121 p. 18½cm.   CSmH   **2486**
     "Part 2d will contain the rebuttal testimony yet to be taken."

Carroll, James Parsons
Report of the Committee appointed to collect testimony in relation to the destruction of Columbia, S.C., on the 17th February, 1865, by Chancellor James Parsons Carroll. Columbia, Bryan print. co., 1893. 20 p. 23cm.
                 TxU   **2487**
     Text signed: J. P. Carroll, Chairman.
     c1890 by Miss S. P. Carroll.

Garber, Michael Christian
Reminiscences of the burning of Columbia, South Carolina. *Magazine of history* xxii (1916) 177–91.   **2488**
     As a boy of fourteen the writer accompanied his father, Chief Quartermaster, on the march through the Carolinas.

Gibbes, James Guiguard, 1829–
Who burnt Columbia?, by Col. James G. Gibbes. Newberry, S.C., Elbert H. Aull co., 1902. 137, iii p. 3 plates (ports.). 23½cm.
     "Index," iii p.   CSmH DLC   **2489**

Hill, James D
The burning of Columbia reconsidered. *South Atlantic quarterly* xxv (1926) 269–82.   **2490**

Rhodes, James Ford, 1848–1927.
Who burned Columbia? *American historical review* vii (1902) 485–93.   **2491**

Sill, Edward
Who is responsible for the destruction of the City of Columbia, S.C., on the night of 17th February, 1865? *LWL* iv (1867/68) 361–9.   **2492**

[Simms, William Gilmore] 1806–1870.
Sack and destruction of the City of Columbia, S.C. To which is added a list of the property destroyed. Columbia, Press of the Daily Phoenix, 1865. 76 p. 20½cm.
     Crandall 2661.   CSmH DLC NN   **2493**

—— —— Second edition, edited with notes by A. S. Salley. [Atlanta] Oglethorpe University press, 1937. xx, 25–106 p. 23½cm.
CSmH NN   **2494**

Trezevant, D   H
The burning of Columbia, S.C. A review of Northern assertions and Southern facts, by Dr. D. H. Trezevant. Columbia, South Carolina press, 1866. 31 p. 21½cm.
CSmH DLC   **2495**
Text in double columns.

*   *   *

A bluecoat's account of the Camden expedition. Edited by Lonnie J. White. *ArHQ* xxiv (1965) 82–90.   **2496**
Originally published in the Lawrence Kansas daily tribune.
"Writer was a member of a negro regiment."

Western Theater

GENERAL REFERENCES

Buell, Don Carlos, 1818–1898.
Major-General W. T. Sherman at the Spring campaign of 1862 in the West. *Historical magazine* s 2 viii (Morrisania, 1870) 74–82.   **2497**
"From The [New York daily] world of September 4, 1865."

—— Statement of Major General Buell in review of the evidence before the Military commission, appointed by the War department in November 1862. Campaign in Kentucky, Tennessee, Northern Mississippi and North Alabama in 1861 and 1862. [n.p., 1862] 71, (1) p. 22cm.   CSmH DLC NN   **2498**
Title from cover.

Catton, Bruce, 1899–
Grant moves South, by Bruce Catton. With maps by Samuel H. Bryant. Boston, Little, Brown and co. [1960] 564 p. front. (port.), maps. 22cm.   CSmH   **2499**

Deaderick, John Barron, 1886–
Shiloh, Memphis and Vicksburg, by Barron Deaderick. Memphis, West Tennessee Historical Society [1960] 32 p. 19cm.
Illus. p. [2] of cover.   DLC NN   **2500**

Fry, James Barnet, 1827–1894.
Operations of the army under Buell, from June 10th to October 30th, 1862, and the "Buell commission," by James B. Fry. New York, D. Van Nostrand, 1884. 201 p. front. (port.), fold. map. 19cm.   NHi NN   **2501**

Green, John Pugh, 1839–1921.
The movement of the 11th and 12th army corps from the Potomac to the Tennessee, read by John P. Green, before the Commandery of the State of Pennsylvania, Military Order of the loyal legion of the United States. . . . Philadelphia, Allen, Lane & Scott's print. house, 1892. 16 p. 23cm.   MB   **2502**

Jones, Archer
Confederate strategy from Shiloh to Vicksburg. *JMH* xxiv (1962) 158–67.   **2503**

—— Tennessee and Mississippi, Joe Johnston's strategic problem. *THQ* xviii (1959) 134–47.   **2504**

McClernand, John Alexander, 1812–1900.
Report of Major General John A. McClernand of the operations of the reserve corps, from the battle of Shiloh to the evacuation of Corinth. 1862. 7 p. 19cm.   IHi   **2505**
Title from cover. Dated: Camp Jackson, July 4, 1862.

Stone, Henry,   –1896.
The operations of General Buell in Kentucky and Tennessee in 1862. *PMHSM* vii (1892) 255–91.   **2506**

Andrews Railroad Raid
April, 1862

Ohio boys in Dixie, the adventures of twenty-two scouts, sent by Gen. O. M. Mitchell [sic], to destroy a railroad, with a narrative of their barbarous treatment by the Rebels, and Judge Holt's report. . . . New York, Miller & Mathews, 1863. 47 p. 23cm.   NN RP   **2507**
"The roll of honor," list of participants, p. [2].

Foraker, Joseph Benson, 1846–1917.
The Andrew raiders. The unveiling of Ohio's monument in their honor in the National cemetery at Chattanooga, Tenn., May 30th, 1891. Address of ex-Governor Foraker. 19 p. 23cm.
Caption title.   OHi   **2508**

Fry, James Barnet, 1827–1894.
Notes on the locomotive chase. *B&L* ii 716.   **2509**

Gregg, Frank Moody, 1864–
Andrews raiders; or, the last scenes and the final chapter of the daring incursion into the heart of the Confederacy. Compiled and published by Frank M. Gregg. Chattanooga, Republican print [1891] 98 p. 2 illus., port. 19½cm.   CSmH DLC   **2510**

—— Andrews raiders . . . [1891] 98 p.   **2511**
"J. B. Foraker's oration delivered at the unveiling of the Andrews monument in National cemetery at Chattanooga, May 30, 1891," [83]–98.

Grose, Parlee Clyde
The case of Private Smith and the remaining mysteries of the Andrews raid, by Parlee

Andrews Railroad Raid, continued

C. Grose. McComb, Ohio, General pub. co.
[1963] (10), 131 p. plates (facsim., illus.).
15½cm.   IHi NcD   **2511A**
Illus. on p. [4] of cover.

McBryde, Randell W
The historic "General," a thrilling episode
of the Civil war [by] Randell W. McBryde.
. . . Chattanooga, MacGowan & Cooke co.
[1904] 55 p. illus., map, ports. 20½cm.
Cover illus. in color.   NN   **2512**

O'Neill, Charles
Wild train, the story of the Andrews raid-
ers, by Charles O'Neill. New York, Random
House [1956] xviii, 482, (1) p. plates (illus.,
ports.). 22cm.   NN   **2513**
"The country in and for which the Andrew raiders
fought, 1861–1865," map on endpaper.
"About the author," (1) p.

Pittenger, William, 1840–1904.
Capturing a locomotive, a history of secret
service in the late war, by Rev. William Pittenger. . . . Philadelphia, J. B. Lippincott & co.,
1882. 354 p. plates (illus., map, ports.). 18cm.
                                 CSmH NN   **2514**

—— —— Washington, National Tribune,
1905. 340 p. front. (port.). 17cm.   **2515**
A reprinting which omits the Appendix.
Coulter 373.

—— Daring and suffering, a history of the
great railroad adventure, by Lieut. William
Pittenger, with an introduction by Rev. Alexander Clark. . . . Philadelphia, J. W. Daugha-
day, 1864. 288 p. front. (port.), plates (illus.),
17½cm.   CSmH NN   **2516**

—— Daring and suffering, a history of the
Andrews railroad raid into Georgia in 1862, a
full and accurate account of the secret journey
to the heart of the Confederacy, the capture of
a railway train in a Confederate camp, the terrible chase that followed, and the subsequent
fortunes of the leader and his party, by William Pittenger. . . . New York, War pub. co.,
1887. 416 p. illus., ports. 21½cm.
                                   NN   **2517**

—— —— Twenty-five years after, being a
supplement to Daring and suffering with official documents. An account of the subsequent
fortunes of the Andrews raiders, etc., by William Pittenger. New York, War pub. co., 1887.
55 p. ports. 21½cm.   NN   **2518**

—— The great locomotive chase, a history of
the Andrews railroad raid into Georgia in
1862, by William Pittenger. Fourth edition.

. . . New York, Western W. Wilson [1893]
490 p. illus., maps, ports. 24cm.
                                 NHi   **2519**
On cover: The great locomotive chase, a historical
romance.

—— In pursuit of the General, a history of
the Civil war railroad raid, by William Pittenger. San Marino, Golden West Books [1965]
416 p. front. (illus.), illus., ports. 22½cm.
                                           2520
A facsimile reprinting of Daring and suffering,
1887.
New material is a "Foreword" signed: Colonel
James G. Bogle, Atlanta, Georgia, 8 June 1965.
Illus. endpapers.

—— The locomotive chase in Georgia. *In* Famous adventures and prison escapes of the
civil war. New York, The Century co., 1898.
83–101.   NN   **2521**

—— —— B&L ii 709–16.   **2522**

United States. War Department.
. . . Robert Buffum. Letter from the Secretary of war ad interim, transmitting a communication from the Judge advocate general, en-
closing a letter from Robert Buffum, late of the
Twenty-first Ohio volunteers, who volunteered
to perform very hazardous service during the
late war. [Washington, 1868] 23 p. 23cm.
                                           2523
At head of title: 40th Congress, 2d session. House
of representatives. Ex. doc. no. 74.
Caption title.
Serial no. 1332.

Wilson, John Alfred, 1832–
Adventures of Alf. Wilson, a thrilling episode
of the dark days of the rebellion, by John A.
Wilson, a member of the Mitchell [sic] railroad
raiders. Toledo, Blade print. co., 1880. xiv,
15–237 p. front. (port.), plates (illus.). 20cm.
                                 NHi   **2524**
"Introduction" signed: C. W. E.

—— Washington, National Tribune, 1897.
xiv, 15–237 p. 21cm.   MB   **2525**
A reprinting.

Wright, D   Thew
Romance of the great locomotive raid. *B&G*
ii (1893) 372–5.   **2526**

The Tennessee River Campaign
and Strategies of Anna E. Carroll
1862

The material bearing of the Tennessee campaign in 1862, upon the destinies of our Civil
war. Washington, D.C. W. H. Moore, printer
[1862] 19 p. 22cm.   CSmH NN   **2527**
Title and imprint from cover.

Blackwell, Sarah Ellen, 1828–
A military genius. Life of Anna Ella Carroll, of Maryland, ("the great unrecognized member of Lincoln's cabinet,") compiled from family records and Congressional documents, by Sarah Ellen Blackwell. . . . Washington, D.C., Judd & Detweiler, printers, 1891–1895. 2 v. I plates (illus., ports.). 17cm.
DLC **2528**
Vol. II has title: Life and writings of Anna Ella Carroll. . . .

Carroll, Anna Ella, 1815–1894.
Miss Carroll's claim before Congress asking compensation for military and other services in connection with the Civil war. [n.p., 1874] 70 p. 22½cm.   NN   **2529**
Caption title.
Text signed and dated: Anna Ella Carroll, March 28, 1874.

——— Miss Carroll's claim before Congress in connection with the Tennessee campaign of 1862. [Washington, 1873] 55 p. 21½cm.
Caption title.   NN   **2530**
Text signed and dated: A. E. C., Washington, D.C., January 15, 1873.

——— Plan of the Tennessee campaign. *North American review* CXLII (1886) 342–7.   **2531**

Greenbie, Majorie Latta (Barstow), 1891–
. . . My dear lady, the story of Anna Ella Carroll, the "great unrecognized member of Lincoln's cabinet". . . . New York, Whittlesey House [c1940] xx, 316 p. front. (port.), 2 maps, 2 plates (3 illus.). 23½cm.
GEU NcD   **2532**
At head of title: Marjorie Barstow Greenbie.

Greenbie, Sydney, 1889–
Anna Ella Carroll and Abraham Lincoln, a biography, by Sydney Greenbie and Marjorie Greenbie. Penobscot, Traversity press [c1952] xvi, (1), 539 p. plates (illus., facsim., ports.). 21½cm.   NcD   **2533**
Imprint on paster covering: Manchester, University of Tampa press in cooperation with Falmouth pub. house.

Scott, Charles M
The origin of the Tennessee campaign, by Capt. Charles M. Scott, as a refutation of the fradulent [sic] claim of Miss Anna Ella Carroll. Terre Haute, Moore & Langen, printers, 1889. 38 p. 22cm.   DLC NN   **2534**
Includes Captain Scott's testimony before the Committee on military affairs of the House of representatives which was also printed as House misc. doc. no. 179, 44th Congress, 1st session.

Williams, Kenneth Powers, 1887–1958.
The Tennessee river campaign and Anna Ella Carroll. *Indiana magazine of history* XLVI (1950) 221–48.   **2535**

Grierson's Raid
April 17 – May 2, 1863

Abbott, John Stevens Cabot, 1805–1877.
. . . Grierson's raid. *Harper's magazine* XXX (1865) 273–81. illus., plan, port.   **2536**

Brown, Dee Alexander, 1908–
Grierson's raid [by] D. Alexander Brown. Urbana, University of Illinois press, 1954. 261 p. illus., ports. 24cm.   NN   **2537**
Keyed map showing route of march with accompanying text, on endpaper.

Grierson, Francis, 1824–1927.
Grierson's raid. *In his* The valleys of shadows. . . . Boston, Houghton, Mifflin and co., 1909, 262–7.   NN   **2538**

Mississippi Valley

Buttgenbach, Walter J
Operations on the Mississippi river. *Journal of the United States artillery* XLI (1914) 191–211.   **2539**

Fiske, John, 1842–1901.
The Mississippi valley in the Civil war, by John Fiske. . . . Boston, Houghton, Mifflin and co. [1900] xxv, 368 p. plates (maps and plans). 19½cm.   DLC NN   **2540**

Greene, Francis Vinton, 1850–1921.
. . . The Mississippi, by Francis Vinton Greene. New York, Charles Scribner's Sons, 1882. ix, (1), 276 p. front. (fold. map); maps, 2 fold. 19cm.   NN   **2541**
At head of title. Campaigns of the Civil war — VIII. See Title 1362.

Sherman's Campaign

Papers of convention between Sherman and Johnston. From the papers of Col. B. S. Ewell. *SHSP* XXXIX (1914) 45–53.   **2542**

Barnard, George N
Photographic views of Sherman's campaign, from negatives taken in the field, by Geo. N. Barnard, official photographer Military div. of the Mississippi. New York, Press of Wynkoop & Hallenbeck, 1866. 30 p. 23cm.
CSmH DLC NN   **2543**

——— Photographic views of Sherman's campaigns, embracing scenes of the occupation of Nashville, the great battles around Chattanooga and Lookout mountain, the campaign of Atlanta, march to the sea, and the great raid through the Carolinas. From negatives taken in the field, by Geo. N. Barnard. . . . [New York, 1866]   CSmH DLC   **2544**
Album of 61 plates with title and "Contents" sheet. 40½ × 52cm.

Sherman's Campaign, continued

Barrett, John Gilchrist
Sherman and total war in the Carolinas. *NCHR* xxxvii (1960) 367–81.   **2545**

Bird, Edward C
. . . Sherman's "march to the sea;" or, fighting his way through Georgia, a realistic romance by Lieutenant E. C. Bird of Sherman's command. . . . New York, Munro's pub. house, 1891. 29 p. illus., ports. 32cm.
                                        CSmH   **2546**

At head of title: Ten-cent edition. Old Cap. Collier library, great detective stories in book form . . . no. 398.
"Prologue. Atlanta to the sea" [biography of Sherman] [3]–7 is an account of the campaign.
Text in triple columns.

Boynton, Henry Van Ness, 1835–1905.
Sherman's historical raid. The memoirs in the light of the record, a review based upon compilations from the files of the War office [by] H. V. Boynton. Cincinnati, Baldwin & co., 1875. 276 p. 22cm. CSmH NB   **2547**

Burt, Jesse C
Sherman's logistics and Andrew Johnson. *THQ* xv (1956) 195–215.   **2548**

Conyngham, David Power, 1840–1883.
Sherman's march through the South, with sketches and incidents of the campaign, by Capt. David P. Conyngham. New York, Sheldon and co., 1865. 431 p. 18½cm.
                                        CSmH NN   **2549**

Author "served all through his [Sherman's] brilliant campaigns, as volunteer aid-de-camp and war correspondent."

Cook, Harvey T
Sherman's march through South Carolina in 1865, by Harvey T. Cook, an ex-Confederate. Greenville, 1938. 25 p. 23cm.   ScU   **2550**

Cox, Jacob Dolson, 1828–1900.
The Sherman-Johnston convention. *Scribner's magazine* xxviii (1900) 489–500.   **2551**

—— The surrender of Johnston's army and the closing scenes of the war in North Carolina. *MOLLUS-Ohio* ii 247–76.   **2552**

Doyle, J   E   Parker
Sherman's sixty days in the Carolinas. *United States service magazine* iii (1865) 511–14.   **2553**

Ewing, Charles, 1835–1883.
Sherman's march through Georgia, letters from Charles Ewing to his father, Thomas Ewing. Edited by George C. Osborn. *GHQ* xlii (1958) 323–7.   **2554**

Force, Manning Ferguson, 1824–1899.
Marching across Carolina, read before the Ohio commandery of the Loyal legion, May 2d, 1883, by M. F. Force. Cincinnati, Robert Clarke & co., printers, 1883. 18 p. 21½cm.
                                        CSmH   **2555**
Also published in *MOLLUS-Ohio* i 1–18.

Hitchcock, Henry, 1829–1902.
Marching with Sherman, passages from the letters and campaign diaries of Henry Hitchcock, Major and Assistant adjutant general of volunteers, November 1864 – May 1865. Edited with an introduction, by M. A. DeWolfe Howe. New Haven, Yale University press, 1927. 322 p. plates (facsim., illus., fold. map, ports.). 23cm.   NN   **2556**
Coulter 235.
"The eighth work published by the Yale university press on the Amasa Stone Mather memorial publication fund."

Howard, Oliver Otis, 1830–1909.
Sherman's campaign of 1864. *US* xiii (1885) 660–73; xiv (1886) 142–7.   **2557**

Johnston, Joseph Eggleston, 1807–1891.
My negotiations with General Sherman. *North American review* cxliii (1886) 183–97.   **2558**

McMaster, Richard H
The Feasterville incident, Hampton and Sherman, by Richard H. McMaster. [Washington, D.C., 1955] 12 p. map on cover. 23cm.
                                        WHi   **2559**

Moulton, Charles William,   –1888.
The review of General Sherman's memoirs examined, chiefly in the light of its own evidence [by] C. W. Moulton. Cincinnati, Robert Clarke & co., printers, 1875. 87 p. front. (port.). 22cm.   CSmH DLC OMC   **2560**

A discussion of H. V. Boynton's Sherman's historical raid, 1875 (see Title 2547) which the author claims is written "in a spirit bitterly hostile to General Sherman."

Nichols, George Ward, 1837–1885.
The story of the great march, from the diary of a Staff officer, by Brevet Major George Ward Nichols, Aide-de-camp to General Sherman. New York, Harper & Brothers, 1865. xii, [15]–394 p. front. (port.), illus., fold. map. 19½cm.
                                        NN   **2561**

"Sixteenth edition," 1865, 408 p., a reprinting with addition of p. 395–401, Appendix XII.
"Twenty-sixth edition," 1866, 456 p., a reprinting with the addition of "After the war, a supplement to the story of the great march, by Col. Geo. Ward Nichol," p. 403–49.

Palfrey, George Carver, 1833–1906.
General Sherman's plans after the fall of Atlanta. *PMHSM* viii (1886) 493–527. **2562**

Senour, Faunt le Roy, 1824–1910.
   Major General William T. Sherman and his campaigns, by Rev. F. Senour. . . . Chicago, Henry M. Sherwood, 1865. xiv, [15]–477 p. front. (port.). 19cm.   CSmH DLC   **2563**

Sherman, William Tecumseh, 1820–1891.
   General Sherman's official account of his great march through Georgia and the Carolinas, from his departure from Chattanooga to the surrender of General Joseph E. Johnston and the Confederate forces under his command. To which is added, General Sherman's evidence before the Congressional committee on the conduct of the war, the animadversions of Secretary Staunton and General Halleck, with a defence of his proceedings, etc. New York, Bunce & Huntington, 1865. 214 p. 19½cm.   CSmH DLC   **2564**
   On cover: The hero's own story. General Sherman's official account of his great march through Georgia and the Carolinas.

—— Major-General Sherman's reports. I. Campaign against Atlanta; II. Campaign against Savannah; III. Campaign through the Carolinas; IV. Johnston's truce and surrender; V. Story of the march through Georgia <by a staff officer.> Official copy-complete. New York, Beadle and co. [1865] 84 p. 16cm.
                                       CSmH   **2565**

Slocum, Henry Warner, 1826–1894.
   Final operations of Sherman's army. *B&L* IV 754–8.   **2566**

—— Sherman's march from Savannah to Bentonville. *B&L* IV 681–95.   **2567**

Snowden, Yates, 1858–1933.
   Marching with Sherman, a review by Yates Snowden of The letters and campaign diaries of Henry Hitchcock, Major and Assistant Adjutant General of volunteers as edited by M. A. De Wolfe Howe and published by the Yale press. . . . Columbia, The State, 1929. 58 p. 23cm.   NcU   **2568**
   "Foreword" signed: E. G. S.

Thompson, Joseph Parrish, 1819–1879.
   The great march. *Hours at home* II (1865/66) 314–20.   **2569**

United States. Army.
   Campaign of the Carolinas. Organization of the Union forces (commanded by Major General William T. Sherman) January – April, 1865. [Washington, War Records office, n.d.] 18 p. 22½cm.   CSmH   **2570**

Ward, Dallas T
   The last flag of truce, by Dallas T. Ward. Franklinton, N. C. [1915] 16 p. 1 col. illus., port. 20½cm.   IHi NcD   **2571**

The author, a civilian trainman, gives "a narration of the flag of truce sent by Governor Z. B. Vance to General W. T. Sherman the day before he reached Raleigh, N.C."

Wilbur, R   H
   One day with Sherman coastward. *Hours at home* II (1865/66) 173–7.   **2572**

Stoneman's Raid
March, 1865

Van Noppen, Ina W
   The significance of Stoneman's last raid. *NCHR* XXXVIII (1961) 19–44, 149–72, 340–61, 500–26. 2 plates (ports.)   **2573**

Streight's Raid
April – May, 1863

Kniffen, Gilbert Crawford, 1832–1917.
   Streight's raid through Tennessee and Northern Georgia in 1863. 1910. 10 p. *MOLLUS-DC* no 82.   **2574**

ALABAMA
General References

Letford, William
   Location and classification and dates of military events in Alabama, 1861–1865, prepared by William Letford and Allen W. Jones. . . . Montgomery Alabama Civil War Centennial Commission, 1961. p. 189–206. fold. map. 23cm.   **2575**
   "Reprinted from the Spring issue, 1961, of the Alabama historical quarterly."

*   *   *

Jones, Allen Woodrow, 1930–
   A Federal raid [February 1862] into Southeast Alabama *AR* XIV (1961) 259–68.   **2576**

Bearss, Edwin Cole, 1923–
   Rousseau's raid on the Montgomery and West Point railroad. *AHQ* XXV (1963) 7–48. 2 maps, 1 fold.   **2577**

Turchin, John Basil, 1822–1901.
   Huntsville, Ala., the seizure of it and a part of the Memphis and Charleston railroad in April, 1862. G.A.R. war papers, papers read before the Fred C. Jones post, no. 401, Department of Ohio, G.A.R., 164–89.   **2578**

Buell, Don Carlos, 1818–1898.
   Operations in North Alabama. *B&L* II 701–08.   **2579**

Fretwell, Mark E
   Rousseau's Alabama raid. *AHQ* XVIII (1956) 526–50.   **2580**

Mobile
March – April, 1865

Allen, Charles Julius, 1840–1915.
Some account and recollections of the operations against the City of Mobile and its defences, 1864 and 1865. *MOLLUS-Minn* I 54–88.   **2581**

Andrews, Christopher Columbus, 1829–1922.
History of the campaign of Mobile, including the cooperative operations of Gen. Wilson's cavalry in Alabama, by Brevet Major-General C. C. Andrews. New York, D. Van Nostrand, 1867. 267 p. plates (illus., plan). 23½cm.
                                      NN   **2582**
Reviewed by General Dabney H. Maury in *SHSP* III (1877) 1–13.

———— ———— Second edition. New York, D. Van Nostrand co., 1889. viii, 276 p. plates (illus., plans). 23½cm.   NN   **2583**
A reprinting with new material in the Preface.

Buttgenbach, Walter J
Operations in Mobile bay. *Journal of the United States artillery* XLI (1914) 317–36. 3 fold. maps.   **2584**

Irwin, Richard Bache, 1829–1892.
Land operations against Mobile. *B&L* IV 410–11.   **2585**

Maury, Dabney Herndon, 1822–1900.
Defence of Mobile in 1865. *SM* XII (1873) 288–95.   **2586**

Nichols, James L
Confederate engineers and the defense of Mobile. *AR* XII (1959) 180–95. map.   **2587**

Page, Richard Lucien, 1807–1901
The defense of Fort Morgan. *B&L* IV 408–10.   **2588**

Palfrey, John Carver, 1833–1906.
The capture of Mobile, 1865. *PMHSM* VIII (1888) 529–57.   **2589**

Parker, Prescott Alphonso
Story of the Tenesaw, Blakely, Spanish fort, Jackson Oaks, Fort Minns, by Prescott A. Parker. . . . Montrose, Ala., P. A. Parker [1922] 19, (9) p. front. (illus.), 1 illus. 21cm.
                                      NN   **2590**
Stephenson, P   D
Defence of Spanish fort on Mobile bay, last great battle of the war. *SHSP* XXXIX (1914) 118–29.   **2591**
For comments by Dabney H. Maury see *SHSP* XXXIX (1914) 130–6.

United States Army.
Operations against Mobile, Ala. Organization of the Union forces (commanded by Major-

General Edward R. S. Canby), March–April, 1865. [Washington, War Records office, n. d.] 7 p. 22cm.   CSmH   **2592**

Wilson, John Moulder, 1837–1919.
"The campaign ending with the capture of Mobile," 1894. 29 p. *MOLLUS-DC* no 17.
                                               2593

*   *   *

Beaumont, Eugene Beauharnois
Campaign of Selma. *US* II (1880) 250–62.
                                               2594
Folmar, John Kent
The war comes to Central Alabama, Ebenezer Church, April 1, 1865. *AHQ* XXVI (1964) 187–202. map.   **2595**

Clinton, Thomas P
The military operations of General John T. Croxton in West Alabama, 1865. *Transactions of the Alabama historical society* IV (1899/1903) 449–63.   **2596**

GEORGIA
General References

Georgia.
Reports of the operations of the militia, from October 13, 1864, to February 11, 1865, by Maj.-Generals G. W. Smith and Wayne, together with memoranda by Gen. Smith, for the improvement of the State military organization. Macon, Boughton, Nesbit, Barnes & Moore, State printers [1865] 29 p. 21cm.
                                      NcD   **2597**
Transmitting message to Governor dated: February 28, 1865.
Harwell 464.

Jones, Charles Colcock, 1831–1893.
Military lessons inculcated on the coast of Georgia during the Confederate war. An address delivered before the Confederate survivors' association, in Augusta, Georgia, at its fifth annual meeting, on Memorial day, April 26, 1883, by Colonel Charles C. Jones, Jr. . . . Augusta, Chronicle print. estab., 1883. 15 p. 22cm.   CSmH DLC NN   **2598**

———— Military operations in Georgia during the War between the States, address delivered before the Survivors' association in Augusta, Georgia, upon the occasion of its fifteenth annual reunion on Memorial day, April 26th, 1893, by Col. Charles C. Jones, Jr., and Chickamauga, by Col. Joseph B. Cumming. . . . Augusta, Chronicle Job print. co., 1893. 32, (1) p. 23½cm.   NN   **2599**

Young, Rogers W
Two years at Fort Bartow, 1862–1864. *GHQ* XXIII (1939) 253–64.   **2600**

Fort Pulaski
January 3 – April 11, 1862

Buttgenbach, Walter J
Fort Pulaski, Georgia. *Journal of the United States artillery* XL (1913) 205–15. map. **2601**

Gillmore, Quincy Adams, 1825–1888.
Official report to the United States Engineer department of the siege and reduction of Fort Pulaski, Georgia, February, March, and April, 1862, by Brig. Gen. Q. A. Gillmore. New York, D. Van Nostrand, 1862. 96 p. plates (col. illus.; fold. maps and 2 fold. plans.) 22½cm.
                CSmH NN   **2602**
At head of title: Papers on practical engineering. no. 8.

——— Siege and capture of Fort Pulaski. *B&L* II 1–12. **2603**

Jones, Charles Colcock, 1831–1893.
The seizure and reduction of Fort Pulaski. *Magazine of American history* XIV (1885) 53–7. **2604**

Chickamauga
September 19–21, 1863

The truth of the battle of Chicamauga, Georgia, fought in the year 1863. [n. p., 189–] broadside, 43 × 22cm.   NN   **2605**
Text signed: E. A. M.
Two captions of text: The battlefield of Chicamauga, Georgia; The last day of the battle of Chicamauga, Georgia.
"In company with General Grant, the writer of this sketch."

Turchin's brigade vs. the Commissioners of the Chickamauga and Chattanooga national park. Published by the Brigade association.... Columbus, Westbote co., printers, 1896. 32 p. fold. map. 23cm.   CSmH OMC **2606**

Anderson, Archer, 1838–
The campaign and battle of Chickamauga, an address delivered before the Virginia division of the Army of Northern Virginia association, at their annual meeting, in the Capitol at Richmond, Va., October 25, 1881, by Archer Anderson, formerly Lieut.-Colonel in the Confederate service, and during the last months of the war, Adjutant-general of the Army of Tennessee, Richmond, William Ellis Jones, printer, 1881. 38 p. 23½cm.
                CSmH NNC   **2607**
Boynton, Henry Van Ness, 1835–1905.
. . . Battle of Chickamauga, Ga., September 19–20, 1863. Organization of the Army of the Cumberland (commanded by Maj. Gen. W. S. Rosecrans) and of the Army of Tennessee (commanded by General Braxton Bragg). Compiled by H. Van Boynton. Washington,

Govt. print. office, 1895. 35 p. plate (map). 22½cm.   NN   **2608**

Bragg, Braxton, 1817–1876.
General Braxton Bragg's report of the battle of Chickamauga. *OLOD* I (1874/75) 122–34. **2609**

——— Official report of the battle of Chickamauga. Published by order of Congress. Richmond, R. M. Smith, Public printer, 1864. 234 p. 23cm.   CSmH DLC **2610**
Bragg's transmitting letter dated: Warm Springs, Georgia, December 28, 1863.
Crandall 1372.

Breckinridge, Joseph Cabell, 1842–1920.
Report of the battle of Chickamauga. *LWL* I (1866) 305–09. **2611**

Burr, Frank A   1843–1894.
The great battle of Chicamauga. [Memphis, Tracy print. co., 1883] 32 p. 19½cm.
                  CSmH   **2612**
Burr's narrative, 3–17; Longstreet's 17–23, quoted by Burr who signs this portion of the text.
Chicamauga, a battle of which the half has not been told, by Capt. W. W. Carnes of Macon, 26–32.

Cleburne, Patrick Ronayne, 1828–1864.
General Cleburne's report of the battle of Chickamauga. *LWL* I (1866) 249–54. **2613**

Cox, Jacob Dolson, 1828–1900.
The Chickamauga crisis. *Scribner's magazine* XXVII (1900) 326–39. **2614**

Cunningham, W   H
A history of the battle of Chickamauga, September 19th and 20th, 1863. [Evergreen, Ala., Press of the Orphans' Call, 1900] 11 p. 14½ × 9cm.   NN   **2615**
Title from cover.
"Introductory" signed: John Cunningham.
Letter dated: Camp near Tyner's station on East Tennessee & Knoxville railroad, Hamilton county, Tenn., September 27th, 1863.

Dolton, George E
Points of dispute regarding Chickamauga. *B&G* II (1893) 402–05. plan. **2616**

Fullerton, Joseph Scott,   –1897.
Reenforcing Thomas at Chickamauga. *B&L* III 665–7. **2617**

Furay, William S
The real Chickamauga. Reprint of articles by W. S. Furay, war correspondent Cincinnati gazette, and Col. G. C. Kniffen. . . . [n. p., 1888] 20 p. 21½cm. CSmH DLC **2618**
Caption title.
Contents: The real Chickamauga, by W. S. Furay, 1–6; On the Tennessee, by G. C. Kniffen, 7–20.

Gilmore, James Roberts, 1822–1903.
Garfield's ride at Chickamauga. *McClure's magazine* V (1895) 357–60. 1 illus. **2619**

Chickamauga, continued

Gracie, Archibald, 1858–1912.
    The truth about Chickamauga, by Archibald Gracie. . . . Boston, Houghton, Mifflin co., 1911. xxxii, (1) 462 p. plates (illus.; maps, partly double and fold.; ports.). 24cm.
                        CSmH DLC   *2620*
Hay, Thomas Robson
    The campaign and battle of Chickamauga. *GHQ* VII (1923) 213–50.   *2621*

Hill, Daniel Harvey, 1821–1889.
    Chickamauga, the great battle of the West. *B&L* III 638–62.   *2622*

—— Gen'l D. H. Hill's report of the battle of Chickamauga. *OLOD* I (1874/75) 205–17.
                                         2623
Joyce, Frederick
    Orphan brigade at Chickamauga. *SB* III (1884/85) 29–32.   *2624*

Kniffen, Gilbert Crawford, 1832–1917.
    The battle above the clouds. 1892. 22 p. *MOLLUS-DC* no 10.   *2625*

Lynde, Francis, 1856–1930.
    Chickamauga and Chattanooga national military park, with narratives of the battles of Chickamauga, Lookout mountain and Missionary ridge, by Francis Lynde. Chattanooga, W. E. Birchmore, c1895. 39, (1) p. illus., 2 fold. maps. 22½cm. CSmH DLC   *2626*

McLaws, Lafayette, 1821–1897.
    After Chickamauga. *In* Addresses delivered before the Confederate veterans association of Savannah, Ga., 1898, 49–72.   *2627*
    See Title 419A.

Marriner, W   M
    Chickamauga, the opening. *SB* III (1884/85) 8–11.   *2628*

Morgan, John M
    Old Steady: the role of James Blair Steedman at the battle of Chickamauga. *Northwest Ohio quarterly* XXII (1950) 73–94. map.
                                         2629
Norwood, Charles W
    The Chickamauga and Chattanooga battlefields, compiled by C. W. Norwood, late First Sergeant Company G, Twenty-first Kentucky infantry. Chattanooga, Gervis M. Connelly [1898] 31, (1) p. illus. fold. map. 29 ×10cm.   CSmH NN   *2630*
Polk, William Mecklenburg, 1844–1918.
    General Polk at Chickamauga. *B&L* III 662–3.   *2631*

Reid, Samuel Chester, 1818–1897.
    Great battle of Chicamauga, a concise history of events from the evacuation of Chatta-

nooga to the defeat of the enemy . . . by S. C. Reid. . . . Mobile, F. Titcomb, 1863. 16 p. 21cm.   CSmH   *2632*
    Dated: Camp before Chattanooga, October 15th, 1863.
    Crandall 2660.

—— The great battle of Chickamauga. (Rebel report.) By S. C. Reid ("Ora"), correspondent of the Mobile Tribune. Reprinted for private circulation. Chattanooga, 1864. 14 p. 20½cm.   NN   *2633*

Shackleton, Robert, 1860–1923.
    The battle-field of Chickamauga, 1863–1893. *B&G* I (1893) 485–9. illus., plan, ports.
                                         2634
Sheridan, Philip Henry, 1831–1888.
    Report of operations of the Third division, 20th army corps, Army of the Cumberland, from September 2 to September 23, 1863, including the battle of Chickamauga, September 19th and 20th, 1863. [n.p., n.d.] 4 p. 23cm.
                                    NN   *2635*
Smith, William Farrar, 1824–1903.
    The battle of Chickamauga. *Galaxy* XX (1875) 641–5.   *2636*

Thruston, Gates Phillips, 1835–1912.
    Chickamauga. *SB* ns II (1886/87) 406–15.
                                         2637
—— Chickamauga, reprint of an article originally published in the Southern bivouac, December, 1886, and republished in the Century war book, "Battles and leaders of the Civil war," vol. III. By Gen'l Gates P. Thruston. Nashville [n.d.] 13 p. 25½cm.
    Text in double columns.   CSmH   *2638*

—— The crisis at Chickamauga. *B&L* III 663–5.   *2639*
Tucker, Glenn
    Chickamauga, bloody battle in the West, by Glenn Tucker. Maps by Dorothy Thomas Tucker. Indianapolis, Bobbs-Merrill co. [1961] 448 p. maps and plans. 21½cm. NN *2640*

Turchin, John Basil, 1822–1901.
    . . . Chickamauga, by John B. Turchin. Chicago, Fergus print. co., 1888. 295 p. 8 fold. maps, 4 in pocket. 25cm.   NN   *2641*
    At head of title: Noted battles for the Union during the Civil war in the United States of America, 1861–5.

—— Turchin's brigade vs. Commissioners of the Chickamauga and Chattanooga military park. [Centralia] Centralia Sentinel print [1895] 8 p. 21cm.   CSmH   *2642*
    Title and imprint from cover, p. [1].

Tydings, Joseph M
    The battle of Chickamauga, Kentucky heroism in the engagement. A Kentuckian com-

memorates the event in verse. *RKHS* xi (1913) 65–7.   **2643**

United States. Army.
. . . Organization of the Army of the Cumberland, commanded by Major-General W. S. Rosecrans, at the battle of Chickamauga, Ga., September 19–20, 1863, and return of casualties. Compiled under the direction of Brigadier General Richard C. Drum, Adjutant General U. S. army. Washington, 1886. 25 p. 23½cm.
CSmH DLC   **2644**
At head of title: Adjutant general's department.

United States. Adjutant General's Department.
. . . Battle of Chickamauga, Ga., September 19–20, 1863. I. Organization of the Army of the Cumberland (commanded by Major-General W. S. Rosecrans) and return of casualties. II. Organization of the army of Tennessee (commanded by General Braxton Bragg). Compiled under the direction of Brigadier General Richard C. Drum, Adjutant General U. S. army. <Second edition.> Washington, 1889. 33 p. 22½cm.   CSmH DLC   **2645**
At head of title: Adjutant general's department.

United States. Army. Cumberland Department.
Chickamauga. Correspondence and orders, September 18 to 23, 1863. Union. [Washington, War Records office, 1884] 76 p. 23cm.
CSmH   **2646**

United States. Chickamauga and Chattanooga National Military Park Commission.
The campaign for Chattanooga. Historical sketch descriptive of the model in relief of the region about Chattanooga, and of the battles illustrated thereon. Washington, Govt. print. office, 1902. 47 p. fold. map. 23cm.
NN   **2647**

—— Report of the . . . on the claim of Gen. John B. Turchin and others that in the battle of Chattanooga his brigade captured the position on Missionary ridge known as the De Long place, and the decision of the Secretary of war thereon. [Washington, Govt. print. office, 1896] 37 p. fold. map. 22½cm.
NN   **2648**

Van Lisle, Arthur
At Chickamauga. *B&G* ii (1893) 195–201. illus., ports.   **2649**

Waggoner, Clark, 1820–1903.
Honors at Chickamauga. The claim of "hero" at that battle. Delayed justice to the memory of a brave and gallant soldier. An examination of the official record. [Toledo, 188–] 16 p. 23½cm.   CSmH NN   **2650**
Title from cover.
"With compliments of C. Waggoner, Toledo, Ohio," inserted slip.

Chickamauga Memorials

Wilder's brigade monument dedication . . . from the Chattanooga daily news, September 20, 1899. *Journal of the Illinois state historical society* xiii (1920) 51–63.   **2651**

Armstrong, Zella
A national memorial park, the battlefields of Chickamauga and Chattanooga. . . . *Munsey's magazine* xxx (1903) 65–72. illus.   **2652**

Bate, William Brimage, 1826–1905.
The dedication of the Chickamauga and Chattanooga national park. Address by Gen. Wm. B. Bate, one of the speakers appointed by the Secretary of war for the above occasion. Delivered on September 20, 1895. Nashville, Brandon print. co., 1895. 38 p. 23cm.
NcD   **2653**

Boynton, Henry Van Ness, 1835–1905.
Dedication of the Chickamauga and Chattanooga national military park, September 18–20, 1895. Report of the Joint committee to represent the Congress at the dedication of the Chickamauga and Chattanooga national military park. Compiled by H. V. Boynton, for the Committee. Washington, Govt. print. office, 1896. 374 p. plates (illus., map). 24cm.
NN   **2654**

—— The National military park, Chickamauga, Chattanooga, an historical guide, by H. V. Boynton. Cincinnati, Robert Clarke co., 1895. xviii, 307 p. illus., maps, plans. 22cm.
NHi   **2655**

—— The National military park (embracing the Chickamauga and Chattanooga battle fields. *Century magazine* l (1895) 703–08. 2 maps, port.   **2656**

Chickamauga Memorial Association.
Proceedings at Chattanooga, Tenn., and Crawfish Springs, Ga., September 19 and 20, 1889. [Chattanooga?] Chattanooga Army of Cumberland Entertainment Committee [1889] 42, (1) p. plates (ports.). 24cm. NHi   **2657**

Colburn, Webster Jay
To the President . . . Narrative and petition of Major W. J. Colburn in re request for resignation as Commissioner and Secretary Chickamauga and Chattanooga national park commission, November 1911. . . . [15] p. 22cm.
Title from cover.   CSmH   **2658**
"Memorandum. Comrades of the Army of the Cumberland," transmitting letter and summary, inserted.

Disbrow, Albert
Glimpses of Chickamauga, a complete guide to all points of interest on this historic battlefield . . . by comrade Albert Disbrow. Chi-

Chickamauga Memorials, continued

cago, Donohue & Henneberry [1895] 136 p.
illus., map, ports., plates (illus., ports.). 20cm.
                                NcD   *2659*

Kilborn, Lawson S
Dedication of the Wilder brigade monument
on Chickamauga battlefield on the thirty-sixth
anniversary of the battle, September 20, 1899.
Souvenir edition, with addresses delivered at
dedication accompanied by pictures of monument and some prominent members of the
Brigade. Marshall, Ill., Herald press, 1900.
60 p. 1 illus., ports. 22½cm.   DLC   *2660*
"Preface" signed: L. S. Kilborn.

McElroy, Joseph C
The battle of Chickamauga. Historical map
and guide book. By Capt. J. C. McElroy, 18th
Ohio infantry. [1895?] 17, (1) p. front. (4
ports.), fold. map. 19½cm.   CSmH   *2661*
Title from cover.

United States. Chickamauga and Chattanooga
    Military Park Commission.
Legislation, Congressional and State, pertaining to the establishment of the Park. Regulations, original and amended, governing the
erection of monuments, markers, and other
memorials. Washington, Govt. print. office,
1897. 28 p. plate (map). 22½cm. NN   *2662*

—— Progress and condition of the work of
establishing the Chickamauga and Chattanooga
national military park. [Washington, 1895]
15 p. plates (illus., map). 22½cm.
                            CSmH NN   *2663*
Transmission date supplied by rubber stamp: January 19, 1895.

—— . . . Report. 23cm.   *2664*
1898/99–1899/1900 are excerpts from the Report
of the Secretary of war.
1908/09–1919/20 have at head of title: Annual
reports, War department.

Indiana

Indiana.
Chickamauga national park. Report of Indiana commissioners. Indianapolis, Wm. B. Burford, 1896. 19 p. 22½cm.   NN   *2665*

—— Indiana at Chickamauga, 1863–1900, report of Indiana commissioners Chickamauga
national military park. Indianapolis, Sentinel
print. co., 1900. 318 p. map in pocket, plates
(illus., ports.). 25cm.   DLC NN   *2666*
Individual sketches of Indiana regiments, 128–310.

Iowa

Iowa.
Report of the Iowa commissioners Chickamauga and Chattanooga national military park.

Together with acts of Twenty-fifth General
assembly, and park regulations by the Secretary
of war and the United States commission. . . .
Des Moines, F. R. Conway, State printer, 1896.
10 p. 22cm.   NN   *2667*

Sherman, Ernest Anderson, 1868–
Dedicating in Dixie, a series of articles
descriptive of the tour of Governor Albert B.
Cummins and staff, the members of the Vicksburg, Andersonville, Chattanooga and Shiloh
monument commissions . . . 1907.   *2668*

Kansas

Kansas at Chickamauga and Chattanooga.
*Transactions of the Kansas state historical
society* VIII (1904) 271–5. 3 plates (illus.).
                                    2669

Michigan

Belknap, Charles Eugene, 1846–1929.
History of the Michigan organizations at
Chickamauga, Chattanooga and Missionary
ridge, 1863. Lansing, Robert Smith print. co.,
1897. 374, (1) p. plates (illus., ports.). 25cm.
                        CSmH DLC   *2670*
"Financial report," (1) p.
Copyright and dedication signed by Charles E.
Belknap.
"Belknap" on spine.

—— —— Second edition authorized by resolution of the Legislature, March 30, 1899.
Lansing, Robert Smith print. co., 1899. 374,
(1) p. plates (illus., ports.). 25cm.
                            CSmH NN   *2671*
A reprinting on heavier paper.

Minnesota

Minnesota.
Report of the Minnesota commissioners
(under Act approved April 10, 1893) to locate
positions and erect monuments on the battle
fields of Chickamauga and Chattanooga and of
the dedication of said monuments, Sept. 18,
1895. [n.p., 1896] 18 p. 1 illus. 21½cm.
                                CSmH   *2672*
Report dated: October 9, 1896.

New York

Colburn, Webster Jay
"The battles of Chattanooga," address of
Major W. J. Colburn . . . at the dedication of
the New York monument in Point park, Lookout monument, Tennessee, November 15th,
1910. [8] p. 22cm.   CSmH   *2673*
Title from cover.
Inserted "Memorandum" describes the text as revised and rewritten from that of an address delivered
"more than twenty years ago."

Ohio

McElroy, Joseph C
Chickamauga, record of the Ohio Chickamauga and Chattanooga national park commission, by Joseph C. McElroy, late Captain 18th Ohio. Cincinnati, Earhart & Richardson, printers, 1896. 199 p. map in pocket, plates (illus.). 23½cm.   CSmH NN   2674
"Errata" slip inserted.

Pennsylvania

Pennsylvania.
An account of the appointment, organization, and proceedings of delegates commissioned by the Governor of the Commonwealth of Pennsylvania, to act with the United States commissioners, for the establishment of the Chickamauga and Chattanooga national military park, in locating the positions of Pennsylvania troops engaged in the battle of Chickamauga and the battles about Chattanooga, in the year 1863 of the War of the rebellion. [Harrisburg, 1894] 15, (1) p. 26cm.   CSmH   2675
Caption title.

—— Roster of applications received at Adjutant general's office, Harrisburg, Pa., for transportation to Chattanooga, Tennessee, under provisions of Act of Assembly, approved July 22, 1897. [Harrisburg, Wm. Stanley Ray, State printer, 1897] 27 p. 20½ x 10cm.
Caption title.   CSmH   2676

Skinner, George Washington
Pennsylvania at Chickamauga and Chattanooga. Ceremonies at the dedication of the monuments erected by the Commonwealth of Pennsylvania to mark the positions of the Pennsylvania commands engaged in the battles . . . 1897. [Harrisburg, Wm. Stanley Ray, State printer, 1900] 500 p. plates (illus., ports.). 23cm.   DLC NN   2677
Copyright "by the editor and compiler, Capt. George W. Skinner, Secretary of the Executive committee of the Pennsylvania-Chickamauga-Chattanooga battlefields commission."
"Roster of applications for transportation to Chattanooga, Tenn," arranged by regiments and supplies addresses of individuals.

South Carolina

Henderson, Daniel Sullivan, 1849–1921.
Address of Daniel S. Henderson at the unveiling of the Palmetto monument at the National park, Chickamauga, May 27th, 1901. Aiken, S. C., Journal and Review press, 1901. 12 p. 23cm.   ScU   2678

South Carolina.
Ceremonies at the unveiling of the South Carolina monument on the Chickamauga battlefield, May 27th, 1901. Together with a record of the Commission who suggested and were instrumental in securing and erecting the monument. [n.p., 1901] 50 p. 2 plates (illus.). 21½cm.   CSmH TxU   2679

Tennessee

Tennessee.
Tennessee monuments and markers, report of the Tennessee Chickamauga park commission. [Nashville, Foster & Webb print.] 1898. 46 p. fold. front. (ports.)., illus. 22cm.
                                    NN   2680

*   *   *

Johnston, Joseph Eggleston, 1807–1891.
Opposing Sherman's advance to Atlanta. B&L iv 260–77.   2681

United States. Staff College, Fort Leavenworth, Kansas.
Campaign in Georgia, 1864. Organization of the Northern and Southern armies. . . . [Fort Leavenworth, 1906] 29 p. 19½cm.
Title from cover.   CSmH   2682

Shackleton, Robert, 1860–1923.
The beginning of Sherman's advance, Rocky Face ridge. B&G ii (1893) 147–52. illus. 2683

Brown, Joseph M 1851–1931.
The mountain campaign in Georgia; or, war scenes on the W. & A. [Buffalo, Art-print. works of Matthews, Northrup & co., 1886] 51 p. front. (illus.), illus., maps, ports., plate (port.). 27½ x 21cm. CSmH DLC   2684
Copyright by Jos. M. Brown.
Cover illus. in color.
"Errata" slip included.

—— —— Sixth edition. [Buffalo, Matthews-Northrup co., 1895] 72, (1) p. illus., maps, ports. 27cm.   TxU   2685
Copyright 1890; "Preface" dated 1886.
On cover: Mountain campaigns in Georgia, Chattanooga-Dalton-Atlanta, 1863–1864. Souvenir Cotton states and international exhibition, Atlanta, 1895.

Johnston, Joseph Eggleston, 1807–1891.
The Dalton-Atlanta operations. AW 330–41.
                                        2686

Shackleton, Robert, 1860–1923.
The beginning of Sherman's advance. Battle of Reseca. B&G ii (1893) 219–23.   2687

Kenesaw Mountain
June 10 – July 2, 1864

The battle of Dead angle on the Kenesaw line, near Marietta, Georgia [June 27, 1864] SB iii (1884/85) 71–4.   2688
Text signed: M.

Kenesaw Mountain, continued

Brown, Joseph Emerson, 1821–1894.
St. Valentine, February XIV, MDCCC-LXXXVIII. [New York, Press of Fleming, Brewster & Alley, 1888] [7] p. illus., ports.
NN(M)   **2689**
The recovery of the wounded with both sides participating at the battle of Kennesaw mountain, June 27, 1864.

Brown, Joseph M. 1851–1931.
Kennesaw's bombardment; or, how the sharpshooters woke up the batteries. Atlanta, Record pub. co., 1890. 172 p. illus., map, 18cm.
"Erratum" slip inserted.   CSmH   **2690**

French, Samuel Gibbs, 1818–1910.
Kennesaw mountain. *SB* I (1882/83) 273–80.   **2691**

Storrs, George S
Kennesaw mountain. *SB* I (1882/83) 135–40.   **2692**

Atlanta
July 22 – September 2, 1864

Colonel L. P. Grant and the defenses of Atlanta. *Atlanta historical bulletin* I 6 (February 1932) 32–5.   **2693**

Archer, W   P
History of the battle of Atlanta. Also, Confederate songs and poems. Knoxville, Ga., C. B. H. Moncrief [c1940] 35 p. plates (illus., ports.). 19½cm.   **2694**
"Introductory" signed and dated: W. P. Archer, Atlanta, Ga., 1900.

Bowman, Samuel Millard, 1815–1885.
Sherman's Atlanta campaign. *United States service magazine* III (1865) 305–22. plate (map).   **2695**

Brown, Joseph M., 1851–1931.
The great retreat. Could Johnston have defended Atlanta successfully? The policy of the great Southern General defended and the field looked over in the light of events. A review of his plan of campaign. By Joseph M. Brown. Atlanta, Railroad record print [188–] 16 p. illus. 23cm.   CSmH DLC   **2696**

Cox, Jacob Dolson, 1828–1900.
. . . Atlanta, by Jacob D. Cox. New York, Charles Scribner's Sons, 1882. vii, (1) 274 p. maps. 19cm.   DLC NN   **2697**
At head of title: Campaigns of the Civil war — IX.
See Title 1362.

Cox, Rowland
"Snake creek gap, and Atlanta," a paper read by Brevet Major Rowland Cox. *MOLLUS-NY* II 7–29.   **2698**

Dodge, Grenville Mellen, 1831–1916.
The battle of Atlanta. *MOLLUS-NY* II 240–54.   **2699**

—— The battle of Atlanta and other campaigns, addresses, etc., by Major-General Grenville M. Dodge. Council Bluffs, Iowa, Monarch print. co., 1910. 183 p. illus., ports. 23½cm.
CSmH NHi   **2700**

—— Society of the Army of the Tennessee, Reunion at Cincinnati, Ohio, Sept. 25–26, 1889. Banquet at Burnet house, Thursday eve., Sept. 26. Sixth regular toast, the battle of Atlanta . . . response by General G. M. Dodge. [Des Moines, State Register press, 1889] 15 p. 26cm.   CSmH   **2701**

Hay, Thomas Robson
The Atlanta campaign. *GHQ* VII (1923) 99–118. map.   **2702**

—— Davis, Bragg, and Johnston in the Atlanta campaign. *GHQ* VIII (1924) 38–48.   **2703**

Hoehling, Adolf A
Last train from Atlanta, by A. A. Hoehling. New York, Thomas Yoseloff [1958] 558 p. plates (facsims., illus., ports.). 24cm.
NN   **2704**

Hood, John Bell, 1831–1879.
The defense of Atlanta. *B&L* IV 336–44.   **2705**
Condensed from the author's *Advance and retreat*. . . . New Orleans, 1880.

Howard, Oliver Otis, 1830–1909.
The battles about Atlanta. *Atlantic monthly* XXXVIII (1876) 385–99, 559–67. maps.   **2706**

—— The struggle for Atlanta. *B&L* IV 293–325.   **2707**

Jamison, Alma Hill
The cyclorama of the battle of Atlanta. *Atlanta historical bulletin* X (July 1937) 58–74. plate (port.).   **2707A**
Running title: A history of the cyclorama.

Johnston, Joseph Eggleston, 1807–1891
Official report of Gen. Joseph E. Johnston, Vineville, Ga., October 20, 1864. [Richmond, 1865.] 14 p. 23cm. CSmH DLC TxU   **2708**
Caption title from p. 2.
"Report of General Hood," 13–14.
Crandall 1316.

Key, William,   –1958
The battle of Atlanta and the Georgia campaign, by William Key. New York, Twayne publishers [1958] 92 p. illus. 23½cm.
NN   **2709**
"First published in the Atlanta journal and constitutionalist."

Kurtz, Wilbur G   1882–
The Atlanta cyclorama, the story of the
famed battle of Atlanta. Compiled and written
by Wilbur G. Kurtz. Published by the City of
Atlanta, Georgia. [Atlanta, Higgins-McArthur
co., 1954] 32 p. illus., partly col.; maps, ports.
28cm.   NN   **2710**

Leggett, Mortimer Dormer, 1821–1896.
The battle of Atlanta, a paper read by Gen-
eral M. D. Leggett, before the Society of the
Army of the Tennessee, October 18th, 1883, at
Cleveland. [Cleveland] John A. Davies, printer,
1883. 28 p. 22cm.   CSmH DLC   **2711**
Title and imprint from cover.

Little, Robert D
General Hardee and the Atlanta campaign.
GHQ xxix (1945) 1–22.   **2712**

Long, Eli, 1837–1903.
Letter from General Long. *JUSCA* iii (1890)
428–30.   **2713**
Commenting upon Kilpatrick's raid around Atlanta
. . . by W. S. Scott, *JUSCA* iii (1890) 263–70 (see
Title 2715).

Rodgers, Robert L.
Report of Robert L. Rodgers, historian to
the Atlanta camp no. 159, U.C.V., on the capture of the DeGress battery, and Battery A, 1st
Ill. light artillery, in the battle of Atlanta, July
22d, 1864, with other papers bearing thereon.
Published by some of the survivors of Manigault's brigade. [Atlanta, 1896] 47 p. 23cm.
                        CSmH NHi   **2714**
On cover: In the battle of Atlanta, July 22d, 1864,
who captured the DeGress battery Manigault's brigade!
Report of Col. Robert L. Rogers. . . .

Scott, William Sherley, 1856–1941.
Kilpatrick's raid around Atlanta, August
18th to 22d, 1864. *JUSCA* iii (1890) 263–70.
map.   **2715**
For comment see Letter from General Long *JUSCA*
iii (1890) 428–30 (Title 2713).

Smith, Gustavus Woodson, 1821–1896.
The Georgia militia about Atlanta. *B&L* iv
331–5.   **2716**

Stone, Henry,   –1896.
The Atlanta campaign, by Henry Stone Lieutenant-Colonel. *PMHSM* viii (1891–94) 341–
92.   **2717**
Contents: Chapter i Opening of the campaign; ii
From the Oostenaula to the Chattahooche; iii The
siege and capture of Atlanta; iv Strategy of the campaign.

United Confederate Veterans. Atlanta Camp.
Battles of Atlanta. Short sketches of the battles around, siege, evacuation and destruction
of Atlanta, Ga., in 1864, with map, historic

places, directory to battle lines, prominent
characters who participated, etc. Prepared
under the direction of the Committee of the
Atlanta camp, United Confederate veterans, for
the information of visitors, and sold for the
benefit of the Camp. Atlanta, 1895. 31 p. front.
(fold. map). 22cm.   IHi   **2718**

United States. Army.
The Atlanta campaign. Organization of the
Union (field) forces (commanded by Major-
General William T. Sherman), May 5–31,
1864. [Washington, War Records office, 1888]
16 p. 23cm.   CSmH   **2719**

—— The Atlanta campaign. Organization of
the Union (field) forces (commanded by
Major-General William T. Sherman) May 3 –
September 8, 1864. [Washington, War Records
office, 1888] 28 p. 23cm.   CSmH   **2720**

              *   *   *

Adams, John Quincy
Hold the fort! By Captain John Q. Adams.
MOLLUS-Iowa ii 164–72.   **2721**

Brown, Joseph M, 1851–1931.
The battle of Allatoona, October 5, 1864, one
of the gamest and bloodiest fights of the war.
. . . Atlanta, Record pub. co., 1890. 24, (1) p.
illus., map, plan. 29½cm.   CSmH   **2722**
Text in triple columns.

Brown, Joseph Emerson, 1821–1894.
The story of a song. Saint Valentine's day,
1889. [New York, Press of Fleming, Brewster
& Alley, 1889] [8] p. illus. 17½cm.
Title from cover.   CSmH   **2723**

Ludlow, William, 1843–1901.
The battle of Allatoona, October 5th, 1864,
a paper read before the Michigan commandery
of the Military order of the loyal legion of the
U. S., by William Ludlow . . . Detroit, Winn
& Hammond, 1891. 42 p. 2 plates (maps).
21½cm.   NHi   **2724**
Also published in *MOLLUS-Mich* i no 17.

Sherman's March to the Sea
November – December, 1864

Bonner, James Calvin, 1904–
Sherman at Milledgeville in 1864. *JSH* xxii
(1956) 273–91.   **2725**

Bowman, Samuel Millard, 1815–1885.
Sherman's Georgia campaign from Atlanta
to the sea. *United States service magazine* iii
(1865) 426–46. plate (map).   **2726**

Sherman's March to the Sea, continued

Bratton, J   R
Letter of a Confederate surgeon on Sherman's occupation of Milledgeville. *GHQ* xxxii (1948) 231–2.   **2727**

Cox, Jacob Dolson, 1828–1900.
. . . The march to the sea. Franklin and Nashville. By Jacob D. Cox. New York, Charles Scribner's Sons, 1882. ix, (1), 265, (1) p. maps. 19½cm.   NN   **2728**
At head of title: Campaigns of the Civil war — x.
"Errata," second (1) p.
See Title 1362.

De Laubenfels, David John
Where Sherman passed by. *Geographical review* xlvii (1957) 381–95. illus.   **2729**
Based on the maps drawn by Captain John Rziha, Chief topographical engineer XIV corps.

Ellis, Robert R
From Atlanta to the sea. *Military engineer* li (1959) 437–44; lii (1960) 37–43, 122–7. illus., plans, ports.   **2730**

Howard, Oliver Otis, 1830–1909.
Sherman's advance from Atlanta *B&L* iv 663–6.   **2731**

Jones, Charles Colcock, 1831–1893.
General Sherman's march from Atlanta to the coast, an address delivered before the Confederate survivors' association, in Augusta, Georgia, at its sixth annual meeting, on Memorial day, April 26, 1884, by Col. Charles C. Colcock, Jr. . . . Augusta, Chronicle print. estab., 1884. 19 p. 22cm.   NN   **2732**

Rziha, John,   –1881.
With Sherman through Georgia, a journal. Edited by David J. de Laubenfels. *GHQ* xli (1957) 288–300. plan.   **2733**
The author later changed his name to John Laube de Laubenfels.

Shackleton, Robert, 1860–1923.
From the Etowah river to Atlanta. *B&G* ii (1893) 442–9. illus., plans.   **2734**

Smith, Gustavus Woodson, 1821–1896.
The Georgia militia during Sherman's march to the sea. *B&L* iv 667.   **2735**

Savannah
November 15 – December 21, 1864

Howard, Charles Henry
Incidents and operations connected with the capture of Savannah, by General Charles H. Howard, read, December 14, 1893. *MOLLUS-Ill* iv 430–50.   **2736**

Hughes, N   C
Hardee's defense of Savannah. *GHQ* xlvii (1963) 43–67.   **2737**

Jones, Charles Colcock, 1831–1893.
The siege and evacuation of Savannah, Georgia, in December 1864, an address delivered before the Confederate survivors' association in Augusta, Ga., on the occasion of its twelfth annual reunion on Memorial day, April 26th, 1890, by Col. Charles C. Jones. Augusta, Chronicle pub. co., 1890. 30, (1) p. 23½cm.
                              NN   **2738**
Also published in *SHSP* xvii (1889) 60–84.

—— The siege of Savannah in December, 1864, and the Confederate operations in Georgia and the Third military district of South Carolina, during General Sherman's march from Atlanta to the sea, by Charles C. Jones, Jr. Printed for the author. Albany, Joel Munsell, 1874. x, 184 p. 21½cm.
                    CSmH DLC NN   **2739**

—— Bombardments and capture of Fort McAllister. *Magazine of American history* xiv (1885) 501–08.   **2740**

Nichols, George Ward, 1837–1887.
How Fort M'Allister was taken. *Harper's magazine* xxxvii (1868) 368–70.   **2741**

United States. Army.
The Savannah campaign. Organization of the Union forces (commanded by Major-General William T. Sherman), November 15 – December 21, 1864. [Washington, War Records office, 1888] 10 p. 22½cm.
                              CSmH   **2742**

Swift, Charles Jewett
The last battle of the Civil war, paper read by Charles Jewett Swift, at the organizing first meeting of the Columbus historical society, Wednesday night, February 10th, 1915. . . . Columbus, Gilbert print. co. [1915] 33 p. plates (illus.). 23cm.   NN   **2743**
Also published in *Journal of the Military service institution of the United States* lvi (1915) 359–75.

KENTUCKY
General References

Collins, Richard H   1824–1888.
Civil war annals of Kentucky (1861–1865) by Richard H. Collins. Edited by Hambleton Tapp. *FCHQ* xxxv (1961) 205–322.   **2744**
"Index," 407–22.

United States. Works Progress Administration.
. . . Military history of Kentucky, chronologically arranged. Written by workers of the Federal writers project of the Works progress

administration for the State of Kentucky. Sponsored by the Military department of Kentucky, G. Lee McLain, the Adjutant general. . . . [Frankfort, Printed by the State Journal, 1939] viii, 493 p. plates (illus., ports.). 22cm.
NN   2745
At head of title: The American guide series. "War between the states," 151–238.

*   *   *

Scalf, Henry P
The battle of Ivy mountain [Nov. 8, 1861] *RKHS* LVI (1958) 11–26.   *2746*

Smith, William Farrar, 1824–1903.
The campaign of 1861–1862 in Kentucky unfolded through the correspondence of its leaders. *Magazine of American history* XIV (1885) 351–74, 764–80, 577–99. map.   *2747*

McMurtey, Robert Gerald, 1906–
Zollicofer and the battle of Mill Springs. *FCHQ* XXIX (1955) 303–19.   *2748*

Walker, Peter Franklin
Holding the Tennessee line, Winter, 1861–62. *THQ* XVI (1957) 228–49.   *2749*

Bragg's Campaign
1862

Bragg, Braxton, 1817–1876.
Report made by General Bragg of the Kentucky campaign. . . . *OLOD* I (1874/75) 15.
2750

Duke, Basil Wilson, 1838–1916.
Bragg's campaign in Kentucky. *SB* ns I (1885/86) 161–7. 232–40. ports.   *2751*

—— Morgan's cavalry during the Bragg invasion. *B&L* III 26–8.   *2752*

Fisher, Horace Newton, 1837–1916.
"The Harris letter" outlining Bragg's plan of campaign for the invasion of Kentucky in 1862, by Col. Horace Newton Fisher. [n.p.] c1953. 15 folios. 28cm.   DLC   *2753*
A facsimile printing of the manuscript.

Gilbert, C   C
Bragg's invasion of Kentucky. *SB* ns I (1885/86) 217–22, 296–301, 336–42, 430–6, 465–77, 550–6.   *2754*

Hammond, Paul F
Kirby Smith's Kentucky campaign. *SHSP* IX (1881) 225–33, 246–54, 289–97, 445–62; X (1882) 70–6, 158–61.   *2755*

McWhiney, Grady
Controversy in Kentucky: Braxton Bragg's campaign of 1862. *CWH* VI (1960) 5–42. *2756*

Messmer, Charles K
Louisville and the Confederate invasion of 1862. *RKHS* LV (1959) 299–324.   *2757*

Otis, Ephraim Allen
Recollections of the Kentucky campaign of 1862, by Captain Ephraim A. Otis. *PMHSM* VII (1903) 227–53.   *2758*
Also published in *MOLLUS-Ill* IV 122–47.

Quisenberry, Anderson Chenault, 1850–1921.
The battles of Big Hill and Richmond, Kentucky, September, 1862. *RKHS* XVI (1918) 7–25. plate (port.).   *2759*

Rankins, Walter Herbert, 1882–
Morgan's cavalry and the Home guard at Augusta, Kentucky. An account of the attack, of a detachment of Morgan's cavalry, on the Home guard at Augusta, Kentucky, September 27, 1862. By Walter Rankins. Louisville, Press of Standard print. co., c1953. 15 p. 27½cm.
CU-SB   *2760*
"Reprinted with the permission of the Filson club from the Filson club history quarterly, volume 27, no. 4, October 1953."

Urquhart, David
Bragg's advance and retreat. *B&L* III 600–09.   *2761*

Wheeler, Joseph, 1818–1879.
Bragg's invasion of Kentucky. *B&L* III 1–25.
2762

Perryville
October 8, 1862

Memoranda of facts bearing on the Kentucky campaign. [n.p., 1862?] 4 p. 22cm.
Caption title.   CSmH DLC   *2763*
Text in double columns.

Buell, Don Carlos, 1818–1898.
East Tennessee and the campaign of Perryville. *B&L* III 31–51.   *2764*

Finley, Luke W
The battle of Perryville . . . by Colonel Luke W. Finley. *SHSP* XXX (1902) 238–50.
2765

Gilbert, Charles Champion, 1822?–1903.
On the field of Perryville. *B&L* III 52–9.
2766

Quisenberry, Anderson Chenault, 1850–1921.
The Confederate campaign in Kentucky. The battle of Perryville. *RKHS* XVII (1919) 31–8.
2767

Sheridan, Philip Henry, 1831–1888.
[Report of the operations of my division, in the action of the 8th [October 1862] instant, near Perryville, Kentucky] 3 p. 20½cm.
CSmH   *2768*

Perryville, continued

At head of text: Headquarters 11th division, Army of the Ohio, (Camp on Rolling Fork, six miles south of Lebanon, Ky.), October 23, 1862.

Tapp, Hambleton
The battle of Perryville, 1862. *FCHQ* IX (1935) 158–81.   **2769**

Wright, John Montgomery
A glimpse of Perryville. *SB* ns I (1885/86) 130–4. plate (map).   **2770**
Also, in condensed form, in *B&L* III 60–1.

LOUISIANA
General References

Louisiana. Governor
Official report relative to the conduct of federal troops in western Louisiana, during the invasions of 1863 and 1864. Compiled from sworn testimony, under direction of Governor Henry W. Allen. Shreveport, April 1865. Shreveport, News print. estab., 1865. 89 p. 21cm.   MBAt   **2771**
Crandall 1638.

——— ——— [Baton Rouge, Otto Claitor, 1939] 89 p. 24cm.   TxU   **2772**
"Notice. This a line-for-line reprint of the original, issued in a limited edition of 76 copies. Otto Claitor. Baton Rouge, Louisiana, January, 1939."

Williams, Thomas Harry, 1909–
The Civil war in Louisiana, a chronology, by T. Harry Williams and A. Otis Hebert, Jr. [Baton Rouge, Louisiana Civil war Centennial Commission, 1961?] 29 p. illus., port. 23cm.
                                              2773

Winters, John D
The Civil war in Louisiana, by John D. Winters. [Baton Rouge] Louisiana State University press [1963] xiv, (1), 534 p. maps and plans, plates (illus., ports.). 24cm.   **2774**

New Orleans
April, 1862

Buttgenbach, Walter J
The passage of Forts Jackson and Saint Philip. *Journal of the United States artillery* XLI (1914) 19–47. plan   **2775**

Confederate States of America. War Department.
Proceedings of the Court of inquiry, relative to the fall of New Orleans. Published by order of Congress. Richmond, R. M. Smith, Public printer, 1864. 206 p. 23cm.
Crandall 1385.   CSmH NN   **2776**

Confederate States of America. War Department.
Correspondence between the War department and General Lovell, relating to the defences of New Orleans, submitted in response to a resolution of the House of representatives passed third February, 1863. Richmond, R. M. Smith, Public printer, 1863. 123 p. 23½cm.
                              CSmH DLC   **2777**
Includes correspondence between the President, War department, and Governor T. Moore, relating to the defence of New Orleans, with separate title page, p. [91]–119.
Crandall 1333.

Dufour, Charles L
. . . The night [April 24, 1862] the war was lost. Garden City, Doubleday & co., 1960. 427 p. plates (illus., plan, ports.). 24cm.
                                       NN   **2778**
"Approaches to New Orleans," map on endpaper. At head of title: Charles L. Dufour.

Parton, James, 1822–1891.
General Butler in New Orleans. History of the administration of the Department of the Gulf in the year 1862; with an account of the capture of New Orleans, and a sketch of the previous career of the General, civil and military. By James Parton. New York, Mason Brothers, 1864. 649 p. front. (port.), 2 plates (plans). 20½cm.   CSmH DLC   **2779**
Later editions are reprintings. The 6th has 2 fronts. (ports.).
"Preface" dated: October 20, 1863.

——— ——— Thirteenth edition. New York, Mason Brothers, 1864. 661 p. 2 fronts. (ports.), 2 plates (plans). 21cm.   **2779A**

——— General Butler in New Orleans, being a history of the administration of the Department of the Gulf in the year 1862. With an account of the capture of New Orleans, and a sketch of the previous career of the General, civil and military. By James Parton. New York, Mason Brothers, 1864. 174 p. 23½cm.
                              DLC NN   **2780**
"In this edition some of the longer documents have been omitted or abridged."
Text in double columns.

Robertson, William B
The water-battery at Fort Jackson. *B&L* II 99–100.   **2781**

*   *   *

Irwin, Richard Bache, 1829–1892.
Military operations in Louisiana in 1862. *B&L* III 582–4.   **2782**

Smith, George Winston
The Banks expedition of 1862. *LHQ* XXVI (1943) 341–60.   **2783**

Williams, G   Mott
The first Vicksburg expedition and the battle
of Baton Rouge, 1862, by Rev. G. Mott Williams. *MOLLUS-Wis* II 52–69   **2784**
On General Thomas Williams by his son.

Port Hudson
1862–1863

Bonham, Milledge Lewis, 1880–1941.
Man and nature at Port Hudson, 1863. *Mili-
tary historian and economist* II (1917) 372–84;
III (1918) 20–38.   **2785**

Cunningham, Edward
The Port Hudson campaign, 1862–1863, by
Edward Cunningham. [Baton Rouge] Louisiana State University press [1963] xiii, 174 p.
map, plates (illus.). 23½cm.   **2786**

Harrington, Fred Harvey
Arkansas defends the Mississippi. *ArkHQ*
IV (1945) 109–17.   **2787**

Irwin, Richard Bache, 1829–1892.
The capture of Port Hudson. *B&L* III 586–
98.   **2788**

Jackson, Crawford
An account of the occupation of Fort Hudson, La. *AHQ* XVIII (1956) 474–85.   **2789**

Kassel, Charles
Opening the Mississippi, a Civil war drama.
Open court XL (1926) 145–54.   **2790**

Palfrey, John Carver, 1833–1906.
Port Hudson, by Lieutenant-Colonel John
C. Palfrey. *PMHS* VIII (1891) 21–63.   **2791**

Red River Campaign
March 10 – May 22, 1864

The Red river campaign. *United States service
magazine* II (1864) 417–31.   **2792**

Barr, Alwyn
The battle of Calcasieu pass. *SWHQ* LXVI
(1962/63) 59–67.   **2793**

—— Texan losses in the Red river campaign,
1864. *TMH* III (1963) 103–10.   **2794**

Byrd, William
The capture of Fort De Russy, La. *LWL* VI
(1868/69) 185–7.   **2795**

Fitzhugh, Lester N
Texas forces in the Red river campaign,
March-May, 1864. *TMH* III (1963) 15–22.
                                           2796

Homans, John,   –1903.
The Red river expedition. *PMHSM* VIII
(1893) 65–97.   **2797**

Hewitt, John Edmond, 1851–1936.
. . . Battle of Mansfield, Louisiana, fought
April eighth, 1864 . . . Published on the 61st
anniversary of the battle, on the occasion of
the unveiling of the monuments to Gen. Rich-
ard Taylor and Gen. Polignac. [Logansport,
La., Interstate Progress] 1949. 18, (2) p. 2
illus., plan, ports. 23cm.
                   LNHT TxU   **2798**
Title and imprint from cover.
At head of title: 1864.
Port and plan, (2) p. Second illus., p. [4] of cover.
"The Kate Beard chapter no. 397 Daughters of the
Confederacy had this History . . . reprinted." Originally published in the *Confederate veteran* XXXIII
(1925) 172–3, 198. The Mansfield Battle Park Museum reports that there was also a separate publica-
tion in 1925.

Irwin, Richard Bache, 1829–1892.
The Red river campaign. *B&L* IV 345–62.
                                           2799

Johnson, Ludwell H
Red river campaign, politics and cotton in
the Civil war, by Ludwell H. Johnson. Baltimore, Johns Hopkins press [1958] 317 p.
maps. 21½cm.   NN   **2800**

Landers, Howard Lee
Wet sand and cotton. Bank's Red river campaign, by Colonel H. L. Landers. *LHQ* XIX
(1936) 150–95.   **2801**

Smith, Edmund Kirby, 1821–1896.
The defense of the Red river. *B&L* IV 369–
74.   **2802**

Texas Historical Foundation.
Red river campaign centennial commemora-
tion. Center, Texas — Mansfield, Louisiana,
April 4, 1964. 36 p. 1 illus., map, ports. 23cm.
Title from cover.   **2802A**
"Publication of the Texas historical foundation,
affiliate of the Texas state historical survey committee."

United States Army.
The Red river campaign. Organization of
the Union forces (commanded by Major-General Nathaniel P. Banks), March 31, 1864.
[Washington, War Records office, 1888] 6 p.
23½cm.   CSmH   **2803**

Williams, Richard Hobson
General Banks' Red river campaign. *LHQ*
XXXII (1949) 103–44.   **2804**

MISSISSIPPI
General References

Bearss, Edwin Cole, 1923–
Calendar of events in Mississippi, 1861–
1865. *JMH* XXI (1959) 85–112.   **2805**

—— Decision in Mississippi. Mississippi's important role in the War between the States.

Mississippi, General References, continued

By Edwin C. Bearss. Jackson, Mississippi Commission on the War between the States [1962] xvi, 636 p. maps, fold. maps. 24cm.   **2806**
"Battles, skirmishes and events in Mississippi, 1861–1865," 581–97.
"Mississippi military units in the Civil war," p. 598–600.

—— Grand Gulf's role in the Civil war. *CWH* v (1959) 5–29. map.   **2807**

Lee, Stephen Dill, 1833–1908.
Index to campaigns, battles and skirmishes, series I., in Mississippi from 1861 to 1865. *PMHS* viii (1904) 23–32.   **2808**

McCardle, William H
William H. McCardle's account of the great war between the States. Edited by Charlotte Capers. *JMH* ix (1947) 174–81.   **2809**

Iuka
September 19, 1862

Gunn, Jack W
The battle of Iuka. *JMH* xxiv (1962) 142–57.   **2810**

Hamilton, Charles Smith, 1822–1891.
The battle of Iuka. *B&L* ii 734–6.   **2811**

McDonald, Lyla Merrill
Iuka's history embodying Dudley's battle of Iuka [by] Lyla Merrill McDonald. . . . [Corinth, Rankin printery, 1923] 32 p. 1 illus. 15cm.   NN   **2812**
Civil war, 12–22.
Unit roster Co. K, 2nd Miss. infantry 12–13.

Snead, Thomas Lowndes, 1817–1897.
With Price east of the Mississippi. *B&L* ii 717–34.   **2813**

Corinth
October 4, 1862

Carpenter, Cyrus Clay, 1829–1898.
The charge on battery Robinet. *Annals of Iowa* s 3 i (1893) 99–106, 214–21.   **2814**

Dudley, G   W
The battle of Corinth, October 3–4, 1862, including also the battle of Davis' bridge, on Hatchie, and skirmish at the Tuscumbia, October 5, 1862. By G. W. Dudley. Iuka, Vidette print [1899] 24 p. 1 illus., map, port., 3 plates (illus., 2 ports.). 23cm.
                         CSmH DLC   **2815**
Title and imprint from cover.
Text in double columns.

—— The lost account of the battle of Corinth and court-martial of Gen. Van Dorn. Introduc-

tion and informal essay on the battle by Monroe F. Cockrell. Jackson, Tenn., McCowat-Mercer press, 1955. 78 p. illus., ports., fold. maps in pocket. 21½cm   NN   **2816**

Force, Manning Ferguson, 1824–1899.
. . . From Fort Henry to Corinth, by M. F. Force. New York, Charles Scribner's Sons, 1881. vii, (2), 204 p. maps. 19cm.   **2816A**
At head of title: Campaigns of the Civil war — ii.
See Title 1362.

Hamilton, Charles Smith, 1822–1891.
Correspondence in regard to the battle of Corinth, Miss., October 3d and 4th, 1862. Major General C. S. Hamilton and Arthur C. Ducat. [Chicago, 1882] 11 p. 24½cm.
                                    CSmH   **2817**
The text of General Hamilton's speech to the surviving officers, October 4, 1882, and the letters exchanged by Generals Ducat and Hamilton.
Text in double columns.

Pope, John, 1822–1892.
Correspondence between General Pope and Halleck in relation to prisoners captured at Corinth. [Washington, D.C., 1865] 3 p. 25½cm.   CSmH   **2818**
Caption title.
Pope disclaims a report credited to him by Halleck published in the press and dated June 4, 1862.

Rosecrans, William Starke, 1819–1898.
The battle of Corinth. *B&L* ii 737–57.
                                              2819

Stanley, David Sloan, 1828–1902.
The battle of Corinth, a paper read by General D. S. Stanley. *MOLLUS-NY* ii 267–79.
                                              2820

*   *   *

Brown, A   F
Van Dorn's operations in Northern Mississippi, recollections of a cavalryman. *SHSP* vi (1878) 151–61.   **2821**

Jackman, John S
Vicksburg in 1862. SB iii (1884/85) 1–8.
                                              2822

Lee, Stephen Dill, 1833–1908.
The campaign of Generals Grant and Sherman against Vicksburg in December 1862, and January 1st and 2nd, 1863, known as the "Chickasaw bayou campaign." *PMHS* iv (1901) 15–36. fold. map.   **2823**

—— Details of important work by two Confederate telegraph operators, Christmas eve, 1862, which prevented the almost complete surprise of the Confederate army at Vicksburg. *PMHS* viii (1904) 51–5.   **2824**

Maury, Dabney Herndon, 1822–1900.
Grant's campaign in North Mississippi in 1862. *SM* xiii (1873) 410–17.   **2825**

—— Recollections of the campaign in North Mississippi in 1862–63 of Generals Van Dorn and Price against Grant. *SM* x (1872) 607–12.
2826

—— Recollections of the campaign against Grant in North Mississippi in 1862–63. *SHSP* xiii (1885) 285–311. **2827**

Morgan, George Washington, 1820–1893.
The assault on Chickasaw bluffs. *B&L* iii 462–70. **2828**

Hartje, Robert
Van Dorn conducts a raid on Holly Springs and enters Tennessee. *THQ* xviii (1959) 120–33. **2829**

Vicksburg
December 20, 1862 – July 4, 1863

The doomed sappers, a night in Vicksburg during the investment. *Onward* Vol 2, no 4 (October 1869) 275–85. plate (illus.). **2830**

Historical Vicksburg and her part in the great drama, a succinct account of the great campaign for the possession of Vicksburg during the Civil war. The number of the troops engaged. Something of the National military park which will commemorate the heroic valor displayed by the American soldier on both sides during that great conflict for possession of the City. 1901. [4] p. map. 28½cm. **2831**
Caption title.

The Vicksburg campaign, by Majors Van Volkenburgh, Perkins, Stuart, and Hogan. *Coast artillery journal* lxxx (1928) 212–31. map.
2832

Alvord, Benjamin, 1864–1924.
Campaign of Vicksburg in 1863, compiled by B. Alvord, 20th infantry. [n.p., n.d.] 9 p. plate (map). 23½cm. **2833**
Caption title.

Bearss, Edwin Cole, 1923–
The campaigns culminating in the fall of Vicksburg, March 29–July 4, 1863. *Iowa journal of history* lix (1961) 173–80, 238–42. plates (facsims., 2 maps). **2834**
List of Iowa troops at Vicksburg with their commanders, 238–9.
"Calendar of actions in which Iowa troops participated during the Vicksburg campaign, March 29–July 4, 1863," 240–2.

—— The Vicksburg river defenses and the enigma of "whistling Dick." *JMH* xix (1957) 21–30. **2835**

Bolling, Eugene S
The bill of fare at the hotel de Vicksburg, 1863. Edited by Mattie Russell. *JMH* xvii (1955) 282–5. **2836**

Carnahan, Earl Clark
The Vicksburg campaign, January 10 to July 4, 1963. *Journal of the United States infantry association* iii 4 (April 1907) 51–69. map. **2837**

Confederate States of America. Army
Organization of the Confederate army of Vicksburg (Lieutenant-General John C. Pemberton commanding), July 4, 1863. [Washington, War Records office, 1885] 4 p. 23cm.
CSmH **2838**

Confederate States of America. President.
Correspondence between the President and General Joseph E. Johnston, together with that of the Secretary of war and the Adjutant and Inspector general, during the months of May, June and July, 1863. Published by order of Congress. R. M. Smith, Public printer, 1864. 64 p. 23½cm. CSmH GEU **2839**
Crandall 605.

Fox, Joe
History of the siege of Vicksburg and map of the Vicksburg national military park, showing Confederate and Union lines, avenue and locations of all memorials, headquarters and camps. Vicksburg, Joe Fox [1909?] 24 p. fold. map. 16cm. LNHT **2840**
Title and imprint from cover.

Grant, Frederick Dent
A boy's experience at Vicksburg. *MOLLUS-NY* iii 86–100. **2841**

Gregory, Edward S   1843–1884.
Vicksburg during the siege. *AW* 111–33.
2842

Hains, Peter Conover, 1840–1921.
"An incident of the battle of Vicksburg," prepared by Lieutenant-Colonel Peter C. Haines. 1891. 9 p. *MOLLUS-DC* no 6. **2843**

Hall, Thomas O
The key to Vicksburg. *SB* ii (1883/84) 393–6. **2844**

Hay, Thomas Robson
Confederate leadership at Vicksburg. *MVHR* xi (1925) 543–60. **2845**

Hogane, J   T
Reminiscences of the siege of Vicksburg, by Major J. T. Hogane of the Engineer corps. *SHSP* xi (1883) 223–7, 291–7, 484–9. **2846**

Hubbard, Lucius Frederick, 1836–1913.
Minnesota in the campaigns of Vicksburg, November, 1862–July, 1863, an address delivered before the Minnesota historical society, by General L. F. Hubbard, September 9th, 1907. Report of the Minnesota Vicksburg mon-

Vicksburg, continued

ument commission. 64 p. illus., 2 maps, fold. map. 23½cm.   CSmH   NeHi   *2847*

Jenney, William Le Baron, 1832–1907.
Personal recollections of Vicksburg. *MOLLUS-Ill* III 247–65.   *2848*

Johnston, Joseph Eggleston, 1807–1891.
Jefferson Davis and the Mississippi campaign. *North American review* CXLIII (1886) 585–98.   *2849*

—— Report of General Joseph E. Johnston of operations in the Departments of Mississippi and East Louisiana, together with Lieut. General Pemberton's report of the battles of Port Gibson, Baker's creek, and the siege of Vicksburg. Published by order of Congress. Richmond, R. M. Smith, Public printer, 1864. 213 p. 23½cm.   CSmH   IHi   *2850*
    Crandall 1418.

Jordan, Thomas, 1819–1895.
The Vicksburg campaign of 1862–1863. *US* XII (1885) 632–49; XIII (1885) 22–33.   *2851*

Lee, Stephen Dill, 1833–1908.
The campaign of Vicksburg, Mississippi, in 1863, from April 15 to and including the battle of Champion hills, or Baker's creek, May 16, 1863. *PMHS* III (1900) 21–53. fold. map.
        2852

—— The siege of Vicksburg. *PMHS* III (1900) 55–71.   *2853*

Livermore, William Roscoe, 1843–1919.
The Vicksburg campaign. *PMHSM* IX (1912) 541–71.   *2854*

Lockett, S   H
The defense of Vicksburg. *B&L* III 482–92.
        2855

Loring, William Wing 1818–1886.
Report of Major General Loring of battle of Baker's creek, and subsequent movements of his command. . . . Richmond, R. M. Smith, Public printer, 1864. 29 p. 23cm.
    Crandall 1423.   CSmH   DLC   *2856*

McClernand, John Alexander, 1812–1900.
Official report of Maj. Gen. J. A. M'Clernand detailing the march of the Thirteenth army corps, from Milliken's bend to Vicksburg, including an account of the battles of Port Gibson, Champion hill, Big Black river and the assault upon the defences of Vicksburg. Springfield, Press of Messrs. Baker & Phillips, 1863. 14 p. 23cm.   IHi   *2857*
    Text in double columns.

Miers, Earl Schenck, 1910–
The web of victory, Grant at Vicksburg. New York, Alfred A. Knopf, 1955. xiv, (2), 320, xii p. maps, plates (illus., ports.). 22cm. "Index," xii p.   *2858*

Mulvihill, Michael Joseph
Vicksburg and Warren county, Mississippi. Tunica Indians. Quebec missionaries. Civil war veterans. Designed and compiled by W. J. Mulvihill, Sr. Published by authority of the Mayor and Aldermen of the City of Vicksburg and the Board of Supervisors of Warren county., Mississippi. [Vicksburg, Van Norman print. co.] 1931. 80 p. illus., plans, ports. 23cm.
        NcD   *2859*
    "Civil war. Vicksburg and Yazoo river. Fort Snyder. C. S. ram Arkansas. Battle of Chickasaw bayou," 25–77.

Oakley, Minnie Myrtle
Selected bibliography of the Vicksburg campaign. *In* Original papers no. 1, Wisconsin history commission, 1908, 85–104.   *2860*

Paxton, Alexander Gallatin, 1896–
The Vicksburg campaign, a story of perseverance, by A. G. Paxton, Colonel 114th F. A. Mississippi National guard. [Grenada, Miss., 1959] 17 p. 21cm.   MsHa   *2861*

Pitzman, Julius
Vicksburg campaign reminiscences. *Military engineer* xv (1923) 112–15. map, plan.   *2862*

Reed, Samuel Rockwell
The Vicksburg campaign and the battles about Chattanooga under the command of General U. S. Grant, in 1862–63, an historical review, by Sam. Rockwell Reed. . . . Cincinnati, Robert Clarke & co., 1882. 201 p. 22½cm.
        CSmH   NN   TxU   *2863*

Rhodes, Charles Dudley, 1865–1948.
The Vicksburg campaign. *JMSIUS* XLII (1909) 193–209. plan.   *2864*

Rigby, William Titus, 1841–
Historic Vicksburg, an epitome of the campaign, siege and defense of Vicksburg, March 29–July 4, 1862. And a brief account of the inception of the Vicksburg national military park and of the work that has been done toward its establishment. Compiled by Capt. W. Rigby. [n.p., n.d.] [16] p. illus., 2 plans. 21½ × 20½cm.   CSmH   *2865*
    Caption title.
    On cover: Siege of Vicksburg and the Vicksburg national military park. Advertisement of Illinois Central railroad, p. [4] of cover.
    Text in double columns, the publication was folded.

—— —— [revised edition. n.p., 1905] [24] p. illus., 2 plans. 21½ × 20½cm.
        CSmH   *2866*

Cover title adds: Revised edition, 1905.
See also notes about earlier edition.

Sanborn, John Benjamin, 1826–1904.
The campaign against Vicksburg, by Brigadier-General John B. Sanborn. *MOLLUS-Minn* II 114–45. **2867**

—— The crisis at Champion's hill, the decisive battle of the Civil war, by Gen. John B. Sanborn. [St. Paul?, 1903?] 32 p. 22½cm.
Title from cover. CSmH DLC **2867A**

—— Memories of Vicksburg. Address of Gen. John Sanborn before St. Paul camp no. 1, Sons of veterans. St. Paul, 1887. 25 p. 22½cm. CSmH **2868**

—— Reminiscences of the campaigns against Vicksburg, by General John B. Sanborn. Read by request at the October meeting of Department of American history of the Michigan historical society. Saint Paul, H. M. Smythe print. co., 1887. 44 p. 22½cm. CSmH **2869**

Smith, William Sooy
The Mississippi raid, by General Wm. Sooy Smith. *MOLLUS-Ill* IV 379–91. **2870**

Swan, Samuel Alexander Ramsey, 1826–1913.
A Tennessean at the siege of Vicksburg, the diary of . . . May–July, 1863. *THQ* XIV (1955) 353–72. **2871**

United States. Army.
Organization of the Union forces operating against Vicksburg (Major-General Ulysses S. Grant, comdg.), May 18 to July 4, 1863. [Washington, War Records office, 1885] 13 p. 23cm. CSmH **2872**

—— War Department.
Correspondence relating to the operations against Vicksburg. [Washington, War Records office, 1885] 60 p. 23cm. CSmH **2873**
Correspondence between E. M. Stanton and Charles A. Dana.

Wilson, James Harrison, 1837–1925.
A staff-officer's journal of the Vicksburg campaign, April 30 to July 4, 1863. *JMSIUS* XLIII (1908) 93–109. plans. **2874**

United States. Vicksburg National Military Park Commission.
. . . Record of the organizations engaged in the campaign, siege, and defense of Vicksburg. Compiled from the official records by John S. Kountz, Secretary and historian of the Commission. Washington, Govt. print. office, 1901. 72 p. fold. map. 23cm. DLC NN **2875**
At head of title: Vicksburg national military park commission.

Vicksburg Memorials

The defenders of Vicksburg, a monument to their memory unveiled at Vicksburg, Mississippi, April 25, 1893. Exercises on the occasion, with the addresses by Lieut.-General Stephen D. Lee, and ex-Governor M. F. Lowry. *SHSP* XXI (1893) 183–206. **2876**

Everhart, William C
Vicksburg National military park, by William C. Everhart. Washington, D.C., 1954. 60 p. illus., maps and plans, ports. 23½cm. NN **2877**
National park service Historical handbook series no. 21.

Folsom, Charles W
Report of an inspection made of cemeterial operations at Vicksburg, Miss., by Brevet Colonel C. W. Folsom, A.Q.M., on the 14th of June, 1867. [n.p., 1867] 22 p. 22½cm.
Caption title. NN TxU **2878**
Dated: Vicksburg, Miss., June 29th, 1867.
NN's copy has ms. note: Inspection reports no. 19.

United States. Vicksburg National Military Park Commission.
. . . Report. Washington, Govt. print. office, 1904–20. 17 nos. 22½cm. CSmH **2879**
At head of title 1907/08–1919/20: Annual reports, War department.
Reports commencing with the first, 1899, are available in the Annual reports of the War department.
1903/04–1919/20 also issued as a separate publication.

Young, Rogers W
Vicksburg Confederate hill, 1862–1863. *JMH* VI (1944) 3–29. **2880**

Alabama

Jones, Walter Burgwyn, 1888–
The Alabama state memorial at Vicksburg. *AHQ* XIV (1952) 135–9. **2881**

Illinois

Illinois. Vicksburg Military Park Commission.
Illinois at Vicksburg. Published under authority of an act of the forty-fifth General assembly by the Illinois-Vicksburg military park commission. [Chicago, Blakely print. co.] 1907. 709 p. facsims., illus., ports., 2 fold. maps. 28cm. CSmH NN **2882**
"Alphabetical roll of names of Illinois soldiers" with regiment, 528–706.

—— —— Addenda and corrections to the book. . . . Chicago, 1910. [5] p. 26cm. CSmH **2883**
"Please paste these names under the tablets," [3] folios.

Vicksburg Memorials, continued

Indiana

Adams, Henry Clay, 1844–1910.

Indiana at Vicksburg . . . by the Indiana-Vicksburg military park commission. Compiled by Henry C. Adams. 1910. Indianapolis, Wm. B. Burford, Contractor for State print., 1911. 476 p. illus., map, ports., fold. map. 23½cm.

DLC NN   **2884**

"Regimental histories," 197–402.

Hanly, James Franklin, 1863–1920.

Vicksburg, by J. Franklin Hanly. Cincinnati, Jennings and Graham [1912] 44 p. front. (port.). 19cm.   CSmH NN   **2885**

Address at the dedication of the Indiana monument, Dec. 29, 1908

Perry, Oran, 1838–1929.

Morton in bronze, Indiana circle, Vicksburg battlefield. Report of Vicksburg state memorial commission, Compiled by Oran Perry, Secretary. Indianapolis, Wm. B. Burford, 1926. 64 p. 1 illus., ports. 23½cm.   NN   **2886**

Iowa

Iowa soldiers interred in the Vicksburg national cemetery. *Iowa journal of history* LIX (1961) 14 unnumbered pages after 242.   **2887**

Abernethy, Alonzo, 1836–1915.

Dedication of monuments erected by the State of Iowa commemorating the death, suffering and valor of her soldiers on the battlefields of Vicksburg, Lookout mountain, Missionary ridge, Shiloh, and in the Confederate prison at Andersonville, November twelfth to twenty-sixth, nineteen hundred and six. Compiled by Alonzo Abernethy, for the Committee. [Des Moines, Emory H. English, State printer, 1908] 301 p. plates (illus., 3 fold. maps, plan, ports.). 25½cm.   NN   **2888**

Letter of transmittal signed by the Secretaries of the four commissions authorized by the General assembly to erect monuments.

Sherman, Ernest Anderson, 1868–

Dedicating in Dixie, a series of articles descriptive of the tour of Governor Albert B. Cummins and staff, the members of the Vicksburg, Andersonville, Chattanooga and Shiloh monument commissions and invited guests, through the South for the purpose of dedicating Iowa memorials on the Southern battle fields and cemeteries, November 12th to November 25th, 1906. By Ernest A. Sherman. Cedar Rapids, Record print. co., 1907. 132 p. plates (group port., illus.). 25½cm.

DLC   **2889**

State emblem in color on front cover.

Thompson, James K   P   1845–1903.

Iowa at Vicksburg and the Vicksburg national military park. *Annals of Iowa* s3 v (1902) 272–92. 2 plates (fold. map, port.).

2890

Missouri

Huling, Polly

Missourians at Vicksburg. *MHR* L (1955/56) 1–15. illus.   **2891**

Missouri.

Report of the Commission appointed by the Governor to determine the position of Missouri troops at Vicksburg. 1901–1902. Jefferson City, Tribune print. co., [1903] 21 p. 23cm.

DLC   **2892**

Ohio

Ohio.

Ohio at Vicksburg, report of the Ohio Vicksburg battlefield commission, by W. P. Gault, late Sergt. Co. F, 78th O.V.I., Secretary to the Commission. [Columbus, 1906] 374 p. 2 maps, 1 double; plates (illus.). 22½cm.

DLC NN   **2893**

Pennsylvania

Cuffel, Charles A

Dedication of the Pennsylvania memorial at Vicksburg, Mississippi, March 24, 1906. An account of the pilgrimage to the Southland by letters to the Doylestown intelligencer, by Lieut. Charles A. Cuffel. 14 p. 23cm.

Title from cover.   CSmH   **2894**
Text in double columns.

Texas

Bearss, Edwin Cole, 1923–

Texas at Vicksburg. Prepared by Edwin C. Bearss in cooperation with the Texas State historical survey committee. Published on the occasion of the dedication of the Texas monument at Vicksburg national military park, November 4, 1961. 31 p. 2 maps. 23cm.   **2895**

Texas.

Commissioners' report, commission appointed to co-operate with the National park commission in locating positions of Texas troops during the siege and defense of Vicksburg. Greenville, Texas, Herald print [1901?] 13 p. 24cm.

Title from cover.   **2896**

Virginia

Dedication of the Virginia tablet in the Vicksburg national military park, Friday evening, Nov. 22, 1907, exercises in the First Baptist

church, Vicksburg, Miss. [Vicksburg, Mississippi ptg. co., 1907] [25] p. 23½cm.
Vi   **2897**
"Miss Mary Johnston's address," included.

West Virginia

West Virginia. Vicksburg Military Park Commission.
. . . Report of . . . . Charleston [Jarrett print.] 1923. 59 p. plates (illus., 1 col. fold.; ports.). 23cm.   **2898**
At head of title: State of West Virginia.
"Roster of the Fourth West Virginia infantry," 36–56.
Pages 57–8 omitted.

Wisconsin

Rood, Hosea Whitford, 1845–1923.
Wisconsin at Vicksburg. Report of the Wisconsin-Vicksburg monument commission, including the story of the campaign and siege of Vicksburg in 1863, with especial reference to the activities therein of Wisconsin troops. Compiled for the Commission by Hosea W. Rood. Madison, 1914. xvii, 501 p., illus., maps, ports. 27½cm.   NN   **2899**
"Names of all Wisconsin soldiers in the campaign and siege of Vicksburg from January 25 to July 4, 1863," listed by regiments, 372–500.

*   *   *

Stovall's brigade at Jackson, Mississippi, July 12th, 1863. *LWL* III (1867) 365–7.   **2900**

Battles of White House, Oct. 3d, and Corinth, Oct. 4th. [n.p., 1863]? broadside, 20 × 15cm.
CSmH   **2901**
Text signed: One of the 2d division.

Lee, Stephen Dill, 1833–1908.
Sherman's Meridian expedition from Vicksburg to Meridian, Feb. 3rd to March 6th, 1863 [sic]. *PMHS* IV (1901) 37–47.   **2902**

United States. Army.
Correspondence, etc., relating to the Meridian expedition, etc. Union. [Washington, War Records office, 1884] 125 p. 23cm.
CSmH   **2903**

Brice's Crossroads
June 10, 1864

Gentry, Claude
The battle of Brice's crossroads, by Claude Gentry. 3rd printing. . . . Baldwyn, Miss., Magnolia pub. [1968] 26 p. plates (illus., map., port.). 20½cm.   **2904**
Front. illus., p. [2] of cover.

Lee, Stephen Dill, 1833–1908.
Battle of Brice's cross roads, or Tishimingo creek, June 2nd to 12th, 1864. *PMHS* VI (1906) 27–37.   **2904A**

Luckett, William W
Bedford Forrest in the battle of Brice's cross roads. *THQ* XV (1956) 99–110. fold. map. **2905**

Morton, John Watson
Battle of Tishimingo creek or Brice's cross-roads. *SB* I (1882/83) 366–83.   **2905A**

Wyeth, John Allen
Major-General Forrest at Brice's cross-roads. *Harpers new monthly magazine* XCVIII (1898/99) 530–45. illus., plan, ports.   **2906**

Harrisburg
July 13–15, 1864

Lee, Stephen Dill, 1833–1908.
The battle of Tupelo, or Harrisburg, July 14th, 1863. *PMHS* VI (1902) 39–52. plan. **2907**

—— Gen. Stephen D. Lee's account of the battle of Harrisburg, read before the Mississippi state historical society, differing in many respects from the version generally accepted. 15 p. 22cm.   NHi   **2908**
Caption title.

*   *   *

Dimick, Howard T
Motives for the burning of Oxford, Mississippi [August 22, 1864] *JMH* VIII (1946) 111–20.   **2909**

TENNESSEE
General References

Deaderick, John Barron, 1886–
Civil war campaigns in Tennessee. *WTHSP* 10 (1956) 53–77.   **2910**

Guerrant, Edward O
Operations in East Tennessee and Southwest Virginia. *B&L* IV 475–9.   **2911**

Walker, Peter Franklin
Building a Tennessee army, Autumn, 1861. *THQ* XVI (1957) 99–116.   **2912**

Forts Henry and Donelson
February 4–16, 1862

Campaigns against Forts Henry and Donelson, February, 1862, by Committee no. 6, C.A.S., 1926–27. *Coast artillery journal* LXVII (1927) 389–404. maps.   **2913**

Forts Henry and Donelson, continued

Bearss, Edwin Cole, 1923–
    The Iowans at Fort Donelson. General C. F.
Smith's attack on the Confederate right, February 12–16, 1862. *Annals of Iowa s* 3 xxxvi
(1961/62) 241–68, 321–43. plan.   **2914**

—— Unconditional surrender, the fall of Fort
Donelson. *THQ* xxi (1962) 47–65, 140–61.
                                          2915

Buttgenbach, Walter J
    Fort Donelson, Tennessee. *Journal of the
United States artillery* xxxix (1913) 210–16.
                                          2916

Casseday, Morton M
    The surrender of Fort Donelson. *SB* ns ii
(1886/87) 694–7.   **2917**

Collyer, Robert, 1823–1912.
    The battle-field of Fort Donelson, narrative
sermon preached in Unity church, Chicago, by
the pastor . . . March 2, 1862. *Monthly journal American Unitarian association* iii (1862)
145–58.   **2918**

Confederate States of America. House of Rep-
        resentatives.
    Report of the Special committee, on the
recent military disasters at Forts Henry and
Donelson, and the evacuation of Nashville. . . .
Richmond, Enquirer press, Tyler, Wise, Allegre
and Smith, 1862. 178 p. 21cm.
    Crandall 602.   CSmH DLC NN   **2919**

Floyd, John Buchanan, 1806–1863.
    The battle at Fort Donelson, General Floyd's
reported. *THM* v (1919) 152–5.   **2920**
    "Reproduced from the Daily Nashville patriot,
March 26, 1862."

Holcombe, John L   and Walter J.
        Buttgenbach
    Fort Henry, Tennessee. *Journal of the
United States artillery* xxxix (1913) 83–90.
                                          2921

Roland, Charles P   1918–
    Albert Sidney Johnston and the loss of Forts
Henry and Donelson. *JSH* xxiii (1957) 45–69.
map.   **2922**

Smith, William Farrar, 1824–1903.
    Operations before Fort Donelson. *Magazine
of American history* xv (1885) 20–43.   **2923**

Stotsenburg, John Miller,   –1899.
    The Fort Donelson campaign. *JUSCA* x
(1897) 417–28. fold. map.   **2924**

Treichel, James A
    Lew Wallace at Fort Donelson. *Indiana mag-
azine of history* lix (1963) 3–18. map. **2925**

United States. General Service Schools, Fort
        Leavenworth, Kansas.
    Donelson campaign sources, supplementing
volume 7 of the Official records of the Union
and Confederate armies in the War of the
rebellion. Compiled for use at the Army service
schools, Fort Leavenworth, Kansas. [Fort
Leavenworth] Army Service Schools press,
1912. xii, 239 p. plates (illus., ports.), fold.
maps in pocket. 22½cm.   NN   **2926**
    The Library of Congress collates as 244 pages thus
including the ten plates with illus. on the rectos that
are at the end of the volume.

—— Fort Henry and Fort Donelson campaigns, February, 1862, source book. . . . Fort
Leavenworth, General Service Schools press,
1923. vii, 1488 p. illus., ports., fold. maps.
22½cm.   NN   **2927**

Walker, Peter Franklin
    Command failure, the fall of Forts Henry
and Donelson. *THQ* xvi (1957) 335–60. **2928**

Wallace, Lewis, 1827–1905.
    The capture of Fort Donelson. *B&L* i 398–
428.   **2929**

Wyeth, John Allen, 1845–1922.
    Lieutenant-Colonel Forrest at Fort Donel-
son. *Harper's new monthly magazine* xcviii
(1898/99) 339–54. illus., port.   **2930**

Cumberland Gap Campaign
March 28 – June 18, 1862

Morgan, George Washington, 1820–1893.
    Cumberland Gap. *B&L* iii 62–9.   **2931**

Shiloh
April 6–7, 1862

The battlefield of Shiloh. [n.p., n.d.] 6 p.
19cm.   CSmH   **2932**
    A letter dated: Field of Shiloh, Tennessee, April
14th, 1862.
    Text signed: W.

—— [another edition] [n.p., n.d.] 8 p. 22½cm.
    Text signed: W. W. W.   CSmH   **2933**

Andreas, A   T   publisher
    Manual of the panorama of the battles of
Shiloh. . . . Chicago, A. T. Andreas, 1885.
15 p. fold. plate (illus.). 23½ cm.
                                  NeHi   **2934**
    "Battle of Shiloh, written expressly for this work
by L. B. Crocker, late Captain 55th Illinois," 8–15.
    Advertising matter included.

Beauregard, Pierre Gustave Toutant, 1819–
        1893.
    The Shiloh campaign. *North American
review* cxlii (1886) 1–24, 159–94.   **2935**

Buell, Don Carlos, 1818–1898.
Shiloh reviewed. *B&L* I 487–536. **2936**

Deaderick, John Barron, 1886–
The truth about Shiloh, by J. B. Deaderick.
[Memphis, Pres of S. C. Toof & co., 1942]
36 p. 1 illus., maps. 15½cm.
　　　　　　　　　　DLC NN **2937**

Duke, Basil Wilson, 1838–1916.
The battle of Shiloh. *SB* II (1883/84) 150–
62, 201–16. **2938**

Eisenschiml, Otto, 1880–
The story of Shiloh, by Otto Eisenschiml,
and decorated by Joseph Trautwein. [Chicago]
Civil War Round Table [Norman press, 1946]
89 p. maps, plates (illus., ports.). 24cm.
　　　　　　　　　　DLC NN **2939**

Elliott, Stephen Habersham,　　–1917.
Battle of Shiloh. *JUSCA* XXII (1911) 157–
66. **2940**
　A review of Joseph W. Rich's The battle of Shiloh.
(See I III. Title 150).

Ewing, Thomas, 1829–1896.
Letter of the Hon. Thomas Ewing to His
Excellency Benj. Stanton, Lieut. Governor of
Ohio, in answer to his charges against our
Generals who fought the battle of Shiloh, on
the 6th of April, 1862. Columbus, Richard
Nevins, printer, 1862. 24 p. 23cm.
　　　　　　CSmH NN OMC **2941**
　Title and imprint from cover.
　Dated: October 4, 1862

——— ——— Columbus, R. Nevins, printer
[1862] 12 p. 23½cm.　　NN OMC **2942**
　Dated: Lancaster, O., Nov. 1, 1862.

Gentry, Claude
Shiloh, by Claude Gentry. Baldwyn, Miss.,
Magolia pub. [c1966] 38 p. fold. map. 20cm.
　　　　　　　　　　　　　　　　2943

Grant, Ulysses Simpson, 1822–1885.
The battle of Shiloh. *B&L* I 465–86. **2944**

Hurst, T　　M
The battle of Shiloh. *THM* v (1919) 81–96.
　　　　　　　　　　　　　　　　2945

Jordan, Thomas, 1819–1895.
The campaign and battle of Shiloh. *US* XII
(1885) 262–80, 393–410. **2946**

——— *US* s 3 VI (1904) 430–50, 576–95. **2947**

LeMonnier, Y　　R
General Beauregard at Shiloh, Sunday,
April 6, '62, by Y. R. LeMonnier, ex-Private,
Company B, Crescent regiment, Louisiana in-
fantry. . . . [New Orleans, Graham press,
1913] 32 p. 23cm.　　　　DLC **2948**
　Caption title from p. [3].

McCook, Daniel, 1834–1864.
The second division at Shiloh, by a staff
officer. *Harper's magazine* XXVIII (1863/64)
828–33. **2949**

McCook, Edward Moody, 1833–1909.
Six weeks in the mud. *Overland monthly* II
(1869) 215–21. **2950**

McWhiney, Grady, 1928–
Braxton Bragg at Shiloh. *THQ* XXI (1962)
19–30. **2951**

Milligan, Mancil A
Seeing Shiloh 1862 and today, an authentic
history of the battle of Pittsburgh Landing,
together with interesting incidents and stories.
. . . [Indianapolis, Jobbers pub. co., 1940]
[47] p. plates (illus.), double map. 23cm.
　　　　　　　　　　　　　NN **2952**
　"Compiled by Mancil A. Milligan."

National Association Battle of Shiloh Survivors.
Proceedings of the re-union. . . . [Topeka,
1915–1923?] 22cm.　　　　KHi **2953**

Otis, Ephraim Allen
The second day at Shiloh, by Captain
Ephraim A. Otis. *PMHSM* VII (1904) 173–
202. **2954**

Putnam, Douglas
Reminiscences of the battle of Shiloh.
MOLLUS-Ohio III 197–211. **2955**

Reed, David Wilson, 1841–
. . . The battle of Shiloh and the organizations engaged. Compiled from the official
records by Major D. W. Reed, Historian and
Secretary, under the authority of the Commission, 1902. Washington, Govt. print. office,
1903. 122 p. fold. maps. 24cm.　IHi **2956**
　At head of title: Shiloh national military park commission.

——— ——— 1902 (revised 1909). Washington,
Govt. print. office, 1909. 122 p. fold. maps.
24cm.　　　　　　　CSmH **2957**
　A reprinting.

Rice, DeLong, 1872–1929.
The story of Shiloh, by DeLong Rice, Superintendent, Shiloh national military park. [Jack-
son, Tenn., McCowat-Mercer, 1924] 70 p.
map, plates (illus.). 19cm. DLC NN **2958**

Roland, Charles P　　1918–
Albert Sydney Johnston and the Shiloh campaign. *CWH* IV (1958) 355–82. **2959**

Sherman, William Tecumseh, 1820–1891.
The battle of Pittsburgh landing, a letter
from General Sherman. *United States service
magazine* III (1865) 1–4. **2960**

Shiloh, continued

Smith, William Farrar, 1824–1903.
Shiloh. *Magazine of American history* xv
(1885) 292–304, 382–90, 470–82. maps. **2961**

Stanton, B
Letter of Lieut. Gov. Stanton in reply to
Thos. Ewing. Columbus, Printed at the Ohio
State Journal, 1862. 25 p. 21cm.
Dated November 4, 1862.   OMC   **2962**
"The battle of Shiloh — was it a surprise?," by
Chas. Whittlesey, p. 21–5.

Steele, Matthew Forney, 1861–1953.
. . . Shiloh campaign, by Matthew W. Steele.
[Fort Leavenworth] Department of Military
Art, Infantry and Cavalry School, 1907. 29 p.
19½cm.   NN   **2963**
At head of title: Strategy and military geography
and history. Lecture no. IX.
Title and imprint from cover.

Throne, Mildred, 1902–1960.
Comments on the "Hornet's Nest," 1862 and
1887. Compiled by Mildred Throne. *Iowa journal of history* LV (1957) 249–74.   **2964**

—— Iowa and the battle of Shiloh. *Iowa journal of history* LV (1957) 209–48.   **2965**

Ulmer, J   B
A glimpse of Albert Sidney Johnston
through the smoke of Shiloh. *Quarterly of the
Texas state historical association* x (1906/07)
285–96.   **2966**

Victor, Orville James, 1827–1910.
. . . Pittsburgh landing, (Shiloh) and the
investment of Corinth, drawn from original
sources, official reports, etc., with anecdotes,
incidents, etc. New York, Beadle and co.
[c1862] iv, 5–96 p. 16cm.
               CSMH DLC NN   **2967**
At head of title: Beadle's American battles ["dime
series"]
"Introductory" signed: O. J. V.

Wallace, Harold Lew
Lew Wallace's march to Shiloh revisited. *Indiana magazine of history* LIX (1963) 19–30.
map.   **2968**

Wheeler, Joseph, 1836–1906.
The battle of Shiloh, a graphic description
of that sanguinary engagement, written by
General Joseph Wheeler. *SHSP* xxiv (1896)
119–31.   **2969**

Whittlesey, Charles, 1803–1886.
Gen. Wallace's division — battle of Shiloh —
was it tardy? By Col. Charles Whittlesey.
[1874] 8 p. 25cm.   CSmH NN   **2970**
Title from cover.
Text in double columns.

Williams, Thomas Harry, 1909–
Beauregard at Shiloh. *CWH* I (1955) 17–
34.   **2971**

Shiloh Memorials

Campbell, Bernard T
Shiloh national military park. *THQ* xxi
(1962) 3–18. illus.   **2972**

United States. Shiloh National Military Park
Commission.
. . . Annual report. Washington, Govt. print.
office, 1904–19. 16 nos. 23cm.   CSmH **2973**
1897–1918/19 in the Annual reports of the War
department; since 1903/04, also issued separately.

Illinois

Illinois. Shiloh Battlefield Commission.
Illinois at Shiloh. Report of the . . . and ceremonies at the dedication of the monuments
erected to mark the positions of the Illinois
commands engaged in the battle. The story of
the battle by Stanley Waterloo. Compiled by
Major George Mason, Secretary of the Commission. [Chicago, M. A. Donohue & co.,
printers, 1905] 187 p. plates (illus., ports.,
2 fold. maps in pocket) 23½cm.
"Errata" slip inserted.   DLC **2974**

Indiana

Beveridge, Albert Jeremiah, 1862–1927.
Address of Albert J. Beveridge . . . at the
dedication of Indiana's monuments on the battlefield of Shiloh, Tennessee, April 6, 1903.
Indianapolis, Press of Levey Bro's & co. [1903]
15 p. front. (mounted port.). 17cm.
                                CSmH **2975**

Iowa

Iowa. Governor.
In the matter of the controversy between
the Shiloh national military park commission
and the Iowa Shiloh commission relating to
inscriptions upon the regimental monuments of
the 15th and 16th Iowa volunteer infantry. Before the Secretary of war. Proof and argument
presented by Albert B. Cummins, Governor of
Iowa. [n.p., 190–] 59 p. 27½cm.
Title from cover.   CSmH NHi **2976**

Sherman, Ernest A
Dedicating in Dixie, a series of articles descriptive of the tour of the Governor Albert B.
Cummins and staff, the members of the Vicksburg, Andersonville, Chattanooga and Shiloh
monuments commissions . . . 1907.
                                 DLC **2977**

Iowa. Shiloh Battlefield Commission.
Report of the . . . to the Governor of Iowa, December 3, 1895. . . . Des Moines, F. R. Conway, State printer, 1895. 22 p. 22½cm.
CSmH **2978**

Michigan

Michigan. Shiloh Soldiers' Monument Commission.
Michigan at Shiloh, report of the. . . . Lansing, 1920. 27, (4) p. plates (illus., ports.). 22½cm. (Bulletin no. 13 Michigan historical commission). **2979**

Ohio

Ohio. Shiloh Battlefield Commission.
Ohio at Shiloh. Report of the Commission, by T. J. Lindsey, Secretary to the Commission. Washington Court House [Cincinnnati, Printed by C. J. Krehbiel & co.] c1903. iv, 226 p. plates (illus.), map in pocket. 23½cm.
CSmH NN **2980**

Pennsylvania

Pennsylvania. Shiloh Battlefield Commission.
Report. Harrisburg, 1908. plates (illus.). *In* The Seventy-seventh Pennsylvania at Shiloh . . . by John Obreiter, [Harrisburg, Pa., Harrisburg pub. co., State printer], 1908, 11–33.
NN **2981**

Wisconsin

Wisconsin. Shiloh Monument Commission.
Wisconsin at Shiloh, report of the Commission. Compiled by Capt. F. H. Magdeburg. Issued by the Wisconsin Shiloh monument Commission. [Madison, Democrat print. co.] 1909. 257 p. 3 fronts. (illus.), illus., plans, ports., 4 fold. maps. 22½cm.
CSmH NN **2982**

*　　　*　　　*

Alexander, Herbert L
The Armstrong raid including the battles of Bolivar, Medon station and Britton Lane. *THQ* xxi (1962) 31–46. **2983**

Beard, Dan W
With Forrest in West Tennessee. Winter campaign of 1862, filled with adventures and incidents. *SHSP* xxxvii (1909) 304–08. **2984**

Hodge, George Baird, 1828–1902.
Report of Brigadier-General George B. Hodge, C.S.A., of the operations of his command, Sept. 9, 1863. [n.p., 188–] [4] p. 22cm.
CSmH **2985**

Report signed: George B. Hodge, Col. commanding cavalry brigade.
Dated: Muscle Shoals, October 11, 1863.

Williams, John Stuart, 1818–1898.
Report of Brig. Gen. John S. Williams of operations in East Tennessee, from 27th September to 15th October, 1863. Published by order of Congress. Richmond, R. M. Smith, Public printer, 1864. 9 p. 23cm.
Crandall 1415. CSmH DLC **2986**

Schurz, Carl, 1829–1906.
Court of inquiry on Maj.-Genl. Hooker's report of the night engagement of Wauhatchie. Argument of Maj.-Gen. Carl Schurz, delivered February 12, 1864. 22 p. 22½cm.
CSmH **2987**

Bickham, William Denison, 1827–1894.
Rosecran's campaign with the Fourteenth army corps, or the Army of the Cumberland, a narrative of personal observations, with an appendix consisting of official reports of the battle of Stone river, by "W.D.B.," correspondent of the Cincinnati commercial. Cincinnati, Moore, Wilstach, Keys & co., 1863. viii, 9–476 p. front. (map). 19cm.
CSmH SLC NN **2988**
"Preface" signed: Wm. D. Bickham.
"Embraces a period beginning with the 30th day of October, 1862 . . . and concludes with the occupation of Murfreesboro, Tennessee."

Davidson, James F
Michigan and the defense of Knoxville, Tennessee, 1863. *ETHSP* 35 (1963) 21–53. **2989**

Longstreet, James, 1821–1904.
Report of operations of part of the First corps, A.N.V. in East Tennessee, November and December 1863. *SHST* ii (1875) 85–98. **2990**

Duke, Basil Wilson, 1838–1916.
The battle of Hartsville. *SB* i (1882/83) 43–51. **2991**

Speed, Thomas, 1841–1906.
Battle of Bean's station, East Tennessee. *SB* ii (1883/84) 112–18. **2992**

Stone's River
December 31, 1862 – January 3, 1863

Bearss, Edwin Cole, 1923–
Cavalry operations in the battle of Stone's river. *THQ* xix (1960) 25–53, 110–44. **2993**

Crittenden, Thomas Leonidas, –1893.
The Union left at Stone's river. *B&L* iii 632–4. **2994**

Hascall, Milo Smith
Personal recollections and experiences concerning the battle of Stone river, a paper read

Stone's River, continued

by request before the Illinois commandery of the Military order of the loyal legion of the U. S., at Chicago, Ill., Feb. 14, 1889, by Milo S. Hascall. . . . Goshen, Ind., Times pub. co., 1889. 22 p. 22cm.   **2995**
Also published in *MOLLUS-Ill* iv 148–70.

Johnson, Richard Washington, 1827–1897.
The battle of Stone river. *US* xiv (1886) 11–19.   **2996**

Kniffen, Gilbert Crawford, 1832–1917.
Army of the Cumberland and the battle of Stone's river. 1907. 24 p. *MOLLUS-DC* no 68.   **2997**

—— The battle of Stone's river. *B&L* iii 613–32.   **2998**

—— The third day at Stone's river. 1907. 22 p. *MOLLUS-DC* no 69.   **2999**

Otis, Ephraim Allen
The Murfreesboro campaign, by Captain Ephraim A. Otis. *PMHSM* vii (1907) 293–320.   **3000**

Paxton, Alexis Rupert, 1849–
The Stone's river campaign. *In* Report of the ninth annual convention of the National guard association of Illinois, 1891, 37–58. 2 plates (maps).   **3001**
"Errata" slip inserted.

Rosecrans, William Starke, 1819–1898.
. . . Report of the Secretary of war, communicating in answer to a resolution of the senate of the 10th instant, a copy of Major General Rosecran's report of the battle of Murfreesboro', or Stone river, Tennessee. [Washington, 1863] 577 p. 2 fold. maps. 23cm.
Caption title.   NN   **3002**
At head of title: 37th [sic] Congress, special session. Senate. Ex. doc. no. 2.
Dated: February 12, 1863.

Seay, Samuel
A Private at Stone river. *SB ns* i (1885/86) 156–60.   **3003**

Sheridan, Philip Henry, 1831–1888.
Report of operations of the Third division, right wing, 14th army corps, Brig. Gen. P. H. Sheridan, commanding, from December 26, 1862, to January 6, 1863. Including the battle of Stone river. 8 p. 20½cm. CSmH   **3004**
"Headquarters 3d division, right wing, 14th army corps, camp on Stone river, Tennessee, January 9th, 1863."

Thruston, Gates Phillips, 1835–1912.
Personal recollections of the battle in the rear at Stone's river, Tenn., by Brevt Brig.-Gen.

Gates P. Thruston. Nashville, Press of Brandon print. co. [1906] 21 p. plate (map). 23cm.
      NHi   **3005**
Also published in *MOLLUS-Ohio* vi 219–37.

United States. Army.
The Stone river campaign, 1862–'63. Organization of the Fourteenth army corps, Department of the Cumberland, (Major-General William S. Rosecrans, Commanding), Dec. 26, 1862–Jan. 5, 1863. [Washington, 1883] 10 p. 23cm.   CSmH   DLC   **3006**

*   *   *

Kniffen, Gilbert Crawford, 1832–1917.
Manoeuvring Bragg out of Tennessee. *B&L* iii 635–7.   **3007**

Pennington, Edgar Legare
The battle of Sewanee. *THQ* ix (1950) 217–43.   **3008**

Rayner, Juan Timoleon, 1844–
An eye-witness account of Forrest's raid on Memphis. *WTHSP* xii (1958) 134–7.   **3009**

Fink, Harold S
The East Tennessee campaign and the battle of Knoxville in 1863. *ETHSP* xxix (1957) 79–117.   **3010**

Kniffen, Gilbert Crawford, 1832–1917.
The East Tennessee campaign, September, 1863. 1905. 26 p. *MOLLUS-DC* no 57.   **3011**
Also published in *PMHSM* vii (1903) 409–32.

Chattanooga and Missionary Ridge
September – November, 1863

Battles of Chattanooga, fought Nov. 23–25, 1863, by the Armies of the Cumberland and Tennessee, under Generals Grant, Thomas, Sherman, and Hooker. General Bragg commanding the Confederate forces. Chattanooga, Lookout mountain, Missionary ridge and localities made famous by the battles of Chickamauga, Wauhatchie, Graysville, Ringgold, etc. A resume of the situations shown in the panorama of Missionary ridge, and very full extracts official reports and papers from the library of William Wehner's panorama studio, Milwaukee, Wisconsin. Chicago, W. J. Jefferson, 1886. 71, (2) p. 2 fold. maps. 24cm.
      DLC   NN   **3012**
"Roster Army of the Cumberland," (2) p.

Comments on General Grant's "Chattanooga." *B&L* iii 714–718.   **3013**
Part I by William Farrar Smith, 714–17; II by Henry M. Cist, 717–18; III Postscript by General W. F. Smith, 718.

Descriptive catalogue of the Cyclorama: "Storming of Missionary ridge" and "Battle above the clouds." Atlanta, Ga., Paul M. Atkinson, manager. Atlanta, J. A. McCown, printer, 1891. 15, (7) p. illus. on cover. 18½cm.					NN	**3014**

Planned by Henry W. Hill, the cyclorama was opened in 1886. The painting was done in Berlin by the artists Eugene Bracht, Karl Roechling, and George Koch.

Advertising matter included.

Maney's brigade after the battle of Missionary ridge. *SB* II (1883–84) 345–8.					**3015**

Text signed: Private Rock city guards.

Maney's brigade at Missionary ridge. *SB* II (1883/84) 298–305.					**3016**

By a "Private soldier."

Boynton, Henry Van Ness, 1835–1905.
. . . Battles about Chattanooga, Tenn., November 23–25, 1863. Orchard Knob, Lookout mountain, Missionary ridge. Organization of the Union forces (commanded by Maj. Gen. U.S. Grant) and of the Confederate forces (commanded by General Braxton Bragg). Compiled by H. V. Boynton. Washington, Govt. print. office, 1893. 35 p. plate (map). 22½cm.					CSmH	**3017**

At head of title: Chickamauga and Chattanooga national military park.
NN has an 1895 reprinting.

—— Chattanooga and Chickamauga, reprint of Gen. H. V. Boynton's letter to the Cincinnati Commercial gazette, August, 1888. Washington, D.C., Gray & Clarkson, printers, 1888. 59 p. 22cm.					CSmH	NcD	**3018**

"Preface" addressed to the "Comrades of the Society of the Army of the Cumberland" and signed: W. S. Rosecrans.

—— —— Second edition, with corrections. Washington, Geo. R. Gray, printer, 1891. 54 p. 6 plates (maps). 23½cm.					**3018A**

Brock, Irving A
Cleburne and his division at Missionary ridge and Ringgold gap. *SHSP* VIII (1880) 464–75.					**3019**

Butterfield, Daniel, 1831–1901.
Major-General Joseph Hooker and the troops from the Army of the Potomac at Wauhatchie, Lookout mountain and Chattanooga, together with General Hooker's military record . . . address by Major-General Daniel Butterfield at the battlefield dedication ceremonies at Chattanooga, September 18, 1895 . . . New York, Exchange print. co., 1896. 48 p. front. (port.). 23½cm.					CSmH	**3020**

Connor, George C
Battles around Chattanooga. Campaign of 1863. Chattanooga, Commercial print [1881] 20 p. front. (port.), fold. map. 22cm.					CSmH	OMC	**3021**

A guide prepared for the meeting of the Army of the Cumberland, September 21–22, 1881.
Front. signed: Courteously G. C. Connor.

Downey, Fairfax Davis, 1893–
Storming of the gateway, Chattanooga, 1863, by Fairfax Downey. New York, David McKay co. [1960] xiv, 303 p. illus., music, plates (illus., ports.). 22cm.					NN	**3022**

Maps on endpapers.

Fitch, John
Chickamauga, the price of Chattanooga. A description of the strategic plans, marches, and battles of the campaign of Chattanooga, by the author of the "Annals of the Army of the Cumberland." Philadelphia, J. B. Lippincott & co., 1864. p. [451]–82, 703–16. front. (double map). 21½cm.					CSmH	DLC	**3023**

"Issued as an addition to the first editions of the "Annals of the Army of the Cumberland." This text was new material to the first four editions and appears in its proper place in the fifth edition.
"General Rosecran's report of the Chickamauga campaign," 703–16.
On cover: Defence of the Army of the Cumberland. Rosecran's last campaign.

Fullerton, Joseph Scott, 1835–1897.
The Army of the Cumberland at Chattanooga. *B&L* III 719–26.					**3024**

Govan, Gilbert E   and James W. Livingood
Chattanooga under military occupation, 1863–1865. *JSH* XVII (1951) 23–47.					**3025**

Gregg, Joseph Olds
Eight Buckeyes at Missionary ridge. *Ohio magazine* II (1907) 54–8.					**3026**

Hardison, Wallace Everett
Chattanooga and her battlefields. [Chattanooga, W. E. Hardison, 1912] 94 p. illus. 23½ x 31cm.					NN	**3026A**

"Published and for sale by W. E. Hardison, Chattanooga, Tenn."

Hay, Thomas Robson
The battle of Chattanooga. *GHQ* VIII (1924) 121–41.					**3027**

Henry, Robert Selph, 1889–
Chattanooga and the war. *THQ* XIX (1960) 222–30.					**3028**

Howard, Oliver Otis, 1830–1909.
Chattanooga. *Atlantic monthly* XXXVIII (1876) 203–19. maps.					**3029**

Chattanooga and Missionary Ridge, continued

—— Grant at Chattanooga, an address. *MOLLUS-NY* I 244–57.   **3030**

Kniffen, Gilbert Crawford, 1832–1917.
The Army of the Cumberland at Missionary ridge. 1900. 28 p. *MOLLUS-DC* no 37. **3031**

—— Assault and capture of Lookout mountain, "the battle above the clouds". . . . Chattanooga, W. E. Hardison [1898?] 31 p. 17½cm.
Title and imprint from cover.   NN **3032**
Caption title: "The battle above the clouds," by Gilbert Kniffen.

Le Duc, William Gates, 1823–1917.
The little steamboat that opened the "cracker line." *B&L* III 676–8   **3033**

McDonald, William Naylor, 1834–1898.
The battle of Lookout mountain. *SB* II (1883/84) 97–105. map.   **3034**

—— The battle of Missionary ridge. *SB* II (1883/84) 193–201. map.   **3035**

Meigs, Montgomery Cunningham, 1816–1892.
The three days' battle of Chattanooga, 23d, 24th, 25th November, 1864, an unofficial dispatch from General Meigs, Quartermaster General of the United States, to the Hon E. M. Stanton, Secretary of war. Now first correctly printed. Washington, D.C., McGill & Witherow, printers, 1864. 8 p. 22½cm.
                            CSmH NN **3036**
—— —— Presented to the U. S. sanitary commission by Julius Bien and Wm. M. Franklin. New York, 1864. 10 p. fold. map. 21½cm.
                            CSmH   **3036A**
Roper, John S
An interesting account of the battle of Missionary ridge. *Journal of the Illinois state historical society* VI (1914) 496–505.   **3037**

Searcher, Victor
An Arkansas druggist [Pat Cleburne] defeats a famous General. *ArHQ* XIII (1954) 249–56.   **3038**

Severance, Margaret A   E
Descriptive and historical guide to Chattanooga, Lookout mountain and Walden's ridge, by Margaret A. E. Severance. [Chattanooga, Times Book & Job office] 1892. 75 p. illus.
                            CSmH **3038A**
Sheridan, Philip Henry, 1831–1888.
Report of operations of the Second division, Fourth army corps, Army of the Cumberland, Maj. Gen. P. H. Sheridan, commanding, from November 23d, to November 26th, 1863, including the battle of Missionary ridge. 9 p. 20½cm.   CSmH **3039**

"Headquarters 2d division, 4th army corps, Loudon, Tennessee, February 20, 1864."

Smith, William Farrar, 1824–1903.
An historical sketch of the military operations around Chattanooga, Tennessee, September 22 to November 27, 1863. *PMHSM* VIII (1894) 149–271.   **3040**

—— The relief of the Army of the Cumberland, and the opening of the short line of communication between Chattanooga, Tenn., and Bridgeport, Ala., in October, 1863 [by] Wm. Farrar Smith. Wilmington, Del., C. F. Thomas & co., printers, 1891. 60 p. 23cm.
                            CSmH NN **3041**
—— The re-opening of the Tennessee river near Chattanooga, October 1863, as related by Major General George H. Thomas and the official record. Compiled and annotated by Bv't Major Wm. Farrar Smith. Wilmington, Press of Mercantile print. co. [n.d.] 40 p. 2 fold. maps. 21cm.   CSmH NB **3042**

United States. Army.
Organization of the United States forces (commanded by Major-General U. S. Grant) in the Chattanooga-Rossville campaign, November 23–27, 1863, and return of casualties. [Washington, 1887] 28 p. 22½cm.
                            CSmH DLC **3043**
United States. Chickamauga and Chattanooga National Military Park Commission.
The campaign for Chattanooga. The theater of movements, and the battlefields, as seen from the point of Lookout mountain. Washington, Govt. print. office, 1902. 9 p. front. (map). 22½cm.   **3044**
Text signed: H. V. Boynton, Chairman.

United States. Smith (William Farrar), Board of Officers upon the Claim of.
Report of a Board of army officers upon the claim of Maj. Gen. William Farrar Smith, U.S.V., Major, U.S. army (retired), that he, and not General Rosecrans, originated the plan for the relief of Chattanooga in October, 1863. Proceedings, conclusions, and opinions of the Board, approved by Elihu Root, Secretary of War. . . . Washington, Govt. print. office, 1901. 226 p. plates (1 illus., 3 fold. maps). 22½cm.   NN **3045**

—— Brown's ferry [October 27] 1863. Part I, report of a Board of army officers; Part II. Review of the report, by Maj. Gen. William Farrar Smith. [Philadelphia, F. McManus, Jr. & co., printers] 19, 38, (1) p. fold. map.
Title from cover.   NB **3046**
In completing this set of an unofficial printing, Part III (Accompanying papers) and the Index of the official printing were used.
"Errata to Part II, (1) p.

Watkins, Samuel R   and J. S. Jackman
Battle of Missionary ridge. *SB* II (1883–84)
49–58.   **3047**

Wood, Thomas John, 1823–1906.
The battle of Missionary ridge. *MOLLUS-Ohio* IV 23–51.   **3048**

Chattanooga Memorials
Alabama

Oates, William Calvin, 1835–1910.
Speech of Governor William C. Oates of Alabama, delivered at Chattanooga, Tenn, September 20th, 1895, on the battles of Chickamauga and Chattanooga. Dedication of the National park. . . . Montgomery, Roemer print. co., 1895. 18 p. 24cm.   DLC NN   **3049**
Title and imprint from cover.
"Errata" on cover.

Illinois

Boynton, Henry Van Ness, 1835–1905.
Remarks of Gen. H. V. Boynton, Chairman of the Chickamauga and Chattanooga national park commission, at Orchard knob, Chattanooga, Nov. 23, 1899, on the occasion of the dedication of the Illinois state monuments. [4] p. 21½cm.   CSmH   **3050**
Caption title.

Iowa

Sherman, Ernest A
Dedicating in Dixie, a series of articles descriptive of the tour of Governor Albert B. Cummins and staff, the members of the Vicksburg, Andersonville, Chattanooga and Shiloh monument commissions . . . 1907.
DLC   **3051**

New York

New York.
Instructions of the New York Board of commissioners for monuments at the battlefields of Chattanooga, comprising Wauhatchie, Lookout mountain, Missionary ridge and Ringgold. Also Chapter 371, Laws of 1894, with Report of the Commissioners to the Legislature of the State of New York, and information for the survivors of organizations interested. . . . [New York, Press of Thomas F. Eagan and Son, 1894] 33 p. 25½cm.   CSmH   **3052**

—— Report on the New York monuments at Chattanooga, and proceedings of dedication of the central historical memorial or peace monument on Lookout monument. Albany, J. B. Lyon co., printers, 1928. ix, 194 p. plates (illus., plans, ports.). 28cm.   NN   **3053**

Pennsylvania

Blakely, Archibald
Address delivered by Col. Archibald Blakely, President of the Pennsylvania commission and Chairman of the Chickamauga and Chattanooga battlefields committee, November 15, 1897, at Orchard Knob, Chattanooga, Tenn., on the occasion of the presentation of the Pennsylvania battlefields monuments to Daniel H. Hastings, Governor of the Commonwealth of Pennsylvania. [4] p. 24½ x 13cm.   CSmH   **3054**
Caption title.

Knoxville
November 4 – December 23, 1863

Alexander, Edward Porter, 1835–1910.
Longstreet at Knoxville. *B&L* III 745–51.
3055

Kniffen, Gilbert Crawford, 1832–1917.
Raising the siege of Knoxville. 1906. 20 p. *MOLLUS-DC* no 65.   **3056**

Poe, Orlando Metcalf, 1832–1895.
The defense of Knoxville. *B&L* III 731–45.
3057

—— Personal recollections of the occupation of East Tennessee and the defense of Knoxville, a paper read before the Michigan commandery of the Military order of the loyal legion of the United States, December 5th, 1888, by Orlando M. Poe. Detroit, Ostler print. co., 1889. 43 p. plate (map). 21½cm.
NHi   **3058**
Also published in *MOLLUS-Mich* I 8.

Fort Pillow
April 12, 1864

Castel, Albert
The Fort Pillow massacre, a fresh examination of the evidence. *CWH* IV (1958) 37–50.
3059

Jordan, John L
Was there a massacre at Fort Pillow? *THQ* VI (1947) 99–133.   **3060**

United States. Conduct of the War, Joint Committee on the.
[Reports in relation to the late massacre at Fort Pillow and on the condition of returned prisoners. Washington, 1864] 128, 34 p. 4 plates (8 ports.). 22cm.   CSmH NN   **3061**
Published as House of representatives Reports, 38th Congress, 1st session: Fort Pillow no. 65; Returned prisoners, no. 67.
Also published from the same plates as Senate committee reports, 38th Congress, 1st session: Fort Pillow, no. 63; Returned prisoners, no. 68.
Cover titles:

Fort Pillow, continued

Senate printing, Reports of the Committee on the conduct of the war. Fort Pillow massacre.
House printing, Returned prisoners.

*   *   *

Stanley, David Sloan, 1828–1902.
The Tullahoma campaign, by David S. Stanley, Brigadier-General. *MOLLUS-Ohio* III 166–81.   *3062*

Holmes, Jack D   L
Forrest's 1864 raid on Memphis. *THQ* XVIII (1959) 295–321.   *3063*

Morton, John Watson
Battle of Johnsonville, by Captain John W. Watson. *SHSP* x (1882) 471–88.   *3064*

—— Raid of Forrest's cavalry on the Tennessee river in 1864. *SHSP* x (1882) 261–8. *3065*

Smith, Henry King, 1910–
Some encounters with General Forrest, compiled and written, by H. K. Smith, Jr. [McKenzie?, Tenn., 1959?] 10 p. 1 illus. 22½cm.
                                      IHi   *3066*
"Deals chiefly with the account of the Johnsonville battle of 1864, with some treatment of the battles of Lexington and Parkers Cross Roads, the skirmish at Beech creek."

Hood's Tennessee Campaign

Hay, Thomas Robson
Hood's Tennessee campaign, by Thomas Robson Hay. . . . New York, Walter Neale, 1929. xv, 17–272 p. plates (maps, 2 fold.) 23cm.   NN   *3067*

Hood, John Bell, 1831–1879.
The invasion of Tennessee. *B&L* IV 425–37.
                                              3068

Sanders, D   W
Hood's Tennessee campaign. *SB* II (1884/85) 97–104, 145–53, 193–203, 241–52, 289–94, 350–66; ns I (1885/86) 6–13, 110–15, 168–76, 244–51. ports., plate (map). *3069*

Stone, Henry,   –1896.
Repelling Hood's invasion of Tennessee. *B&L* IV 440–64.   *3070*

Wilson, James Harrison, 1837–1925.
The Union cavalry in the Hood campaign. *B&L* IV 465–71.   *3071*

Watkins, Samuel R   1839–1901.
Reminiscences of Hood's Tennessee campaign. *SB* II (1883/84) 399–402.   *3072*

*   *   *

Hay, Thomas Robson
The cavalry at Spring hill. *THM* VIII (1924/25) 7–23.   *3073*

Franklin
November 30, 1864

Burr, Frank A   1843–1894.
The battle of Franklin. [Philadelphia, 1883] 30 p. 18cm.   CSmH   *3074*
"From the Philadelphia press of March 11th, 1883."
The preface announces the proposed publication of a large work with the same title.
A form for subscription, p. 5.

Cox, Jacob Dolson, 1828–1900.
The battle of Franklin, Tennessee, November 30, 1864, a monograph, by Jacob D. Cox. New York, Charles Scribner's Sons, 1897. x, (2), 351 p. 4 plates (maps, 2 fold.). 21cm.
                              CSmH NN   *3075*

Crownover, Sims
The battle of Franklin. *THQ* XIV (1955) 291–322. plates (plans, 1 fold.; 2 ports.). *3076*

Field, Henry Martyn, 1822–1907.
The battle of Franklin. *In his* Bright skies and dark shadows, 1890, 209–56.   *3077*

Kendall, Henry Myron
The battles of Franklin and Nashville, prepared by Major Henry M. Kendall. 1902. 22 p. *MOLLUS-DC* no 42.   *3078*

Lee, Stephen Dill, 1833–1908.
Johnson's division in the battle of Franklin. *PMHS* VII (1903) 75–83.   *3079*

Morgan, Marshall
The battle of Franklin, by Marshall Morgan. [Franklin, Press of the News] c1931. [20] p. port. 22½cm.   NcD   *3080*
Advertising matter included.

Stanley, David Sloan, 1828–1902.
. . . General Stanley's sharp retort. A rattling reply to an insinuation by General Jacob D. Cox. [1889] 6 p. 19cm.   CSmH   *3081*
At head of title: New York Sun, September 22, 1889.
Caption title.
Text signed: D. S. Stanley, Brigadier-General, U.S.A., San Antonio, Texas, September 10, 1889.

Stewart, Alexander Peter, 1821–1908.
General Stewart's report [dated April 3, 1865, operations of his corps on the 29th of November, 1864] *SB* I (1882/83) 199–201.
                                              3082
Includes a letter by J. B. Hood denying any intention of reflection on Stewart's conduct.

Stone, Henry,   –1896.
The battle of Franklin, Tennessee, November 30, 1864. *PMHSM* VII (1883) 433–77.
                                              3083

Nashville
December 1-16, 1864

Ayres, Stephen Cooper, 1840–1921.
The battle of Nashville, with personal recollections of a field hospital. *MOLLUS-Ohio* v 284–300. **3084**

Brooke, John Rutter, 1838–1926.
The battle of Nashville, by Major General John R. Brooke. *MOLLUS-Nebr* i 141–4. **3085**

De Peyster, John Watts, 1821–1907.
Nashville, the decisive battle of the rebellion [address delivered before the annual meeting of the New York historical society, January 4, 1876] 14 p. 21½cm. CSmH NN **3086**
Caption title.
Text in double columns.

Horn, Stanley Fitzgerald, 1889–
The decisive battle of Nashville, by Stanley F. Horn. Baton Rouge, Louisiana State University press [1956] xii, (2), 181 p. plates (illus., maps, ports.). 21cm. NN **3087**

Johnson, Richard Washington, 1827–1897.
The battle of Nashville, General George H. Thomas. *US* ii (1880) 23–6. **3088**

Lynne, Donald M
Wilson's cavalry at Nashville. *CWH* i (1955) 141–59. maps. **3089**

Otis, Ephraim Allen
The Nashville campaign, paper read by Ephraim Otis, before the Commandery of the State of Illinois, Military order of the loyal legion, February 14, 1895. . . . Chicago, Dial press, 1899. p. [267]–88. 22½cm.
CSmH **3090**
"Reprinted from volume iii. Military essays and recollections."

Rusling, James Fowler, 1834–1918.
The victory at Nashville. *United States service magazine* iii (1865) 113–23. **3091**

Schofield, John McAllister, 1831–1906.
[Letter to General Henry M. Cist, Corresponding secretary, Society of the Army of the Cumberland, dated Sept. 15, 1880, on the Nashville campaign. West Point, 1880] 8 folios. 25cm. CSmH **3092**
Preceded by leaf with text on verso, "This letter having been evidently mislaid and not received until after the meeting at Toledo, cannot be presented to the Society as published until the next meeting. A few copies are therefore distributed privately."

Stone, Henry, –1896.
The battle of Nashville, Tennessee, December 15 and 16, 1864. *PMHSM* vii (1884) 479–542. **3093**

United States. Adjutant General.
[An abstract from the returns of troops under the command of Major General George H. Thomas, on November 20 and 30 and December 10, 1864. Washington, 1882] 6 p. 23½cm. CSmH **3094**

United States. Army.
Battle of Nashville, Tenn. Organization of United States forces (commanded by Major-General George H. Thomas), December 15–16, 1864. [Washington, D.C., 189–] 9 p. 22½cm. CSmH **3095**

Nashville Memorials

Minnesota.
Report of the Minnesota commission appointed to erect a monument in the Nashville National cemetery at Madison, Tenn. [1921] 32 p. 3 plates (2 illus., port.). 24cm. MnHi **3096**
Roster of burials by regiments included.

United States. Military Affairs Committee (House, 70:1).
National military park at Fort Negley on the battlefield of Nashville, Tenn. Hearings before the Committee on military affairs, Seventieth Congress, first session on H.R. 10291. Statement of Mrs. E. Gillentine [and] Joseph W. Byrns, February 2, 1928. Washington, Govt. print. office, 1928. 7 p. 22½cm. NN **3097**
Title from cover.

INDIANA AND OHIO

The Hines raid, invasion of the State, June, 1863. *Indiana history bulletin* xxxvi (1959) 53–6. **3098**

Morgan's Raid
July 2-26, 1863

The great Indiana-Ohio raid by Brig.-Gen. John Hunt Morgan and his men, July 1863. An authentic account of the most spectacular Confederate raid into Union territory during the War between the States . . . The capture and subsequent escape of Brig.-Gen. Morgan, as seen and told by Brig.-Gen. Basil W. Duke, Brig.-Gen. Orlando B. Willcox and Captain Thomas H. Hines . . . With an introduction and commentary by Don D. John. Louisville, Book Nook press [1955] 32 p. illus., 2 maps, port. 24½cm. NN **3099**
"A romance of Morgan's rough riders [p. 9–31] is an exact reproduction as it appeared in the Century magazine, January, 1891."
On cover illus. in color: Morgan's great Indiana-Ohio raid, July 1863.

Morgan's Raid, continued

Humors of the Morgan raid into Indiana and Ohio. *LWL* II (1866/67) 405–07, III (1867) 36–7, 233–6; IV (1867/68) 535–8.   **3100**

The John Morgan raid in Ohio. *Magazine of history* XI (1910) 209–19.   **3101**
"Written by a veteran of the Civil war . . . and was printed in the Lima (O.) Times democrat."

Operations of the Indiana legion and minute men, 1863–64. Documents presented to the General assembly, with the Governor's message, January 6, 1865. Indianapolis, W. R. Holloway, State printer, 1865. iv, 104 p. 22½cm.   DLC NHi   **3102**

A romance of Morgan's rough riders. *Century magazine* XLI (1891) 403–25.   **3103**
Contents: Part I The raid, by Basil W. Duke, 403–12; II The capture, by Orlando B. Willcox, 412–17; III The escape, by Thomas H. Hines, 417–25.

The truth of the raid of the Confederate General John Morgan and command through portions of the States of Kentucky, Indiana and Ohio, during the War of the rebellion. By a United States army officer who was present and assisted in the capture. 1894. [21] p. 23cm.   OMC   **3104**
Title and imprint date from cover.

Benedict, James Bell
General John Hunt Morgan, the great Indiana-Ohio raid. *FCHQ* XXXI (1957) 147–71.   **3105**

Blair, John L
Morgan's Ohio raid. *FCHQ* XXXVI (1962) 242–71.   **3106**

Boyer, Margarette
Morgan's raid in Indiana. *Indiana magazine of history* VIII (1912) 149–65.   **3107**

Butler, Lorine Letcher
Morgan and his men, by Lorine Letcher Butler. Philadelphia, Dorrance & co. [1960] 357 p. plates (illus., ports.). 24cm.   NN   **3108**

Cone, Mary
Morgan's raid. *Magazine of Western history* IV (1886) 748–66.   **3110**

Duke, Basil Wilson, 1838–1916.
Morgan's Indiana and Ohio raid. *AW* 241–56.   **3111**

Enn, C   C [pseud.]
The bloody first; or, twelve days with the 1st Pickaway throwing "paw paws" at John Morgan, by C. C. Enn. Circleville, Printed at the office of the Circleville Democrat, 1863. 16 p. 17cm.   OHi   **3112**

"The author identifies himself as "Third Sergeant of Co. E, 1st Pickaway regiment" who was C. C. Neibling.

Ewbank, Louis Blasdel, 1864–
Morgan's raid in Indiana. *Indiana historical society publications* VII (1923) 133–83.   **3113**

Ford, Mark, editor
The Brandenburg story, with particular reference to John Hunt Morgan's crossing of the Ohio, July 8, 1863. Prepared for the centennial celebration being held in Brandenburg, July 13, 1963, by the Methodist Men's Club, Brandenburg, Kentucky. Centennial booklet committee: Mark Ford, editor . . . [3 names] 30, (1) p. illus., 2 maps, port. 23cm.   NN   **3114**

Gard, Ronald Max, 1913–
The end of the Morgan raid, by R. Max Gard. Foreword and conclusion plus photographs, by Foster B. Shattuck. . . . [Lisbon, Ohio, Printed by the Buckeye pub. co., 1963] 22 p. illus., double map. 21½cm.   **3115**

——— Morgan's raid into Ohio, by R. Max Gard. Lisbon, Ohio, Author, 1963. xvii, 62 p. plates (illus., map, 2 ports.). 23½cm.   NN   **3116**

Hinkle, Thornton Mills, 1840–1920.
My war experience. *Yale literary magazine* XXVIII (1862/63) 4–11.   **3117**

Jordan, Lewis
Report of Colonel Lewis Jordan commanding 6th regiment Indiana legion. *Indiana history bulletin* XXXVIII (1961) 115–17.   **3118**

Keller, Allan
Morgan's raid, by Allan Keller. Indianapolis, Bobbs-Merrill co. [1961] 272 p. plates (2 illus., map, ports.). 23½cm.   NN   **3119**

King, Charles P
The important part the squirrel hunters played in the War of the rebellion in Ohio, delivered at the first reunion of the Squirrel hunters of Ohio at Buckeye lake, Newark, Ohio, on Wednesday, September 12, 1906, by Chas. P. King. [4] p. 24cm.   OHi   **3120**
Title from cover.

Quisenberry, Anderson Chenault, 1850–1921.
Morgan's men in Ohio. *SHSP* XXXIX (1914) 91–9.   **3121**

Read, Thomas Buchanan, 1822–1872.
The siege of Cincinnati. *Atlantic monthly* XI (1863) 229–34.   **3122**

Reid, Samuel Chester, 1818–1897.
A full account of the capture and wonderful escape of Gen. John H. Morgan with Captain

T. Henry; thrilling and interesting incidents; by 290. Atlanta, Intelligencer presses, 1864. 16 p. 22cm.   GEU   *3123*
    Crandall 2659.

—— The capture and wonderful escape of General John H. Morgan, as reported by Samuel C. Reid, Jr., of the Atlanta intelligencer. Edited by Joseph J. Matthews. Atlanta, The Library Emory University, 1947. 20 p. 21½cm.   DLC NN   *3124*
    Half-title: Emory University publications sources & reprints series IV [no. 2].

Senour, Faunt le Roy, 1824–1910.
    Morgan and his captors, by Rev. F. Senour. Cincinnati, C. F. Vent & co., 1865. x, 11–389 p. front. (port.). 19½cm.
                              CSmH DLC NN   *3125*
Simmons, Flora E
    A complete account of the John Morgan raid through Kentucky, Indiana and Ohio, in July, 1863. [Louisville] Flora E. Simmons, 1863. 94 p. 15½cm.   OMC MB   *3126*
    "Introductory" signed: Flora E. Simmons "offers this singular book for your perusal" and mentions the author's support of her aged mother "by selling various articles on the cars."
    "To the public" is a testimonial for the author signed by officials representing four railroads.

—— —— [Louisville] Flora E. Simmons, 1863. 108 p. 13½cm. CSmH DLC   *3127*
    The type has been reset without change in the text.

Simms, Jeremiah H
    Morgan's raid and capture, the story from its inception to the last night and last camp at Bergholz, formerly "Old Nebo," chronicled by J. H. Simms, of East Liverpool Morning tribune. [East Liverpool, Ohio, c1913] 40 p. illus., ports. 39cm.   NN   *3128*
    Caption title.
    Text in triple columns.

Stern, Joseph S
    The siege of Cincinnati. *Bulletin of the historical and philosophical society of Ohio* XVIII (1960) 163–86. illus.   *3129*

Still, John S
    Blitzkrieg, 1863, Morgan's raid and rout. *CWH* III (1957) 291–306.   *3130*

*   *   *

Carrington, Henry Beebe, 1824–1912.
    Military movements in Indiana in 1864, designed to supplement the military history of Indiana and correct several errors in relation to the raids of Forrest, Morgan and Johnson in 1864, by reference to omitted official documents, orders, telegrams, etc., of that period.

By Henry B. Carrington. [Boston, For sale by De Wolfe, Fiske & co., 189–] 12 p. 19½cm.
                              InHi   *3130A*
    The text has references to the War of the rebellion records XXXIX which was published in 1892.
    "Military zones of the Civil war, by H. B. Carrington," double map, laid in.

Trans-Mississippi

GENERAL REFERENCES

Confederate victories in the Southwest. Prelude to defeat. From the official records. Edited by the publishers. Albuquerque, Horn & Wallace, 1961. 201, (1) p. front. (plan), 4 plans. 23½cm.   NN   *3131*
    "Produced verbatim [direct facsimile process] from: The War of the rebellion, a compilation of the official records of the Union and Confederate armies."
    Colophon, (1) p.

Bearss, Edwin Cole, 1923–
    From Rolla to Fayetteville with General Curtis. *ArHQ* XIX (1960) 225–59. 2 maps.
                                          3132
Bundy, Jonas Mills, 1835–1891.
    The last chapter in the history of the war. *Galaxy* VIII (1869) 113–21.   *3133*

Castel, Albert Edward, 1928–
    Order no. 11 and the Civil war on the border. *MHR* LVII (1962/63) 357–68. 1 illus., 2 ports.   *3134*

Colton, Ray Charles, 1907–
    The Civil war in the Western territories, Arizona, Colorado, New Mexico and Utah, by Ray C. Colton. Norman, University of Oklahoma press [1959] ix, 230 p. maps and plans, plates (facsims., illus., ports.). 23½cm.
                              DLC NN   *3135*
Curtis, Samuel Prentis
    The army of the South-west and the first campaign in Arkansas, by Sam'l Prentis Curtis, late Lieutenant and Aide-de-camp to Major-General Curtis. *Annals of Iowa* IV/V (1866/67) 625–45, 721–37, 769–85, 817–83, 865–76, 917–33; VI (1868) 1–12, 69–84, 141–60, 249–70; VII (1869) 1–20, 113–32, 209–25, 305–16. plates (ports.).   *3136*

Dodge, Grenville Mellen, 1831–1916.
    The Indian campaign of Winter of 1864–65. Written in 1877 by Major General Grenville M. Dodge and read to Colorado commandery of the Loyal legion of the United States at Denver, April 21, 1907. 20, (1) p. 23cm.
                              IaCb   *3137*
Hartje, Robert G
    A Confederate dilemma across the Mississippi. *ArHQ* XVII (1958) 119–31.   *3138*

Hindman, Thomas Carmichael, 1828–1868.
Report of Major General Hindman of his
operations in the Trans-Mississippi district. . . .
Richmond, R. M. Smith, public printer, 1864.
26 p. 23cm.   CSmH DLC   *3139*
    Dated: Richmond, Va., June 19, 1863; a supple-
mental report, June 29, 1863.
    Crandall 1422.

Hunt, Aurora
The Army of the Pacific, its operations in
California, Texas, Arizona, New Mexico, Utah,
Nevada, Oregon, Washington, Plains region,
Mexico, etc., 1860–1866, by Aurora Hunt.
Glendale, Arthur H. Clarke co., 1951. 455 p.
plates (illus., fold. map, ports.). 25cm.
                                      NN   *3140*
Jones, Robert Huhn
The Civil war in the Northwest, Nebraska,
Wisconsin, Iowa, Minnesota and the Dakotas
[by] Robert Huhn Jones. Norman, University
of Oklahoma press [1960] xvi, 216 p. maps,
plates (illus., ports.). 23½cm. NHi   *3141*

Lewis, Oscar, 1893–
The war in the Far West, 1861–1865 [by]
Oscar Lewis. Garden City, Doubleday & co.,
1961. 263 p. 22cm.   NN   *3142*

Marmaduke, John Sappington, 1833–1887.
General Marmaduke's campaign against
Maj.-Gen. Steele. *SM* x (1872) 445–52. *3143*

Monaghan, James, 1891–
Civil war on the Western border, 1854–
1865, by Jay Monaghan. Boston, Little, Brown
and co. [1955] x, 454 p. 22cm. NN   *3144*

Rea, Ralph R
Sterling Price, the Lee of the West, by Ralph
R. Rea. Little Rock, Pioneer press [1959] xii,
229 p. plans, plates (illus., 2 plans., ports.).
23½cm.   NN   *3145*
    "Price's route to and from the Missouri invasion of
September, October, November, 1864," 2 maps on
endpaper.
    Orders of battle, 214–20.

Scheiber, Harry N
The pay of troops and Confederate morale
in the Trans – Mississippi West. *ArHQ* xviii
(1959) 350–65.   *3146*

Stuart, Edwin Roy
. . . The Federal cavalry with the armies in
the West, 1861–1865. *JUSCA* xvii (1906)
195–259.   *3147*
    At head of title: Prize essay, 1905.

ARIZONA TERRITORY

Donnell, F   S
The Confederate territory of Arizona, as
compiled from official sources. *NMHR* xvii
(1942) 148–63.   *3148*

Hunsaker, William J
Lansford W. Hastings' project for the invasion and conquest of Arizona and New
Mexico for the Southern Confederacy. *Ari HR*
iv 2 (1931/32) 5–12. plate (port.).   *3149*

Hall, Martin Hardwick
The skirmish of Picacho. *CWH* iv (1958)
27–36.   *3150*

ARKANSAS
General References

Jones, Allan W   and Virginia Ann Buttry
Military events in Arkansas during the Civil
war, 1861–1865. *ArHQ* xxii (1963) 124–70.
                                      3151
Smith, Jodie Arnold
Battle grounds and soldiers of Arkansas,
1861–65. *ArHQ* vi (1947) 180–6.   *3152*

Wright, Marcus Joseph, 1831–1922.
Arkansas in the war, 1861–1865. Batesville,
Ark., Independence county historical society
[1963]. 104 p. ports, facsim. 23cm.
                                      NN   *3153*
    Includes a list of battles, campaigns and skirmishes.

Pea Ridge
March 6–8, 1862

Battlefield of Pea ridge, Arkansas, the clamor-
ous struggle behind the battle of Pea ridge.
[Garfield, Ark., Battlefield Museum, 194–]
16 p. map. 19½cm.   MoHi   *3154*
    Title from cover.

The opposing forces at Pea ridge, Ark., March
7th and 8th, 1862. The composition and losses
as here stated give the gist of all the data available in the Official records. [Rogers, Ark., Pea
Ridge National Park Association, 1926] broadside, 32 x 21½cm.   *3155*
    Printed in connection with a reunion of the armies
of the frontier, October 26, 1926.

Baxter, William, 1820–1880.
Pea ridge and Prairie Grove; or, scenes and
incidents of the war in Arkansas, by William
Baxter. Cincinnati, Poe & Hitchcock, 1864.
262 p. 18cm.   NHi   *3156*

—— —— Cincinnati, Hitchcock & Walden
[c1864] 262 p. 15½cm.   NHi   *3157*

—— Pea Ridge and Prairie Grove, by William Baxter. Reprint of the original volume published in 1864. Introduction by Hugh Park. Van Buren, Ark., Press-Argus, 1957. xv, 262 p. port. 16½cm. (Arkansas historical series, no. 5). NN **3158**

Bearss, Edwin Cole, 1923–
The battle of Pea ridge. *Annals of Iowa s* 3 xxxvi (1961–63) 569–89. **3159**

—— —— *ArHQ* xx (1961) 74–94. map. **3160**

—— The first day at Pea ridge, March 7, 1862. *ArHQ* xvii (1958) 132–54. **3161**

Benton County Historical Society.
100th anniversary battle of Pea ridge. 75 p. facsim., plates (illus., ports.). 28cm. mimeo. *Benton county pioneer* vii 3 (March 1962).
Page 75 printed on p. [3] of cover. **3162**
Includes rosters.

Bond, John W
The history of Elkhorn tavern. *ArHQ* xxi (1962) 3–15. plate (2 illus.). **3163**

Brown, Walter L
Pea ridge, Gettysburg of the West. *ArHQ* xv (1956) 3–16. fold. map. **3164**

Clifford, Roy A
The Indian regiments in the battle of Pea ridge. *CO* xxv (1947) 314–22. plan. **3165**

Ford, Harvey S
Van Dorn and the Pea ridge campaign. *Journal of the American military institute* iii (1939) 222–36. **3165A**

Maury, Dabney Herndon, 1822–1900.
Recollections of the Elkhorn campaign. *SHSP* ii (1876) 180–92. **3166**

Moody, Claire Norris
Battle of Pea ridge or Elkhorn tavern, by Claire N. Moody. Little Rock, Arkansas Valley print. co., c1956. vii, 40 p. illus., map, ports. 21cm. NN **3167**
"Letter to Washington Telegraph, published Apr. 2, 1862, at Washington, Arkansas," 22–7, signed: R. K. G. [Rufus K. Garland].

Sigel, Franz, 1824–1902.
The Pea ridge campaign. *B&L* i 314–34. **3168**

Stewart, Faye L
Battle of Pea ridge. *MHR* xxii (1927/28) 187–92. **3169**

Pea Ridge Memorials

Memorial services at Pea ridge, March 11, 1962. *ArHQ* xxi (1962) 158–65. plates (illus., ports.). **3170**

Willett, John T
Development of Pea ridge national military park. *ArHQ* xxi (1962) 166–9. **3171**

*   *   *

Vaught, Elsa
The battle of Maysville, Oct. 22, 1862. *Benton county pioneer* v 3 (March 1960) 14–19. **3172**
Includes an account of the battle by T. F. Potts, Confederate soldier, and the Official report of Brig.-Gen. J. J. Blunt.

Oates, Stephen Berry, 1936–
Cavalry fight at Cane hill [Nov. 28, 1862] *ArHQ* xx (1961) 65–73. **3173**

Prairie Grove
December 7, 1862

. . . Army of the frontier commemorating the fiftieth anniversary of the battle of Prairie Grove, Ark., at Milwaukee, December 7th, 1912. 24 p. fold. plate (illus.). 21½cm.
At head of title: 1862   1912. NN **3174**

Abercrombie, Irene
The battle of Prairie Grove. *ArHQ* ii (1943) 309–15. **3175**

Jones, Samuel, 1819–1887.
The battle of Prairie Grove, December 7, 1862. *SB* ns i (1885/86) 203–11. **3176**

Logan, Robert R
Addresses at dedication of Prairie Grove battlefield monument, December 7, 1956. Compiled by Robert R. Logan. *ArHQ* xvi (1957) 257–80. fold. plate (2 illus., map.). **3177**

Oates, Stephen Berry, 1936–
The Prairie Grove campaign, 1862. *ArHQ* xix (1960) 119–41. plate (2 plans). **3178**

Snead, Thomas Lowndes, 1817–1897.
The conquest of Arkansas. *B&L* iii 441–59. **3179**
Prairie Grove, Arkansas Post, Helena and Little Rock.

*   *   *

Bearss, Edwin Cole, 1923–
The battle of the Post of Arkansas [Jan. 10–11, 1863]. *ArHQ* xviii (1959) 237–79. **3180**

Scroggs, Jack B   and Donald E. Reynolds
Arkansas and the Vicksburg campaign. *CWH* v (1959) 390–401. **3181**

Wright, V   C
The battle of Chalk Bluff which occurred during the Civil war, May 1 and 2, 1863. Battle

Arkansas, miscellaneous, continued

location four miles northwest of St. Francis,
Arkansas, and four miles southwest of Campbell, Missouri. Other early historical events
about northeast Arkansas and southeast Missouri. Co-authors: V. C. Wright & Laud Payne.
Piggott, Ark., 1953. 17 p. 1 illus., ports., 2
plates (illus.). 22cm.   NcD   *3182*
Title and imprint from cover.
Text in double columns.

Bearss, Edwin Cole, 1923–
    The battle of Helena, July 4, 1863. *ArHQ*
xx (1961) 256–97.   *3183*

Huff, Leo E
    The Union expedition against Little Rock,
August – September, 1863. *ArHQ* xxii (1963)
224–37. 3 plates (2 maps, 4 ports.).   *3184*

Bearss, Edwin Cole, 1923–
    Steele's retreat from Camden and the battle
of Jenkins' ferry, by Edwin C. Bearss. With
an introduction by Lou Oberste. [Little Rock,
1967] xiv, 190 p. maps, ports. 24cm.   *3184A*
"Published by Arkansas Civil war centennial commission and Pioneer press, Little Rock, by arrangement
with the Grant county chamber of commerce, Sheridan, Arkansas."

McLeod, Edward S
    The Frontier division in the Camden expe-
dition. [Cincinnati, 1912] 24 p. 23cm.
                          CSmH   TxU   *3185*
Author's name signed to introductory note on p. [2]
of cover.
Text of General orders no. 33, Department of
Arkansas, May 9, 1864, p. [3] of cover.

Atkinson, J   H
    The action at Prairie de Ann. *ArHQ* xix
(1960) 40–50. 2 plates (plans.)   *3186*

Richards, Ira Don
    The battle of Poison Spring. *ArHQ* xviii
(1959) 338–49. 2 plates (maps).   *3187*

——— The engagement at Marks' Mills. *ArHQ*
xix (1960) 51–60. plate (plan).   *3188*

McDonald, Harold L
    The battle of Jenkins' ferry. *ArHQ* vii
(1948) 57–67.   *3189*

Richards, Ira Don
    The battle of Jenkins' ferry. *ArHQ* xx
(1961) 3–16. plan.   *3190*

Lisenbee, Payne
    Trapped. *B&G* i (1893) 183–6.   *3191*
Skirmish at Canehill, November 6, 1864.

CALIFORNIA

Clendenen, Clarence C
    The expedition that never sailed. *CHSQ*
xxxiv (1955) 149–56.   *3192*

Gilbert, Benjamin Franklin
    California and the Civil war, a bibliographi-
cal essay. *CHSQ* xl (1961) 289–307. 3 plates
(facsim., illus., 2 ports.).   *3193*

Grant, Ulysses Simpson, 1822–1885.
    A threatened invasion of California. Letter
[January 8, 1865] addressed to Major General
McDowell by General U. S. Grant. *CHSQ* xiii
(1934) 38–42.   *3194*

Kennedy, Elijah Robinson, 1844–1926.
    The contest for California in 1861. How
Colonel E. D. Baker saved the Pacific states
to the Union, by Elijah R. Kennedy. Boston,
Houghton Mifflin co., 1912. xiv, (1) 361 p.
plates (ports.). 21½cm.   CSmH   *3195*

Kibby, Leo P.
    California soldiers in the Civil war *CHSQ*
xl (1961) 343–50.   *3196*

——— Some aspects of California's military
problems. *CWH* v (1959) 251–62.   *3197*

Moore, Avery C
    Confederate California?, by Avery C. Moore.
Sonora, Cal., Mother Lode press [1956] 29 p.
port. 22½cm.   TxU   *3198*

Virden, William
    The affair at Minter's ranch [November 29,
1861] *San Diego historical society quarterly*
vii (1961) 23–5. 1 illus.   *3199*

Watford, Wilbur H, 1914–
    The Far-Western wing of the rebellion,
1860–1865. *CHSQ* xxxiv (1955) 125–48.
                                         3200

COLORADO TERRITORY

Smith, Duane Allan
    The Confederate cause in the Colorado terri-
tory, 1861–1865. *CWH* vii (1961) 71–80.
                                         3201

INDIAN TERRITORY

Debo, Angie
    The site of the battle of Round mountain,
1861. *CO* xxvii (1949) 187–206. plate (illus).
                                         3202

Freeman, Charles R
    The battle of Honey springs. *CO* xiii (1935)
154–68.   *3203*

Hancock, Marvin J
The second battle of Cabin creek [September 19] 1864. *CO* xxxix (1961) 414–26. *3204*

Russell, Orpha
Ekvn-hv'lwuce, site of Oklahoma's first Civil war battle. *CO* xxix (1951) 401–07. map, plate (illus., port.). *3205*

Trickett, Dean
The Civil war in the Indian territory. *CO* xvii (1939) 315–27, 401–12; xviii (1940) 142–53, 266–80; xix (1941) 55–69, 381–96. 3 plates (illus., 2 maps). *3206*

Wright, Muriel H
Colonel Cooper's Civil war report on the battle of Round mountain [November 19, 1861] *CO* xxxix (1961) 352–97. maps, ports., illus. *3207*

KANSAS

Quantrell's Raid
August 20–28, 1863

Bailey, Lawrence Dudley, 1819–1891.
Border ruffian troubles in Kansas. Some newspaper articles written for the Garden city Sentinel and Kansas cultivator in 1887, by Judge L. D. Bailey . . . [edited] by Charles R. Green. Lyndon, 1899. 101, (1) p. front. (port.). 21½cm. NN *3208*
Quantrell's raid on Lawrence, 52–73.

—— Quantrell's raid on Lawrence, by L. D. Bailey and others, with names of victims of the raid. Edited and reprinted by C. R. Green. Lyndon, 1899. 52 p. 18cm. DLC NN *3209*

Boughton, Joseph S   1839–
The Lawrence massacre by a band of Missouri ruffians under Quantrell, August 21, 1863. 150 men killed, eighty women made widows and 250 children made orphans. . . . Lawrence, J. S. Boughton [1885?] 36 p. 15½cm.
Title from cover.   DLC   *3210*
Based on a letter furnished by Rev. R. Cordley to the *Congregational record* in 1863.

Clarke, Henry S
Incidents of Quantrell's raid on Lawrence, August 21, 1863. The remarkable and heretofore unpublished personal experiences of Hon. Henry S. Clarke. By S. W. Brewster. Lawrence, Jeffersonian print, 1898. 17 p. port p. [2] of cover. 23cm.   NN   *3211*
Title and imprint from cover.
"As given in an interview with S. W. Brewster."

Ridenour, Peter D   1831–1904.
Quantrell's raid, Aug. 21, 1863, from the Autobiography of Peter D. Ridenour. Reprinted . . . for the benefit of the Douglas county Historical society. [1963] 32 p. 1 illus., ports. 22½cm.   *3211A*
Cover title adds: An eyewitness account.
Reprinted from the Autobiography of Peter D. Ridenour . . . 1908.

Shea, John C
. . . Reminiscences of Quantrell's raid upon the City of Lawrence, Kas. Thrilling narratives by living eye witnesses. Compiled and arranged by John C. Shea, editor and publisher. Kansas City, Isaac P. Moore, printer, 1879. 27 p. 22½cm.   CSmH   *3212*
At head of title: The only true history of Quantrell's raid ever published.

MISSOURI

St. Louis in the Civil war, Camp Jackson, and General D. M. Frost, its commander. *Magazine of Western history* xi (1890) 267–76. *3213*

Adamson, Hans Christian
Rebellion in Missouri, 1861, Nathaniel Lyon and his Army of the West [by] Hans Christian Adamson. . . . Philadelphia, Chilton co. [c1961] xix, 305 p. plates (illus., ports.). 21cm.
          DLC NcD   *3214*
"St. Louis, Mo. and its fortifications, 1861–1865;" "Battlefield of Wilson's creek, Mo., August 10, 1861," maps on endpapers.

Blair, Francis Preston, 1821–1875.
"Fremont's hundred days in Missouri." Speech of F. P. Blair, Jr., of Missouri, on Fremont's defense, delivered in the House of representatives, March 7, 1862. Washington, Printed at the Congressional Globe office, 1862. 16 p. 24cm.   CSmH   *3215*
Text in double columns.

Bundy, Martin Luther, 1817–
Missouri in '61, by Brevet Lieutenant-Colonel M. L. Bundy. *MOLLUS-Ind* 207–11. *3216*

Castel, Albert Edward, 1928–
Kansas Jayhawking raids into Western Missouri in 1861. *MHR* liv (1959/60) 1–11. 1 illus., ports. *3217*

Cheavens, Henry Martyn, 1830–1920.
Journal of the Civil war in Missouri: 1861, Henry Martyn Cheavens. Edited by Virginia Easley. *MHR* lvi (1961/62) 12–25. port. *3218*

Colfax, Schuyler, 1823–1885.
Fremont's hundred days in Missouri. Speech of Schuyler Colfax, of Indiana, in reply to Mr. Blair, of Missouri, delivered in the House of representatives, March 7, 1862. [Washington, D.C. Scammell & co., printers, 1862] 15, (1) p. 24½cm.   CSmH   *3219*

Missouri, miscellaneous, continued

Caption title.
Text in double columns.

Covington, James W
The Camp Jackson affairs, 1861. *MHR* LV
(1961) 197–212. illus.   *3220*

Dorsheimer, William, 1832–1881.
Fremont's hundred days in Missouri. *Atlantic monthly* IX (1862) 115–25, 247–58, 372–84.   *3221*

Drake, Charles Daniel, 1811–1892.
Camp Jackson: its history and significance.
Oration of Charles D. Drake, delivered in the
City of St. Louis, May 11, 1863, on the anniversary of the capture of Camp Jackson. To
which is subjoined his reply to the Missouri
Republican's attack upon him, on account of
that oration. St. Louis, Printed at the Missouri
Democrat office, 1863. 16 p. 23cm.
Text in double columns.   CSmH   *3222*

Fremont, John Charles, 1813–1890.
In command in Missouri. *B&L* I 278–88.
                                        3223

Herklotz, Hildegarde Rose
Jayhawkers in Missouri, 1858–1863. *MHR*
XVII (1922/23) 266–84, 505–13; XVIII (1923/
24) 64–101.   *3224*

Kirkpatrick, Arthur Roy
Missouri on the eve of the Civil war. *MHR*
LV (1960/61) 99–108. illus.   *3225*

—— Missouri in the early months of the Civil
war. *MHR* LV (1960/61) 235–66.   *3226*

Knox, Thomas Wallace, 1835–1896.
The lost army, by Thomas W. Knox. New
York, Merriam co. [1894] 296 p. plates (illus.).
20cm.   CSmH DLC   *3227*

McCulloch, Benjamin, 1811–1862.
The military operations in Missouri, in the
summer and autumn of 1861, an unpublished
report of General Ben McCulloch, communicated with a supplementary note, by General
Franz Siegel. *Historical magazine* s 3 I (Morrisania 1872) 129–34.   *3228*
Also *in MHR* XXXI (1931/32) 354–67.

McElroy, John, 1846–1929.
The struggle for Missouri, by John McElroy.
. . . Washington, D.C. National Tribune co.,
1909. ix, 342 p. 3 illus., 3 ports, map, plates
(2 col. illus., maps, ports.). 20½cm.   *3229*

McNamara, J   H
My knapsack. *Land we love* VI (1868/69)
316–19.   *3230*
Seizure of the Confederate forces at Camp Jackson.

Minnesota.
Report of the Minnesota commission
appointed to erect a monument in the National
cemetery at Jefferson barracks, Mo. [1922]
38 p. 2 plates (illus., port.). 24cm.
                        MnHi   *3231*
Roster of burials by regiments included.
"Errata" slip inserted.

Musser, Richard H
The war in Missouri [1861] *SB* ns I (1885/
86) 678–85, 745–82; ns II (1886/87) 43–8,
102–07.   *3232*

[Paynter, Henry Martyn] 1827–1893.
Brief narrative of incidents in the war in
Missouri, and of the personal experience of
one who has suffered. Boston, Press of the
Daily Courier, 1863. 28 p. 23½cm.
                        CSmH DLC   *3233*

Peckham, James
Gen. Nathaniel Lyon and Missouri in 1861,
a monograph of the great rebellion, by James
Peckham, formerly Lt.-Col. 8th infantry, Mo.
vols. New York, American News co., 1886.
xvii, [21]–447 p. front. (port.), 2 plates
(illus.). 19½cm.   CSmH NN   *3234*
"Roll of the Union legion, organized January,
1861," [433]–47.

Snead, Thomas Lowndes, 1828–1890.
The fight for Missouri, from the election of
Lincoln to the death of Lyon, by Thomas L.
Snead. New York, Charles Scribner's Sons,
1886. viii, 322 p. front. (fold. map). 18½cm.
                        CSmH NN   *3235*
Contents: Part I Political; II Military.

Stewart, Douglas
When the Civil war invaded Livingston
county. *MHR* XXI (1926/27) 50–5.   *3236*

Webb, William Larkin, 1856–1931.
Battles and biographies of Missourians; or,
the Civil war period of our State, by W. L.
Webb. Kansas City, Mo., Hudson-Kimberly
pub. co., 1900. 369, (1) p. plates (ports.).
20cm.   CSmH DLC   *3237*

—— —— Kansas City, Mo., Hudson-Kimberly pub. co., 1903. 404 p. plates (ports.).
18cm.   MoHi   *3238*
At head of title: Second edition.
A reprinting with additional biographies, 370–404.

Wherry, William Macky, 1836–1918.
General Nathaniel Lyon and his campaign
in Missouri in 1861, by Brevet Brigadier-General William M. Wherry. *MOLLUS-Ohio* IV
68–86.   *3239*

Schrantz, Ward L
The battle of Cathage [July 5, 1861] *MHR*
XXXI (1936/37) 140–9.   *3240*

Athens
August 5, 1861

Dixon, Ben F
Battle on the border, Athens, Missouri, August 5, 1861. *Annals of Iowa* s 3 xxxvi (1961/62) 1–15. plate (illus., 2 ports.). *3241*

Garretson, Owen Albright
The battle of Athens. *Palimpsest* viii (1927) 138–49. *3242*

McCrary, George W
The battle of Athens. *MOLLUS-Mo* i 169–76. *3243*

Wilson's Creek
August 10, 1861

The battle of Springfield, August 10th, 1861. Official reports. *In* Public documents of the State of Kansas for the year 1862, 65–80. *3244*

Austin, Robert A
Battle of Wilson's creek. *MHR* xxvii (1932/33) 46–9. *3245*

Bearss, Edwin Cole, 1923–
The battle of Wilson's creek. *Annals of Iowa* s 3 xxxvi (1961/62) 81–109, 161–86. 2 plates (map, 2 ports.). *3246*

Flournoy, George M
An unofficial account of the battle of Wilson creek, August 10, 1861. Edited by Willard E. Wright. *ArHQ* xv (1956) 360–4. *3247*

Holcombe, Return Ira, 1845–1916.
An account of the battle of Wilson's creek, or Oak hills, fought between the Union troops commanded by Gen. N. Lyon, and the Southern, or Confederate troops, under command of Gens. McCulloch and Price, on Saturday, August 10, 1861, in Greene county, Missouri. Written and compiled from authentic sources by Holcombe and Adams. Published on the twenty-second anniversary of the battle, as a full and faithful account, and as a memorial of the reunion of the survivors of the engagement of both sides, held August 8, 9, and 10, 1883. Springfield, Mo., Dow & Adams, 1883. 104 p. 2 fronts. (ports.). 23½cm.
　　　　　　CSmH DLC NN　*3248*
—— An account of the battle of Wilson's creek, by Holcomb and Adams. Centennial edition. Springfield, Mo., Springfield Public Library and the Greene County Historical Society, 1961. xii, 111 p. 2 fronts. (ports.). 22½cm.　　　　DLC　*3249*
"Introduction" signed: Fred De Armond.
A photographic reprinting.

Hulston, John K
West Point & Wilson's creek. *CWH* i (1955) 333–54. map. *3250*

Lobdell, Jared C
Nathaniel Lyon and the battle of Wilson's creek. *BHMS* xvii (1961) 3–15. *3251*

McDonald, William Naylor, 1834–1898.
Battle of Wilson's creek. *SB* iii (1884/85) 49–54. *3252*

McNamara, J　H
My knapsack. General Sterling Price's report of the battle of Oak hills. *SM* ii (1869) 99–104. *3253*
Report was first published in the Springfield, Mo. Mirror, August 12, 1861.

Neville, H　Clay
Wilson's creek. Monument to be erected to heroes who fell there. *SHSP* xxxviii (1910) 363–72. *3254*

Sons of Union Veterans of the Civil War. Wilson Creek Camp N. 30.
Souvenir program of battle of Wilson creek, seventy-fifth anniversary, August 10–11, 1938, sponsored by. . . . Springfield, Mo. [1938] [40] p. ports., fold. map. 22½cm.
　　　　　　　　　　　　NN　*3255*
"History of the battle of Wilson creek, by L. E. Meador."
Advertising matter included.

Upton, Lucile (Morris)
Battle of Wilson's creek, reprinted from articles by Lucile Morris Upton in the Springfield news and leader. Springfield, Mo., Printed and distributed by Wilson's Creek Battlefield Foundation [195-] 15 p. 22cm. NN　*3256*
Text in double columns.

Wilkie, Franc Bangs, 1832–1892.
The battle of Wilson's creek. *Palimpsest* ix (1928) 291–310. *3257*
"Adapted . . . from the account written by Franc B. Wilkie . . . published in the Dubuque Herald on August 21," 1861.

Lexington
September 18–20, 1861

Lexington Historical Society.
The battle of Lexington, fought in and around the City of Lexington, Missouri, on September 18th, 19th and 20th, 1861, by forces under command of Colonel James A. Mulligan and General Sterling Price. The official records of both parties to the conflict, to which is added memoirs of participants with maps and cuts. Printed for the Lexington historical society. [Lexington] Intelligencer print.

Lexington, continued

co., 1903. 68 p. illus., plan, ports., 3 plates
(illus., fold. map). 20cm.   CSmH   **3258**

McDonald, William Naylor, 1834–1898.
    Capture of Lexington, Missouri, by Price's
army. *SB* III (1884/85) 105–10.   **3259**

Smith, Harold F
    The 1861 struggle for Lexington, Missouri.
CWH VII (1961) 155–66. plate (illus., port.).
                                             3261
Snyder, J   F
    The capture of Lexington. *MHR* VII (1912/
13) 1–9.   **3262**

                    *   *   *

Polk, Leonidas, 1806–1864.
    General Polk's report of the battle of Bel-
mont. Columbus, Ky., 1861. 8 p. 20½cm.
                        CSmH   **3263**
    Dated: Headquarters, 1st division, Western depart't
Columbus, Ky. November 10th, 1861.
    Crandall 1352.

Buttgenbach, Walter J
    Island number 10. *Journal of the United
States artillery* XXXIX (1913) 331–8. map.
                                             3264
Dial, Marshall
    The Bootheel swamp struggle, by Marshall
Dial. Lilbourn, Mo., Lloyd publications, 1961.
66 p. illus., 2 ports. 22½cm.
                        DLC NN   **3265**
    Partial contents: The siege of Madrid; The battle
of Island number Ten; Marmaduke's raid and Jeff's
surrender.
    Plates are paged.
    Pages 63–5 are blank.
    Map on front cover.

Pope, John, 1822–1892.
    Report of operations which resulted in the
capture of Island no. 10. [n.p., n.d.] 2 folios.
25cm.   CSmH   **3266**

——— Report of operations which resulted in
the capture of New Madrid. [n.p., n.d.] 3 p.
25cm.   CSmH   **3267**
    Caption title.
    Dated: Headquarters, District of the Mississippi,
New Madrid, March 14, 1862.

Byam, W   W
    The Lieutenant's confession. *B&G* V (1895)
214–18.   **3268**
    Pineville, Mo., August, 1862.

Clarke, Charles W
    Address of Senator Chas. W. Clarke at the
anniversary of the battle of Lone Jack, August 6th, 1903. 16 p. 23cm.   MoHi   **3269**
    Caption title.

Violette, E   M
    The battle of Kirksville, August 6, 1862.
MHR V (1910/11) 94–112.   **3270**

Palmyra
November 18, 1862

The Palmyra massacre. *SM* X (1872) 485–8.
                                             3271
Palmyra Confederate Monument Association.
    The Palmyra massacre, a short concise but
true history of the execution of ten Confederate
soldiers, at Palmyra, Mo., October 18th, 1862.
Written, published and circulated by the Palmyra Confederate monument association. Palmyra, Sosey Bros., printers [190–] 15, (1) p.
24½cm.   NB   **3272**

Marmaduke's Expeditions
December 31, 1862 – January 25, 1863
April 17 – May 2, 1863

Oates, Stephen Berry, 1936–
    Marmaduke's first Missouri raid. *BHMS*
XVII (1961) 147–53.   **3273**

Blue, B   B
    General Marmaduke's expedition into Mis-
souri, April and May, 1863. *SM* IX (1871)
333–9.   **3274**
    "General Marmaduke's report, Jacksonport, Ark.,
May 19, 1863," 336–9.

Oates, Stephen Berry, 1936–
    Marmaduke's Cape Girardeau expedition,
1863. *MHR* LVII (1962/63) 237–47. 2 illus.,
map, port.   **3275**

                    *   *   *

——— Shelby's great raid, 1863. *BHMS* XVII
(1961) 337–45.   **3276**

Price's Raid
August 29 – December 2, 1864

Cabell, William Lewis, 1827–1911.
    Report of the part Cabell's brigade took in
what is called "Price's raid into Missouri and
Kansas in the Fall of 1864." [1900] 16 p.
23cm.   LNHT ViHi   **3277**
    Title from cover.

Castel, Albert Edward, 1928–
    War and politics: the Price raid of 1864.
Kansas historical quarterly XXIV (1958) 129–
43. plate (3 illus.).   **3278**

Curtis, Samuel Ryan, 1807–1866.
    Report of campaign against Major General
Sterling Price in October and November, 1864.
Annals of Iowa VIII/IX (1870/71) 50–94, 184–

97, 315–30, 491–506, 617–31; x/xi (1872/73)
207–26; xii (1874) 53–79, 125–34, 299–319.
                                          3279

Grover, George S
   The Price campaign of 1864. *MHR* vi (1911/
12) 167–81.   3280

Price, Sterling, 1809–1867.
   Gen. Price's report of the Missouri campaign,
1864. *LWL* v (1868) 379–97.   3281

Tucker, Samuel, 1872–
   Price raid through Linn county, Kansas,
October 24, 25, 1864, by Samuel Tucker.
[n.p., c1958] 17 folios. map. 28cm.
   Title from cover.   DLC   3282

          *   *   *

Monnett, Howard N
   The origin of the Confederate invasion of
Missouri, 1864. *BHMS* xviii (1961/62) 37–48.
                                          3283

Sanborn, John Benjamin, 1826–1904.
   The campaign in Missouri in September and
October, 1864. *MOLLUS-Minn* iii 135–204.
                                          3284

—— Reminiscences of the war in the Depart-
ment of Missouri. Paper read at meeting
of the Military order of the loyal legion at
Ryan hotel, St. Paul, Nov. 3, 1886, by Bvt.
Maj. Gen. John B. Sanborn. 31 p. 23cm.
   Title from cover.   CSmH   3285
   Also published in *MOLLUS-Minn* L 224–57.

Pilot Knob
September 26, 1864

Mackey, T   J
   A lady of Arcadia, the doomed garrison of
Pilot Knob and how it was saved, by T. J.
Mackey, late Captain engineers, C.S.A. *Home
and country* xi (1895/96) 319–29. 1 illus.,
map, 2 ports.   3286

Peterson, Cyrus Asbury, 1848–
   Pilot Knob, the Thermopylae of the West,
by Cyrus A. Peterson and Joseph Mills Hanson.
New York, Neale pub. co., 1914. 324 p. 21cm.
                          CSmH NN   3287

Pilot Knob Memorial Association.
   Meeting of . . . on the . . . anniversary of
the battle of Pilot Knob. [St. Louis, Press of
A. R. Fleming, 1904–06] 3 nos. 22cm.
                          NN   3288

          *   *   *

Todd, W   C
   The Centralia fight, by W. C. Todd. The
killing of Jesse James, by Maj. J. N. Edwards.
[n.p., n.d.] [17] p. 19½cm.   MoHi   3289

Title from cover.
   "Not to permit a book published in 1882, titled
'The history of Boone county' to stand unchallenged
and undenied with its partial and biased statements
and hatreds of the Confederate cause."

Monnett, Howard N
   The Confederate advance to Lexington,
1864. *BHMS* xix (1962/63) 260–72. 3289A

Westport
October 23, 1864

Crittenden, Henry Huston, 1859–
   The battle of Westport and National memorial park, by H. H. Crittenden. Kansas City,
Mo., Lowell press, 1938. xiii, 202 p. plates
(illus., 1 fold.; ports.). 22cm.
                          DLC NN   3290

Jenkins, Paul Burrill, 1872–
   The battle of Westport, by Paul B. Jenkins.
. . . Kansas City, Mo., Franklin Hudson pub.
co., 1906. 193 p. front. (port.), illus., maps,
ports. 20½cm.   NN   3291
   Plates are paged.

Monnett, Howard N
   Action before Westport, 1864, by Howard
N. Monnett. Paintings and maps by George
Barnett. Kansas City, Mo., Westport Historical
Society, 1964. xxi, 190 p. 3 maps, plates (illus.,
ports.). 24cm.   NN   3292

United States. Military Affairs Committee
   (House, 70:1).
   National military park to commemorate the
battle of Westport, State of Missouri. Hearing
before Subcommittee no. 4 Committee of military affairs, House of representatives, Seventieth Congress, first session on H.R. 5781.
Statements of George H. Coombs, Jr. [and]
H. H. Crittenden, February 8, 1928. Washington, Govt. print. office, 1928. 8 p. 22½cm.
                          NN   3293

Westport Improvement Association, Kansas
   City, Mo.
   Westport, 1812–1912. Commemorating the
centennial of the Sante Fe trail. Westport's
history from its beginning as a frontier military
post until its annexation to Kansas city. . . .
Kansas City, Mo., Press of Franklin Hudson
pub. co. [1912] 76 p. front. (6 ports.), illus.,
ports. 20cm.   NN   3294
   Partial contents: The Upton Hays brigade, by
Albert N. Doerschuk, 45–8; Battle of Westport, 50–63;
Personal reminiscences of Maj. H. J. Vivian [2nd Mo.
Cavalry C.S.A.] of the last day of the battle of Westport, 69–70; Recollections of the second day's fight in
the battle of Westport, by P. I. Bonebrake, 71–5.

NEW MEXICO

Armstrong, Andrew F   H 1910–
The case of Major Isaac Lynde. *New Mexico
historical review* xxxvi (1961) 1–35.   *3295*

Brayer, Herbert O
The fall of Fort Filmore, 1861. *In* The Westerners Denver posse Brandbook, 1951, 411–56.
fold. facsims., plates., (1 illus., 3 ports.).
                                         3296

Crimmons, Martin Lalor, 1876–
Fort Filmore. *New Mexico historical review*
vi (1931) 327–33.   *3298*

Dunford, A   H
'The Gray brigade' the success and failure
of Confederate arms in New Mexico. The English Westerners brand book ii 1 (October
1959) 11, (1) p. map.   *3299*

Hall, Martin Hardwick
Sibley's New Mexico campaign, by Martin
Hardwick Hall. Austin, University of Texas
press [1960] xv, 366 p. facsim., maps and
plans, plates (facsims., illus., ports.). 23½cm.
                        DLC NN   *3300*
"The muster rolls of the Army of New Mexico,"
227–329.

——— The skirmish at Mesilla [July 25, 1861]
Arizona and the West i (1959) 343–51. plate
(port.).   *3301*

Hayes, Augustus Allen, 1837–1892.
The New Mexico campaign of 1862, a stir-
ring chapter of our late Civil war. *Magazine of
American history* xv (1885) 171–84.   *3302*

Keleher, William A
Turmoil in New Mexico, 1846–1868, by
William A Keleher. . . . Sante Fe, Rydal press
[1952] xii, 534 p. illus., map on endpaper,
plates (illus., ports.). 22cm.   NN   *3303*
Partial contents: The Confederates invade Mexico,
[141]–210; Carleton's California column, [211]–74.

Kerby, Robert Lee
The Confederate invasion of New Mexico
and Arizona, 1861–1862, by Robert Lee Kerby. Los Angeles, Westernlore press, 1958. xix,
(1), 23–159 p. illus., maps, ports., plates (facsims., 2 illus.). 21cm.   NN TxU   *3304*
Half-title: Westernlore great West and Indian
series XII.
"Civil war in the Southwest . . . ," map on endpaper.
Appendices: I Table of organization of the Sibley
brigade; II Battle statistics of the campaign; III Documents.

McClure, C   B
The battle of adobe walls, 1864. *Pan-handle
plains historical review* xxi (1948) 18–65.
                                         3305

McKee, James Cooper,   –1897.
Narrative of the surrender of a command
of U. S. forces at Fort Filmore, N. M., in July,
A.D. 1861, at the breaking out of the Civil
war, between the North and the South, by
James Cooper McKee. Prescott, A. T., 1878.
15 p. 20½cm.   CSmH NN   *3306*

——— ——— Second edition revised and corrected. New York, 1881. 30 p. 18½cm.
Title from cover.   CSmH NN   *3307*

——— Narrative of the surrender of a command
of U.S. forces at Fort Filmore, N.M., in July
A.D., 1861, by Major James Cooper McKee.
Boston, Printed by John A. Lovell & co., 1886.
2 plates (map, plan). 27½cm.   NN   *3308*
"Third edition. 300 copies for private circulation."

——— ——— by James Cooper McKee, Surgeon,
U.S. army with related reports by John R. Bay-
lor, CSA, & others. Houston, Stagecoach press,
1960. viii, 64 p. front. (map). 18cm.   *3309*

McMaster, Richard K   and George Ruhlen
The guns of Valverde. *Password of the El
Paso historical society* v (1960) 21–34. 1 illus.,
plan, 2 ports.   *3310*

Santee, J   F
The battle of La Glorieta pass. *New Mexico
historical review* vi (1931) 66–75.   *3311*

Sonnichsin, Charles Leland, 1901–
Major McMullen's invasion of New Mexico.
Password of El Paso historical society ii (1957)
38–43.   *3312*

Spencer, Elma Dill Russell
Famous fugitives of Fort Union. *New Mexico historical review* xxxii (1957) 1–9. *3313*

Waldrip, William I
New Mexico during the Civil war. *New
Mexico historical review* xxviii (1953) 163–
82, 251–90.   *3314*

Walker, Charles S.
Causes of the Confederate invasion of New
Mexico. *New Mexico historical review* viii
(1933) 76–97.   *3315*

Whitford, William Clarke, 1828–1902.
Colorado volunteers in the Civil war, the
New Mexico campaign in 1862. Denver, State
Historical and Natural History society, 1906.
159 p. front. (illus.), illus., maps, ports.
23½cm.   CSmH NN   *3316*

——— ——— Boulder, Pruett press, 1963. 159,
(15) p. front. (illus.), illus., maps, ports.
23cm.   NN   *3317*
New material: A salute to the Centennial, by Agnes
Wright Spring; Suggested additional reading; and
Index.

TEXAS

General References

How Texas was surrendered, a military sketch. *Northern monthly* i (1867) 40–8.   *3318*

Barr, Alwyn
Texas coastal defense, 1861–1865. *SWHQ* LXV (1961/62) 1–31. maps, plates (2 illus.).
3319

Connor, Daniel A
Civil war operations in West Texas and New Mexico, 1861–62. *Password of the El Paso historical society* i (1956) 90–8. map, 2 ports.
3320

Fitzhugh, Lester N
Saluria, Fort Esperanza, and military operations on the Texas coast, 1861–1864. *SWHQ* LXI (1957/58) 66–100. 2 maps.   *3321*

Havins, Thomas R
The Texas mounted regiment at Camp Colorado. *TMH* IV (1964) 67–69.   *3321A*

Jones, Allen W
Military events in Texas during the Civil war. *SWHQ* LXIV (1960/61) 64–70.   *3322*
Also in *TMH* II (1962) 126–30.

Kellersberger, Getulius, 1821–1900.
Erlebnisse eines schweizerischen Ingenieurs in Californien, Mexico und Texas zur Zeit des amerikanischen Bürgerkrieges, 1861–1865, von G. Kellersberger. Zurich, Buchdruckerei Juchli & Beck, 1896. 196, (1) p. front. (port.).
"Inhaltsverzeichnis," (1) p. TxU(P)   *3323*

—— Memoirs of an engineer in the Confederate army in Texas. Translated from German by Helen S. Sundstrom. [Austin?, 1957?] 48 p. 24cm.   TxU   *3324*

Cumberland, Charles C
The Confederate loss and recapture of Galveston, 1862–1863. *SWHQ* LI (1947/48) 109–30.   *3325*

Nueces River
August 10, 1862

Newcomb, James Pearson, 1837–1907.
Address of Hon. James P. Newcomb, delivered at Comfort, Texas, on the 10th of August, 1887, the twenty-fifth anniversary of the Nueces massacre. San Antonio, Press of Johnson Brothers, printers, 1887. 10 p. 18cm.
Title and imprint from cover. TxU   *3326*

Sansom, John W
Battle of Nueces river in Kinney county, August 10th, 1862, as seen and reported by John W. Sansom. [San Antonio, 1905] 14 p. plate (port.). 22½cm.   TxU   *3327*
Title from cover.

Shook, Robert W
The battle of the Nueces, August 10, 1862. *SWHQ* LXVI (1962/63) 31–42. map, plate (2 illus.).   *3328*

Williams, Robert H   1831–
The massacre on the Nucas river, the story of a Civil war tragedy, as related by R. H. Williams and John W. Sansom, both of whom participated in the battle, Williams on the Confederate side and Sansom with the Unionists. Grand Prairie, Frontier Times pub. house [1954] 36 p. 22cm.   Tx   *3329*
"Foreword" signed: J. Marvin Hunter, Sr.

*   *   *

Ashcraft, Allan C   1928–
The defense of Houston, October, 1962. *TMH* IV (1964) 189–91.   *3330*

Franklin, Robert M
Battle of Galveston, January 1st, 1863, by Robert M. Franklin. [Galveston, 1911] 11 p. front. (port.). 23½cm.   TxU   *3331*
An address before Camp Magruder, U.C.V., post 105, April 2, 1911.

Sabine Pass
September 4–11, 1863

Barr, Alwyn
Sabine Pass, September, 1863. *TMH* II (1962) 17–22. map.   *3332*

Muir, Andrew Forest
Dick Dowling and the battle of Sabine pass. *CWH* IV (1958) 399–428.   *3333*

Pray, May M   (Brewer) "Mrs. R. F. Pray," 1876–
Dick Dowling's battle, an account of the War between the States in the eastern Gulf region of Texas, by Mrs. R. F. Pray. San Antonio, Naylor co., 1936. xii, 143 p. 3 plates (map, 2 ports.). 21½cm.
DLC NN   *3334*

Tolbert, Frank X
Dick Dowling at Sabine pass, by Frank X. Tolbert. New York, McGraw-Hill [1962] 159 p. map. 21cm.   NN   *3335*

Young, Jo
The battle of Sabine *SWHQ* LII (1948/49) 398–409. map.   *3336*

*   *   *

Ashcraft, Allan C   1928–
San Antonio defenses, 1863. *TMH* IV (1964) 25–6.   *3337*
Directive of Major General John B. Magruder to Major A. G. Dickinson, December 20, 1863.

Texas, miscellaneous, continued

Hunter, J   Marvin
    Midnight battle at Fort Lancaster. *Frontier times* (Bandera, 1944) 366–70.   *3338*

Pool, William C
    The battle of Dove creek. *SWHQ* LIII (1949/50) 367–85. map.   *3339*

Index of Authors

Index of Authors

Numbers refer to entries in Volume III. This is primarily an index of individual authors, with titles listed only for entries which lack an author. The publications of bodies corporate and governmental agencies are not indexed.

Abbot, George Maurice 1
Abbot, Willis John 1365–67
Abbott, John Stevens Cabot 174–75 2536
Abdill, George B 705
Abel, Annie Heloise 285–86
Abercrombie, Irene 3175
Abernethy, Alonzo 2888
Acme haversack of patriotism and song 336
Adams, George Worthington 926–27
Adams, Henry Clay 2884
Adams, John Quincy 2721
Adams, Julius Walker 315
Adamson, Hans Christian 3214
Ages of U. S. volunteer soldiery 1121
Albaugh, William Archibald 995 1138–41
Alden, Henry M 540
Alexander, Charles Wesley 396A
Alexander, Edward Porter 818 1217–18 1478
   1577–78 1732 1798 2010 3055
Alexander, Herbert L 2983
Allan, Francis D 557
Allan, William 996 1516–18 1534 1594–96
   1632 1944–47 2011–12
Allen, Charles Lewis 2581
Alms, Frederick H 1066
Alvord, Benjamin 2833
Ambler, Charles Henry 2301–02
Ambrose, Stephen E 76 1615
American heritage picture history of the Civil
   war 530
Ames, Adelbert 1616 2404–05
Anderson, Archer 2607
Anderson, Charles Carter 1102
Anderson, Ephraim F 1984
Anderson, Galusha 928
Andrews, Christopher Columbus 2582–83
Andrews, George Leonard 1607
Anecdotes of the rebellion 376
Angle, Paul McClelland 77 1368
Annals of the Army of Tennessee and early
   Western history 337
Annals of the war 377
Anthony, William 2013
Appler, Augustus C 265–67
Aptheker, Herbert 316–17
Archer, Fletcher H 1799
Archer, G   W 1197
Archer, W   P 2694
Armstrong, A   F   H 3297
Armstrong, Andrew F 3295
Armstrong, William Jackson 146
Armstrong, Zella 17 2652

Army and Navy official gazette 338
Army reunion . . . 1869 752
Arthur, Robert 1561
Asche, S   W 620
Ashcraft, Allan C 706 895 3330 3337
Ashe, Samuel A'Court 2014–15 2448
Ashmore, Otis 162
Atchinson, Ray M 348
Atkinson, J   H 3186
Atwater, Dorence 621–23
Austin, Robert A 3245
Ayres, Stephen Cooper 3084

Bachelder, John Badger 2016–18 2250–57
Bachtell, Samuel 1067
Badeau, Adam 1103
Bailes, Clarice Lorene 2303
Bailey, Lawrence Dudley 3208–09
Bain, William E 720A
Baker, Lafayette Curry 872–75
Balch, William Ralston 2019
Baltzell, George F 2377
Bankston, Marie Louise Benton 397
Barbee, David Rankin 163
Barber, John Warner 176
Barber, Joseph 362
Barlow, Francis Channing 1754
Barnard, George N 2543–44
Barnard, John Gross 748 1272 1479–80 1535–
   36 1918
Barnes, Eric Wollencott 177
Barnes, Frank 2425
Barney, Caleb Henry 1987
Barnwell, Robert W 2413
Barr, Alwyn 819 1246 2793–94 3319 3332
Barr, Thomas Francis 295
Barrett, John Gilchrist 2385 2545
Barringer, Rufus 1857
Barstow, Charles Lester 398
Barter, George W 1104
Bartlett, John Russell 2 600 2190
Bate, William Brimmage 2653
Bates, Samuel Penniman 1665–66 2020
Battle of Fort Sumter and first victory of the
   Southern troops 2421–22A
Battle-fields of the South, from Bull Run to
   Fredericksburg 1356–57
Battles and leaders of the Civil war 1358–
   61
Baxter, Jedediah Hyde 929
Baxter, William 3156–57
Beard, Dan W 2984